INFORMATION TECHNOLOGY
and the
Criminal Justice System

INFORMATION TECHNOLOGY
and the
Criminal Justice System

Editor

APRIL PATTAVINA

University of Massachusetts at Lowell

SAGE Publications
Thousand Oaks ▪ London ▪ New Delhi

For information:

 Sage Publications, Inc.
2455 Teller Road
Thousand Oaks, California 91320
E-mail: order@sagepub.com

Sage Publications Ltd.
1 Oliver's Yard
55 City Road
London, EC1Y 1SP
United Kingdom

Sage Publications India Pvt. Ltd.
B-42, Panchsheel Enclave
Post Box 4109
New Delhi 110 017 India

Printed in the United States of America on acid-free paper.

Library of Congress Cataloging-in-Publication Data

Information technology and the criminal justice system / edited by April Pattavina.
        p. cm.
Includes bibliographical references and index.
ISBN 0-7619-3018-3 (cloth) — ISBN 0-7619-3019-1 (pbk.)
    1. Criminal justice, Administration of—Data processing. 2. Criminal justice,
Administration of—Information services. 3. Information storage and
retrieval systems—Criminal justice, Administration of. I. Pattavina, April.
HV7412.4.I54 2005
364'.0285—dc22   2004013903

04   05   06   07   08   09   10   9   8   7   6   5   4   3   2   1

Acquiring Editor:	Jerry Westby
Project Editor:	Claudia A. Hoffman
Copy Editor:	D. J. Peck
Typesetter:	C&M Digitals (P) Ltd.
Indexer:	Molly Hall
Cover Designer:	Janet Foulger

Contents

Preface

This book is about the impact that advances in information technology (IT) have had on the criminal justice system over the past several decades. Given the substantial investments that federal, state, and local criminal justice agencies are making in IT, the time is appropriate to begin synthesizing the growing body of information about IT and criminal justice in a way that frames the discussion in terms of what we have learned from past experiences, what the current state of IT is in various components of the criminal justice system, and what challenges lie ahead.

From this perspective, the goal of this book is to inform readers that computer and IT should be understood as more than just a set of tools designed to accomplish a discrete set of job tasks. As the chapters in this book illustrate, there are many technical, analytic, legal, and organizational issues related to advances in computer technology and IT. Therefore, IT must be considered as an integral component of understanding how our criminal justice system works.

There are many types of IT that could be topics of discussion for a book of this sort. Any attempt to enumerate and describe each in detail would likely be outdated by the time this work is published. The specific types of IT that are described in this book were selected because they address some perennial questions regarding IT and criminal justice and because they span across a variety of agencies, including police, courts, and corrections. These questions are as follows:

1. How has IT changed the way in which we monitor criminal behavior?

2. How has IT changed the way in which we examine patterns of criminal behavior?

3. How have criminal justice organizations adapted to the use of IT?

4. What is the future of IT in criminal justice?

The first section of the book deals with advances in criminal justice IT. In Chapter 1, Terence Dunworth provides an historical overview of advances in IT in criminal justice and describes some of the important advances that have been made during the past several decades. He also discusses some of the benefits and risks associated with IT advancement. In Chapter 2, Lois Davis and Brian Jackson provide an in-depth investigation of the major sources of IT support for criminal justice agencies and how those developments have shaped the current state of IT in agencies as well as how agencies have managed the acquisition and implementation of IT projects. They also discuss some lessons learned from past experiences with IT implementation in criminal justice agencies.

The second section of the book deals not only with how criminal justice agencies use the Internet but also with how *criminals* use the Internet. The subject of Chapter 3, by Roberta Griffith, is a discussion of various ways in which the Internet has changed the way that criminal justice agencies manage information. In Chapter 4, David Wall describes the transformative impacts of the Internet on criminal activity. He also analyzes the construction of our understanding of cybercrime and its relationship to enforcement.

The third section of the book focuses on IT and crime reporting and analysis. In Chapter 5, Donald Faggiani and David Hirschel discuss how advances in IT have affected official crime reporting, with a particular emphasis on the National Incident-Based Reporting System (NIBRS). In Chapter 6, crime analysis is covered by Phyllis McDonald, who describes the relationship between the development of IT and crime analysis and the policy implications of IT advances for police practices and policies. In Chapter 7, April Pattavina discusses geographic information systems (GIS) and crime mapping in criminal justice agencies. In addition to GIS applications in criminal justice, she pays specific attention to issues of data quality.

The fourth section of the book includes chapters that provide in-depth analysis into IT development in specific agencies. In Chapter 8, Glenn Pierce and Roberta Griffith discuss how the Bureau of Alcohol, Tobacco, Firearms, and Explosives' (ATF) communications and information system structure evolved to support ATF's ability to collect and manage information on firearms recovered by law enforcement. In Chapter 9, Kathleen Snavely, Faye Taxman, and Stuart Gordon describe an integrated consent-driven system to monitor offender flow through the criminal justice system and how the information can be used. They also describe the legal context of information sharing across agencies, with a focus on issues related to privacy. In Chapter 10, Peter Manning illustrates the importance of organizational context in understanding how IT is implemented and used by those who work in police agencies.

The final section of the book addresses the future of IT in criminal justice. In Chapter 11, James Byrne and Eve Buzawa discuss the need for a criminal justice curriculum that focuses on developing the knowledge, skills, and analytic tools available in the area of IT. The final chapter, by April Pattavina, includes a discussion of the future prospects and challenges of IT in the criminal justice system.

The ultimate purpose of this book is to enhance our understanding of IT in criminal justice as a continuous process that will constantly challenge us to think about how we turn criminal justice information into knowledge, who can use that knowledge, and for what purposes. The incredible pace at which IT advances are being made is fascinating, and the opportunities for involvement undoubtedly will grow. Any person who is interested in criminal justice issues must develop the capacity to understand, use, and challenge current IT practices if he or she wishes to successfully contribute to the future of the field.

Section I

ADVANCES IN CRIMINAL JUSTICE INFORMATION TECHNOLOGY

CHAPTER 1

Information Technology and the Criminal Justice System

An Historical Overview

TERENCE DUNWORTH

The purpose of this chapter is to provide an historical perspective for the most prominent changes in information technology (IT) use that have taken place in the criminal justice field over the past several decades. Given that the field consists of more than 18,000 police departments and several thousand prosecutorial, court, and corrections agencies, it is clear that the objective can be met only in the most general terms. The agencies that comprise the criminal justice "system" are at highly varying stages of IT sophistication and use. They also have different motivations for initiating IT change. To illustrate, we may consider that an agency's objectives when making IT decisions fall into one or more of four general categories: to better understand the problems with which they must deal, to manage day-to-day operations more effectively, to reduce operating costs, and to engage in more informed strategic and tactical planning and decision making. These objectives will not have equal weight with every agency. For instance, police departments are strongly motivated by the need to gain greater understanding of the problem of crime, whereas courts need effective management at a reasonable cost. Thus, the nature of these two agencies' IT focus will inevitably differ. Their respective choices of hardware and software will be guided by their objectives, and what works in one place might not work in the other. Because of this, the reader should bear in mind that any claims made, or any examples provided, in the text that follows will rarely have universal application. Nevertheless, I argue that the field in general

AUTHOR'S NOTE: Earlier versions of some of the sections in this chapter were published in the following: Terence Dunworth, "Criminal Justice and the IT Revolution," *Federal Probation* (2nd Quarter 2001); *Criminal Justice 2000*, vol. 3: *Policies, Processes, and Decisions of the Criminal Justice System* (Washington, DC: U.S. Department of Justice, 2000).

has made very substantial movement toward practical and effective use of a wide range of IT capabilities, and that the pace of this movement is accelerating.

The movement began during the mid-1960s when two powerful forces combined to stimulate transformations in information management and processing that criminal justice agencies would have found inconceivable during earlier decades. The first of these forces derives its strength from changes in federal policy toward state and local governments, and the second derives its strength from seminal changes in IT. Although the focus of this book is on the latter, it is important to recognize that federal policy shifts and the specific federal actions that resulted have at least contributed to, and have perhaps in some ways been essential to, the changes in IT that are identified.

Prior to 1965, the responsibility for dealing with crime—especially street crime—rested with local governments. Except for the relatively narrow jurisdiction of the Federal Bureau of Investigation (FBI), both the legislative and executive branches of the federal government had a "hands-off" attitude, and federal courts dealt with only a tiny proportion of the nation's criminal matters. Cities or towns, even in small jurisdictions, were responsible for funding law enforcement activities. Prosecution, adjudication, and jails operated largely at county levels.

During the 1960s, however, crime increased rapidly and became a more pressing social problem. The consequence was that national political attention began to focus on the issue. A common view was that the local criminal justice system was in fact not a "system" and was not performing effectively. It was seen as fragmented, underfunded, and poorly informed. Most jurisdictions paid attention only to the events that took place within their boundaries, shared little or no information, and were rarely involved in cross-jurisdictional cooperation.

The immediate outcome of this new national focus on local crime was the federal Law Enforcement Assistance Administration (LEAA).[1] This agency was proposed by the National Commission on Crime, established by the Johnson administration during the mid-1960s, and brought into existence by the Safe Streets Act of 1968. Its mission was to provide technical assistance and support to state and local criminal justice agencies, and it was funded over the subsequent 10 years at levels that, in adjusted dollars, were as high as any that have been devoted to crime control by the federal government since then. Among the act's most significant objectives were the stimulation and management of improved information gathering and sharing. Considerable sums of federal money were devoted to the acquisition of hardware, the development of software, and the creation of regional information-sharing systems. Although there are few who would argue that the LEAA met all of its goals, it seems clear that the agency greatly assisted state and local agencies in beginning to move along the path toward vastly better use of IT than had been the case previously. Although it is true that this stimulus faded for several years when the LEAA was shut down in 1982, federal assistance was resumed by the 1986 and 1988 Anti-Drug Abuse Acts,[2] and an even stronger federal IT push was introduced when the Crime Act of 1994 was passed.[3] This legislation created the Office of Community-Oriented Policing Services and put more than $1 billion of federal money into IT acquisition for local police departments, based on the principle that improved IT constitutes a "force multiplier."

As these adjustments in federal policy were taking place, the second stimulus for change was taking shape outside the criminal justice system. This was, of course, the revolution in IT that began with the invention of the transistor in 1949 and then underwent warp-speed acceleration during the 1970s and 1980s when desktop computers were first produced. The significance of these developments for criminal justice is that they provided the technical capacity to implement the policy objectives that national legislation embodied. In this sense, the political and technical developments were complementary and, for the criminal justice field at least, mutually supportive.

Thus, we can reasonably assert that this combination of policy changes and technological advances has initiated a transformation of the criminal justice field. There has been significant movement from the highly fragmented structure of thousands of unconnected agencies toward a more integrated system in which agencies not only are able to generate better information about their own operations but also can share and integrate that information with the activities of other organizations. This is taking place not only within and between agencies that perform common functions (e.g., police departments), which I would characterize as horizontal integration, but also between the various elements of the system (i.e., law enforcement, prosecution, courts, and corrections), which I would characterize as vertical integration.

This transformation is nowhere near completion. In fact, in many respects, it is still in its infancy. There are still many agencies—probably thousands—whose adoption of the new IT capabilities is modest at best. Some unknown but not trivial number of agencies still operate IT systems that predate the introduction of the desktop computer. Others have made hardware and software changes but have not yet realized the information processing potential that such changes promise. In short, the movement of the criminal justice field into a new IT world is a work in progress—a journey that is under way. Nevertheless, the journey has begun, and the distance traveled is impressive.

In the remainder of this chapter, I first present a more complete review of historical IT developments. I then consider some of the major manifestations of IT change that have taken place in law enforcement, courts, and corrections. To conclude, I consider some of the impacts of these changes and review the benefits and risks that accompany them.

HISTORICAL BACKGROUND

Acquisition of state-of-the art IT has become a dominant theme in criminal justice during the past decade. However, this is not without precedent. In fact, a desire to develop systematic information about crime has existed in the United States in one form or another for more than 150 years.[4] In 1834, Massachusetts became the first state to collect data on crimes. The U.S. federal government soon followed, first in conjunction with the 1850 census and subsequently with later censuses. By the early 1900s, data from police reports were being compiled in a few places into criminal statistical summaries, and federal prisoner data and federal judicial statistics were being accumulated, printed, and disseminated by the office of the U.S. attorney general.

These early efforts, although modest, were used for decision making about federal budgeting, facilities construction, and resource allocation issues. However, many local police departments lacked the resources and interest needed to compile comprehensive and accurate statistics. The result was questionable knowledge at best about nonfederal crime and the local criminal justice environment.

An effort was made to address this shortcoming during the 1920s when the International Association of Chiefs of Police (IACP) developed, and in 1929 implemented, a Uniform Crime Reporting (UCR) system to which local police departments were urged to voluntarily contribute crime data in a standardized format. In 1930, the IACP transferred this system to the FBI, where it is still housed.[5] Substantial participation quickly followed. The 1930 UCR report covered 1,002 cities, with 83% participation of all cities with populations greater than 25,000.

Commissions: 1931–1965

In 1929, the same year that the UCR system was launched, President Hoover established a National Commission on Law Observance and Enforcement that later came to be known as the Wickersham Commission.[6] Although there had been a few locally based studies of criminal justice during the previous 10 years,[7] this was the first national review of justice administration in the United States. The commission published 13 reports in June 1930.[8] One of these, the Report on Criminal Statistics, was an assertion of the need for accurate nationwide statistics on crime and the criminal justice system. Members of the commission advocated creation of a comprehensive system of national data encompassing penal, judicial, and police data under one umbrella federal agency that would have both the mandate and the resources to achieve these objectives. The UCR system became the formal manifestation of this principle and over the subsequent three and a half decades came to be the nation's barometer of crime levels.

In 1965, President Johnson convened the President's Commission on Law Enforcement and Administration of Justice to examine criminal justice information systems and statistics and to make recommendations about the role that the federal government could and should play. Henry Ruth, deputy director of the commission, stated, "Practically no data on the criminal justice system existed when the commission began work. Not much police data existed. Court data were a mess."[9] In addition, the commission's survey of 10,000 households indicated that crime of all kinds was being seriously underreported to police.

The inevitable conclusion was that the UCR system could not be relied on as an accurate measure of crime levels in the country.[10]

This led to a reaffirmation and clarification of the principles and approaches that had been promulgated earlier by the Wickersham Commission but had never been fully implemented. Primary among these were that the federal government should provide support and guidance to local governments to aid the development, collection, and compilation of crime statistics at the local level; that a National Criminal Justice Statistics Center should be set up to manage and disseminate the information that local governments would collect; that state statistical centers should be established both to provide information and support to the federal agency and to generate locally useful data; and that appropriate levels of federal funding should be provided to help accomplish these goals.

Federal Legislation: 1968–1994

The immediate outcome of the President's Commission on Law Enforcement and Administration of Justice was the passage of the Omnibus Crime Control and Safe Streets Act of 1968, which has been the foundation for virtually all subsequent federal legislation on state and local criminal justice matters. This act created the LEAA, which from 1968 to 1979 housed the National Institute of Law Enforcement and Criminal Justice (the precursor agency to today's National Institute of Justice) and the National Criminal Justice Information and Statistics Service (the precursor to today's Bureau of Justice Statistics).

Despite the promise inherent in the commission's report and the subsequent legislation, the operational manifestation of the principles the commission espoused did not generate long-term acceptance by Congress or the criminal justice community. Congressional willingness to fund the agency dwindled, and appropriations were effectively zero in 1980 after an all-time high in 1976.[11]

In 1979, Congress passed the Justice System Improvement Act, which took the building blocks created by the LEAA and converted them into the federal system for dealing with state and local criminal justice issues that we know today. An independent National Institute of Justice (NIJ) and Bureau of Justice Statistics (BJS) were created within the LEAA framework. An oversight office, the Office of Justice Assistance, Research, and Statistics (OJARS), was also established. When the LEAA was formally abolished in 1982, the other three offices survived and the Comprehensive Crime Control Act of 1984 created a new structure retaining the NIJ as the research entity, retaining the BJS as the statistics entity, renaming the OJARS the Office of Justice Programs with similar oversight responsibilities, and creating two new agencies: the Bureau of Justice Assistance (BJA) to manage block grants and the Office for Victims of Crime to handle victim issues. This organizational structure has survived to this day.

An important exception was the Crime Control Act of 1994,[12] which among other things created an independent agency, the Office of Community-Oriented Policing Services (OCOPS), to manage the 100,000 Cops on the Street program of the Clinton administration. This legislation formalized federal IT development aid to local jurisdictions at an unprecedented level. Under the MORE (Making Officer Redeployment Effective) program, the OCOPS delivered more than $1.3 billion to nearly 4,500 police departments for the acquisition and implementation of IT systems.[13] The principle behind this commitment was the notion that improved information systems would work as force multipliers by reducing the time burdens imposed on police officers by data-gathering requirements. Participating departments were required to commit to increased street time for police officers to secure the MORE funding. Initially, the OCOPS reserved the right to withdraw funding, or to require reimbursement for funds disbursed, if departments were unable to live up to their commitments. This condition was later relaxed, but the principle that more effective use of IT enhances police performance was well established and accepted.[14]

Summary

This short historical summary has highlighted the primary administrative and legislative actions that the federal government has taken in its efforts to come to terms with the informational demands of the problem of crime. In some respects, these efforts can be considered a success. The federal BJS now produces an impressive array of data series covering a large variety of criminal justice topics. The NIJ sponsors a wide range of empirical research and has managed significant data collection efforts focusing on drugs and crime.[15] The FBI produces UCR reports on a nationwide scale, and every state has a criminal justice Statistical Analysis Center.[16] The National Crime Victimization Survey captures both unreported and reported crime in ways that most observers consider to be highly credible and dependable.

At the local level, many police departments have replaced paper records with computerized information systems that would have been infeasible a decade or so ago. The development of these local systems has often been a consequence of federal support, particularly during their early stages. As IT sophistication has increased and become more affordable, most jurisdictions are now funding their own systems, but the federal role has been clear.

I now turn to a more specific review of the salient changes that have taken place.

PROMISES AND ADVANCES IN IT

In this section, I review what has taken place in the criminal justice system with respect to IT and information system development in a number of important areas during the past three decades or so. The overarching theme is that the rapid technological advances that have taken place outside criminal justice have promised, and sometimes delivered, significant improvements in the information processing capabilities of criminal justice agencies. In addition, my argument is that the incorporation of these advances into police department, court, and corrections operations will at least radically improve, and perhaps revolutionize, criminal justice. Such advances span virtually all of the information-gathering requirements pertaining to crime measurement, control, and response that these agencies might need. A side effect of these advances has resulted in the systemization of criminal justice agencies. Although law enforcement agencies, courts, and departments of correction have experienced IT advances individually, they have in some instances collectively experienced a shift from being completely separate agencies to becoming information-sharing partners in the working components of a criminal justice system.

The reader should keep in mind that some of the technologies presented are of recent vintage and so have not yet stood the test of time. It is common for agencies to express concern and dissatisfaction that hardware or software does not seem to be living up to its promise. This is to be expected. Criminal justice agencies do not operate at the cutting edge of change, and one of the well-known effects of new IT is that operational and institutional change is often entailed by adjustments in information processing. That is, IT changes are not simply a way of doing old tasks faster or more cheaply (although that is usually a desired outcome). They also often require a new way of doing business to fully use the innovative capabilities that have been introduced. What seems certain, however, is that IT changes will continue to be implemented and that they will have profound impacts on the criminal justice system.

This section is divided into four subsections on law enforcement, courts and prosecution, corrections, and criminal justice agency integration. Law enforcement agencies have experienced the widest-ranging changes in information processing and so are given greater coverage than the other elements.

Law Enforcement

Crime Analysis

Crime analysis serves four specific functions in criminal justice. Reuland identifies these as supporting resource deployment, assisting investigations and apprehending offenders, preventing crime, and meeting administrative needs.[17] Crime analysis may also serve strategic purposes for planning agencies, crime prevention units, patrol and investigative commanders, and community relations units in terms of their programmatic, planning, development, and evaluation functions.

Law enforcement agencies have been doing some form of crime analysis for as long as they have been in existence. Policing has always been focused rather than random, and it has never simply been reactive rather than proactive. In short, crime analysis has always guided strategic and tactical decision making in police departments, even when the analysis was paper based because that was the only option available. However, IT advances have increased the domain of crime analysis tremendously, and the crime analysis that takes place today differs dramatically from what was performed even a decade ago. Because of the low-cost proliferation of information processing capacity, it is now rare for even a small police department to have no crime analysis capability. In fact, most departments now consider automated management information systems, computer-aided dispatch (CAD), computerized case management systems, and Internet access by citizens as technologies that are prerequisites to effective policing.[18]

The five stages of crime analysis illustrate the natural fit with the IT revolution:

1. *Data collection.* Most local crime data are generated by crime reports made to police departments, officer investigations of those reports, and any subsequent arrests. Initial reports are handled primarily by CAD systems, which are now virtually universal. Officers follow up with field interviews, offense reports, investigative reports, arrest reports, evidence technician reports, criminal history records, offender interviews, and so forth. For some criminal justice agencies, information is also likely to come from non-police sources such as schools, utility companies, city planners, parks departments, social service agencies, courts, probation and parole agencies, other police agencies, and the Bureau of the Census (e.g., for demographics of a given area).

2. *Data collation.* Departments create databases capable of automated searches and comparisons. Basic database requirements include completeness, reliability, and timeliness.

3. *Analysis.* Departments analyze crime data to detect descriptive patterns of activity that may also predict future crimes. Crime mapping has become an increasingly popular analysis approach.

4. *Dissemination.* Departments prepare data for internal and external users. Face-to-face contact between crime analysts and officers and investigators, as well as some other users, can be important for developing a mutual understanding of the data and their usability.

5. *Feedback.* Measuring user satisfaction with the information that police are given is essential. Crime analysts need to find out which products and formats work and which ones do not work. They must also learn how end users plan to use their products. Analysts can use a simple, closed-ended survey form to obtain feedback as well as personal contact.

Historically, the most common form of crime analysis has involved tabular presentation of aggregate data, hand-drawn charts, and pin maps. With the advent of high-speed computer processing, however, automated spatial crime mapping (often referred to as geographic information systems [GIS]) has become dominant. Although computers have been used to display and manipulate maps since the 1960s, the use of sophisticated mapping software in criminal justice is a relatively new phenomenon. Its growth is due largely to the recent development of inexpensive, yet effective and sophisticated, PC-based mapping software packages as well as to the emphasis that the federal government has placed on it.[19]

The most well-known agency implementation of spatial analysis has been in New York City, where the New York Police Department (NYPD) has used these techniques on a regular and systematic basis for more than a decade.[20] The NYPD approach, known universally as CompStat (derived from the phrase "computer statistics"), is used for both performance management and crime analysis. On a weekly basis, top-level NYPD command staff members hold a CompStat meeting at which borough and precinct staff members report on recent crime trends. Crime analysis reports (both spatial and tabular) are displayed on wall-size screens as the meeting proceeds. These meetings are highly visible assessments of unit performance, generally focusing on the precinct level, and may involve as many as 100 people from various divisions and sections within NYPD. Outsiders, such as members of district attorney offices, community organizations, and corrections departments, may also be invited to attend. There are many who attribute the recent crime reductions in New York City in part to the accountability approach of CompStat.

More recently, in a significant number of other departments, spatial mapping has been used to detect crime trends and displacement and to predict future crime incidents. In October 2002, as the Washington, D.C., metropolitan area sought answers to the sniper shootings, law enforcement agencies called on the Department of Justice to use mapping techniques to predict the snipers' next target.[21] Yet gathering spatial data from the surrounding police jurisdictions became a much more difficult task than was originally thought. Although the process of data collection was expedited, it still took several weeks to receive data from the relevant jurisdictions. And upon receipt, it was clear that the data quality, standards, and street names and addresses did not correspond across jurisdictions. Regional, or interjurisdictional, crime mapping was not yet possible in this particular context.

In response, officials at the NIJ partnered with the University of Virginia's Department of Systems and Information Engineering to develop the Geospatial Repository for Analysis and Safety Planning (GRASP). The GRASP program essentially acts as a central database for regional spatial analysis, enabling local authorities to upload and analyze detailed spatial data for regional events. According to Bryan Vila, chief of the NIJ's Crime Control and Prevention Research Division, the GRASP program is designed to standardize and link interjurisdictional data.[22] It has a Web-based interface that allows researchers and relevant agencies to transfer and access data easily and in a timely manner.[23] Currently, data repositories are being developed or are already available for Baltimore County, Maryland;

Charlotte–Mecklenburg, North Carolina; the San Francisco Bay Area; and the Washington, D.C., metropolitan area.

Despite the capabilities that programs such as GRASP and spatial analysis offer, use of such programs is by no means universal. In 1994, 30% of 280 member departments of the IACP Law Enforcement Management Information Section (including the most active users of computer technology among local departments in the nation) reported having used mapping software. A 15-month survey of 2,000 law enforcement agencies conducted by the NIJ Crime Mapping Research Center found that 261 used some computerized crime mapping. Not surprisingly, larger departments (i.e., those having more than 100 sworn officers) were much more likely to use the technology (36%) than were smaller departments (3%).[24] These statistics are now dated, of course. Since the OCOPS began funding IT acquisition programs, many more departments have implemented spatial analysis. However, the Washington, D.C., experience in 2002 illustrates an important consideration. The value, or usefulness, of crime analysis is contingent on both the quality of input data and the capacity of the hardware and software used. The overall message is that traditional data quality standards that police departments have been able to maintain may very well be inadequate in light of more sophisticated IT. This is another example of the way in which IT developments mandate changes in longstanding operating procedures.

Uniform Crime Reporting/National Incident-Based Reporting System

During the mid-1970s, it was clear that a revised and enhanced UCR system was needed for the 21st century. This coincided with advances in IT that made a more sophisticated system feasible. The BJS and the FBI funded a substantial examination and reassessment of the UCR program that culminated in the 1985 publication of a *Blueprint for the Future of the Uniform Crime Reporting System.*[25]

The *Blueprint* proposed that a National Incident-Based Reporting System (NIBRS) replace the existing UCR system. The plan called for "incident-based" reporting, rather than aggregate reporting, represented by two levels of reporting complexity, the more detailed of which would be followed by only 3% to 7% of law enforcement agencies nationwide. Ultimately, the law enforcement community endorsed the NIBRS framework but elected to institute the more complex reporting level for all participating agencies.

Representing both an expansion of the UCR system and a major conceptual shift, the NIBRS is an incident-based system that collects detailed information on individual crimes, including data on location, property, weapons, victims, offenders, arrestees, and law enforcement officers injured or killed. In addition, under the NIBRS, the scope of reporting is widened to cover 22 crime categories that include a total of 46 specific offenses known as "Group A" offenses. For an additional 11 "Group B" offenses, the NIBRS collects detailed data on persons arrested.

Whereas the UCR system requires local law enforcement agencies to report monthly aggregate figures on crimes and arrests, the NIBRS asks local agencies to submit data on individual incidents for compilation at the state and federal levels. As agencies have improved their automated systems, this level of detail is in fact present (in principle) in most police department record management systems. This offers a potential for analysis that would be impossible using only the UCR aggregates, but it also decreases local agencies' control over dissemination of information.

Despite the potential benefits of the NIBRS to law enforcement management, training, and planning, law enforcement agencies have been relatively slow to adopt the system. As of May 1997, only 10 states were certified to report NIBRS data and only 4% of U.S. criminal incidents were reported under the NIBRS. Large law enforcement agencies have been especially reluctant to make the transition to the NIBRS; as of May 1999, the Austin (Texas) Police Department was the only agency serving a population of more than 500,000 to report NIBRS data.

According to a recent study by SEARCH, the National Consortium for Justice Information and Statistics, law enforcement agencies cite lack of funding as the primary obstacle to full adoption of the NIBRS.[26] Indeed, the costs associated with the transition can be substantial for those law enforcement agencies that have existing records management systems (RMSs) that either are too antiquated to function effectively or are incompatible with NIBRS requirements.

Of course, the technical and cost problems are not created by NIBRS information needs. They are a consequence of the outmoded and inadequate IT systems that are supposed to produce NIBRS-quality data but do not. Nevertheless, as departments upgrade and automate record-keeping systems, they do generate computerized data that would easily meet all NIBRS needs provided that the requirement for cross-jurisdictional standardization of definition of offenses and other data elements can be achieved. Most big city departments, for instance, now have data systems that contain substantially more data elements than does the NIBRS and perform analyses that are significantly more sophisticated than those contemplated by NIBRS advocates. This suggests that the main obstacles to more widespread implementation of the NIBRS are not so much technical or financial as they are related to the perception that the NIBRS contributes little to local needs for crime analysis and information. In this sense, the potential contribution of the

NIBRS seems destined to be greatest at the regional, state, and national levels. It remains to be seen whether the perceived value of this potential will be sufficient to mobilize the voluntary local commitment to participation on which the NIBRS depends.[27]

Records Management Systems

An RMS is the informational heart of any police department's operations. It provides for the storage, retrieval, retention, manipulation, archiving, and viewing of information, records, documents, and files about every aspect of police business. A comprehensive and fully functioning RMS should include crime and arrest reports, personnel records, criminal records, and crime analysis data.

Prior to the 1970s, nearly all police department record keeping was paper based. Gradual conversion to mainframe computer record keeping began during the 1970s, particularly for crime and arrest information, and by the mid-1980s an estimated 1,500 of the nation's 17,000 police agencies were using mainframe computers to a limited extent. More recently, departments have begun to move to fully automated RMSs. Some of these departments have gone beyond simply automating record-keeping procedures to implementing dynamic relational databases as an integral element in information management.

In such departments, RMSs are no longer stand-alone systems. They can be interfaced to other systems in the city or county and to state law enforcement systems, which in turn provide access to national crime databases. More recent systems provide graphical user interface with menus, buttons, icons, and other easily recognizable screen images. Built-in editing and error checking can reject incorrect information as it is entered, thereby prompting correction before data are stored.

Incident address records are a good example of this capability. When entered by hand, addresses frequently contain mistakes; in fact, error rates of 30% to 40% are not uncommon. Now, some departments have every legitimate city address stored in a master file that is scanned whenever an address is entered. Addresses not found are rejected, and a prompt for correction is issued. This produces percentage accuracy rates in the high 90th percentile, a critical accomplishment for use with other computer-based applications such as crime mapping and the NIBRS. For example, in Los Angeles County, which averages more than 500,000 arrests per year, the integrated system purportedly verifies a suspect's identity and accesses criminal and case histories in less than 2.5 seconds, even though the county receives data from 50 law enforcement agencies, 62 additional authorities, 21 different city attorney/prosecutor offices, and 24 municipal court districts. Thus, state-of-the-art RMSs can be integrated with other systems, such as CAD. They can track all the functions of a police precinct—not just arrests and bookings—in one complete package. For example, the latest breed of RMS will manage budgets; keep an active inventory of supplies, property, and evidence; schedule K-9 care and vehicle maintenance; organize intelligence; track 9-1-1 data; and automate many other departmental functions.

These RMSs also support access to a wide range of external databases, such as the National Crime Information Center (NCIC) and the NIBRS, and have the ability to share information with other justice agencies at all levels of government. These capabilities create significant new potential for police departments to conduct advanced crime analysis, ground strategic and tactical decision making on sound information, determine resource deployment on a proactive rather than a reactive basis, and execute many other functions that either were impossible to perform under earlier systems or were performed under conditions of extreme uncertainty.

Criminal Histories and Offender Identification

A critical component of record keeping involves criminal histories and offender identification. These have always been problematic for police departments for two principal reasons. First, definitive identification at the time of arrest is sometimes difficult to achieve. Some arrestees simply give false names and carry no documents. A survey conducted in 1997 found that only 25 states had final dispositions for at least 70% of arrests from the previous 5 years.[28] Computerization clearly offers the potential to overcome these problems quickly and efficiently, yet the results of this survey suggest that this potential has not yet been realized.

Nevertheless, both federal and state criminal history and identification systems have evolved significantly over the past few decades. States have established criminal history repositories that contain information about arrests occurring throughout their jurisdictions. The FBI maintains criminal history systems for federal offenders and a national criminal records system, including the NCIC and the Interstate Identification Index (III). Individual law enforcement agencies can query them by way of remote terminals. At the national level, the FBI is currently moving toward an automated National Fingerprint File (NFF).

Perhaps of greater significance are the mandates imposed by the Brady Handgun Violence Prevention Act, the National Child Protection Act of 1993, and "Megan's Laws."[29] These significantly expanded the importance of criminal history records for determining eligibility to purchase a firearm, screening child care facility employees,

and registering sexual offenders. Although controversy continues to surround the constitutionality and efficacy of this process, some evidence exists that it has had an effect. The BJS reported that from March 1, 1994, to November 29, 1998, approximately 12,740,000 applications for handgun purchases were made. There were 312,000 rejections as a result of the background checks required by the Brady Act law.[30] The ability to perform such checks is a remarkable IT achievement. Given the growing public and political attention being paid to gun violence, there seems little doubt that the process of background checks will become increasingly sophisticated.

The BJS currently manages a major federal initiative, the National Criminal History Improvement Program (NCHIP), that provides funding to the FBI and state criminal history repositories. The goal of the NCHIP is to ensure that accurate records are available for use in law enforcement, including sex offender registry requirements. The objective is to give states the ability to identify persons who are ineligible to buy firearms or hold positions involving children, persons who have outstanding warrants or who are subject to protective orders, and persons who have been arrested or convicted of stalking and/or domestic violence. The NCHIP also provides funding to the FBI to operate the National Instant Criminal Background Check System (established pursuant to the permanent provision of the Brady Act), the National Sex Offender Registry (NSOR), and the National Protective Order File.

These developments move law enforcement closer to the goal of rapid identification and accurate recovery of history information. The key, in the end, will be the extent to which individual police departments develop the capacity to take advantage of the state and federal systems that are being created.

Mobile Data Terminals

During the past decade, another important enhancement for law enforcement response capability has been developed through mobile data terminals (MDTs). These allow wireless receipt and transmission of information to and from officers on foot or in patrol cars. Initially, MDTs were basically unsophisticated terminals that permitted transfer of rudimentary information between station and officer. Dispatch instructions, for instance, could be sent to the terminal rather than being put out over police radio. Officers could automatically record and transmit arrival times at the dispatch location. During the past few years, however, technological advances have led to the introduction of laptop and notebook computers, voice-activated computers, personal digital assistants (PDAs), and handheld ticket-issuing computers. These now match desktop machines in sophistication and in the future will continue to expand in capability. As miniaturization progresses, for instance, handheld devices that do not require patrol car installation seem certain to proliferate. This will free officers from patrol car dependence and increase the scope and sophistication that officers on the street can exercise with respect to two-way information flow. In this sense, MDTs are becoming much more than just aids to response.

Although there are few empirical studies of the impacts of MDTs, their reported benefits include speed of information dissemination, saving officers time and effort, facilitating information sharing, increasing reporting accuracy and uniformity, enhancing response time, and increasing officer safety.

In 1997, the NIJ sponsored a study by the National Law Enforcement and Corrections Technology Center on the ability of different agencies to communicate with each other across jurisdictions (so-called "interoperability"). A total of 1,344 agencies responded to the questionnaire. The agencies that were currently using MDTs employed these devices primarily for database information and free text (e.g., reports, queries). However, for budgetary reasons, the use of MDTs was far less common in smaller agencies—as low as 4% of agencies that employed fewer than 10 sworn officers.

Despite current limitations, more departments can be expected to use MDTs. Some federal funds are being provided to assist in the purchase of MDTs. In addition, the technology now enables officers on the street to take advantage of the FBI's new NCIC 2000 and Integrated Automated Fingerprinting Identification System (IAFIS) initiatives, providing an added impetus for implementation. MDTs will also assist departments in conforming to the new incident-based reporting standards of the NIBRS. These clear advantages, coupled with declining cost and increasing ease of use, suggest that it will not be long before virtually every department uses MDTs.

Forensic Technology

DNA databases are an emerging technology that seems likely to substantially enhance the investigative work of law enforcement and prosecutorial agencies. The DNA Identification Program and DNA Laboratory Improvement Program, both of which receive federal funding, have prompted interest in implementing these programs on the local, regional, and state levels.

An NIJ-funded study of the application of DNA technology in England and Wales indicated the critical assistance that such forensic databases can provide in the apprehension and prosecution of offenders. The National DNA Database of England and Wales contains DNA profiles of more than 2 million individuals. The study found that, when DNA is available from the crime scene, the suspect identification rate for domestic burglary rises from 14% to 44%. It also found that use of the database prevents 7.8 crimes for each custodial sentence resulting from a DNA-based conviction. By March 2004, the national database was expected to include profiles of the entire "criminally active population." Even in its current state, the database has a 40% match rate in linking crime scene DNA profiles to "criminal justice" (arrestee or suspect) profiles in the database.[31] It is clear that DNA technology offers tremendous potential to criminal justice agencies. The principal cautionary note is that the expense of such databases and the specialized skills required to match DNA profiles that might delay nationwide implementation in the United States.

Courts, Prosecution, Public Defenders, and Corrections

Technology in Courtrooms

The introduction of technology in the courts has improved court functions and efficiency, yet it has not brought the wide-sweeping change experienced by law enforcement. Nonetheless, with the advent of closed-caption television (CCTV) in the courtroom, the courts were able to respect the constitutional rights of offenders while simultaneously guarding against causing further trauma to victims, particularly young victims. In 1990, the U.S. Supreme Court approved CCTV use in the courtroom in *Maryland v. Craig.*[32] In its decision, the court recognized the critical importance of CCTV in the courtroom in that it allows young victims of abuse or assault to present courtroom testimony without having to appear in the same room as the accused.

Courts are only more recently using CCTV, whereas law enforcement agencies have been using some form of CCTV to prevent and solve crimes for years. A survey conducted by the IACP found that 80% of responding police agencies use some form of CCTV.[33] The most common settings were in police cars, in interrogation rooms, and at access points to government buildings. Fully 63% of respondents reported that CCTV was useful in conducting investigations, and 54% said it was helpful in gathering evidence. More recently, there has been a growing acceptance of CCTV in schools that have public safety problems. Given the public concern about high-profile violence in schools (e.g., Columbine High School in Littleton, Colorado), this trend seems likely to continue to expand.[34]

The introduction of digital technology in the courts has expanded to digital evidence presentation systems. Such systems are becoming an entrepreneurial venture, with private companies offering elaborate systems to county and state courtrooms nationwide. These systems include laptop computers, DVD players, videocassette recorders (VCRs), cassette players, printers, and document cameras allowing legal teams to display exhibits instantly. For example, using a touch screen located in the witness box, a doctor can draw a circle on a magnetic resonance image (MRI) where he or she sees a problem that was misdiagnosed. At the same time, the same circle can be seen by the entire courtroom on multiple large plasma screens, by the attorneys and judges on their touch screens, and by each juror on his or her own plasma screen. More than 300 courtrooms nationwide are currently using this technology.[35]

The National Task Force on Court Automation and Integration is a partnership with SEARCH, the National Center for State Courts, the National Association for Court Management, and the Conference of State Court Administrators and is funded by the Department of Justice. The task force studied county-level integrated systems in 34 states and concluded in its *Court Technology Survey Report,* issued in November 2001, that benefits were tremendous. Among the benefits were reduction of repetitive tasks, improved quality of decision making, enhancement of data quality, increased information accessibility, increased organizational integration, enhanced statistics and monitoring, and increased effectiveness.[36]

The Justice Information Management System (JIMS) exemplifies the benefits of such a system. Harris County, Texas, is one of many jurisdictions that have established integrated information systems to end miscommunications between sentencing agencies and jails that can result in the prolonged incarceration of inmates after their sentences expire. Harris County currently uses the nation's largest fully integrated, automated, county-level justice information system, serving 144 county-level courts and other agencies, 111 non-county agencies (including municipalities and school districts), 11 state agencies, 15 federal agencies, and more than 800 subscriber access companies. The JIMS allows any Harris County law enforcement station to file cases electronically 7 days a week, resulting in a first court appearance within 24 hours for felony and misdemeanor suspects. The benefits of such a system are realized by the accused (the amount of time that suspects spend behind bars prior to trial is reduced dramatically) as well as by the county (the system reportedly saves Harris County more than $6.5 million annually).[37]

Case Tracking and Case Management Systems

All participants in criminal (and civil) cases have a need for effective case tracking and management systems. Most cases involve multiple parties (e.g., judges, prosecutors, defendants) and several events (e.g., arraignments, hearings, trials), all of which have to be carefully scheduled and organized for the court system to work. Prior to the 1960s, systems for tracking cases were nearly entirely paper based. During the early 1960s, however, the federal government began funding the Prosecutor's Management Information System (PROMIS), which was the first major automated case management system in the United States.[38] This system was first introduced in the District of Columbia but was extended to several other major metropolitan jurisdictions over the subsequent two decades (e.g., borough of Manhattan in New York, Los Angeles in California). Stored on computers, the system provided comprehensive automated information about cases, including offender names and addresses, witness identification and location, lawyers' mailing addresses, schedules for court events, and automatic notice generation. Since the 1970s, similar systems have been introduced, and courts today typically have some automated case tracking and management capability.

A good example of such a system on the prosecution side is RACKETS, a case tracking and mapping system that was developed for the U.S. Attorney's Office of the Southern District of New York (SDNY). According to the system's final report,

> RACKETS was initially designed to collect information on the cases, defendants, investigations, wiretaps, and warrants for the violent gangs, narcotics, organized crime, and general crime units. The system was developed to collect information either not handled, or not handled at sufficient enough detail, by the office's existing case management system. The system was implemented to overcome the episodic way of handling cases to a comprehensive and strategic method.[39]

As the federal prosecuting office for Manhattan, Bronx, and other counties in and around New York City, SDNY works with numerous local, state, and federal agencies.

In many cases, information collected by one agency is often relevant to another agency's investigation. RACKETS was designed to collectively house data related to all of the office's investigations, thereby linking related cases and streamlining investigations.

Indigent Defense and Technology

Technology has, in addition to supporting the court system as a whole, made indigent defense more efficient and cost-effective. The BJA recently commissioned a special report on the way in which technology has affected the work of public defenders. The report found that "technology is improving client access to attorneys and attorney access to information. It is improving case information management, attorneys' presentation of evidence in court, and attorneys' access to routine pleadings." [40] Online technology has also been shown to improve litigation, management of case-related information, and case tracking.

For example, in 1997 in Knoxville, Tennessee, the District Public Defender's Office, together with its IT specialist, developed a case management system for case-related multimedia known as *Virtual Casefile:*

> *Virtual Casefile* digitizes and stores video and audiotapes, photographs, and documents on a powerful workstation. These data are categorized, cross-referenced, and integrated with a graphical user interface. The data are then stored permanently on a recordable CD-ROM. The attorney can read the original police report or search warrant, view a lineup or photo of physical evidence, listen to a recording of a 911 call, navigate a virtual reality crime scene, or watch a clip from the local news using the *Virtual Casefile*'s simple point-and-click interface. [41]

Public defender offices are increasingly using case-tracking software applications that allow updating and monitoring of individual cases as well as the generation of statistics on aggregate case trends. "Using these systems, public defender managers can determine much more accurately whether case processing problems are emanating from outside the office (for example, from the practice of judges or prosecutors), [are emanating from] within the office (inefficient attorneys or case-flow glitches), or are specific to a particular type of case." [42] These systems also provide a significant cost savings to public defenders. For example, a system implemented throughout West Virginia saved its counties more than $100,000 in voucher errors during its first year of implementation between 1998 and 1999.

Corrections–Offender Supervision with Electronic Monitoring

Corrections and correctional officials are currently taking advantage of the potential offered by new technologies to reduce the costs of supervising criminal offenders. Known today as "technocorrections," this field uses emerging technologies in the areas of electronic tracking, pharmacological treatments, and genetic and neurobiological risk assessments to minimize the risk that offenders pose to society. [43]

Most jurisdictions across the country use some form of electronic monitoring to locate persons on probation and parole. Introduced during the mid-1980s, this technology minimizes the use of court or police officers, whose effort is replaced by a monitoring agency, saves correctional dollars, enhances supervision, and arguably encourages offender accountability. Tremendous advances in tracking technology have been made in other fields, and so modern electronic monitoring can vary dramatically, from wrist bracelets that communicate through a device connected to telephone lines to updated versions based on cellular or satellite tracking. Both of these methods offer correctional officials the means to continuously

track offenders' locations and supervise their movements.

The technology is now capable of far more than tracking an individual's location and will enable correctional officials to define geographic zones from which an offender is prohibited, alerting officials instantly when an offender has entered those areas. Some jurisdictions are also exploring the provision of tracking devices to an offender's previous or potential victims. These devices will set "safe zones" that trigger alarms or warning notices on approach of the offender. In addition, tiny cameras could be attached to tracking devices to provide live video of an offender's location and circumstances.[44]

Criminal Justice Agency Integration

Integrated Criminal Justice Information Systems

Arguably the most valuable application of networking technology has led to integrated justice information systems. The cited benefits of integrated justice information systems are clear. They improve the quality of data available to all users, save time and money by eliminating redundant data entry, facilitate timely access to information, and permit accurate information sharing across distance and time. For many years, the fragmentation and lack of coordination among criminal justice agencies has been deplored; the criminal justice system, according to many, is not a system. Networking seems to offer the potential for addressing this problem.

Setting up an integrated system typically demands an extended planning process requiring the participation of all stakeholders. The planning process involves building support for the project, establishing needs assessment and strategic planning for the project, setting standards for data collection, identifying technological solutions, and establishing an oversight board for acquisitions and implementation.

During the planning phases, particular attention must be paid to establishing information systems standards, which have been called "the linchpin to integration."[45] For successful integration, standardization is required in several areas: data definitions, a common language for use between information systems, communications protocols used between agencies, procedures for transferring different types of information (e.g., photos, fingerprints), and security.

The foregoing indicated that regardless of the advantages of integration, it should not be undertaken lightly. Rather, it is an extended process that requires substantial financial and human resources, as well as a sustained commitment from all involved agencies, to be completed successfully. A qualitative study conducted by SEARCH indicated the following primary obstacles to adoption of integrated justice information systems: persistence of entrenched information processing systems and data at local agencies, difficulty of coordinating interagency projects, limited understanding of technological issues and capabilities, need for systems to be private and secure, fundamental interagency differences in recording/reporting systems, and shortage of IT professionals.

Computer Networking Technology and the Internet

Advances in IT, combined with criminal justice agencies' increasing emphasis on crime prevention, problem solving, and community credibility, is redefining the pursuit and use of criminal justice information. The development of incident-based reporting systems and increasingly sophisticated techniques of communication has resulted in sharp increases in the volume and complexity of collected data. As this has occurred, new technologies have begun to play a crucial role in agencies' efforts to disseminate, share, and manage this torrent of criminal justice information.

Computer networking plays a valuable and expanding role in facilitating communication at all levels—among the local, state, and federal agencies; between local agencies and constituent communities; and across agencies within a given region or locality—and this is particularly relevant to the operations of courts.

Establishing websites is one of the most common applications of IT networking and offers tremendous benefits to the community (facilitating communication and centralizing important information for residents) and to justice agencies (lending credibility to the agencies). As of August 1997, more than 500 local law enforcement agencies maintained websites, and the establishment and expansion of sites has continued at a rapid pace.[46] By allowing agencies to interact cheaply and easily with members of their constituent communities, an effective website can significantly enhance police–community relations and further community policing objectives.[47]

Yet the Internet is not a completely satisfactory way of dealing with criminal justice agencies' information dissemination problems. First, not all residents use or have access to the Internet, and some do not even have computers. In general, these distinctions are associated with income and education. Therefore, relying on the Internet risks bias against the poorest residents, that is, those who arguably have the greatest need for information. For this reason alone, agencies should continue to pursue traditional methods of public education to reach everyone in the community.

IMPACT OF IT ADVANCES ON THE CRIMINAL JUSTICE SYSTEM

Although criminal justice agencies have stood to gain from the IT advances of the past 30 years, the reality for many has been, and still is, quite different. In reality, only a handful of new IT systems have been implemented at anything that approaches the level that is technologically feasible. Despite agencies' desire to improve, which is the principal stimulus for IT changes, IT advances carry risks in addition to benefits. I elaborate on these in this section.

Benefits

Strategic and Tactical Decision Making

This benefit is readily apparent. The more information an agency has, and the better its methods of processing that information, the greater the likelihood that decision making will be rationally based and impact driven.

Cross-Jurisdictional Cooperation and Collaboration

Quality data and access to regional information will create a better foundation for effective cross-jurisdictional interaction. Departments will be able to make a more effective contribution to their own knowledge and experience while also better using information provided by other jurisdictions. Cooperation and collaboration on matters of common interest will be enhanced.

For example, San Diego has grappled with the increased criminal activity that has resulted from criminals' use of technology. In a joint undertaking, the law enforcement community has formed CATCH, a task force that investigates and prosecutes criminals who commit crimes using or targeting sophisticated IT. CATCH consists of investigators from numerous agencies, including the San Diego Sheriff's Department, the San Diego Police Department, the FBI, the San Diego County District Attorney's Office, the California Department of Justice, the Internal Revenue Service, the Imperial County District Attorney's Office, and the Riverside County Sheriff's Department. CATCH, which became operational on June 1, 2000, is one of many joint law enforcement and prosecutorial efforts around the

United States that use advanced IT to prevent crimes that use IT opportunities for identity theft, online fraud, and the like.

Information Sharing

In 2002, the Law Enforcement Information Technology Standards Council was established to promote information sharing and establish relevant protocols. The council, which consists of the IACP, the National Organization of Black Law Enforcement Executives, the National Sheriffs' Association, and the Police Executive Research Forum, recently collaborated with the Global Justice Information Sharing Initiative Advisory Committee (known as GLOBAL). GLOBAL acts as a central warehouse of IT standards with the goal of resolving issues that arise among criminal justice agencies—specifically courts, corrections, parole, and police—during information sharing.[48]

Today, there are several national databases, administered by the FBI, that permit interstate access to the criminal records maintained in all 50 states. These systems include the NCIC, the III, the IAFIS, the National Protection Order File, and the National Sex Offender Registry.

Technology standards and information-sharing protocols are time-consuming and expensive to establish and implement. They place information generation and processing demands on participating agencies that generally exceed what have previously been considered necessary for the conduct of "normal" business. However, they are a prerequisite for interagency communication and cooperation.

Aggregation at the State, Regional, and National Levels

Aggregate statistics, such as those produced by the UCR system, are of no higher quality than data provided by individual police departments. Improved data at the local level leads to improved aggregations at higher levels. Better compilations and more accurate statements of trends will result.

Stimulation of Research

A common complaint among researchers is that the research they conduct is often not used. There are a number of reasons for this. Some are ideological and not susceptible to easy change.[49] Others, however, are a consequence of the informational impediments that researchers have characteristically faced. These have tended to mean that research costs too much, takes too long, and produces results that are too often equivocal.[50] This is particularly true of research that has focused on police departments.[51] However, with more dependable and more comprehensive computerized data, policing research will be better positioned to increase our basic knowledge about crime and to inform policymaking at the local, state, and national levels.

Few would resist the assertion that these improvements are desirable, and many would agree that they are necessary. Looked at from that point of view, these are side effects of the IT revolution that we can applaud. But we cannot leave it at that. We have to look at the other side of the coin. As information about crime, criminals, and suspects becomes more detailed and more easily accessible and manipulable, we must consider whether potential misuses of such information are possible and, if so, what steps we should take.

Risks

The proliferation of information, although potentially valuable in streamlining the efforts of local, state, and federal criminal justice agencies as well as in enabling collaboration among these groups, could lead to problems relating to privacy and security.[52]

Inaccuracy of Data

As more and more information about individuals is accumulated, it becomes increasingly important that the information be accurate and dependable. Of course, this is also true outside the law enforcement world. For example, no one wants a good credit report to be reported as bad due to data errors. Yet in a law enforcement context, the negative effects of inaccurate or incomplete data about individuals can be devastating. In one scenario, a police department that collects data on potential gang members might use a series of subjective indicators to assess the likelihood of gang membership (e.g., clothing, nicknames, tattoos, associates). Above a certain threshold (e.g., three of four matched "hits"), an individual is flagged as a gang member. There might be no known criminal activity associated with such a person, but regardless, the individual may subsequently be treated differently. An argument can be made that this identification procedure might help to prevent or control crime. Nevertheless, the approach is troubling because it bears a significant potential for misidentification, which in turn has adverse effects for the individual.

Unrestrained Official Use

Police files are filled with personal information, most of which is gathered through crime investigations that are a normal and proper exercise of police power and responsibilities. When this information is paper based, access to it is easily restricted. But when such information becomes computerized, it is more difficult to limit access and to maintain exclusive oversight of information. It is nearly too easy to transmit electronic records and otherwise confidential information to other law enforcement agencies, businesses, and (in some cases) individuals. An official reason that receives approval is all that is necessary for transmission, and such a reason can vary from an application for a driver's license to an application for employment. The danger is that once the information is transmitted, control over the information is lost. Is this what we want?

Unauthorized Access

A paper file in a police department filing cabinet or in an officer's desk drawer has a symbolic boundary around it. Not only is it inaccessible to outsiders, it is not likely that unauthorized insiders will go looking through it. Such barriers disappear when the file is computerized. Insiders and outsiders have opportunities to access it, sometimes without leaving any trace once the file is accessed. If there is any doubt about this, it is only necessary to reflect on the number of known breaches of supposedly secure national databases. If hackers can gain access to files that are protected by national security systems, it is hard to conceive of a police database that is not equally vulnerable.

Critical concerns about data quality and integrity, and about internal and external access to sensitive information, require appropriate consideration. Unrestrained or improper access seems certain to lead to abuses and, thus, warrants careful attention. Addressing these concerns may limit the amount and type of information that can be maintained in computerized police, court, or corrections files and may require safeguards that result in less than optimal use of burgeoning IT capability. Currently, the rapid movement toward computerization stands to jeopardize protections of individual privacy.

Cybercrime

With the onset of technological advances, criminals have also found innovative ways in which to exploit technology to commit crimes. The Internet, although an extremely effective means of disseminating information to a wide audience and of enhancing communications and criminal justice operations, has also opened a plethora of criminal opportunities. Despite firewalls, antivirus software, verification channels, and other protective tactics, enterprising individuals continually find ways in which to overcome security barriers. Access to secure databases can be jeopardized, confidential identifying information can be compromised, and a host of companies can become vulnerable to fraudulent activity.

A recent study analyzing the computer security incidents experienced by U.S. companies serves as a rough measure of the security threats presented to criminal justice agencies. The BJA collaborated with the U.S. Bureau of the Census to conduct a Computer Security Survey (CSS) pilot in 2001. The CSS pilot sample consisted of 500 companies drawn from 5.3 million companies nationwide. Of these, 42% responded to the survey, and among the respondents, 74% reported detecting at least one computer security incident in 2001. Computer viruses were the most common type of incident (64.1%), followed by denial of service attacks (25.3%) and vandalism or sabotage (13.1%). Many companies reported that in the case of embezzlement (87.5%), fraud (52.9%), and theft of proprietary information (66.7%), the majority of the incidents were committed by employees. In the case of incidents designated as computer attacks, companies reported that denial of service (82.0%), vandalism or sabotage (83.8%), and computer viruses (72.4%) were committed by nonemployees.[53]

Identity theft is also becoming dangerously prevalent. In a report on fraud complaints released by the Federal Trade Commission (FTC) in January 2004, identify theft accounted for 42% of all complaints. In 19% of those cases, criminals used stolen identities to apply for credit cards in the victims' names. In 12%, criminals used the victims' existing credit card accounts. Unspecified employment-related motives accounted for 11% of identity thefts, and the victims' bank accounts were entirely depleted in nearly 8% of the cases.[54]

Cost of Cybercrime

In the survey mentioned previously, the responding companies reported a total of $61 million in losses and recovery costs for 2001. Computer viruses accounted for losses of nearly $22 million, fraud for more than $18 million, and denial of service for another $14 million. If the 500 sample companies accounted for 16% of the nation's payroll and 42% of the companies responded, the responding sample would account for, generally speaking, 6.72% of the nation's payroll. Broadly speaking, then, the $61 million in losses accounts for only approximately 6.72% of American companies' losses. By this logic, total losses to American companies amounted to nearly $1 billion (approximately $907 million) in 2001.

Furthermore, a California state-sponsored study released in February 2000 found that a conservative estimate of the impact of technology crime in California over the past few years was $6.5 billion in industry losses and $358 million in tax revenue losses.

According to a report released by the FTC in January 2004, American consumers filed more than 500,000 fraud reports, totaling more than $437 million in losses, the previous year. The report indicated that the Internet was responsible for 55% of all the fraud reports, up from 45% in 2002, and accounted for approximately $200 million in losses.[55]

These estimates, although sobering, are modest when compared with the economic impact of viruses and spam. The Blaster

worm and SoBig virus that attacked during the summer of 2003 are reported to have caused an estimated $35 billion in losses worldwide.[56]

The Current Nonexistence of Cyber-Law

A major obstacle that criminal justice agencies face is the extremely limited laws that cover cybercrime. An individual can inflict costly damage that constitutes only a technical (prosecutable) violation with modest penalties. According to Lawrence Lessig, a professor at Stanford University and an expert on cyber-law, "Policymakers have so far shown themselves to be consistently 'stupid and bribable.'" How else, he asks, can one explain the curious hierarchy of their current priorities? Online copyrights come at the top due to the powerful lobbying of music companies, which are better described as "firms faced with a rapidly eroding business model than as victims of crime. Near the bottom comes the online privacy of millions of consumers."[57] Without laws that clearly demarcate acceptable and legal uses of the Internet, criminal justice agencies are paralyzed. Furthermore, Alan Nugent, the chief technologist at Novell, argues that anonymity allows cybercrime not only to persist but also to flourish:

> The issue boils down to the question of how much anonymity society can tolerate on the Internet. Driver's licenses and registration plates dramatically reduced the incidence of hit-and-run accidents. Crack cocaine is never bought by credit card because the card can be tracked. If everybody on the Internet were easily traceable, would that deter hackers? "I'm kind of a fan of eliminating anonymity," says Alan Nugent, "if that is the price for security."

According to Lessig, the challenge that policymakers face is to "set the legal hurdles for online search warrants high enough so that governments cannot abuse their power. But at the same time, they have to be kept low enough so that criminals can be found and stopped. In this respect, the online world should be no different from the real one."[58]

Criminal Justice Agencies and the Private Sector

Developing proactive security strategies and technologies to guard against attacks is a business's mandate but traditionally a criminal justice agency's afterthought. One editorial noted,

> Drafting policies, investing in protective tools, establishing a response team, auditing security mechanisms once in place, updating patches, using a system to detect and prevent intrusion all these things demand constant diligence and an enduring commitment by everyone—equally. Executives in both private and public arenas are predicting more innovative and harsh attacks will assail us in coming years. And while they continue to debate who's following what leader and what must be done to secure the country's infrastructure, malicious hackers are sharing information. They are working together in ways that government and industry have yet to perfect.[59]

CONCLUSION

To characterize the IT developments of the past 50 years as a revolution would not be an overstatement. The changes in IT that have taken place are revolutionizing our lives, and even more rapid change is surely at hand. For the foreseeable future, we can expect the pace of IT innovation and development to continue to be extraordinarily rapid. This will be particularly noticeable within what can be thought of as the current IT paradigm. For instance, further miniaturization and

increased speed of components will likely characterize most advances.[60] Memory and storage capacity of machines will increase even as the machines themselves shrink in size. So long as monopolistic or oligopolistic conditions do not prevail, the unit cost of these developments will continue to fall as installations proliferate.[61] We are able to do now what was prohibitively expensive just a decade or so ago. During the early 21st century, it will be possible to do routinely and cheaply what is technically or financially infeasible now.

Although the criminal justice system is not at the forefront of the revolution (and probably should not be), it is nevertheless moving inexorably in the same direction. The IT revolution is bringing change in our way of doing business that cannot be avoided. I would argue that it should not be avoided because the change, if managed properly, can be beneficial. But as criminal justice agencies make these changes, there will be side effects that bring rewards and risks. Assessing these risks and harnessing these benefits is a burden that the criminal justice system must bear.

NOTES

1. The Omnibus Crime Control and Safe Streets Act of 1968 allocated federal funds to the states to bolster local and state crime reduction efforts. The act also established the LEAA to stimulate the computerization of policing that would assist local law enforcement agencies.

2. Anti-Drug Abuse Act of 1986 and Anti-Drug Abuse Act of 1988. The provisions of these acts were designed to curb drug violations and grant the federal government greater control in this arena. Among the acts' provisions were source country certification requirements and mandatory minimum sentences. In addition, the acts established money laundering as a federal crime and also established the Office of National Drug Control Policy.

3. Violent Crime Control and Law Enforcement Act of 1994.

4. S. H. Decker, "Evolution of Crime Statistics as a Police Problem." *Journal of Police Science and Administration* (March 1978): 67–73. This article provides a useful, albeit brief, overview of the historical development of statistical reporting on crime.

5. A helpful summary of the UCR system can be found on the FBI website (www.fbi.gov/ucr/ucrquest.htm). An additional crime reporting system that has the potential for at least supplementing, and perhaps replacing, the UCR system was proposed and adopted during the mid-1980s. It came to be called the National Incident-Based Reporting System and is discussed later.

6. Publications on the Wickersham Commission are numerous. For an Internet reference, see the University Publications of America website (www.upapub.com/guides/wickersham.htm). This excerpts from Samuel Walker, *Popular Justice: A History of American Criminal Justice,* 2d ed., rev. (New York: Oxford University Press, 1997). For other selections, see James D. Calder, *The Origins and Development of Federal Crime Control Policy: Herbert Hoover's Initiatives* (Westport, CT: Praeger, 1993) and National Commission on Law Observance and Enforcement, *Reports* (Washington, DC: Government Printing Office, 1931).

7. The most significant of these was the Cleveland Survey of Criminal Justice. Led by Felix Frankfurter and Roscoe Pound, this inquiry produced *Criminal Justice in Cleveland* (Cleveland, OH: Cleveland Foundation, 1922).

8. National Commission, *Reports.* A 14th report, on a particular case of abusive police behavior, was suppressed at the time of the original publications but was later released.

9. Reported by Joseph Foote, "An Overview for the Symposium on the 30th Anniversary of the President's Commission on Law Enforcement and Administration of Justice," in *The Challenge of Crime in a Free Society: Looking Back, Looking Forward* (Washington, DC: U.S. Department of Justice, 1997), 3.

10. "Summary," *The Challenge of Crime in a Free Society.*

11. The LEAA was officially terminated on April 25, 1982. A vast literature on the LEAA exists. For an entry to it, see Richard S. Allinson, "LEAA's Impact on Criminal Justice: A Review of the Literature," *Criminal Justice Abstracts* (December 1979): 608–648; Robert F. Diegelman, "Federal Financial Assistance for Crime Control: Lessons of the LEAA Experience," *Journal of Criminal Law and Criminology* (3rd Quarter 1982): 994–1011; Malcolm Feely and Austin Sarat, *The Policy Dilemma: Federal Crime Policy and the Law Enforcement Assistance Administration* (Minneapolis: University of Minnesota Press, 1980).

12. Violent Crime Control and Law Enforcement Act of 1994; U.S. Department of Justice, "Violent Crime Control and Law Enforcement Act of 1994" *Fact Sheet* (Washington, DC: U.S. Department of Justice). (NCJ FS000067)

13. Office of Community Oriented Policing Services, "Making Officer Redeployment Effective (MORE): Using Technology to Keep America's Communities Safe," *COPS Fact Sheet* (Washington, DC: U.S. Department of Justice), 26 December 2002.

14. Jeffrey A. Roth, Joseph F. Ryan, Stephen J. Gaffigan, Christopher S. Koper, Mark H. Moore, Janice A. Roehl, Calvin C. Johnson, Gretchen E. Moore, Ruth M. White, Michael E. Buerger, Elizabeth A. Langston, and David Thacher, *National Evaluation of the COPS Program: Title I of the 1994 Crime Act* (Washington, DC: U.S. Department of Justice, 2000); Jeffrey A. Roth, Calvin C. Johnson, Gretchen Maenner, and Daryl E. Herrschaft, "The Flow of COPS Funds," in *National Evaluation of the COPS Program,* 63–100; Jeffrey A. Roth, Christopher S. Koper, Ruth White, and Elizabeth A. Langston, "Using COPS Resources," in *National Evaluation of the COPS Program,* 101–148; Michael L. Victor, "Relations between Known Crime and Police Spending in Large United States Cities," *Sociological Focus* (2nd Quarter 1977): 199–207.

15. I refer here to the Arrestee Drug Abuse Monitoring (ADAM) program, the successor to the Drug Use Forecasting Program (DUF), which systematically collects and analyzes urine samples from arrestees in jails in 35 U.S. cities and then correlates the results with interviews of those arrestees. Currently, future funding from the NIJ for the ADAM program has not been secured.

16. Bureau of Justice Statistics, *State Justice Statistics Program for Statistical Analysis Centers: Application Guidelines 2003* (Washington, DC: U.S. Department of Justice, 2003). (NCJ 200219)

17. M. M. Reuland, *Information Management and Crime Analysis: Practitioners' Recipes for Success* (Washington, DC: Police Executive Research Forum, 1997).

18. For further information see Terence Dunworth, Gary Cordner, Jack Greene, Timothy Bynum, Scott Decker, Thomas Rich, Shawn Ward, and Vince Webb, *Police Department Information Systems Technology Enhancement Project (ISTEP)* (Cambridge, MA: Abt Associates, 2000); Tom McEwen, Randall Guynes, Julie Wartell, and Steve Pendleton, *Information Technology Acquisition: Final Report* (Alexandria, VA: Institute for Law and Justice, 2004). (NCJ 204026)

19. See, for instance, National Partnership for Reinventing Government, *Providing 21st Century Tools for Safe Communities: Report of the Task Force on*

Crime Mapping and Data-Driven Management (Washington, DC: U.S. Department of Justice), 12 July 1999.

20. Paul E. O'Connell, *Using Performance Data for Accountability: The New York City Police Department's CompStat Model for Police Management* (Arlington, VA: PricewaterhouseCoopers Endowment for the Business of Government, 2001).

21. Sara Michael, "Justice to Create Regional Data Store," *Federal Computer Week,* 11 August 2003.

22. Ibid.

23. Donald E. Brown and James Dalton, "The Production and Deployment of Grasp: A Geospatial Repository for Analysis and Safety Planning," in *IEEE Systems and Information Design Symposium, University of Virginia,* 169–174.

24. C. D. Mamalian and N. G. La Vigne, "The Use of Computerized Mapping by Law Enforcement: Survey Results," *Research Preview* (Washington, DC: National Institute of Justice, 1999). (FS000237)

25. Eugene Poggio, Stephen Kennedy, Jan Chaiken, and Kenneth Carlson, *Blueprint for the Future of the Uniform Crime Reporting System: Final Report of the UCR Study* (Washington, DC: Bureau of Justice Statistics, 1985). (NCJ 98348)

26. D. J. Roberts, *Implementing the National Incident-Based Reporting System: A Project Status Report* (Washington, DC: Bureau of Justice Statistics, 1997). (NCJ 165581)

27. As of September 2003, the FBI had certified 22 state programs. The proportion of the U.S. population covered had reached 19%, and 15% of crime was reported through the NIBRS. Of the nation's law enforcement agencies, 27% were reporting crime statistics by way of the NIBRS (www.search.org/nibrs).

28. SEARCH, *Survey of Criminal History Information Systems, 1997* (Washington, DC: Bureau of Justice Statistics, 1999). (NCJ 175041)

29. Brady Handgun Violence Prevention Act; National Child Protection Authority Act of 1993; Linda Greenhouse, "States' Listings of Sex Offenders Raise a Tangle of Legal Issues," *The New York Times,* 4 November 2002.

30. Bureau of Justice Statistics, *Presale Handgun Checks: The Brady Interim Period, 1994–98* (Washington, DC: Bureau of Justice Statistics, 1999). (NCJ 175034)

31. Christopher H. Asplen, *The Application of DNA Technology in England and Wales* (London: Smith Alling Lane, 2004). (NCJ 203971)

32. 497 U.S. 836 (1990).

33. International Association of Chiefs of Police, *The Use of CCTV/Video Cameras in Law Enforcement: Executive Brief* (Alexandria, VA: IACP, 2001). Available: www.theiacp.org/documents/index.cfm?fuseaction=document&document_id=164

34. Mary W. Green, *The Appropriate and Effective Use of Security Technologies in U.S. Schools: A Guide for Schools and Law Enforcement Agencies* (Washington, DC: National Institute of Justice, 1999). (NCJ 178265) Cited in Dave Hayeslip, Kate France, and Karen Beckman, *School Based Drug Abuse and Violence Prevention Programs: A Review of Whole-School Environmental Prevention/ Reduction Strategies* (Washington, DC: Urban Institute, 2004).

35. Thomas C. Moore and Paul Neale, "New York Lawyers Lead Way in Taking Technology to Court," *New York Law Journal* (2nd Quarter 2003). See also Ira Breskin, "A Stage for Court Rehearsals," *The New York Times,* 6 July 2003. For more information on DOAR, the court technology and litigation support firm, see its website (www.doar.com).

36. SEARCH, "Metro/Davidson County, Tennessee: Criminal Justice Information System—Project Overview and Keys to Success," in *Case Study Series: A Report of the National Task Force on Court Automation and Integration* (Sacramento, CA: SEARCH).

37. Ibid.

38. S. H. Brounstein, J. M. Firestone, J. W. Hogg, J. S. Robinson, and J. A. Roth, *National Evaluation Program: Phase I—Summary Report Prosecution Management Information Systems* (Rockville, MD: Westat, 1980). (NCJ 90083)

39. Colin Reilly and Victor Goldsmith, *RACKETS: Case Tracking and Mapping System* (Washington, DC: U.S. Department of Justice, 1999). (NCJ 182918)

40. Robert L. Spangenberg, Marea L. Beeman, David J. Carroll, David Freedman, Evelyn Pan, David J. Newhouse, and Dorothy Chan, *Indigent Defense Technology: A Progress Report* (Washington, DC: U.S. Department of Justice, 1999). (NCJ 179003)

41. Ibid.

42. Ibid., 9–10.

43. Tony Fabelo, "Technocorrections: The Promises, the Uncertain Threats," in *Sentencing and Corrections: Issues for the 21st Century* (Washington, DC: U.S. Department of Justice, 2000).

44. Ibid.

45. D. J. Roberts, *Integrated Justice Information Systems for State and Local Jurisdictions: An Overview of Planning Activities for the Office of Justice Programs, U.S. Department of Justice* (Washington, DC: U.S. Department of Justice, 1998).

46. M. D. Goodman, "Working the Net: Exploiting Technology to Increase Community Involvement and Enhance Service Delivery," *Police Chief* (August 1997): 45–53.

47. K. E. Sulewski, "Faxback Response: Previous Question—How Has the Internet Helped Your Agency?" *FBI Law Enforcement Bulletin* (January 1997): 23–25.

48. Terry Chowanec, "Toward Integrated Justice Information Systems," in *Police Executive Research Forum* (June 2003).

49. Jeremy Travis, "Criminal Justice Research and Public Policy in the United States." Paper presented at the Ninth United Nations Congress on the Prevention of Crime and the Treatment of Offenders, Cairo, Egypt, May 1995.

50. For comments on the general problems associated with research, see Terence Dunworth, "National Assessment of the Byrne Formula Grant Program," *Research in Brief* (Washington, DC: National Institute of Justice, 1977).

51. For an illustration of the particular difficulties associated with policing research, see Terence Dunworth, *Crime in Public Housing: A Three City Analysis* (Washington, DC: National Institute of Justice, 1993). This study began as a five-city inquiry using police department data. Two of the five cities had to be dropped because the data did not support the spatial analysis that the project performed. In the other cities, Thomas maps were used to manually correlate police department data with housing development boundaries. In a more recent project, the advances made in police department data are illustrated by the fact that longitude/latitude coordinates were developed for more than 90% of specific incidents contained in citywide databases in five cities for which such databases were obtained. See Terence Dunworth, *The National Evaluation of the Youth Firearms Violence Initiative: Research in Brief* (Washington, DC: National Institute of Justice, 1999).

52. A cross-national discussion of privacy and security issues can be found in Peter Csonka, "Council of Europe and Data Protection: Free Flow of Information versus Privacy," in *Ninth United Nations Congress on the Prevention of Crime and the Treatment of Offenders,* 103–112.

53. Bureau of Justice Statistics, *Cybercrime against Businesses* (Washington, DC: U.S. Department of Justice, 2004). (NCJ 200639)

54. Kevin Poulsen, "Online Fraud, I.D. Theft Soars," *Security Focus,* 23 January 2004.

55. Ibid.

56. "Fighting the Worms of Mass Destruction," *The Economist* (November 2003): 65–68.

57. Ibid.

58. Ibid.

59. Illena Armstrong, "Let's Work Together Like the Cyber Attackers Do," *SC Magazine,* January 2003.

60. Gordon E. Moore, "Cramming More Components onto Integrated Circuits," *Electronics,* 19 April 1965. Moore made the observation, dubbed "Moore's Law," that the number of transistors per integrated circuit had grown exponentially, and he predicted that this trend would continue. Moore's Law, the doubling of transistors every couple of years, still holds true.

61. The cost of desktop and laptop computers has declined steadily since their introduction. Innovations in technology, such as transistors, integrated circuits, and microprocessor chips, have consistently and drastically reduced the cost of computers. See David Reed, *Balanced Introduction to Computer Science and Programming* (Upper Saddle River, NJ: Prentice Hall, 2004).

CHAPTER 2

Acquiring, Implementing, and Evaluating Information Technology

LOIS M. DAVIS AND BRIAN A. JACKSON

In pursuit of public safety, the application of information technology (IT)[1] to criminal justice applications has many potential benefits. Improved availability and use of information can increase the efficiency of police operations, resulting in more effective crime control at lower cost or reduced risk to law enforcement officers. In the court system, IT has the potential to facilitate court operations and improve application of the large body of legal precedent and knowledge to prosecution and sentencing. In a corrections environment, IT systems can make important contributions to the operation of correctional facilities, helping to ensure that the prison population is managed both safely and appropriately. In addition, integrating justice agencies' information systems, such as those of the courts, probation, and law enforcement, has the potential to improve decision making throughout the justice system and to streamline the flow of information (SEARCH, 1999).

Historically, the federal government's role in supporting the acquisition of IT by justice agencies has been through providing funding for technology equipment, training, and technical assistance through a variety of programs. Funding from federal departments and agencies, such as the Department of Justice program COPS MORE (Community-Oriented Policing Services/Making Officer Redeployment Effective), the Local Law Enforcement Block Grants program, and the Edward Bryne Grant program, have tended to focus on specific programmatic objectives. The result has been the implementation of a patchwork of various computer systems that often are applicable only for very specific purposes, are unable to share information with other justice agencies, and serve only individual components of state and local governments (Office of Justice Programs, 2001).

The acquisition and use of IT by law enforcement is a relatively recent phenomenon. In the 1967 report of the President's

AUTHORS' NOTE: We acknowledge the support received from RAND's Public Safety and Justice Program and its Science and Technology Program. We also thank John Baker and Debra Knopman for their careful review of a draft of the chapter. The conclusions and opinions expressed herein are solely those of the authors.

Commission on Law Enforcement and Administration of Justice, criminal justice agencies were criticized for lagging in acquiring technologies that could help them to do a better job of policing and conducting other criminal justice operations. The commission's Science and Technology Task Force noted several reasons for this lag, including the fact that "procurement funds have been scarce, industry has only limited incentive to conduct basic development for an uncertain and fragmented market, and criminal justice agencies have very few technically trained people on their staffs" (Seaskate Inc., 1998, p. 3). The commission's Police Task Force specifically called for the "development of computer-based information system[s] [that] would aid the police in such functions as patrol, criminal investigations, manpower deployment, the arrest process, and budgeting" (p. 29).

In response, state and local criminal justice and law enforcement agencies began to receive federal funding through a small research and demonstration program run by the Department of Justice. Within a few years, this program grew into the Law Enforcement Assistance Administration (LEAA), created by the Omnibus Crime Control and Safety Streets Act of 1968. The LEAA served as an important catalyst for the computerization of policing during the 1970s. The LEAA's mandate was broad: "to curb organized crime and control urban civil disorders" (DiIulio, Smith, & Saiger, 1995, p. 453). The LEAA functioned primarily as a grant-making agency that sponsored law enforcement training institutes, developed national criminal justice data-gathering and information-sharing networks, developed criminal rehabilitation programs, and funded local community-based crime control initiatives (DiIulio et al., 1995). Over its multiyear lifetime, the LEAA provided nearly $8 billion to state and local criminal justice and law enforcement agencies, with a significant portion being focused on management

science and information systems (p. 454). As summarized by Colton (1980), the expectations regarding the potential of computer technology for law enforcement were high, with advocates hypothesizing that technology would improve the efficiency and effectiveness of law enforcement and, thus, reduce response times, improve apprehension rates, and reduce crime rates. Although the LEAA was later sharply criticized for having had little impact on reducing crime and was deestablished in 1982 (Morgan, 2003), it still served as a catalyst for police organizations to acquire computer technology. The development of the Federal Bureau of Investigation's (FBI) National Crime Information Center (NCIC) also helped to encourage the adoption of computer technology by law enforcement (Rosen, 1982).

According to Colton (1980), the growth in the use of computers by police between the mid-1960s and 1980s was slower than projected, and information systems were used primarily for routine applications such as police patrol and inquiry systems and administrative uses. For applications where computers provided decision support or aided strategic planning, such as resource allocation and computer-aided dispatch (CAD), the results were more mixed. During the late 1980s, the acquisition of IT by police focused primarily on two types of systems: CAD and Automated Fingerprint Identification Systems (AFISs) (Sparrow, 1993).

During the years since the LEAA, a variety of other initiatives have sought to improve the application of technology, and specifically management science and information systems, to criminal justice and law enforcement operations. As summarized by Northrop, Kraemer, and King (1995), the foci of these initiatives have varied and include extending techniques to improve the deployment of police resources, applying analytic techniques to understand the systematic character of the criminal justice system, developing and implementing complex systems to support prosecution, and maintaining criminal history information. However, these authors note that less attention has been paid to understanding the effects of information systems on police operations.

In 1995, the Clinton administration established the COPS program. A component of the COPS program was a grant program called COPS MORE, whose objective was to save officer time. One strategy to do so was by using new grant-funded IT (Roth et al., 2000). According to Roth and colleagues (2000), between 1995 and 1998, technology accounted for more than half of the COPS MORE funds distributed to law enforcement agencies.[2] This funding allowed many smaller law enforcement agencies to purchase their first computers. In addition, President Clinton proposed a 21st Century Policing Initiative to provide law enforcement with crime mapping and other technologies (U.S. Department of Justice, 1999).

The most recent focus has been on facilitating the integration of justice information systems and the connection of law enforcement organizations to database resources. In 1998, Congress passed Public Law 105-251 that included the Crime Identification Technology Act (CITA), which authorized spending $250 million per year for 5 years to help integrate justice system technology (SEARCH, 2001a). This assistance came in the form of state grants to help upgrade criminal justice information systems (CJISs) and identification technologies in 17 specified areas. CITA funds also can be used to support state and local participation in national databases such as the National Instant Check System (NICS), the Combined DNA Information System (CODIS), and the Interstate Identification Index (III) (Office of Justice Programs, 2003).

The degree of automation of information systems by the courts varies significantly across the United States. Although many courts have been automated for years, historically automation efforts have tended to focus on improving internal agency operations with less emphasis being placed on integration of information systems across the courts and justice agencies (SEARCH, 1999). More recently, the increased caseloads and the increased reporting requirements associated with a number of federal and legislative initiatives have been important factors driving toward automation, increased information sharing, and integration of courts' and other justice agencies' information systems (SEARCH, 1999). For example, CITA authorized $1.25 billion over a 5-year period (1999–2003) in state grants to facilitate the integration of information, identification, and forensic technologies (SEARCH, 1999). In addition, the legislation included grant funding to help states upgrade their information systems so that they can participate in national justice initiatives such as the Integrated Automated Fingerprint Identification System (IAFIS) (SEARCH, 1999). Legislation such as the National Child Protection Act of 1993, the Brady Handgun Violence Prevention Act, the Lautenberg Amendment to the Appropriations Act of 1997, the Immigration and Naturalization Service Alien Conviction Notification, and various state sex offender registration and notification statutes included mandated reporting requirements that required increased information sharing across justice agencies and helped to further spur the drive toward integration of information systems (SEARCH, 1999). In addition, federal initiatives such as the FBI's IAFIS, the III, and the NCIC 2000 project require timely reporting of information by justice agencies, further spurring the drive toward improved IT capabilities (Johnson, 1997). More recently, homeland security concerns have renewed interest in developing integrated CJISs at the local, regional, state, and federal levels.

In the remainder of this chapter, we examine recent trends in criminal justice agencies' acquisition of IT systems, IT acquisition and implementation, the evaluation of IT projects, and challenges for the future in using IT systems.

RECENT TRENDS IN ACQUIRING AND APPLYING IT

Given the significant federal involvement in funding the acquisition of IT, where does the criminal justice community currently stand in terms of acquiring and using IT? Although IT has made inroads across the criminal justice community, data on IT deployment are most readily available for law enforcement organizations. The acquisition of IT has occurred at different rates among law enforcement agencies, varying by type of technology and its applied functions. As shown in Table 2.1, law enforcement's use of IT has been concentrated in municipal areas.[3] During the past 10 years or so, the acquisition of IT by large municipal police departments has increased, particularly in areas such as the use of in-field computer systems or terminals and access to an AFIS. Whereas 73% of police departments in 1990 were using in-field computers or terminals, 92% of them reported having this capability by 2000. Municipal police departments' access to an AFIS also grew from 60% in 1990 to 97% by 2000. The percentage of departments that exclusively owned or shared ownership of an AFIS increased from 57% to 71% during this time period (data not shown) (Reaves & Hickman, 2002b).

In 1990, approximately three quarters of municipal police departments participated in enhanced 9-1-1 systems capable of automatically pinpointing the location of a caller. By 2000, nearly all of the departments used enhanced 9-1-1 systems. Although most municipal police departments (90%) were using CAD in 1990, its use further increased during the 1990s and by 2000 all of the municipal police departments in the Law Enforcement Management and Administrative Statistics (LEMAS) survey reported having a CAD system. Overall, between 1990 and 2000, the use of computers and IT had increased so that by 2000 most municipal police departments were using CAD, were using in-field computers or terminals, and participated in enhanced 9-1-1 systems.

In comparison, the use of these technologies by local police departments in general and sheriffs' offices is less widespread, as shown in Table 2.2. Overall, in 2000, much smaller percentages of local police departments and sheriffs' offices reported using in-field computers or terminals, having access to an AFIS, and participating in an enhanced 9-1-1 system than was the case with municipal departments.

Table 2.1   Use of Computers and Information Systems by Police Departments Serving Cities With Population of 250,000 or More: 1990 and 2000 (percentages)

Type of Computer/ Information System	Percentage Use in 1990	Percentage Use in 2000
CAD	90	100
Enhanced 9-1-1 systems	76	97
In-field computers or terminals	73	92
AFIS capability (owned system or remote terminal)	60	97

SOURCE: Hickman, M. J., & Reaves, B. A. (2002b). *Police departments in large cities, 1990–2000* (NCJ 175703). Washington, DC: Bureau of Justice Statistics.

Table 2.2   Use of Computers and Information Systems by Local Police Departments and
Sheriffs' Offices: 2000 (percentages)

Type of Computer/ Information System	Percentage Use by Local Police Departments (all sizes)	Percentage Use by Sheriffs' Offices (all sizes)
Enhanced 9-1-1 systems	71	66
In-field computers or terminals	40	32
AFIS capability (owned system or remote terminal)	20	31

SOURCES: Hickman, M. J., & Reaves, B. A. (2003a). *Local police departments, 2000* (NCJ 196002). Washington, DC: Bureau of Justice Statistics, Law Enforcement Management and Administrative Statistics; Hickman, M. J., & Reaves, B. A. (2003b). *Sheriffs' offices, 2000* (NCJ 196534). Washington, DC: Bureau of Justice Statistics, Law Enforcement Management and Administrative Statistics.

Whereas 97% of municipal police departments participated in enhanced 9-1-1 systems in 2000, only 66% of sheriffs' offices and 71% of local police departments did so. Also, less than half of local police departments and sheriffs' offices used in-field computers or terminals compared with 92% of municipal police departments that did so. Finally, only 20% of local police departments and 31% of sheriffs' offices had access to an AFIS, compared with 97% of municipal police departments that had such access.

Table 2.3 shows the functions for which computer technologies were used by local police departments and sheriffs' offices in 2000. Overall, two thirds of police departments and sheriffs' offices reported using computers for routine administrative tasks such as records management, and between 40% and 46% also used computers for managing personnel records. Other common uses included crime investigations and access to the Internet. Although approximately 30% of police departments and sheriffs' offices used computers for crime analysis, only approximately 14% used computers to do crime mapping.[4] Just 10% of police departments and sheriffs' offices used computers for resource allocation purposes. In general, local police departments and sheriffs' offices were similar in their use of computer technology, with two exceptions: use of computers for dispatching calls for service and use of computers for doing automated booking. In 2000, sheriffs' offices were more likely than local police departments to be using computers for automated booking (60% vs 18%) and for dispatching calls for service (47% vs 32%).

The use of computer technology and geographic information systems (GIS) by law enforcement for crime mapping deserves further comment. In 1994, the New York City Police Department (NYPD) began initial steps toward developing a computer-supported crime statistics mapping and management system called CompStat.[5] Using this system, the NYPD began to do more and more geographic mapping and analysis of crime statistics, and this in turn enabled the department to target their crime-fighting resources more effectively and to improve the accountability of precinct commanders (Silverman, 1996). Computerized mapping of crime statistics to support similar analyses have begun to be used by a number of police departments across the United States (U.S. Department of Justice, 1999).

Other uses of computer technology by law enforcement and corrections include the use of global positioning systems (GPS) as part of

Table 2.3 Functions of Computers in Local Police Departments and Sheriffs' Offices: 2000 (percentages)

Type of Department	Records Management	Internet Access	Crime Investigations	Personnel Records	Dispatch	Crime Analysis	Interagency Information Sharing	Automated Booking	Fleet Management	Crime Mapping	Resource Allocation
Local police departments	60	56	44	40	32	30	28	18	16	15	10
Sheriffs' offices	63	67	48	46	47	27	33	60	22	13	11

SOURCES: Hickman, M. J., & Reaves, B. A. (2003a). *Local police departments, 2000* (NCJ 196002). Washington, DC: Bureau of Justice Statistics, Law Enforcement Management and Administrative Statistics; Hickman, M. J., & Reaves, B. A. (2003b). *Sheriffs' offices, 2000* (NCJ 196534). Washington, DC: Bureau of Justice Statistics, Law Enforcement Management and Administrative Statistics.

electronic monitoring[6] and tracking systems to enable correctional personnel to track offenders' movement and the use of GPS in patrol cars to help guide law enforcement personnel to specific locations. For example, GPS to track offenders on community supervision are currently being used in Florida and Michigan in an effort to provide increased protection to crime victims (e.g., from domestic violence or sex offenders) (Petersilia, 2002). However, the use of GPS—as opposed to regular electronic monitoring—is more costly, and the greater potential benefit might not be worth the additional cost in all cases (Petersilia, 2002).

A novel application of GIS for corrections is also currently being developed by the National Law Enforcement and Corrections Technology Center–Southeast (NLECTC–Southeast) and is referred to as correctional mapping (CORMAP). This system uses a combination of computer-assisted drawing and GIS to display multilevel living areas in a three-dimensional layout. For example, within a prison, each cell and each bed within a housing unit can be displayed with information about an individual inmate linked to an assigned bed. This new technology is designed to enable institutional staff members to monitor and track the geographic locations of inmates as well as to display other relevant information that may be helpful to correctional personnel in managing incidents (Justice Technology Information Network [JUSTNET], n.d.).

As part of an assessment of the use of information systems by state and federal correctional facilities, the Association of State Correctional Administrators (ASCA) undertook an inventory in 1998. The inventory was intended to assess what data departments collect and maintain in electronic form on most adult sentenced prisoners and to what extent the departments can use these data to respond to requests for statistical information about groups of offenders.

The assessment found that most of the 52 departments of corrections collected and maintained a common core of data elements that could be used to describe and profile offenders, measure recidivism in terms of returns to prison, and measure aspects of public safety related to offender registry requirements. However, not all departments defined and collected these data equally. For example, 12 departments did not collect any data on released offenders. Obstacles that corrections departments identified in using their information systems to generate statistical information about offenders included lack of experienced programming staff members, software problems, and institutional and legal restrictions. Few departments cited hardware problems as representing an obstacle (ASCA, 1998).

With respect to the acquisition of IT by the courts, the National Center for State Courts (NCSC) in 1998 did a comprehensive assessment of court automation, gathering data from the 50 states and the District of Columbia. For each state court system, the NCSC gathered information on the status of automation for the different levels of court, from the state's highest court down to courts of limited jurisdiction such as traffic courts. The assessment included questions about what agency had primary responsibility for automation, whether a uniform case management system existed for most courts, who developed the court's software and who was responsible for maintaining it, and what platform was in use. Responsibility for automation varied from state to state. Of the 51 respondents, 45 indicated that their state judicial branch was responsible for automation of their appellate courts. However, for general jurisdiction courts, 27 of the 51 respondents indicated that their state judicial branch was responsible for automation, 12 indicated that it was a local responsibility, and 8 indicated that it was a mixture of state and local responsibility. For limited jurisdiction courts, nearly half of the respondents indicated that their state judicial branch was responsible for automation and approximately half indicated that it was a local responsibility (SEARCH, 1999, Appendix C, Table 4). In terms of case management systems, 36 of the 51 respondents indicated that they had a uniform case management system for most of their courts at the appellate court level, 30 indicated that they had a uniform case management system at the general jurisdiction level, and 19 indicated that they had such a system at the limited jurisdiction level. In addition, the National Task Force on Court Automation and Integration report found that although many courts and justice agencies had been working on integrating their information systems for a number of years, at the time of the 1998 assessment, few integrated systems were fully operational (SEARCH, 1999).

IT ACQUISITION AND IMPLEMENTATION

Challenges to IT Acquisition and Implementation

Whether it is a local police department that has not used IT before or used it on only a very limited basis, or a municipal police department that is acquiring a new IT system or replacing one already in use, studies have shown that there can be significant obstacles to law enforcement organizations acquiring IT systems. Such obstacles include the following (Seaskate Inc., 1998):

♦ IT can be confusing, especially to those who are unfamiliar with computers and computer terminology. Combined with a large array of technologies available, this has made it difficult for police departments to identify their organizations' needs and determine the most appropriate IT solutions.
♦ Many police departments have small equipment budgets, with IT acquisition often

done on a department-by-department basis with little pooled purchasing.
♦ Most police departments are too small to have IT staff experts or individuals who can evaluate IT options. Thus, awareness and information about IT has diffused at different rates among police departments.

These types of barriers are equally relevant to IT acquisition in correctional and court environments.

Characteristics of the court system in the United States also present some additional challenges to IT acquisition and implementation:

♦ "States are frequently dissimilar in the structure of the judicial branches and jurisdictions assigned to their courts, making it difficult to develop transferable automation solutions and create national data standards that are relevant from state to state" (SEARCH, 1999, p. 7).
♦ Leadership tends to be more fragmented among the courts than among other criminal justice agencies, such as law enforcement, making it difficult to gain senior leadership support for IT initiatives in the court environment (SEARCH, 1999).
♦ Variation in state courts' organizational and funding structures also can complicate IT acquisition. In some states, the courts do not control the resources related to their operations. Also, in some states all of the court staff members may work for a centralized state court administrative office, whereas in other states the administrative office plays only a minor role in court operations. Courts' funding also varies from state to state and by type of court, with some courts being funded nearly entirely at the state level, others being funded at the local level, and most having a mixture of funding at the state and local levels (SEARCH, 1999).

Initiatives to integrate information systems across the courts and different types of justice agencies also face some unique challenges in IT acquisition and implementation. The development of integrated information systems requires that the development costs be spread over a number of different justice agencies. However, the stakeholder agencies may place different priorities for improving IT systems and may be at different stages in their acquisition cycle. Statewide court automation projects have the drawback of large and small courts being stuck with a "one size fits all" system that might not be optimized for either size of court (SEARCH, 1999). Participation in large-scale CJISs that are designed to meet the needs of many different types of justice agencies might not allow a particular agency, such as the courts, from integrating other applications within their department or agency. In these situations, for example, courts might have to run separate IT systems for criminal cases and civil cases or might have to maintain separate financial systems (SEARCH, 1999).

Furthermore, to the computer industry, the criminal justice market represents a very small fraction of the total market when compared with private sector and commercial uses (Seaskate Inc., 1998). In the United States in June 2000, there were approximately 18,000 state and local law enforcement agencies with 1,019,496 full-time employees and 708,022 sworn officers, and approximately 75% of them had 24 or fewer full-time sworn personnel (Reaves & Hickman, 2002a). In other words, the vast majority of law enforcement agencies in the United States are small departments with limited equipment budgets. There are even smaller numbers of court and prison systems. For example, in 1998, there were 208 statewide general and limited jurisdiction trial court systems in the United States and 132 courts of appeal (Rottman, Flango, Cantrell, Hansen, & LaFountain, 2000). This translates into more than 17,000 courts within the United States, with the vast majority being state trial courts (SEARCH, 1999). In 2000, there were a total of 1,668 federal, state, and private correctional facilities in

the United States (Stephan & Karberg, 2003).

As a result, computer manufacturers historically have been reluctant to invest in developing application software or specialized hardware for the criminal justice community. In addition, given limited equipment budgets, law enforcement has had difficulty in garnishing support for major computerization projects. Instead, law enforcement agencies have tended to purchase IT when existing systems were being replaced by new technologies and when the price had dropped, making these systems affordable for policing (Seaskate Inc., 1998). As a result, the computer systems purchased by police departments can become obsolete relatively quickly. In addition, vendors initially tended to sell police software programs designed for other occupations and only slightly modified for the law enforcement market. Thus, departments would end up trying to adapt their ways of doing business to the software programs rather than having programs designed to meet their departmental needs (Seaskate Inc., 1998).

In general, key factors that have adversely affected the implementation of IT include the following (Dawes et al., 2003; SEARCH, 2001b):

- Unrealistic expectations about what the new technology can achieve
- Lack of organizational support and acceptance
- Failure to evaluate and redesign business processes to accommodate the new technology
- Unclear objectives
- Lack of measurable alignment between organizational goals and project objectives
- Failure to understand the strengths and limitations of the new technology
- Having too specialized or too ambitious projects to manage successfully
- Incomplete requirements definition and changing requirements
- Unrealistic time frames

♦ Underestimation of costs
♦ Failure to involve end users in the planning and development process

Furthermore, public sector organizations face other risks and constraints in addition to those just listed, and the challenges that law enforcement agencies face are not dissimilar to those faced by other public sector organizations (Dawes et al., 2003). These additional risks and constraints for public sector organizations include the following:

♦ Limited authority to make decisions, with authority divided across multiple decision makers within and/or across agencies
♦ Multiple stakeholders and competing goals with IT initiatives, for example, integrating CJISs involving not only law enforcement but also the court system, probation, and so forth
♦ One-year budgets and uncertainty about the size and availability of future resources, thereby limiting the ability of agencies to do long-term planning
♦ Highly regulated procurement that tends to rely on traditional competitive bidding processes that can lead to time delays, cost overruns, and lengthy negotiations
♦ Limited ability to design or operate integrated or government-wide programs
♦ High degree of risk aversion, with the success or failure of IT projects possibly subject to intense scrutiny by government officials and the general public

Characteristics of Well-Designed IT Implementation Efforts

In 2001, SEARCH, the National Consortium for Justice Information and Statistics, held a series of national technical assistance workshops in law enforcement information technology planning and implementation for the top 100 COPS MORE grantees (i.e., grantees with the largest dollar amounts in grants) (SEARCH, 2001b). The workshops focused specifically on mobile computing issues and technologies, CAD, and records management systems. In addition to describing obstacles similar to those included in the previous section, workshop participants identified lessons learned based on their own experiences, including the following:

♦ Ensure upper management buy-in and support.
♦ Plan for adequate and continuous training.
♦ Know what you want before submitting a grant.
♦ Identify and secure adequate personnel to implement and maintain.
♦ Conduct a needs assessment.
♦ Use a comprehensive request for proposal (RFP).
♦ Conduct thorough vendor research.
♦ Do not assume that technology will save time.
♦ Do not overkill with technology.
♦ Develop a maintenance approach.
♦ Identify a skilled project manager.
♦ Consider outsourcing.
♦ Involve users heavily.
♦ Talk to others and learn from their experiences.
♦ Develop a detailed vendor contract.
♦ Assess the project risks.

The preceding lessons learned are congruent with guidance provided by various experts, including the National Law Enforcement and Corrections Technology Center (NLECTC), regarding "best practices" with respect to IT acquisition and implementation. The NLECTC recently developed a guide for law enforcement agencies to use in developing and/or improving their IT systems that identified 12 steps in the acquisition and implementation process. Importantly, it emphasizes the need to establish the scope of a project based on a review of an agency's goals and long-term objectives. Such a review helps to identify cost and performance expectations as well as who the end users will be.

As the NLECTC (2001) noted, "Defining system expectations will help educate and prepare management for the system, personnel, and financial impacts" (p. 3).

Forming a working group that includes both technical and nontechnical personnel is also an important step, with this group being responsible for conducting the IT assessment and developing the system needs, RFP, interfaces, cost estimates, and schedule. In addition, all key stakeholders, as well as how they can influence or be influenced by the project, need to be identified. Stakeholders include not only those directly involved in developing the system and the end users but also "strategic" partners that might not be system users per se but may eventually need to approve the design of and funding for the project (e.g., other county agencies, city council members).

Another key step is conducting an IT assessment that involves identifying core business processes that are key to the agency's operations and how information is processed within the agency. The assessment should include a review of the agency's current policies and procedures, business policies, IT infrastructure, software, and hardware. Information from the review not only provides a detailed overview of the existing system but also can be used to identify ways in which to streamline business processes. In addition, the assessment should include a comparison of best practices of other agencies. The NLECTC and other experts caution that the new system could provide capabilities that may force operational changes; for example, significant shifts in the way in which activities are managed or organizational activities are documented. Thus, part of the assessment should determine whether the organization can tolerate the scope of change. Information from the technology assessment allows the working group to begin developing overall system needs and a detailed system design.

Dawes and colleagues (2003) outlined a three-phase process for government organizations to follow in deciding which IT investments to make. Phase 1 involves specifying the program or business objective(s), identifying and assessing stakeholders, and analyzing the problem(s) or process(es) to be addressed. Phase 2 involves identifying and testing solutions, including finding relevant practices, tools, and techniques. Phase 3 involves evaluating alternatives by comparing risks, costs, and expected performance.

Two overarching principles guide IT implementation. The first is that any IT effort must be driven by service objectives and the underlying business practices of the organization(s) involved rather than by the technology itself. As stated by Dawes and colleagues (2003), "The best technology will not correct outdated policies, inadequate management practices, or poorly designed workflows" (p. 2). The second guiding principle is the importance of identifying all of the internal and external stakeholders and understanding their different needs, resources, and expectations. Dawes and colleagues also emphasized the importance of considering best and current practices and of learning from the experiences of other agencies in implementing IT systems. In addition, they encouraged agencies with proposals that are complex or that involve unknown parameters to develop prototype systems to be tested under field conditions. One benefit of such tests is that they might help to identify nontechnology solutions and priorities that may fill the agency's needs, for example, improvements in business processes or information flow versus the application of new technologies.

In addition, IT implementation of integrated information systems between criminal justice agencies requires a detailed understanding of the business practices that govern information flow between different types of justice agencies, the type of information being exchanged, the events that trigger such exchange, and an ability to model the nature of the information exchange. SEARCH (2002) has developed a conceptual framework and a Justice Information Exchange Model (JIEM) tool to help inform IT integration planning, design, and implementation at the local, regional, state, and federal levels. This modeling tool is intended to enable justice agencies in state and local jurisdictions to model justice system information flow and business rules by "identifying, describing, documenting, and defining key inter-agency information exchanges" (SEARCH, 2002). Some states, such as Minnesota, New Mexico, Wisconsin, and Kentucky, have begun to use the JIEM tool in their integrated planning efforts.

Case Studies of Law Enforcement's Implementation of IT

Insights From the LEAA Program

Colton (1980) reported on the deployment of a CAD system in San Diego, California. This system was jointly funded by the LEAA and the City of San Diego and was to serve three city departments: police, fire, and water utility. Initial efforts to implement a CAD system failed for three reasons:

1. The users of the system were not generally involved in its design and implementation.

2. A specified schedule was not established and maintained.

3. Hardware purchases were made without detailed specifications, requiring vendors to conform to agreed-on standards. Because the hardware was purchased without consultation with user departments, the system did not match well with actual needs and requirements.

In a second attempt to implement a CAD system, San Diego benefited from the lessons learned from the earlier effort. The first step

was a detailed systems analysis to identify communications needs that looked broadly at all aspects of the communications system—including telephone and dispatch—although the initial objective of the project was to improve the dispatching system. In addition, the implementation approach was modified in this second attempt to include the following:

♦ Involvement of the key stakeholders and end users in the design process, including the establishment of a city task force that included both representatives within the police department and representatives from other municipal agencies and that involved the end users

♦ Emphasis placed on training of operators and dispatchers who would be involved

♦ Development of a specific and detailed RFP that required bidders to demonstrate prior experience in designing and implementing a CAD system in a law enforcement environment, with the RFP outlining in detail both the system to be installed and the specifications that needed to be met

♦ Decision to make one vendor responsible for the performance of the overall system, with the "turnkey contract" holding the vendor responsible for all elements of the CAD system, including the hardware, software, radio communications, communications console equipment, and interface between the telephone subsystem and the CAD system

♦ Negotiation of a fixed-price contract, with payment being tied to successful implementation and final payment not to be made until the entire system was installed and operational

San Diego's second attempt at implementing a CAD system is a good example of the application of a number of the key principles just outlined for successful IT design and implementation. As noted by Colton (1980), an important dimension to the implementation process was the emphasis placed on human factors such as involving the users in the design process and training dispatch and telephone personnel. San Diego also significantly revised its strategy in working with the vendor and handling the RFP process. Ironically, the greatest productivity improvements in San Diego's communications systems appear to have come more from the implementation of the new telephone system and procedures (which focused on getting needed information from callers more rapidly) than from the more costly CAD installation, illustrating the point that it is difficult to assess "success" or to predict which changes or innovations will ultimately produce the greater benefits.

Insights From the COPS MORE Program

A 3-year evaluation of the COPS MORE program by Roth and colleagues (2000) provides a useful overview of the type of implementation challenges that law enforcement agencies have experienced. Over the time period of the program, funding was provided in several areas. The most commonly awarded technology was for mobile computers, with 79% of COPS MORE grantees being awarded mobile computer technology by 1998. Specifically, this included either laptop or notebook computers carried by officers or mounted in vehicles or modular units with separate keyboards, monitors, and CPUs mounted in vehicles. Units permanently mounted in vehicles were used primarily for mobile data terminal (MDT) functions such as computerized dispatch, queries to automated databases (e.g., state vehicle registration, driver's license, and stolen auto files), and the FBI's NCIC as well as for car-to-car and car-to-station messaging. Mobile units not permanently mounted in vehicles were used for automated field reporting. "Reporting software ranged from well-known word processing packages for writing narratives to elaborate locally developed software using

menus to navigate through agency-specific reporting forms" (p. 123).

Another 45% of COPS MORE grantees also had received awards for management/administration computers (desktop or mainframe) that were used to do basic administrative functions such as correspondence, records management, payroll, and keeping track of staff hours (Roth et al., 2000). Some of the management/administration computers also were used to develop new databases such as those for wanted notices and warrants or computerized arrest records. In addition, by 1998, 12% of COPS MORE technology grantees had received awards for CAD systems (Roth et al., 2000). In general, larger law enforcement agencies were more likely than smaller ones to request and receive the COPS MORE funding.

Evaluation of the COPS MORE program identified a number of implementation challenges. Roth and colleagues (2000) noted that different technologies varied in the length of time required to become operational, with each depending on its complexity, size of the project, and novelty of the technology and its applications. Although smaller police departments may have fewer acquisition needs, those funded for stand-alone computers for office work were able to purchase the computers and software off the shelf.

Agencies installing more complex systems, such as mobile computer systems, tended to experience longer delays. In general, Roth and colleagues (2000) postulated that smaller agencies had an easier time in implementing mobile and desktop computers because they had less equipment and software to procure, possibly less complex procurement procedures to follow, and fewer personnel to train on using the computers. In contrast, larger agencies tended to implement more complex computer systems, and this often required upgrading telecommunications technology or integrating the new computer technology with existing record management systems.

Other implementation challenges included unanticipated technology-related costs. COPS MORE technology grantees reported unexpected technology-related costs in the areas of additional computer staff time, installation time, and training time that were not covered by their COPS MORE grants (Roth et al., 2000). For example, some agencies had to hire or redirect staff members for installing and maintaining equipment. Grantees noted that the amount of staff time needed for installing the technology was often extensive. In addition, the COPS MORE funding did not cover the costs of staff and/or vendor time needed to maintain the new equipment. In general, agencies with more sophisticated grant-writing abilities (usually larger agencies) were better able to use their COPS MORE grants to fund consultants, hire civilian computer personnel, and cover the time of existing staff members. In general, the evaluation found that as the implementation process proceeded, the likelihood of COPS MORE grantees experiencing unexpected costs also increased. For example, the percentage of grantees reporting unexpected costs rose from 21% of agencies with mobile computers not fully implemented to 31% of agencies that had completed implementation (Roth et al., 2000).

Brown (2001), in her case study of the Charlotte–Mecklenburg (North Carolina) Police Department's (CMPD) implementation of an ambitious IT initiative, reported similar challenges. The CMPD used its COPS MORE funds to develop and implement a Knowledge-Based, Community-Oriented Problem-Solving System. This initiative had three stages:

- ♦ *Stage 1:* An in-depth needs analysis
- ♦ *Stage 2:* Implementation of much of the system architecture (including a wide area network, a local area network, 19 servers, and 2,000 laptop computers) and several software applications
- ♦ *Stage 3:* An upgrade of the CMPD's most frequently used data sets

At the time of Brown's (2001) assessment endeavors, only Stages 1 and 2 had been completed. She noted that transitioning from a relatively simple system (involving a single mainframe, 200 dumb terminals, and 6 support staff members) to a more complex IT system (involving a 19-server, 2,000-client operation requiring 26 support staff members) required a lot of capital, time, and energy. Although the annual IT operating budget more than tripled, the increase in the number of computers meant that support requirements increased by a factor of 10.

The project experienced cost overruns and schedule delays. Cost overruns resulted primarily from shifting user requirements that expanded the scope of the original project. Other contributing factors included shortages of qualified technical personnel and high turnover among these personnel as well as equipment malfunctions and incompatibilities. As a result, the project had to adopt an incremental, iterative deployment process.

Brown (2001) noted that this, in turn, had ripple effects on other aspects of the organization such as higher demands placed on the human resources section of the agency to do continuous recruitment and hiring due to the high turnover of personnel. Contract changes also placed high demands on the contracting and procurement section of the agency. In addition, the expansion of the scope of the project required ongoing heavy involvement of users. In turn, this required the ongoing engagement of top-level leadership to ensure continued management support and horizontal commitment requirements to the project.

Lessons Learned From Integration of CJ Information Systems

Development and implementation of integrated information systems across different justice agencies within a locality or state present similar but also additional challenges compared with implementation of IT systems within a single agency or department. Delaware was the first state to implement an integrated CJIS, the Delaware Justice Information System (DELJIS), which came into formal existence in 1990. Although Delaware had the advantage of being a small state to attempt integration of its CJISs, it did not have the benefit of learning from others' prior experience. The Delaware system evolved over time, with the initial step being the integration of the state's law enforcement's Computerized Criminal History (CCH) database with the corrections department's system for inmate tracking in 1989 followed by the merging of the courts' Disposition Reporting System with the CCH in 1990. The formal creation of Delaware's CJIS occurred in 1990, with subsequent development of additional system components. In total, the DELJIS evolved to link five separate databases at the state level funded by a patchwork of state and federal grants beginning in 1982 to develop and expand the system. Lessons learned from Delaware's experience in implementing an integrated CJIS, included the following (from Holmes, 1999–2000):

♦ People, not technology, were the biggest obstacles to integration. System developers had assumed that there would be widespread cooperation. However, personnel in different agencies had their own views about how the project should move forward and tended to focus more on their own agencies than on the overall system. In retrospect, formal agreements at the policy and operational levels would have helped to ensure cooperation and to ensure continuity in the commitment of the various agencies by taking into account changes in administration during the course of the project.

♦ Top-level commitment was viewed as essential. Without the support of all the agency heads, it was difficult to move the project along in a coordinated and efficient manner.

♦ User involvement throughout the process was seen as critical for ensuring stakeholder buy-in. For example, during the initiative, one police department installed a computer system that was unable to communicate with the CJIS or to share data with the other justice agencies in real time.

♦ Training of users was important, with some problems encountered being more a result of improper training on the system than of system gaps.

♦ Planning has to be comprehensive, with technology not being viewed as the solution to business problems. In Delaware, a key lesson learned was the need to form a committee to oversee the process of defining business relationships, objectively looking at strengths and weaknesses of the system, defining data ownership and data quality issues, reengineering, building cooperative agreements among criminal justice agencies, and building new automated systems. Another lesson was the need to clearly establish database-sharing rules before system implementation.

In addition to the preceding lessons learned, the Delaware case study analysis noted several system weaknesses that remained after implementation of the CJIS, underscoring the need for continual development. In some instances, data quality had been compromised, indicating a need to improve overall data quality of the system. For example, in the superior courts, there was a lack of standardization among the different courts in how they produce sentencing orders. Also in some courts, clerks did not consistently enter sentencing data into the system. Another weakness was that at some key information exchange points, the necessary information was not being shared among CJIS entities. For example, juvenile case information maintained by the family court was not being shared through the CJIS, although there was no statutory proscription against doing so. In addition, there was the lack of real-time information sharing with agencies that should be participating in the CJIS. For example, information from the Department of Probation and Parole was not available to CJIS participants because the department operated a stand-alone system. Another weakness cited was related to governance structure and the need for high-level support. Delaware's CJIS oversight committee consisted of a mixture of policymakers and technical staff members. Committee members who were technical staff members often were unable to speak with full authority for their respective agencies.

Colorado's experience in developing an integrated CJIS highlighted similar implementation challenges. Colorado's CJIS, which began formal operations in 1998, combined the systems of five separate entities: the Colorado Judicial Branch, the Bureau of Investigation (Department of Public Safety), the District Attorneys Council, the Department of Human Services–Division of Youth Corrections, and the Department of Corrections. Some of the lessons learned from Delaware's experience were echoed in Colorado's experience at implementing its integrated CJIS, including the following (from Holmes, Usery, & Roper, 2000–2001):

- Senior leadership in all agencies affected by the proposed changes needed to be involved to ensure that they would be invested in the project and that the system would meet all of their concerns. For example, when warrant data transfers were attempted at a pilot site, there was strong resistance to changing current business practices due in part to the personnel's ambivalence toward the change, the lack of testing of the system, and CJIS design flaws. In addition, users in one agency were reluctant to give up control of information to another agency.
- In hindsight, Colorado's implementers assessed that the most effective governance structure was one that includes all constituent organizations, providing a neutral forum for resolving issues as they arise.

- Problem resolution needed to be handled at the operational level, with local work groups or committees established to focus on the business practices within a jurisdiction. In addition, such working groups needed to meet often. Those Colorado jurisdictions that had working groups that met frequently were better able to address problems as they arose during the implementation process.
- Documenting the system from a business and technical perspective is critical to successful maintenance and future development.
- A careful analysis of business rules—agreed-on protocols for sharing information—before implementing an integrated system was seen as a critical initial step that should include reassessment by participating agencies of their own business processes.
- Colorado implementers, in hindsight, indicated that it was important to develop an integrated information system incrementally and, when possible, to minimize technical changes. Colorado's CJIS built on existing legacy systems so that agencies and departments were not forced to migrate to other platforms. This allowed Colorado to minimize project costs and development time, maximize the technical expertise of existing staff, and keep the focus on business issues.
- Buy-in from all system stakeholders needed to be established, with IT acquisition being viewed as a continuing investment and with agency funding allocated accordingly.
- Adequate resources for the implementation phase needed to be ensured. In Colorado, following the development phase, implementers found that the resources were scattered and, in some instances, redirected to projects that had been put on hold while the CJIS was being developed. During the implementation phase, this made it difficult to refine and correct some of the initial problems with the CJIS.
- The primary planners and implementers needed to have good "people" skills, be committed to the project, and have the ability to

reprioritize projects and resources. This helps to ensure that resources are not redirected elsewhere and that the "point people" have the authority to redirect the project when necessary. Otherwise, the project will be subject to differing internal priorities among agencies and departments.

♦ Users need to be trained on the technology and business impacts of the new system, with training being viewed as critical in helping to break down political and organizational barriers.

♦ Benchmarking against the project's goals and objectives is important for continued marketing of the project. Integrated IT projects are not a one-time investment but rather require ongoing and continuous development. Thus, document progress in meeting project goals and objectives will help individual stakeholders to make the business case justification for additional resources.

EVALUATING IT PROJECTS

After acquiring any new technology, particularly one as complex as information systems, a formal process of evaluation is often required to fully understand the outcome of the acquisition process. From the organizational perspective, evaluating an IT project can be very important. Evaluation is a key component of management processes to ensure that IT systems are being used effectively and to improve their application to an organization's goals. Such an understanding is also needed to learn from past technology implementation efforts and improve later attempts by the organization to acquire or use other technologies (Willcocks & Lester, 1997). For public organizations, evaluation may also be needed to substantiate that public monies are being used responsibly or satisfy legislative requirements (Chan, Brereton, Legosz, & Doran, 2001) and to support future attempts to gain funding for other

technology acquisition efforts (Johnson & Rivers, 2001).

As discussed previously, research has indicated that IT systems can have significant benefits in criminal justice organizations. However, because many of the benefits and costs associated with new IT systems are difficult to express monetarily, they are often not amenable to standard "business case" assessment methods such as cost–benefit analysis and calculations of returns on investment (Northrop et al., 1995). In addition, a significant fraction of the potentially positive impacts, and some of the potential costs, of IT systems may be intangible or qualitative. They may be spread throughout the organization or might not be clearly linked to the implementation of the technology (Anandarajan & Wen, 1999; Serafeimidis & Smithson, 1999). And as noted previously, IT may also cause ripple effects, affecting other parts of the organization or other organizations (Wen & Sylla, 1999).

Assessing IT deployment is further complicated by the fact that the absolute effects of the technology are affected by a range of factors, including how well the IT system was designed to meet organizational needs, whether individuals are using the system appropriately, structural and managerial factors that affect the way in which the system or its outputs are used, and details regarding how the system was implemented and deployed. As a result, beyond simply evaluating the technology itself, IT technology assessment inherently involves an evaluation of organizational activities and capabilities that either support or detract from the effect of the information systems themselves. These additional concerns have been summarized as the organization's "conversion effectiveness," that is, how well it realizes the potential benefits provided by the IT system (McKeen, Smith, & Parent, 1999).

Potential Effects of
IT in Law Enforcement,
Courts, and Corrections

The potential complexity of the impact of IT on an organization and its activities makes it critical to broadly define and explore the potential impacts—positive and negative, tangible and intangible—that could arise from the IT project of interest. As discussed in the earlier sections, the intended effects of a well-designed implementation effort (and their relationship to the organization's goals and objectives) will be identified during the planning and technology adoption process. However, a rigorous evaluation process must go beyond the intended effects to include the unintended impacts that these changes can have on the organization. Such unintended impacts, which can be either positive or negative, could significantly affect the overall assessment of the IT system. Because IT can affect both what an organization does and how it does it, evaluation must consider the impacts of IT on organizational activities, workforce, management, finances, and the structure of the organization itself.[7]

Effects on Organizational Activities

In many cases, the primary intent of deploying IT systems is to affect the way in which an organization performs tasks and carries out its missions. IT can have two primary impacts on organizational activities: (a) affecting the processes through which established activities are performed and (b) making possible new capabilities or potential activities that were not available previously. For example, in the first category, an IT system might provide more efficient ways in which to process booking or docket information. In the second, a GIS might allow a police department to target its efforts in ways that would not be possible without it. For a particular IT project, these classes of impacts are not mutually exclusive. Whether by design or as a consequence of deployment, many systems will both affect an organization's current activities and provide new or different capabilities.

In applying IT to current organizational processes,[8] the goal is improvement. The intent of technology use is to perform activities faster, cheaper, easier, and/or better. Some effects on current organizational processes are relatively straightforward to identify and measure. For example, decreasing the time required for the organization to carry out activities and deliver service to the public is a common goal of process improvement (Chabrow, 2002; Tien, 1988). Other examples of such process effects relevant across law enforcement, court, and corrections institutions include reducing the amounts of paperwork required for activities, reducing processing times for individuals or transactions within the system, and reducing the costs of organizational activities. It should be noted that although a system may have benefits in some areas, those benefits might come at the expense of costs in others. For example, Chan and colleagues (2001) reported on a case where the introduction of IT systems was perceived to increase the paperwork burden of officers.

Other potentially very important effects of IT deployment on current organizational processes and tasks can be more difficult to identify and assess. A major effect of many IT systems is to change the way in which individuals within an organization have access to information sources. For example, mobile data terminals make available to officers on the street databases that previously were accessible only at a police station terminal or from a clerk searching a paper filing system. Similarly, decision support or information management systems could provide judges with more ready access to legal data to support deliberation and/or sentencing.

The effects of such shifts in access are more difficult to identify. At one level, their impact could be viewed as reducing the time required for officers to perform critical tasks during investigations, thereby providing an increase in productivity compared with previous modes of operation. However, from another perspective, such access can provide new capabilities in that easier manual searching can enable investigators to query databases in ways that increase their effectiveness. Determining all such effects and making judgments about their relative importance will depend on the specific characteristics of the organization involved and must be addressed early in the evaluation process.

IT systems can also provide law enforcement organizations with new capabilities that would not be available in the absence of the systems. Examples include crime analysis and mapping efforts that enable better targeted community intervention initiatives (Brown, 2001), the use of IT methods to provide new training options for officers (Lingerfelt, 1997), and systems that allow coordination of effort among different organizations and allocate response resources (Johnson & Rivers, 2001). Beyond operational capabilities, information technologies can also provide law enforcement organizations with additional mechanisms, such as Internet websites and electronic mail, to communicate with the public (LeBeuf, 2000).

Workforce Effects

Both the capabilities and requirements of IT systems can significantly alter an organization's workforce requirements. In many cases, IT-generated improvements in efficiency may result in less demand for certain types of workers within the organization. In other words, if IT systems simplify record keeping or other tasks, fewer personnel may be required for data management-related tasks. For example, in Queens, New York, the district attorney's office directly connected its data management systems to police department IT systems. The result was a reduction in the number of data entry personnel required to carry out office functions from 17 to 3 (Chabrow, 2002).

The capabilities of IT systems may also allow changes in the type of personnel required to perform certain tasks. In the police department in Washington, D.C., the new systems allowed the movement of some work from sworn personnel to nonsworn personnel, making it possible for sworn officers to spend more time on the street and less time involved in management and record-keeping activities (Lingerfelt, 1997). Another shift in personnel involves the increased need for technical personnel and support staff members (Brown, 2001; Nunn, 2001). New IT systems can have other, less quantifiable impacts on an organization's workforce such as shifts in worker morale (Colton, 1980) and impacts on officer safety. For example, increased availability or more rapid access to information about particular vehicles, suspects, and/or evolving situations could allow officers to alter their tactics to reduce the risk associated with their activities. Such effects would, however, be difficult to measure quantitatively.

Management Effects

Because a major function of IT systems is the organization and delivery of relevant information, these technologies can have significant impacts on management and decision making. More timely and accurate information can enable managers to make better decisions on both tactical and strategic issues. The ability to collect and maintain data on law enforcement activities can facilitate accountability to political leadership and the public and can enable better management of organizational risks. However, because more information is not always positive from the perspective of management decision making, IT also has the potential to generate information overload (Colton, 1980). If the information provided by a system is not well crafted to the needs of commanders, new systems could actually slow decision making and reduce effectiveness.

Financial Effects

Because all organizations are constrained by the financial resources available to carry out their activities, the potential budgetary impacts of IT acquisition on an organization are considerable. In most cases, new IT systems will require substantial initial investments of organizational resources. Whereas organizations may obtain outside support for technology purchases through grants and supplemental funding, additional resources may be drawn from organization budgets to fully fund technology acquisition. Beyond their initial procurement, IT systems can have continuing financial effects over their operating lifetimes. Many of the impacts described in previous sections, such as changes in productivity and workforce requirements, could also affect organizational budgets either positively or negatively.

Organizational Effects

Because organizational routines and procedures are frequently embedded in the design of IT systems, their deployment can cause changes in the structures and processes within organizations. In some cases, making changes in the way in which an organization approaches its activities is a goal of system deployment. In others, these changes occur inadvertently as a result of the new technology (Lingerfelt, 1997). An IT system can also stabilize existing organizational characteristics. For example, by reinforcing existing organizational modes, an information system can make organizational processes inflexible and more difficult for future change efforts (Brown, 2001; Chan et al., 2001).

Measures in Criminal Justice IT Evaluation

Although developing an understanding of the potential impacts of an IT system is a critical first step in IT evaluation, practical management efforts require that those impacts be quantified. Without reducing potential impacts to numerical measures, it is difficult to compare positive and negative effects or to monitor how the IT system's performance changes over time. In constructing performance measures for IT systems, evaluators must consider both the system's functionality (i.e., whether it is available and used by the organization's members) and its effects.

Measures of IT Functionality

Although measures aimed at assessing the internal functioning of an IT department within an organization are not the focus of this discussion, understanding the IT impacts does require information on the availability and functionality of the system for use. Such measures address the reality that if a system is not up and functioning or is not used for the tasks it is designed to perform, its potential benefits might not be realized. Therefore, it is important to capture the effect of human and management elements on IT outcomes. Assessing these effects requires measures of system availability, reliability, and use.

Although appropriate functionality measures must be selected with the specifics of a particular system in mind, a range of potentially relevant metrics can be readily identified. What fraction of the time is a system up and working? How frequent are outages? Are outages predictable? When the system is down, how long is the average downtime? In addition to measuring the overall availability of the system, measures must address the effect that outages have on user perceptions of system reliability. For police organizations in particular, where officers operate in the field under a wide variety of conditions, how does the performance of the system hold up under varied conditions? For example, if a communications system functions well for routine operations but fails under demanding use at large-scale events, this must be addressed in performance measurement.

Beyond the technical availability and functionality of a system, measures must also address how the members of the organization are using the technology in practice. In some cases, employees will have little choice but to use a new information system deployed in their organization. For example, if employees have no choice but to log on and use a system to carry out critical parts of their jobs or to receive their paychecks, they are essentially forced to use it. In such "coercive" situations, the linkage of organizational requirements to the IT itself eliminates the opportunity to circumvent the system. In other cases, however, there can be considerable variety in how employees use a new system. Assessment must then begin by asking whether a technology is actually being used and how employees are using it.

If a system (or capability within a larger system) is not used, it might have no impact on organizational activities. For example, McRae and McDavid (1988) described a case where officers did not use a nonverbal messaging capability provided by a new communications system, although other portions of the system were used.[9] Beyond use of a system, a second area of concern is how well the technology "fits" and is applied as a component of employees' activities (Brown, 2000). For example, if users use a system capability only for activities that are peripheral to their main missions (e.g., using a search function to perform pro forma examinations of events that would otherwise be ignored), its potential impact would be negligible. Because the use of an IT system can change significantly over time, these issues can be viewed as assessing the learning and

innovation activities of the organization associated with the system (U.S. General Accounting Office, 1998).

Measure of IT Impact

Because information technologies are adopted by organizations to assist them in carrying out their responsibilities and routine activities, evaluation of their impact should ideally be tied to the goals and missions of the organization. As a result, both the positive and negative impacts of IT adoption should be evaluated based on their effect on the organization's ultimate outcomes and outputs. Drawing on the example of commercial organizations, a fundamental goal of investment evaluation is directly linking the investment—in this case the capital investment in IT—to the profits made by the firm. Because the central goal of all law enforcement organizations is control of crime, the fundamental outcome measure for evaluating changes in organizational processes and the deployment of IT would be reductions in crime rates or in the seriousness or distribution of observed criminal activity. However, because of the wide range of factors that can influence such overall outcome measures, it is difficult at best to use them as components of assessment efforts (Benson, 1993; McRae & McDavid, 1988). In practice, it is similarly difficult to directly link private sector IT investments with firms' "bottom line" performance.

The difficulties in tying IT directly to organizational outcomes often result in evaluators using intermediate measures to assess the impacts of new systems. For technologies aimed at existing organizational processes or activities, the situation that exists before the deployment of the new system can be used as a baseline for measurement. For example, if a new IT system is adopted for managing traffic tickets or keeping track of jail populations, specific performance improvements—drops in processing time, limitation of paperwork, reductions in record errors, and so forth—might be appropriate intermediate metrics.[10] Systems that provide new capabilities require significantly different evaluation approaches from those predominantly intended to improve current processes. Because new capabilities lack a baseline for direct comparison, intermediate measures that provide a link between them and the overall missions and outputs of the organization must be defined. Such measures must be chosen based on the characteristics and goals of the IT system, and examples include increased collection of fines (McRae & McDavid, 1998), recovery of stolen property (Nunn, 1994), arrests, case clearance, and dismissal or conviction rates (Chabrow, 2002).

From a practical perspective, intended output and outcome metrics will be defined based on the goals of the IT system. However, as described previously, if evaluation is restricted to only the systems' intended impacts, an evaluation effort might miss a range of unintended or incidental effects. To enable fair evaluation of an IT system, a range of measures are required to capture both the costs and benefits associated with its use (Willcocks & Lester, 1997). In addition, the measures that are selected must be relevant to the target audiences for evaluation. For example, it is unlikely that the same set of metrics will be equally useful and persuasive to policymakers, the general public, law enforcement leadership, and IT specialists (U.S. General Accounting Office, 1998). Measures that capture the intangible impacts of IT deployment should also be explored. Some of these more abstract effects are relatively straightforward to capture (e.g., effects on employee morale), whereas others are much less so (e.g., assessing changes in the quality of decision making or impacts on officer safety).

Measurement Issues

In developing measures for IT evaluation, the ideal is developing unambiguous numerical measures for behaviors and effects. For example, to ensure accuracy and uniformity in measurement, system logs are preferable to user recollections for assessing system use. Quantitative measures are often easier to develop for transaction-based IT processes than are more abstract ones such as decision support and knowledge management (Brown, 2000). It should be noted, however, that evaluation should not be limited to measures that are the most straightforward to quantify. Doing so risks ignoring elements of performance that might be critically important in assessing the net benefits and costs of the system. In all cases, the metrics and measurement methods that are developed should limit additional burdens on system users to help ensure validity over time and reduce increases in system costs (U.S. General Accounting Office, 1998).

Because of the difficulties in defining objective measures for components of system productivity, evaluation efforts may rely on user perceptions—obtained through focus groups, surveys, and/or other mechanisms—to assess system performance. These mechanisms are particularly important given that user perceptions can have a significant impact on system use.[11] Furthermore, it is impossible to assess some impacts (e.g., changes in employee morale) without asking users directly. In designing an evaluation, it is critical to be aware that user perceptions and satisfaction might not directly correspond to the interests of the organization. Therefore, they might not be the best measure of system performance (Powell, 1992). Such survey methods also can impose a burden on users that limits their usefulness in ongoing evaluation activities.

The spread of the effects of IT through an organization and the evolution of the effects over time also present challenges for evaluation. Because of the types of effects that IT systems can have, their impacts may go beyond the parts of the organization that are intended to be affected. Examples include increased burdens on contracting staffs to support the new systems and new demands placed on human resources to recruit and retain the needed technical personnel (Brown, 2001). If the potential for such ripple effects is not included in evaluation, costs and benefits of a system may be missed. Similarly, the fact that the use of IT systems changes over time limits the effectiveness of static evaluation efforts. Because many attempts to evaluate technologies are done at a single point in time, it is difficult to address the fact that significant changes can occur as an organization continues to use a new system and gains experience with it (Northrop et al., 1995). These effects can be particularly important for information systems where the expertise of users, and the integration of the new capabilities into organizational processes and routines, can have significant impacts on the presence (and size) of benefits (McKeen et al., 1999).

The design of IT impact measures must also contend with the fact that other, non-IT-related events or organizational shifts can cause changes in organizational productivity and effectiveness. In the absence of metrics that directly connect observed changes to the IT system itself, evaluators must be aware of these external effects that can obscure or confound analysis. This includes the need to disaggregate the effects of the IT system from other procedural changes that might be made at the same time it is put into place. For example, one goal for a new telephone and CAD system installed by the San Diego Police Department during the 1970s was to reduce the average length of time spent by dispatchers on each call for service so that they could serve more citizens and reduce caller wait times. After installing the systems, the average length of time spent per call did indeed drop from 3 minutes to 1 minute 17 seconds. However, during the implementation, operators were also specifically trained to prevent a conversation from wandering by

directly asking whether the caller needed an officer dispatched, and this could have contributed to the improvement even in the absence of the other parts of the system (Colton, 1980).

To assess the impacts of the technology more effectively, evaluation should be approached from an experimental perspective whenever possible. Groups of employees using the technology should be compared with control groups not using the technology to isolate technology-specific effects.[12] However, the realities of implementing technologies in public sector agencies often make such an analytic approach difficult (Nunn & Quinet, 2002).

Making IT Assessment Decisions

From a traditional business case approach to evaluation, judgments about investments are made by a variety of financially centered decision criteria. Prominent among these methods is the notion of cost–benefit analysis, whose terminology and concepts were used implicitly in the earlier portions of this discussion. Beyond cost–benefit, methods include return on investment, return on management, and others. Because such approaches focus on monetary measures, they can lead to a desire to express all costs and benefits in monetary terms. Although this is not problematic for some of the impacts of IT deployment, such as acquisition or maintenance costs, staffing changes, and increases in efficiency, it is much more difficult for new capabilities or intangible benefits (Wen & Sylla, 1999).

Difficulties in reducing IT assessments to a single measure or scale do not apply only to monetary approaches. Across the range of potential impacts described previously, relevant measures range from user perceptions of utility to reductions in the time required to process court documents. Although established methods to normalize and combine such disparate measures do exist, the resulting numerical indexes are often much less useful in management or much less compelling to decision makers. As a result, combinations of different measures and assessment methods may be required to better capture the complexities of system evaluation.

One method, advanced as a best practice by the U.S. General Accounting Office (1998), is the use of a "balanced scorecard" to bring together different measures and metrics for areas such as financial performance, user satisfaction, outcomes, organizational learning, and internal business practices. While attempting to limit the number of measures included so as to reduce the chance of information overload, a scorecard approach seeks to address the fact that "no single measure provides clear performance targets or places attention on critical mission areas" and that a range of measures are needed to be relevant for management from the IT project level up to the organization's strategic management (p. 32).

IT AND POLICY CHANGE: FUTURE CHALLENGES

Different organizations within the criminal justice system—police departments, courts, and correctional facilities—have disparate roles and significantly different uses for IT. As a result, efforts to deploy IT systems to meet their needs must be matched to the characteristics of the organizations involved. Similarly, in evaluating the impacts of these IT deployment efforts, the different goals and requirements of these organizations must be considered so that the impacts of any new technology can be measured appropriately. Although the diversity in the criminal justice system defies simplified approaches to IT adoption and evaluation, a set of basic principles have been developed within the community to guide implementation efforts:

- Matching system requirements to organizational goals
- Ensuring organizational buy-in and commitment
- Considering the full acquisition and life cycles of the technology
- Involving users
- Systematically assessing the potential positive and negative impacts of the systems
- Planning to incorporate evaluation into ongoing management efforts

These concepts provide a strategy to help overcome the potential obstacles that can complicate organizational attempts to acquire new technology systems and are equally relevant to law enforcement organizations that are acquiring their first IT systems and to those that already have efforts under way to apply these technologies to their operations.

Over the past decades, IT has been broadly deployed in some portions of the criminal justice system. In others, these technologies are not as widespread. During the era following the terrorist attacks of September 11, 2001, the United States and its law enforcement organizations face additional challenges associated with the prevention and investigation of terrorist activities. The new emphasis on homeland security has increased the demand for information sharing across multiple agencies and the urgency of integrating justice information systems at the federal, state, and local levels. This need for interoperability among law enforcement organizations in different jurisdictions and different levels of government has been an ongoing challenge for some time. Because of the need for information sharing and cooperation among law enforcement, justice, immigration, and other types of agencies—the need to connect many individual pieces of evidence or intelligence information so as to provide warning or understanding of a planned terrorist attack—broader use of IT by law enforcement organizations could play an important role in keeping the United States safe from terrorism.

As federal, state, and local resources are devoted to improving the capabilities of law enforcement organizations to share information and carry out their critical duties, it is important to ensure that those resources are expended prudently in ways that produce the greatest possible benefits for the nation as a whole. At the same time, the changed homeland security environment has resulted in shifts in funding to many areas. This shift has also revealed many competing priorities for security and investigative resources. As a result, in efforts to apply IT tools to law enforcement activities, it is increasingly critical to design technology adoption well and to incorporate appropriate evaluation systems to ensure that such activities contribute to public safety effectively.

NOTES

1. This chapter adopts a broad definition of IT encompassing systems and technologies devoted to the collection, processing, manipulation, storage, management, display, communication, and use of data. In the law enforcement context, this includes varied technologies such as database systems, communications systems, computer-aided dispatch, decision support or expert systems, inmate management systems, and crime mapping systems.

2. These funds were not distributed evenly across law enforcement organizations. Of the agencies that served jurisdictions with populations less than 25,000, only 5.4% received a MORE grant, compared with 53% of jurisdictions with populations exceeding 1 million. In addition, the award of MORE grants was concentrated in the very largest cities.

3. Data are from the 1990 and 2000 Law Enforcement Management and Administrative Statistics (LEMAS) surveys.

4. The Task Force on Crime Mapping and Data-Driven Management noted in its report on the use of crime mapping that although a National Institute of Justice (NIJ) survey found that only 36% of police departments with more than 100 sworn officers and only 13% of smaller departments reported using computerized mapping in 1997, this technology was spreading rapidly. Moreover, 20% of law enforcement agencies that were not using computerized GIS at the time of the NIJ survey reported plans to purchase mapping software. (U.S. Department of Justice, 1999, Section 2).

5. CompStat originally started out as a book that included current year-to-date crime statistics compiled on a citywide, patrol borough, and precinct basis. It eventually grew more sophisticated over time, evolving into computer-assisted mapping (Silverman, 1996).

6. Electronic monitoring systems are used by community corrections to supervise high-risk violent probationers and parolees.

7. The potential areas of IT impacts listed are adapted from Wen and Sylla (1999).

8. It should be noted that the deployment of IT will result in new sets of internal processes within an organization—the processes required to manage, service, and support the IT systems themselves (U.S. General Accounting Office, 1998). Assessing how well these processes meet the needs of their internal customers is also a key component of IT management but is not the focus of this chapter.

9. Similarly, Nunn and Quinet (2002, p. 91) described a case where officers engaged in problem-oriented policing frequently did not use in-car database search capabilities because they were frequently not necessary for their activities.

10. The difficulty associated with devising such metrics for existing organizational functions clearly differs among the particular systems and functions involved. For example, primarily record-keeping functions are much more straightforward to examine than are functions such as criminal investigation where specific tasks, and the impacts of IT on them, are much harder to define (Northrop, Dutton, & Kraemer, 1982).

11. For example, Brown (2001) used surveys to assess concepts such as changes in productivity, effectiveness, and efficiency. Northrop and colleagues (1995) used recollection surveys as well.

12. An example might be comparing a test group of officers provided with new handheld computers with an equivalent group not provided with the technology so as to identify differences in productivity and/or activities (Pilant, 1999).

REFERENCES

Anandarajan, A., & Wen, H. J. (1999). Evaluation of information technology investment. *Logistics Information Management, 12,* 329–337.

Association of State Correctional Administrators. (1998). *State and federal corrections information systems: An inventory of data elements and an assessment of reporting capabilities* (NCJ 170016). Washington, DC: National Institute of Justice.

Benson, D. (1993). The police and information technology. In G. Button (Ed.), *Technology in working order: Studies of work, interaction, and technology* (pp. 81–97). London: Routledge.

Brown, M. (2000). Criminal justice discovers information technology. In National Institute of Justice, *The nature of crime: Continuity and change* (Vol. 1). Washington, DC: National Institute of Justice. Retrieved July 24, 2003, from www.ncjrs.org/criminal_justice2000/vol_1/02e.pdf

Brown, M. (2001). The benefits and costs of information technology innovations: An empirical assessment of a local government agency. *Public Performance & Management Review, 24,* 351–366.

Chabrow, E. (2002, October 14). A new take on law enforcement. *Information Week,* pp. 58–60.

Chan, J., Brereton, D., Legosz, M., & Doran, S. (2001). *E-policing: The impact of information technology on police practices.* Queensland, Australia: Queensland Criminal Justice Commission. Retrieved July 24, 2003, from www.cmc.qld.gov.au/library/cmcwebsite/epolicing26.pdf

Colton, K. W. (1980, March). Police and computer technology: The case of the San Diego computer-aided dispatch system. *Public Productivity Review,* pp. 21–42.

Dawes, S. S., Pardo, T. A., Simon, S., Cresswell, A. M., Lavigne, M. F., Anderson, D. F., & Bloniarz, P. A. (2003). *Making smart IT choices: Understanding value and risk in government IT investments* (2nd ed.). Albany, NY: University of Albany, Center for Technology in Government.

DiIulio, J. J., Jr., Smith, S. K., & Saiger, A. J. (1995). The federal role in crime control. In J. Q. Wilson & J. Petersilia (Eds.), *Crime: Twenty-eight leading experts look at the most pressing problem of our time* (pp. 445–464). San Francisco: Institute for Contemporary Studies Press.

Hickman, M. J., & Reaves, B. A. (2003a). *Local police departments, 2000* (NCJ 196002). Washington, DC: Bureau of Justice Statistics, Law Enforcement Management and Administrative Statistics.

Hickman, M. J., & Reaves, B. A. (2003b). *Sheriffs' offices, 2000* (NCJ 196534). Washington, DC: Bureau of Justice Statistics, Law Enforcement Management and Administrative Statistics.

Holmes, A. (1999–2000, Fall/Winter). *Delaware Criminal Justice Information System: The evolution of integration.* Report of the National Task Force on Court Automation and Integration, SEARCH Case Study Series.

Holmes, A., Usery, D., & Roper, R. (2000–2001, Fall/Winter). *Colorado Integrated Criminal Justice Information System: Project overview and recommendations.* Report of the National Task Force on Court Automation and Integration, SEARCH Case Study Series.

Johnson, E. C. (1997). *Court automation and integration: Issues and technologies.* SEARCH Technical Bulletin No. 2. Retrieved July 7, 2004, from www.search.org/publications/tech.asp

Johnson, T. A., & Rivers, E. A. (2001). Information technology: A critical addition to the law enforcement arsenal. *Sheriff, 53*(4), 18–19.

Justice Technology Information Network. (n.d.). *GIS for corrections (CORMAP).* Retrieved July 24, 2003, from www.nlectc.org/assistance/cormap.html

LeBeuf, M-E. (2000). *Policing and use of information technology: An assessment.* Ottawa: Canadian Police College. Retrieved July 24, 2003, from www.cpc.gc.ca/research/mel_e.pdf

Lingerfelt, J. (1997). Technology as a force multiplier. In *Proceedings of the Conference on Technology Community Policing.* Retrieved July 24, 2003, from www.nlectc.org

McKeen, J. D., Smith, H. A., & Parent, M. (1999). An integrative research approach to assess the business value of information technology. In M. A. Mahamood & E. J. Szewczak (Eds.), *Measuring information technology investment payoff: Contemporary approaches* (pp. 5–23). Hershey, PA: Idea Group Publishing.

McRae, J. J., & McDavid, J. (1988). Computer-based technology in police work: A benefit–cost analysis of a mobile digital communications system. *Journal of Criminal Justice, 16,* 47–60.

Morgan, M. O. (2003). *Federal juvenile anticrime programs.* Washington, DC: National Center for Policy Analysis. Retrieved August 22, 2003, from www.ncpa.org/hotlines/juvcrm/jj4new/programs.html

National Law Enforcement and Corrections Technology Center. (2001). *A guide for applying information technology in law enforcement* (NCJ 185934). Washington, DC: U.S. Department of Justice.

Northrop, A., Dutton, W. H., & Kraemer, K. L. (1982, May/June). The management of computer applications in local government. *Public Administration Review,* pp. 234–243.

Northrop, A., Kraemer, K. L., & King, J. L. (1995). Police use of computers. *Journal of Criminal Justice, 23,* 259–275.

Nunn, S. (1994). How capital technologies affect municipal service outcomes: The case of police mobile digital terminals and stolen vehicle recoveries. *Journal of Policy Analysis and Management, 13,* 539–559.

Nunn, S. (2001). Police information technology: Assessing the effects of computerization on urban police functions. *Public Administration Review, 61,* 221–234.

Nunn, S., & Quinet, K. (2002). Evaluating the effects of information technology on problem-oriented policing: If it doesn't fit, must we quit? *Evaluation Review, 26,* 81–108.

Office of Justice Programs. (2001). *An overview of OJP bureaus, offices, and cops information technology initiatives.* Washington, DC: U.S. Department of Justice.

Office of Justice Programs. (2003). *Crime identification technology.* Retrieved August 21, 2003, from http://it.ojp.gov/fund/files/cita.html

Petersilia, J. (2002). Community corrections. In J. Q. Wilson & J. Petersilia (Eds.), *Crime: Public policies for crime control* (pp. 483–508). Oakland, CA: Institute for Contemporary Studies Press.

Pilant, L. (1999, January). Going mobile in law enforcement technology. *National Institute of Justice Journal*, pp. 11–16.

Powell, P. (1992). Information technology evaluation: Is it different? *Journal of the Operational Research Society, 43*, 29–42.

Reaves, B. A., & Hickman, M. J. (2002a). *Census of state and local law enforcement agencies, 2000* (NCJ 194066). Washington, DC: Bureau of Justice Statistics.

Reaves, B. A., & Hickman, M. J. (2002b). *Police departments in large cities, 1990–2000* (NCJ 175703). Washington, DC: Bureau of Justice Statistics.

Rosen, M. D. (1982, September). Police and the computer: The revolution that never happened. *Police Magazine*, p. 5.

Roth, J. A., Ryan, J. F., Gaffigan, S. J., Koper, C. S., Moore, M. H., Roehl, J. A., Johnson, C. C., Moore, G. E., White, R. M., Buerger, M. E., Langston, E. A., & Thacher, D. (2000). *National Evaluation of the COPS Program—Title I of the 1994 Crime Act* (NCJ 183643). Washington, DC: U.S. Department of Justice.

Rottman, D. B., Flango, C. R., Cantrell, M. T., Hansen, R., & LaFountain, N. (2000). *State court organization 1998* (NCJ 178932). Washington, DC: U.S. Department of Justice.

SEARCH. (1999). *Report of the National Task Force on Court Automation and Integration* (NCJ 177601). Prepared for the Bureau of Justice Assistance, Office of Justice Programs, U.S. Department of Justice. Retrieved August 21, 2003, from www.search.org/leit/workshops.asp

SEARCH (2001a). *Integration in the context of justice information systems: A common understanding*. Retrieved August 21, 2003, from www.search.org/leit/workshops.asp

SEARCH (2001b). *Strategic planning, CAD/RMS technology initiatives: Issues and Technologies Workshop, San Diego, CA, September 19, 2001*. Retrieved August 21, 2003, from www.search.org/leit/workshops.asp

SEARCH (2002). *Planning the integration of justice information systems: Developing the Justice Information Exchange Model—Final project report*. Retrieved August 21, 2003, from www.search.org/integration/pdf/jiem.pdf

Seaskate Inc. (1998). *The evolution and development of police technology*. Technical report prepared for the National Committee on Criminal Justice Technology.

Serafeimidis, V., & Smithson, S. (1999). Rethinking approaches to information systems investment evaluation. *Logistics Information Management, 12*, 94–107.

Silverman, E. B. (1996, December 15). Mapping change: How the New York Police Department re-engineered itself to drive down crime. *Law Enforcement News*. Retrieved August 21, 2003, from www.lib.jjay.cuny.edu/len/96/15dec/html/ 12.html

Sparrow, M. K. (1993). Information systems and the development of policing. *Perspectives on Policing, 16*, 1–11. (Washington, DC: U.S. Department of Justice)

Stephan, J. J., & Karberg, J. C. (2003). *Census of state and federal correctional facilities, 2000* (NCJ 198272). Washington, DC: U.S. Department of Justice.

Tien, J. M. (1988). Computer applications in U.S. law enforcement. *Computational, Environmental, and Urban Systems, 12*, 37–48.

U.S. Department of Justice. (1999). *Mapping out crime: Providing 21st century tools for safe communities*. Retrieved August 21, 2003, from http://govinfo.library.unt.edu/npr/library/papers/bkgrd/crimemap/content.html

U.S. General Accounting Office. (1998). *Executive guide: Measuring performance and demonstrating results of information technology investments* (GAO/AIMD-98–89). Washington, DC: Author.

Wen, H. J., & Sylla, C. (1999). A road map for the evaluation of information technology investment. In M. A. Mahamood & E. J. Szewczak (Eds.), *Measuring information technology investment payoff: Contemporary approaches* (pp. 182–201). Hershey, PA: Idea Group Publishing.

Willcocks, L. P., & Lester, S. (1997). In search of information technology productivity: Assessment issues. *Journal of the Operational Research Society, 48*, 1082–1094.

Section II

THE CRIMINAL JUSTICE SYSTEM AND THE INTERNET

CHAPTER 3

How Criminal Justice Agencies Use the Internet

Roberta E. Griffith

The Internet was developed during the late 1960s as a direct result of the Advanced Research Projects Agency (ARPA) under the Department of Defense. ARPA wanted to take advantage of computer technology and the computing power of several supercomputers of the time and implemented the Advanced Research Projects Agency Network (ARPANET). The first node of the network was a super-computer at the University of California, Los Angeles. The network served two primary functions: to allow people to communicate with each other in case of a nuclear attack or other disaster and to allow other researchers and scientists to use computer power from the supercomputers. The network, now known as the Internet, had 15 nodes on the network as of 1971, was demonstrated publicly in 1972, and was connected to other countries in 1973 (Schmalleger, 2002). Any computer could connect to the Internet so long as it could "speak" the right language, Transmission Control Protocol/Internet

Protocol (TCP/IP). TCP allowed for the message to be separated and passed through the phone lines and reassembled at the message's destination, whereas IP handled the address of the intended destination.

The importance of TCP/IP was that it was free and easy to use (Sterling, 1993). The intended design and infrastructure was to have no central authority or hierarchical structure, so that if one computer were knocked off the network, information still could be transmitted by way of other computer hubs or nodes. Another novel concept was that it cost taxpayers nothing because the costs were picked up by each user; that is, each user supplied his or her own computer, electricity, phone line, and so forth.

Although academic researchers used the Internet initially, it was not until the development of Hypertext Markup Language (HTML) and the World Wide Web (the Web or WWW) during the early 1990s that the Internet achieved popularity. Coincidentally, ARPANET officially disbanded in 1989

(Sterling, 1993). It is important to note that the Internet is the backbone of the Web; that is, they are not the same thing, but they are often used interchangeably. It can be said that the Web is the most used application on the Internet given that the Web is basically a database of websites using a graphical user interface (GUI) and can combine multimedia.

The Web uses HyperText Transfer Protocol (HTTP) to communicate with other computers on the network, and it uses the HTML programming language to support links to other documents as well as graphics, audio files, and video files. The Web received significant popularity when the Clinton administration placed the Web high on its agenda and used the term "information superhighway" to describe this new communication tool (Schmalleger, 2002). The Web offered a friendly and easy way in which to search, download/upload documents, communicate with other people, shop, and do research all by way of computers.

With the advent of the Web in 1990, it became easier to conduct business (e-commerce), talk to people around the globe (e-mail), and do research (online libraries) (Schmalleger, 2002). This functionality had a large impact on nearly every aspect of society, perhaps even more so than the invention of the telephone. Nearly everyone probably can remember when the Web was just becoming popular. One could not watch television, read a magazine, or go anywhere without seeing someone's website address being advertised. This type of marketing gave people the opportunity to look up information about nearly anything—and right from their very own personal computers. The technology made it easy to display products, services, hours of operation, and just about anything one's organization did. It was not long before government, nonprofit, and service organizations began to create websites.

Criminal justice has always been an information-intensive industry. Investigating criminal activity, implementing problem-oriented policing, processing court cases, and managing correctional facilities all are heavily dependent on information for their successful operation. Until recently, however, implementing information systems on the Internet to better manage available data has typically been beyond the technical and fiscal reaches of most organizations within the criminal justice system. Not surprisingly, the technical and fiscal constraints experienced by the criminal justice system are similar for many other organizations in the public sector. The result is significant variation in how criminal justice agencies use the Internet. Some agencies are quite sophisticated, whereas others are just beginning. The extent of this variation and level of use among the Web uses is not well documented. The purpose of this chapter is to give a general overview of how criminal justice as a field, primarily law enforcement, courts, prosecution, pretrial services, corrections, and social agencies, use the Internet and the Web.

Criminal justice agencies have access to local area networks (LANs), wide area networks (WANs), the Internet, telecommunications, and radio frequencies as their primary information infrastructure for communications. However, for the purposes of this chapter, the primary focus is on discussing the uses of the Internet and the Web and not much on discussing the uses of LANs, WANs, telecommunications, and radio frequencies.

LAW ENFORCEMENT

Over the past 20 years or so, there has been a shift toward community-oriented policing in law enforcement. Community policing, or problem-oriented policing, is based on the notion that law enforcement cannot control crime alone and needs help from the community. Law enforcement can generate citizen participation by becoming better connected to the public. Community policing takes a proactive approach instead of reactive stance, and for this theory to work, every aspect of the criminal justice system needs to be involved: law enforcement, courts, corrections, pretrial, probation, and social agencies.

> Community policing emphasized that the police should work closely with the community in addressing crime and disorder issues, that genuine partnerships should be created, and that individual citizens and community groups should play a larger role in maintaining public safety. Achieving these goals requires that the police engage in much more information sharing with community groups (both providing information to the community and obtaining information from the community). (Abt Associates, 2000, p. 5)

With the advent of the Internet, it seems as if the best way in which to share information is through electronic means, the use of connected networks, and the Web. The Internet and the Web offer the law enforcement community avenues for information seeking, dissemination, and management as well as investigative methods.

INFORMATION SEEKING

There are several websites on the Internet that offer advice, e-mail, publications, and information on policies, conferences, ordinances, programs and innovations to the law enforcement community. Three general examples are the Justice Technology Information Network (JUSTNET, www.justnet .org), the International Association of Chiefs of Police (IACPNet, http://services.login-inc .com/iacpnet), and the National Criminal Justice Reference Service (NCJRS, www .ncjrs.org). All offer information to the criminal justice community and promote

information collection and dissemination. JUSTNET is aimed at law enforcement professionals; however, anyone can access the website to find information on technology issues affecting criminal justice such as equipment and techniques, view the testing and evaluation of products such as body armor and handcuffs, find resources about training for crime mapping and prison riots, use it as an outlet to buy equipment, and access the virtual library. In addition, this website offers links to other criminal justice-related sites.

IACPNet is similar to JUSTNET; however, one has to pay a fee and become a member first before gaining access to a plethora of information the IACPNet website. NCJRS is a website devoted to the dissemination of publications and research concerning all matters of criminal justice, from substance abuse to fraud against the elderly. Other websites, such as Thomas.loc.gov, allow users to complete legal research. The Thomas website provides bill summary and status, access to the congressional record, and committee information.

INFORMATION DISSEMINATION

Police websites offer several benefits. First and foremost, they increase public relations by enhancing communication between the public and police departments. It is commonly thought that through better communication between the police and citizens, each party is more apt to share crime information with the other, thereby allowing the community to become more involved and the police to become more connected to the community (Malinowski, Kalish, & Parks, 2000). For example, police websites can allow the public to file complaints, offer employment qualifications and opportunities, distribute crime alerts, and serve as a link to many other civil and social services available.

Knowing how to protect your home against burglars, identifying the proper location for vehicle inspections, finding out the cost of your traffic citation, and determining the employment qualifications to become a police officer in one's own community are all routine functions performed by law enforcement agencies. Posting current information on the WWW relative to these issues is an efficient method of making the information available to citizens at their convenience. (Haley & Taylor, 1998, p. 131)

A good example is the Tempe (Arizona) Police Department's website, which has interactive capability for the public to use and also distributes information for analysts, community managers, and department personnel (www.tempe.gov). "Posting crime analysis material on the Internet would provide timely information with nearly instantaneous updates and would conserve time and resources by reducing mailing and virtually eliminating printing and duplicating costs," according to Boba (1999, pp. 6–7). Among sex offender registry and general information, the Crime Analysis Unit links users to demographics, calls for service, crime trends, and crime hot spots, all of which are enabled with computer mapping technology.

Some departments offer unique features on their websites. For example, Los Angeles has a section devoted to stolen art and objects. Bulletins with suspects' pictures, as well as images of recovered and stolen art, books, photographs, and other objects, all are listed in this section along with a small description of each object and incident. Another feature on many local and state police websites is a link to sexual offender registries in an effort to comply with "Megan's Law." Here, users can submit a name and/or address to see the status of an offender and his or her current location. Most of the files have offender photographs, physical descriptions, identifying information, the offenses committed, and last known addresses.

Another feature is the listing of local, state, and federal wanted individuals. "One of the reasons for a WWW presence is to distribute information that helps to extend the 'eyes and ears' of the police department, hoping to locate wanted criminals and missing persons," according to Haley and Taylor (1998, p. 140). For instance, the Lake County (Illinois) Sheriff's Office lists a "Deadbeat Parents Wanted" section (www.co.lake.il.us/sheriff). This site also has photographs, physical descriptions, addresses, amounts of child support owed, dates of birth, and other identifying information. Finally, some websites include an e-mail function for users to report crimes, crime tips, and other comments anonymously (e.g., Papillion, Nebraska: www.sarpy.com; Arlington, Texas: www.arlingtonpd.org).

Local law enforcement departments have begun to implement analytic information system capabilities into their operations, for example, embedding geographic information systems (GIS) into their routine functions. GIS have been used for crime prevention and analysis by identifying crime "hot spots" and "forecasting" possible crime areas, for example, identifying and predicting areas of burglary and drug use. It is interesting to note that although GIS have proven to be effective, larger departments (i.e., more than 100 sworn officers) were much more likely to use the computerized crime mapping technology (36%) than were smaller departments (3%) (Mamalian & La Vigne, 1999). Moreover, of the local police agencies that did have computers in 1999, only 16% reported using them for crime mapping (Hickman, 2001).

Although a number of departments may use GIS within their respective agencies, very few currently provide crime mapping capabilities by way of the Internet. Larger departments are active users of GIS. For example, the Portland (Oregon) Police Department offers maps that shade the geographic areas by number of all crimes per area, or users can select a particular type of crime (e.g., assault, arson, burglary) and have the incidence of such crime displayed at the census block level (www.portlandpolicebureau.com). Other advanced website components, including crime stopper tips, stolen property, online incident reporting, crime mapping, data analysis, public surveys, and e-commerce, is available in the form of being able to purchase copies of reports and local record checks.

INFORMATION MANAGEMENT

Some departments are using the Internet to manage their record systems and disseminate information. The Boston Police Department uses the "out of the box" application software, Criminal Justice Information System (CJIS) Web (Kanable, 2000). The benefit of this software is that it implements standard Internet protocols and a common Web browser (Netscape or Internet Explorer) to provide access to networked databases with scanned fingerprints, mug shots, other scanned documents, and text data. Access is controlled by log-ins set up by the system administrator. It is networked and generally used on intranets,[1] but it does have the capability to be used on the Internet. This type of software can allow anyone connected to the network to view the data, whether it is someone in the physical confines of an office within the department or an officer out on the street with a handheld computer or a computer in a patrol car. CJIS Web can be connected to the Federal Bureau of Investigation's (FBI) fingerprint database, the Integrated Automated Fingerprint Identification System (IAFIS).

The purpose of the IAFIS is to "sustain the FBI's mission to provide identification services to the nation's law enforcement community and organizations where criminal background histories are a critical factor in consideration for employment" according

to the FBI (2003a). The IAFIS will provide 10-print, latent print, subject search, and criminal history request services; document submission; and image request services. The total system is being implemented in three segments: the Automated Fingerprint Identification System (AFIS) segment, the Interstate Identification Index (III) segment, and the Identification, Tasking, and Networking (ITN) segment.

CYBERCRIME AND INVESTIGATIVE METHODS

With personal computers and Internet connections now commonplace, certain types of crime, referred to as cybercrime, can be committed even more easily. "Cybercrime can be regarded as computer-mediated activities which are either illegal or considered illicit by certain parties and which can be conducted through global electronic networks," according to Thomas and Loader (2000, p. 3). Some examples of crimes committed by way of computer that constitute cybercrime are drug trafficking, e-commerce fraud (counterfeited prescription drugs and goods), sex crimes and child pornography, illegal arms trafficking, computer network break-ins, industrial espionage, viruses, and denial of service attacks. Identity theft, intellectual property violations (e.g., copyright infringement, software and music piracy), money laundering, credit card fraud, and other bank fraud all are types of crime that can be accomplished on an international scale because the global market exploits "information" as a commodity being bought and sold on the Web (Thomas & Loader, 2000).

Most of these crimes are committed using hackers to steal personal information (e.g., passwords, credit card numbers, banking information) or to steal corporate information (e.g., trade secrets, security codes). Two common methods that hackers use are password sniffers, which are programs released on the Web to seek out passwords and other data, and spoofing, which is impersonating a computer to make another party think that one is indeed the original computer.

One way in which to combat being a victim is to use encryption, which helps both sides of the law by increasing privacy from prying eyes. Law enforcement can encrypt e-mail and stored data, whereas criminals use it to conceal their activities (Thomas & Loader, 2000). However, the use of encryption can seriously stall or altogether halt investigations because evidence on computers may be unattainable due to encrypted files.

Law enforcement is having a difficult time investigating and taking full advantage of the Web because it is moving at such a fast pace, making it hard for law enforcement to keep up. Also, the lack of skilled and knowledgeable officers in cybercrime seriously inhibits their success rate for investigations. Moreover, more times than not, cybercrime is a nonviolent crime, meaning that it does not have as high a priority as violent crime and that people might not know they were victims until months later, when it may be virtually impossible to trace the crime back in time. However, the national government and some select cities are on the right track. For example, New York has implemented the New York Electronic Crimes Task Force, and the federal government has the U.S. Secret Service Electronic Crimes Task Force (www.ectaskforce.org). And with the passage of the Patriot Act, a national network of task forces "for the purposes of preventing, detecting, and investigating various forms of electronic crimes, including potential terrorist attacks against critical infrastructure and financial payment systems" (Sec. 105) are currently being implemented.

Two current investigative techniques that do not require extensive computer expertise and that are used widely in law enforcement are DCS1000 and LexisNexis.

The FBI developed a diagnostic tool to "wiretap" Internet communications. The tool, called Carnivore, recently underwent a name change to DCS1000 (CNN, 2001). The software is installed on an Internet service provider's (ISP) network. Once installed, it can provide the FBI "with a 'surgical' ability to intercept and collect the communications which are the subject of the lawful order while ignoring those communications which they are not authorized to intercept" (FBI, 2003b). For example, if a court order allows only the interception of e-mail, DCS1000 will look only at e-mail and other activities on the Internet by the user will be ignored.

Another investigative tool available to law enforcement is the use of online databases. One great example is LexisNexis, which can search

> 840 metropolitan and large city daily newspapers and wire services of the Associated Press. In addition, it can search corporate and limited partnership registrations, doing-business-as and fictitious name registrations,[2] obituaries and death notices, professional licenses, aircraft and boat registrations, deed transfers and tax assessor records, bankruptcy filings, liens and judgment filings, crime indexes, and Social Security Administration death benefit lists. (Paynter, 1999, p. 89)

Access to these types of databases has a cost, but the fee is nominal.

Law enforcement is not the only group having a difficult time in keeping up with cybercrime; lawmakers and prosecutors are having a difficult time as well. The technology moves too quickly for regulations to come into effect given that it could take years for a bill to become law, and by that time it would be too late to get a handle on a particular type of crime. For example, consider the incidents of identity theft. This is one of the fast-growing crimes in America, and until recently there were no laws to stop it.

Another reason is that what is illegal in some countries is not illegal in others. For example, it was not until recently that Japan banned the production and sale of child pornography (Price & Verhulst, 2000). Moreover, there is no hierarchy, that is, no board of directors to sue, prosecute, or investigate in matters concerning the Internet and the Web. The most basic principle of the Web is anonymity, which is achieved through the flow of information over several million computers. Because information is sent in packets (i.e., one e-mail message could be broken up into several packets of information), and each packet is sent to the intended destination using different computers only to be reunited with other packets at the recipient's computer, it is entirely possible that each packet traveled on different computer networks and that other networks could be used if the same message were sent again. This leaves no one "responsible" for information being sent.

FUTURE USES

Police departments often have internal networks that are called intranets. Many of these departments either have plans in the works or are waiting for funding and the like to expand their intranets by connecting them to the Internet.

For example, in Florida, Broward County has an internal database (Pawn Trac) of merchandise sold to pawn stores. Pawn Trac has proven to be effective for recovering stolen property and leading to the arrests of burglars. It currently works by local pawnshops collecting data (e.g., serial numbers, descriptions, sellers) and then giving the data, usually on disk, to their local police departments. However, there are future plans for being able to submit this information over the Internet. This option would be less costly and more "real time." But there are a few

glitches that need to be overcome; not all pawnshops have access to the Internet, and privacy concerns are still being worked out (Perez, 2000).

Another example is the Reno (Nevada) Police Department, which has future plans for installing new Panasonic mobile computer terminals (MCTs) in its police cars. The MCTs "will provide in-car access to the report-writing tool, to information contained on the department's LAN—such as standard operating procedures, city ordinances, and Internet-based information—and to the National Crime Information Center (NCIC) and state of Nevada motor vehicles database" (Abt Associates, 2000, p. 103).

Courts, Prosecution, and Probation/Pretrial Services

The Internet, and more specifically the Web, can be a viable resource to the public for obtaining information and providing services concerning filings of reports, court dates, fee and fine collection, registration of vehicles, and applications for permits, to name just a few. Specifically, many court systems have attempted to automate court records and implement information systems for the purpose of improved record keeping. As a result, such systems typically were not designed to support the overall operations of the court systems or to support the broader law enforcement objectives of courts.

> According to Polansky (1996), by the early 1970s, many major urban courts had begun building court information systems. But there was little systems analysis and planning, and systems—designed and programmed by people who knew little about courts—never showed the results to justify the high costs. Despite these difficulties, the first court-operated, computer-aided transcript system was installed in Allegheny County, [Pennsylvania], in 1973. (Brown, 2000, p. 231)

Polansky found that, as of 1996, no court system had initiated an information technology (IT) project with a specific objective of improving services or reducing costs (Brown, 2000).

Prosecutorial and public defense agencies typically use the Internet to check the docket status of court cases and/or to process forms. This is unfortunate because these types of systems could help court personnel by reducing paperwork and by allowing them to manage case workloads without being physically present in courtrooms (Brown, 2000).

Currently, some courts use Web-enabled case flow management software by way of the Internet to help process dockets and allow electronic filing, but such systems are still rare. One of the more advanced current approaches to statewide court system automation has been undertaken by the state of Wisconsin, which has developed and implemented an information system called the Circuit Court Automation Program (CCAP). The CCAP is used to improve day-to-day operations of courts such as case records management, calendar/docket planning, jury selection, and financial management (http://wcca.wicourts.gov).

At the federal level, there are two court systems that allow Internet access to record keeping. First is the U.S. Supreme Court's website (http://www.supremecourtus.gov), which allows tracking cases (both pending and decided) by accessing online the docket, argument calendar, slip opinions, and so forth. The second system is the Public Access to Court Electronic Records (PACER), which offers

an inexpensive, fast, and comprehensive case information service to any individual with a personal computer (PC) and Internet access. The PACER system permits you to request information about a particular individual or case. The data [are] displayed directly on your PC screen within a few

seconds. The system is simple enough that little user training or documentation is required. (Administrative Office of the U.S. Courts, 1996)

Information on this website comes from the federal appellate, district, and bankruptcy courts as well as from the U.S. Party/Case Index. "Currently, most courts are available on the Internet. . . . However, a few systems are not available on the Internet and must be dialed directly using communication software (such as ProComm Plus, pcAnywhere, or HyperTerminal) and a modem" (PACER Service Center, n.d.).

Privacy concerns mounted as the courts moved to make electronic access to information a priority. Some believed that access to files by way of the Internet would encourage abuses such as identity theft. Therefore, the U.S. Judicial Conference decided to have a public forum about personal data abuses, and after much debate and many comments were heard, restrictions were implemented. Each user on PACER has to log in, and to do this a registration form must be completed to establish an account. Using log-ins allows the creation of an electronic trail of who accessed which case file and when. Also, as in the case of civil and bankruptcy case files, when a social security number has been recorded, only the final four digits will be made available in electronic format. The same goes for dates of birth; only the years will be available. When minors are involved in a case, only their initials will be included. The conference's Court Administration and Case Management Committee also decided that criminal cases would not be uploaded at this time given that the "information could then be very easily used to intimidate, harass, and possibly harm victims, defendants, and their families" (Judiciary Privacy Policy, n.d., p. 2).

Overall, the current status of general court information that is accessible by way of the Internet is not currently available. However,

SEARCH, the National Consortium for Justice Information and Statistics, completed a study on drug courts' information systems. Importantly, these findings should not be very different from those of general courts so far as information systems and Internet use are concerned. In the SEARCH (2003) study, it was found that 67.8% of small jurisdictions, 63.4% of medium-sized jurisdictions, and 59.8% of large jurisdictions have Internet access. Also, a majority of drug courts have access to database management software, spreadsheet applications, and antivirus programs.

> However, access drops off noticeably when it comes to programs specifically tailored to court tasks. When asked if there was software specific to their job functions, respondents were less positive. For example, only 49 percent of small, 57 percent of medium, and 66 percent of large jurisdiction courts have links to other justice system database[s] as appropriate to job function[s] such as arrest records, criminal histories, and court dockets. (p. 39)

Corrections

The corrections system encompasses a variety of criminal justice operations, including jails, prisons, probation, parole, restitution/ fines, and substance abuse treatment brokers. Typically, corrections systems, from local and county jails to the state and federal prisons, have implemented some type of information system(s). These range from systems that simply indicate who is currently in custody and are accessible only by personnel to more elaborate, online, Internet-accessible systems such as the Federal Bureau of Prisons (www.bop.gov). These information systems can vary from highly sophisticated systems with network links that integrate jail/prison systems with their partner probation and parole departments to much more limited stand-alone information systems.

The most basic corrections information systems collect data on booking and release status, housing assignments, case management status, criminal charges and sentencing, and time served (Kichen, Murphy, & Levinson, 1993). "Approximately 80% of adult facilities, nearly 70% of community corrections agencies, and approximately 60% of large jails had access to a local area network with electronic mail capability. The majority of the facilities also had access to the [NCIC] and local or state online offender information," according to Brown (2000, p. 239).

Some jails at the city and town levels, as well as state and federal prisons, have Internet-based inmate locators. The Federal Bureau of Prisons maintains a database that includes all federal inmates from 1982 onward. Users can search by identification number of offender, first and last name, middle initial, race, age, and sex. The query will return either the location of the offender (which prison, halfway house, etc.) or when he or she was released (http://inmateloc.bop. gov). Many states also have their own inmate locator systems, with Arkansas and Florida being noteworthy examples. Arkansas allows searches by identification number of offender, first and last name, race, age, sex, county, and facility, or users can search for all of the people convicted of committing a particular type of crime. This function allows for a minidatabase to be downloaded. The information available contains inmate details: identification number, name, race, sex, hair color, eye color, height, weight, birth data, initial receipt data, current facility, amount of time sentenced, alias, scars, marks and tattoos, current and prior prison sentence history, detainers, and photograph. The Florida Department of Corrections has a similar search capability, including an "Inmate Escape Information Search" and a "Supervised Population Information Search."

Another way in which the corrections system uses the Internet is through the monitoring of offenders, whether they have been restricted to their homes, placed on curfew, or given court-ordered conditions and sanctions. Some agencies are using the "Internet-based Central Monitory Station [to provide] supervising parties with 24/7 access to the alcohol readings of each subject. The supervising agency can print a variety of reports for periods of one day or one year" (Phillips, 2001, p. 43). This system allows each probation, parole, or pretrial services officer to monitor an offender's alcohol intake, and it can immediately notify the officer of a violation. Other remote location monitoring systems can notify the case manager immediately if a violation has occurred, and "notifications could be sent to others (e.g., officer's supervisor, potential victim, or law enforcement agency) via pager or e-mail" (Gowen, 2001, p. 40). The benefits include efficiency, timeliness through real-time monitoring, accuracy, and cost efficiency on behalf of case management.

Another example of remote monitoring by way of the Internet is the use of kiosks. Kiosks, similar to the size and workings of ATM machines, allow probationers, parolees, and pretrial defendants to report to their case managers. Identification is matched by way of a bar-coded card/log-in and a biometric sample (finger/palmprint). The offenders are then guided through a series of questions, receive notices from their case managers by way of e-mail, are able to submit employment records, and so forth. Case managers then can access their clients' new input by way of "middleware" software[3] located on the Internet. Some cities whose caseworkers tend to have larger caseloads (e.g., New York, Los Angeles) are using these kiosks for low-risk/nonviolent offenders ("It Has Come to Our Attention," 2001). The obvious benefits are time efficiency on behalf of case managers, decreased data entry time, increased accuracy, and provision of real-time access to monitoring data.

One final point of discussion for pretrial and probation officers is how they go about using the Internet to monitor their high-tech defendants and offenders. The Internet has enhanced communications capability, but it also has created new opportunities for criminal activity. Cyber-criminals often commit the same types of ordinary crime, but they are now doing it with the help of computers. "The cyber criminal can be defined as someone whose knowledge and use of computers and/or the Internet has enabled him or her to commit the crime of choice," according to Kelly (2001, p. 8). Sexual predators, embezzlers, addicted gamblers, and those who commit fraud all are using the Internet to commit their crimes. Therefore, the monitoring of behavior by case managers becomes particularly burdensome. Case managers require special knowledge and skills of how computers and the Internet work.

The two methods by which case managers use the Internet to supervise their clients are through remote monitoring and recording software as well as investigative tools. For example, software can be placed on a sexual predator's computer, where it will maintain a photographic record of what the user has been looking at and will log websites previously viewed. The case manager can receive updates of these images by way of e-mail. Moreover, case managers can use databases available on the Internet to gain valuable knowledge about offenders. For example, Whois.com is a database that can reveal who is registered to a particular website. This is useful if an offender is starting a website to perform his or her illegal activities. Other databases, such as LexisNexis, national phone directories, address locators, and Anywho.com, can perform searches and reveal potentially important information about offenders.

The federal judiciary has also played a large role in making sure that correctional agencies come online by supporting the development of the Probation and Pretrial Services Automated Case Tracking–Electronic Case Management System (PACTS^ECM). The new system was introduced in fiscal year 2001 (Office of Probation and Pretrial Services, 2003). The system allows

> a total information system. It includes functionality for: 1) electronic generation, storage, and retrieval of all investigation and supervision case information; 2) electronic retrieval for judiciary personnel of vital case information, including the pre-sentence report, pretrial services report, and chronological records; 3) integrated access to the criminal component of the Case Management–Electronic Case Files (CM-ECF) project; and 4) electronic imaging of defendants/offenders—their tattoos, homes, vehicles, or other appropriate images. (Cadigan, 2001, p. 25)

PACTS^ECM is a Web-enabled application that can be accessed through the federal judiciary's intranet. The connection also allows for a link to Mapquest.com to map a client's address. This type of all-encompassing system allows elimination of data redundancy, accuracy of data, and an increase in productivity for officers.

The implementation of this task is enormous, and the Administrative Office of the U.S. Courts has been overseeing the project. As of fiscal year 2002, 17 of 94 courts/districts were online (Office of Probation and Pretrial Services, 2003). This alone was a daunting task considering all of the information necessary to incorporate as well as to make accessible and user-friendly to officers and court staff members. Because the infrastructure of the program alone is quite involved, using a mentoring system has furthered the training and execution of new courts going online. Districts that are already online are then able to direct and support newly added districts. Moreover, pilot projects that are currently being undertaken involve

providing the same versatility that an officer would have from a desktop to the field by way of a personal digital assistant (PDA) (Office of Probation and Pretrial Services, 2003).

Also on the Internet are several websites serving as information portals to the corrections community. For example, Corrections.com and the National Institute of Corrections (www.nicic.org) offer document search, e-learning/distance education, an online library database, e-mail, listservs about current topics, and much more information. Other comprehensive websites, such as that for Illinois, offer a Probation Officers Internet Resources page (www.19thcircuitcourt.state.il.us). This site consists of many links to other state corrections departments, including all available online inmate locators, crime prevention information, crime victim information, and reference sources.

Social Agencies

There are many national and local websites on the Internet that are devoted to victims. Most offer general information to victims and links to services.

> Victims today can readily access information about rights, services, statutes, victim compensation, civil remedies, and other important resources through the WWW. Criminal and juvenile justice and allied professionals, as well as victim service providers, are often linked to each other so victims know whom to turn to for information and supportive services. Victims' choices about *where to go* and *what to do* in the aftermath of a crime are tremendously expanded by the volume and quality of information available in both paper-based and electronic formats. (National Victim Assistance Academy, 2000, p. 5)

There is information available for a wide range of services: laws and regulations, civil litigation, referrals, document searches, stalking, identity theft, homicide survivors, teen bullying, and the like.

IMPLEMENTATION ISSUES

Using the Internet is a powerful, global, fast, and inexpensive way in which to enhance communication and share information among agencies and within each agency. The basic infrastructure is already in place. One major benefit of using networks and the Internet is that doing so reduces the total cost of ownership. "Internet applications are relatively inexpensive to implement, yet they can significantly increase revenue collections by cross-referencing databases (e.g., no permit issued or renewed until all parking tickets or court fines are paid). They can potentially generate substantial income at a fraction of the cost of manual services," according to Malinowski and colleagues (2000, pp. 71–72). For example, the use of networks within agencies, at either the department or federal level, "reduces reliance on the desktop computer by moving software and data onto the network" (Fielding, 2001, p. 4). However, there is one potential drawback to complete reliance on networks: When the network is down, the user is down.

Some possible reasons why cities, towns, and state agencies do not have good websites or use the Internet include the lack of funds, expertise, privacy, vision, and/or coordinating committees as well as ethical considerations (i.e., accuracy of data) (Brown, 2000). Most of these reasons are self-explanatory; however, the concern about privacy is probably the most hotly debated topic. Even though there has been significant advancement in the areas of encryption, firewalls, passwords, and registration methods that have been used to decrease instances of hacking, privacy concerns still emanate. Issues and policies relating to citizen privacy can present barriers to criminal justice systems integrating or using the Internet to connect, collect, or disseminate information. Citizens, whether criminals or not, value their privacy. Privacy is a major policy and operational issue for any criminal justice system. Privacy must be considered at every level of information systems design, and the impact of privacy policies will vary across regions because privacy laws differ from state to state (Office of Justice Programs, 2000). "The law in more than a dozen states restricts criminal history record information from being integrated or combined with intelligence and investigative information," according to the Bureau of Justice Assistance (1999, p. 68). Moreover, beyond the impact of specific privacy laws, there is a more general concern regarding the linking of criminal justice databases because some observers and citizens believe that this would allow "citizen tracking" (Abell, 1988).

Some cities, towns, states, and federal agencies have websites specifically designated to police or the courts or pretrial/probation services, and some have overcome the compatibility, privacy, data accuracy, and funding concerns to create comprehensive or integrated websites that include all different functions of criminal justice agencies. The Colorado Integrated Criminal Justice Information System (CICJIS) provides a good example of an information system approach that provides integrated support for the criminal justice system. The CICJIS links the individual legacy information systems from five state criminal justice agencies: the Colorado Bureau of Investigation, the Judicial Branch, the Department of Corrections, the Division of Youth Corrections, and the Colorado District Attorneys Council. The primary goal of the system is to provide a complete record of a criminal case through the various stages in different agencies without redundancy of data collection, storage, or data entry. Colorado implemented the system in 1998 and was the first state to have such a system (Report of the State Auditor, 2003). The system allows data transfers and queries to be moved and/or viewed across the five criminal justice agencies within the state and greatly reduces the need for multiple entries of the same data (e.g., offender name and address) across different agencies (Holmes, Usery, & Roper, 2000–2001). As of July 2003, there were few problems with the system because it was working as intended, but there had been some complaints by users, in particular that not all historical data for each system were available. This seems to be a common complaint for any type of system that uses historical data. Problems can arise quickly if not all of the wanted information is in electronic format; even if the information has been captured electronically, it might not be compatible across systems and platforms, and this can result in data quality errors (Boba, 2000). Other complaints cited inadequate training opportunities and the ability for one department to "overwrite" another department's information. The CICJIS board was undertaking measures to fix these problems at the time of this writing. Also, during the annual audit, users expressed a desire for access to the sex offender registry, for data to be kept on misdemeanor and traffic offenses, and for access to information from municipal courts and Denver County Court. The auditors agreed, and measures were being undertaken to connect these systems at the time of this writing (Report of the State Auditor, 2003).

Kansas is also very progressive about using the Internet. Kansas operates its own public network, KANWIN, consisting of state and local government agencies, primary education and universities, and hospitals (Rohrer, n.d.). Kansas decided that using a TCP/IP network with connection to the Internet would provide the most affordable electronic access to criminal justice information. "Today, the KBI [Kansas Bureau of Investigation] is the first, and still the only, agency in the nation approved by the FBI to use the Internet to transmit national criminal justice information" (p. 2). At the regional level, several states pool their resources to apprehend criminals. For example, the western states have a consortium, the Western Identification Network (WIN), whose primary purpose is to use a linked AFIS; however, when the IAFIS becomes fully functional, this system will probably be upgraded. Nearly a dozen western states comprise the Southwest Border States Anti-Drug Information System (SWBSADIS), which is used to combat drug trafficking.

Technical advances continue to facilitate information systems development and integration. The recent emergence of eXtensible Markup Language (XML) provides a new approach to help realign different data standards. Some agencies had electronic information systems in the past; however, these systems were too difficult to upgrade or upload on the Web due to different standards. XML is designed specifically for Web-based documents. XML allows links to point to multiple documents (whereas HTML does not), and XML allows easier communication between systems because it can see images, sound, video, and text. In addition, XML supports several data formats and can cover all existing data structures. Because the Web is now becoming a major backbone for criminal justice agencies to communicate with one another, XML can help to encourage the communication and sharing of information.

CONCLUSION

From the advent of the Internet during the early 1960s to the explosion of the Web during the early 1990s, it is easy to see that computers, technology, and the linking of information through networks are indispensable. Today's society has become knowledge based, and every person in criminal justice, from law enforcement to corrections, must have the necessary skills not only to keep up with high-tech criminals but also to be able to share information and communicate with others inside and out of the criminal justice arena because it is highly decentralized.

The information infrastructure is divided along local, state, and federal levels of government. At each level of government, agencies are further divided along functional lines such as law enforcement, courts, prosecution, probation, pretrial services, corrections, and social agencies. In addition, various state and local jurisdictions operate under different administrative systems and, very often, under different legal and regulatory systems. For much of history in the United States, this was more than adequate because most serious public safety problems typically were localized. However, today this loosely coupled system has had a difficult time in keeping up with public safety problems that often traverse geographic boundaries. This occurs when individuals are highly mobile. Criminal organizations typically cross geographic boundaries, and today criminal acts can easily be initiated from distant locations with the help of technology.

Technology represents a major key to helping criminal justice meet these new challenges because IT offers new methods of integration and organization that were not possible in the past. Fortunately, information integration has become theoretically easier because the technical, fiscal, and management barriers to implementing integrated information systems have fallen dramatically. Both hardware and application software costs continue to decline, provide greater performance, and are becoming easier to manage. Equally important, de facto standards that have emerged over the past decade or so significantly reduce the fiscal and technical management costs of data communications (e.g., TCP/IP, HTML, XML),

operating systems (e.g., UNIX, Windows, Linux), and applications software (U.S. Department of Commerce, 2000). These factors are converging to offer new opportunities for systems development and integration for public sector organizations.

A few industries have already accomplished this task. Selected sectors of corporate America have been perfecting the strategy of information management and the potential of computers and networks for years. It has been a testing ground of innovative techniques for information management. For example, Wal-Mart was one of the first stores to revolutionize inventory control, database design, and data quality in the industry by using bar code technology. These types of techniques and knowledge have trickled down and been altered to work in the criminal justice field. Although criminal justice may move at a slower pace than does corporate America, this is probably better in the long run because most of the initial development and testing costs of ideas have been eliminated. One good example of information management is the inmate locator software used by jails and prisons discussed previously.

Early innovators within the criminal justice system also provide examples. States and local agencies often look to the federal government for guidance, for example, smaller courts using the same software as the U.S. Supreme Court for docket management. Smaller agencies sometimes have exceptional ideas, and the federal government follows suit. For instance, New York's Electronic Crimes Task Force was modeled by the U.S. Secret Service and is being implemented all over the country. Either way, these initial systems allow all of the initial costs of brainstorming and standards to be worked out.

On a much larger scale, the trend in criminal justice, as seen in Colorado and Kansas, is to create integrated information systems. It is imperative to have information from all sectors of criminal justice and public agencies together in one place for easier analysis as well as more efficient decision making and policymaking. It has often been said that data alone mean nothing; however, when data are connected together, they provide information, which in turn creates knowledge and ultimately power to give one the advantage (Fayyad, 1996).

Finally, with integration and increased use of the Internet come new threats. Agencies and personnel in criminal justice need to be aware of how not to be a victim or to let their agencies become vulnerable by using firewalls, controlling access through passwords, keeping passwords secret, changing passwords regularly, and protecting data by employing cryptography and encryption software and making sure that an audit system is installed to monitor log-ins/log-outs. Audit systems are necessary because they are generally the first indication of whether a system has been hacked into or whether an attempt to gain access has been made. And if a system or website has been hacked into, it is imperative to find a solution quickly to resolve the problem and prevent future break-ins.

NOTES

1.   An intranet is "a network based on TCP/IP protocols belonging to an organization… accessible only by the organization's members, employees, or others with authorization. An intranet's Web sites look and act just like any other Web Sites, but the *firewall* surrounding an intranet prevents unauthorized access," according to Margolis (1999, p. 287).

2.   When a sole proprietor or partnership conducts business using a company name other than his or her first and surname, a form usually must be completed, including the sole proprietor's full name or, in the case of a partnership, each partner's full name.

3.   Middleware is "software that connects two otherwise separate applications. [It] is used to describe separate products that serve as the glue between two applications. [It is] sometimes called *plumbing* because it connects two sides of an application and passes data between them," according to Margolis (1999, p. 349).

REFERENCES

Abell, R. B. (1988, November). Effective systems for regional intelligence sharing. *The Police Chief*, pp. 58–99.

Abt Associates. (2000). *Police Department Information Systems Technology Enhancement Project (ISTEP)*. Washington, DC: U.S. Department of Justice.

Administrative Office of the U.S. Courts. (1996). *Summary on current electronic public access programs in the federal judiciary*. Retrieved July 24, 1996, from www.uscourts.gov/press_releases/summ.htm

Boba, R. (1999). Using the Internet to disseminate crime information. *Law Enforcement Bulletin, 68*(10), 6–9.

Boba, R. (2000). *Guidelines to implement and evaluate crime analysis and mapping in law enforcement agencies*. Washington, DC: U.S. Department of Justice.

Brown, M. (2000). Criminal justice discovers information technology. In National Institute of Justice, *The nature of crime: Continuity and change* (Vol. 1, pp. 219–259). Washington, DC: National Institute of Justice.

Bureau of Justice Assistance. (1999). *Report of the National Task Force on Court Automation and Integration.* Washington, DC: U.S. Department of Justice.

Cadigan, T. P. (2001). PACTS. *Federal Probation, 65*(2), 25–30.

CNN. (2001). *"Carnivore" Internet wiretap gets new name.* Retrieved February 14, 2001, from www.cnn.com

Fayyad, U. M. (1996, October). Microsoft research, data mining, and knowledge discovery: Making sense out of data. *IEEE Expert,* pp. 20–25.

Federal Bureau of Investigation. (2003a). *IAFIS builds.* Retrieved August 26, 2003, from www.fbi.gov/hq/cjisd/iafis/iafisbuilds.htm

Federal Bureau of Investigation. (2003b). *Programs and initiatives: Carnivore diagnostic tool.* Retrieved September 2, 2003, from www.fbi.gov

Fielding, E. W. (2001). Technology forecast for the federal judiciary. *Federal Probation, 65*(2), 3–7.

Gowen, D. (2001). Remote location monitoring: A supervision strategy to enhance risk control. *Federal Probation, 65*(2), 38–41.

Haley, K. N., & Taylor, R. W. (1998). Police stations in cyberspace: A content analysis of law enforcement homepages. In L. J. Moriarty & D. L. Carter (Eds.), *Criminal justice technology in the 21st century* (Chap. 9). Springfield, IL: Charles C Thomas.

Hickman, M. J. (2001, January). Computers and information systems in local police departments, 1990–1999. *The Police Chief,* pp. 50–56.

Holmes, A., Usery, D., & Roper, R. (2000–2001, Fall/Winter). *Colorado Integrated Criminal Justice Information System: Project overview and recommendations.* Report of the National Task Force on Court Automation and Integration, Case Study Series. Retrieved August 20, 2003, from www.search.org/integration/default.asp

It has come to our attention. (2001). *Federal Probation, 65*(2), 69.

Judiciary Privacy Policy. (n.d.). *Court Administration and Case Management Committee of the Judicial Conference of the United States.* Retrieved August 8, 2003, from www.privacy.uscourts.gov

Kanable, R. (2000). Weaving databases with the Web. *Law Enforcement Technology, 27*(3), 96–100.

Kelly, B. J. (2001). Supervising the cyber criminal. *Federal Probation, 65*(2), 8–10.

Kichen, C. C., Murphy, J., & Levinson, R. B. (1993). *Correctional technology: A user's guide.* Washington, DC: U.S. Department of Justice.

Malinowski, S. W., Kalish, D. J., & Parks, B. C. (2000, September). From Dragnet to the Internet: One police department extends its reach. *The Police Chief,* pp. 62–72.

Mamalian, C. A., & La Vigne, N. G. (1999). *The use of computerized mapping by law enforcement: Survey results.* Washington, DC: U.S. Department of Justice. Retrieved August 8, 2003, from www.ncjrs.org/pdffiles1/fs000237.pdf

Margolis, P. E. (1999). *Random House Webster's computer and Internet dictionary* (3rd ed.). New York: Random House.

National Victim Assistance Academy. (2000). The WWW has numerous sites devoted to victim information and assistance. *Innovative Technologies and the Information Age.* Retrieved August 15, 2003, from www.ojp.usdoj.gov/ovc/assist/nvaa2000/academy/u-21-tec.htm

Office of Justice Programs. (2000). *Privacy design principles for an integrated justice system.* Working paper, Office of the Ontario Information and Privacy Commissioner and the U.S. Department of Justice. Retrieved June 10, 2003, from www.ojp.usdoj.gov/integratedjustice/pdpapril.htm

Office of Probation and Pretrial Services. (2003). *U.S. Probation and Pretrial Services System: Year-in-review report.* Retrieved January 20, 2003, from www.uscourts.gov/year-in-review02-final.pdf

PACER Service Center. (n.d.). *Public access to court electronic records.* Retrieved August 8, 2003, from http://pacer.psc.uscourts.gov/pacerdesc.html

Paynter, R. (Ed.). (1999). CertiFinder uses news, public records to help locate suspects. *Law Enforcement Technology, 26*(7), 88–92.

Perez, J. C. (2000, December 11). Sheriff's office uses technology to catch the crooks. *InfoWorld,* p. 47.

Phillips, K. (2001). Reducing alcohol related crime. *Federal Probation, 65*(2), 42–44.

Polansky, L. (1996). The long and winding road. *Court Technology Bulletin, 8*(2). Retrieved August 19, 2003, from www.ncsconline.org/d_tech/bulletin/v08n02.htm

Price, M. E., & Verhulst, S. G. (2000). In search of the self: Charting the course of self-regulation on the Internet in a global environment. In C. T. Marsden (Ed.), *Regulating the global information society* (pp. 57–78). London: Routledge.

Report of the State Auditor. (2003). *Colorado Integrated Criminal Justice Information System: Performance audit.* Retrieved January 20, 2004, from www.state.co.us/auditor

Rohrer, R. (n.d.). *Securing Kansas criminal justice information.* Retrieved August 12, 2003, from www.nascio.org/scoring/files/2001kansas2.doc

Schmalleger, F. (2002). *The definitive guide to criminal justice and criminology on the World Wide Web.* Upper Saddle River, NJ: Prentice Hall.

SEARCH. (2003). *Drug court monitoring, evaluation, and management information systems: National scope and needs assessment.* Washington, DC: U.S. Department of Justice.

Sparrow, M. K. (1991, April). Information systems: A help or hindrance in the evolution of policing? *The Police Chief,* pp. 26–44.

Sterling, B. (1993). *Complete Internet history.* Retrieved November 27, 2003, from http://www.acs.ucalgary.ca/~dabrent/art/internet.his

Thomas, D., & Loader, B. D. (Eds.). (2000). *Cybercrime.* London: Routledge.

U.S. Department of Commerce. (2000). *Digital economy 2000.* Washington, DC: Author.

CHAPTER 4

The Internet as a Conduit for Criminal Activity

DAVID S. WALL

Although there appears to be a common view that the Internet has had a major impact on criminality, there is much less consensus as to what that impact has been. Many sources make claims about the prevalence of cybercrime (i.e., networked computer crime) without clarifying what is precisely the issue at hand. Indeed, when so-called cases of cybercrime come to court, they often have the familiar ring of the "traditional" rather than the "cyber" about them. Fraud, pornography, pedophilia, and the like are already covered by substantive areas of law in most jurisdictions. Even more confusing is the gap between the many hundreds of thousands of estimated incidents and the relatively small number of known prosecutions, a gap that questions the early predictions that cybercrime, if not checked, could effectively bring criminals into every home. In fact, the confusion has led some authors to question whether or not "there are indeed such things as cybercrimes" (Brenner, 2001, p. 1). Others have questioned whether cybercrime is actually a category of crime in need of new theory or whether it is better understood by existing theories (Jones, 2003, p. 98). These contrasting viewpoints expose a large gap in our understanding and beg a number of questions. For example, are our concerns about cybercrime driven solely by the media sensationalization of one or two novel events and effectively fabricated into a crime wave? Or are the dramatic news stories the product of information sources created by the cyber-security industry that has a vested interest in sensationalizing cybercrimes? Alternatively, could it simply be the case that the criminal justice processes are woefully inefficient at bringing wrongdoers to justice? There again, are we perhaps looking at an entirely new phenomenon through the wrong lens?

There is clearly a lot to discuss on this topic, and this chapter provides some answers to the preceding questions by drawing on a corpus of work (Wall, 1999, 2001, 2002a, 2002b, 2003) and associated literature to explore whether, and if so how, the

AUTHOR'S NOTE: I thank April Pattavina for her constructive comments on an early draft of this chapter.

Internet has become a conduit for criminal activity. The first section of the chapter reflects on the transformative impacts of the Internet on social and criminal activity. The second section maps out the new criminal opportunities that give rise to what we understand to be cybercrime. The third section outlines the impediments to the production of criminological knowledge about cybercrime that pose a challenge to criminologists when trying to make sense of the divergent range of behaviors that are being called cybercrimes. The fourth section discusses the challenges to the maintenance of order and law on the Internet by arguing that, on the one hand, the Internet creates considerable challenges for criminal justice systems and that, on the other hand and contrary to the commonly held view, these challenges arise from a system that is characterized by order and not disorder. The fifth and final section draws some conclusions about the role of the Internet in enabling criminal activity.

TRANSFORMATIVE IMPACTS OF CYBERSPACE ON SOCIAL AND CRIMINAL ACTIVITY

The origins of the Internet and its associated information technologies (ITs) are well documented elsewhere[1]; however, it is important to briefly explore the impacts of the Internet on society to understand further the origins of cybercrime. A particularly noticeable impact of the rapid colonization of cyberspace has been the way in which it has accelerated the qualities that have come to characterize high modernity, particularly the "discontinuities" highlighted by Giddens (1990, p. 6) that separate modern and traditional social orders. The social orders that bind time and space have become disembedded and distanciated, that is, "lifted out of local contexts of interaction and restructured across indefinite spans of time-space" (p. 14; see also Bottoms & Wiles, 1996).

Social and Economic Impacts

The social impact of cyberspace on individuals is only beginning to be understood. In principle, individuals are freer now than ever before to develop social relations that are commensurate with their own interests or lifestyles and that are potentially more meaningful than they could be otherwise. Individuals can now work in three dimensions instead of two, meaning that it is possible, for example, to do office work at a distance without needing to deal with office politics and to work where abilities can be maximized rather than where they are physically situated. However, the practical realities are quite different and less ideological. Although the virtual social relationship has the advantage of avoiding the pitfalls of "destructive gemeinschaft"[2] (Sennett, 1992, p. 238), it does have a dark side in that it encourages the social deskilling[3] of the individual, specializing and compartmentalizing modes of interaction. As access to the Internet becomes more widely available through falling prices and public access policies, major divisions in society come to be based on inequality of access to information as much as on socioeconomic grounds. Those who do not engage with the technology will become excluded, and the knowledge gap—or information exclusion—will put a new spin on our understanding of social exclusion.

Furthermore, cyberspace is a virtual environment in which economic value is attached to ideas rather than to physical property (Barlow, 1994). Consequently, a new order is emerging in the much contested information society, as described by Castells (2000) and others. One expression of this new order has been an increase in the overall numbers and intrusiveness of intellectual property laws to establish ownership over these ideas. Not only is information becoming commodified, but the commodification process is creating a new political economy of information capital

(Boyle, 1996; Wall, 2004). Because of this characteristic, these ideas or properties, as well as their value, are constantly faced with the threat of being misappropriated, damaged, or distorted. In other words, as business and social opportunities increase, entirely new realms of criminal opportunity emerge.

Transformative Impacts of Internet Technology on Deviant Behavior

If cyberspace today challenges our conventional understanding of ownership and control, the traditional boundaries between criminal and civil activities, as well as between public and private law, become blurred, as do many of the principles on which our conventional understandings of criminal harm and justice are based. Consequently, a number of important questions emerge as to what exactly cybercrimes are and to what extent they differ from other activities that we currently recognize as crime.

Cybercrime is a term that has long symbolized insecurity in cyberspace. But in itself, the term is fairly meaningless because it tends to be used emotively rather than scientifically, usually to signify the occurrence of a harmful behavior that is somehow related to the misuse of computers, with more recent uses suggesting that it be used with regard to networked computers (National Criminal Intelligence Service [NCIS], 1999). Largely an invention of the media, cybercrime has no specific reference point in law, and in fact many of the so-called cybercrimes that cause concern are not necessarily crimes in law. Perhaps the term *cyberspace crime* would have been a more precise and accurate descriptor; however, not only has the term *cybercrime* acquired considerable linguistic agency, but during recent years cybercrimes have become firmly embedded in the public crime agenda as something that must be policed. This is an interesting happenstance given that analysis of the word *cyber* reveals that its origins lie in the Greek *kubernetes,* or "steersman," which is also the root of the word *govern,* as in the French use of the term *cybernétique* (the art of governing).[4] The word *cyber* entered the English language in *cybernetics* (the study of systems of control and communications, which is linked with computers), so linguistically, and more by coincidence than by design, the words *cyber* and *crime* actually sit well together. This interpretation suggests that cybercrimes are crimes that are mediated by networked computers and not just related to computers. If this is the case, the test will be what is left after the Internet is removed from the equation—the elimination test.

To be able to understand further how the Internet has become a conduit for criminal activity, it is important to look first at what have been the key transformative impacts of Internet technologies and distributed systems. Drawing on contemporary sources of literature and social commentary, the following is a list of key transformations along with brief summaries of the ways in which they affect criminal behavior:

♦ *Globalization and "glocalization."* The globalization of crime opportunities across cultures and jurisdictions has extended the reach of criminals beyond the traditional boundaries. From a law enforcement point of view, globalization also shapes the relationship between the global and the local (i.e., the glocal), thereby shaping local enforcement and policing cultures (Robertson, 1995).

♦ *Distributed networks and grid technologies.* These create new forms of commercial and emotional relationships between individuals that engender new opportunities for victimization. Unfortunately, these same qualities also generate multiple-information flows of data that cannot be easily captured to make coherent summaries of deviant behavior and to identify new forms of risk.

♦ *Synopticism and panopticism.* The simultaneous synoptical and panoptical qualities of Internet technologies generate new forms of victimization. Offenders can surveil their victims and offend from afar. Yet the same qualities also provide considerable potential for identifying patterns of offending as well as individual offenders (Wall, 2004).

♦ *Asymmetric rather than symmetric relationships.* These relationships between offenders and victims and the justice processes arising from the changes in the organization of criminal activity have profound implications for the justice process. For example, the problem of small-impact multiple victimizations distributed across jurisdictions collectively constitutes significant criminal activity but individually does not justify the expenditure of resources in investigation or prosecution.

♦ *Data trails (data doubling, data trails, and the disappearance of disappearance).* The creation and retention of data traffic on the Internet mean that we are increasingly experiencing the "disappearance of disappearance" (Haggerty & Ericson, 2000, p. 619). Every time an electronic transaction takes place, an individual leaves a data traffic trail. On the one hand, this aids law enforcement; on the other hand, this combines with the requirement of access technologies to recreate "data doubles" of the individual's identity in cyberspace, and a threat to the maintenance of privacy and human rights arises. Furthermore, the concept of the data double also begins to change the relationship between the self and the state through the creation of new forms of subservience to maintain levels of access and privilege. Because of the desirability (and value) of access to restricted resources, data doubling

generates new opportunities for identity theft.

♦ *Changes in the organization of criminal activities.* Just as there have been some quite profound changes in the nature of criminal opportunity, there have also been some interesting transformations in the organization of criminal behavior on the Internet. The main rationale behind the development and use of technology, as always, is basically financial—to increase the rational efficiency of capital. Offices become more efficient as ITs concentrate workers' skills, provide coordinated management systems, and so forth. It is also the case that as individual tasks become rationalized, degraded, and deskilled (Braverman, 1976), there is a simultaneous reskilling process whereby basic tasks are automated and workers overview whole production processes. Interestingly, these same developments also apply to criminal behavior, and the combination of technological processes with the Internet result in some quite profound transformations in opportunities for the organization of criminal activity. One of the more profound examples of the deskilling and reskilling processes just described is the emergence of "empowered single agents" (Pease, 2001, p. 22). These are lone offenders who are enabled by networked technology to carry out incredibly complex and far-reaching tasks that can be repeated countless times over a global span bordered only by levels of online use and language. Therefore, these offenders are able to commit crimes that were previously beyond their financial and organizational means and reaches. Along with empowered small agents come new dimensions of organized crime; technology links the criminal activities of lone offenders across a global span. Hacking and "cracking" are good examples of how the Internet, mainly through newsgroups, enables individuals to identify a common need to conduct ephemeral activities together. These activities might include teaming up individuals with specific skills to commit a common act or to reproduce their skills and knowledge. For a good example of this process, see the research into the operation of "cracker" newsgroups (Mann & Sutton, 1998; Wall, 2000). At the other end of the spectrum of organized crime on the Internet are, of course, the more traditional transnational crime organizations, whose mode of operation online largely mirrors that of corporate organizations in terms of communication and operation.

These six transformative impacts of the Internet, working either in isolation or in combination, support the argument that the Internet provides a new conduit for committing criminal and harmful behaviors. They change the traditional relationships among offenders, victims, and the state by potentially creating entirely new opportunities for harmful or criminal behaviors by widening offenders' reach of opportunity globally, enabling offenders to engage victims in new ways, and providing new means for the organization of criminal behaviors. So, although the fundamental nature of the victimization might be familiar (e.g., deception, theft), when the behavior has been transformed by the Internet, it is referred to as a cybercrime. The simple principle for defining cybercrimes is the elimination test mentioned previously); in other words, would these crimes disappear if the Internet were taken away? But what exactly are they? Without a systematic clarification of the nature of cybercrimes, dystopian and often inapt concerns about them can result in misplaced or exaggerated public demands for policy responses from criminal justice agencies.

IMPACTS OF THE INTERNET ON CRIMINAL OPPORTUNITIES AND BEHAVIOR

Clearly, the impacts of the Internet on crime are fairly wide-ranging and so require further explanation, especially when many of the so-called cybercrimes appear, on their face, to be similar to traditional crimes covered by the penal code and falling within the existing experience of the criminal justice processes. Having said that, other cybercrimes are very unfamiliar. Drawing on research into computers, crime, and the Internet (e.g., Wall, 1997, 1999, 2000, 2001, 2002a, 2002b, 2003, 2004), a matrix can be drawn to map out offending behaviors that fall under the rubric of cybercrime (Table 4.1).

Impacts on Criminal Opportunity

On the *y* axis of our cybercrime matrix are the different impacts of the Internet on opportunity. The Internet has transformed criminal opportunity in three different ways, although in practice the range spanned by the three is probably more of a continuum. However, it is useful for the purposes of this exploration to break them down into three distinct levels.

First, the Internet has become an advanced vehicle for communications that sustains existing patterns of harmful activity through the circulation of information. For example, newsgroups and websites circulate information about "chipping," that is, bypassing the security devices in mobile telephones or digital television decoders (Mann & Sutton, 1998; Wall, 2000). They also provide information about how to manufacture and distribute synthetic drugs and their precursors (Schneider, 2003, p. 374). But if the Internet is removed from the equation, although these activities will be reduced in number, they will still persist and be conducted through alternative forms of communication (e.g., telephone, postal service). Radical book retailers such as Loompanics (www.loompanics.com), for example, have for many years specialized in the selling of books that prescribe the technologies and techniques of criminal actions.

Table 4.1 The Matrix of Cybercrimes: Level of Opportunity by Type of Crime (with selected examples)

	Integrity-related (Harmful Trespass)	Computer-related (Acquisition theft/deception)	Content-related 1 (Obscenity)	Content-related 2 (Violence)
More opportunities for tradional crime (eg., through communications)	Phreaking Chipping	Frauds Pyramid schemes	Trading sexual materials	Stalking Personal Harassment
New opportunities for traditional crime (e.g., organization across boundaries)	Cracking/Hacking Viruses Hactivism	Multiple large-scale frauds 419 scams Trade secret theft ID Theft	Online Sex trade Camgirl sites	General hate speech Organized paedophile rings (child abuse)
New opportunities for new types of crime	Spams (list constuction and content) Denial of Service Information Warfare Parasitic Computing	Intellectual Property Piracy Online Gambling E-auction scams Small-impact bulk fraud	Cyber-sex Cyber-pimping	Online Grooming Organised Bomb talk/Drug talk Targeted hate speech

Source: Wall, D. S. (2003). Mapping out cybercrimes in a cyberspatial surveillant assemblage. In F. Webster & K. Ball (Eds.), *The intensification of surveillance: Crime, terrorism, and warfare in the information age* (pp. 112–136). London: Pluto, p. 115 (subsequently amended and updated). Reprinted with permission of Willan Publishing.

Second, the Internet has created a transnational environment that provides entirely new opportunities for harmful activities currently the subject of existing criminal or civil law. Examples of such activities include trading in sexually explicit materials, such as through interactive hardcore websites (including child pornography), but also many types of fraudulent activity (Grabosky & Smith, 2001, p. 30; Levi, 2001). The increasing prevalence of deception through Internet auctions, for example, is a vivid example of this level of opportunity (Newman & Clarke, 2003, p. 94). Take away the Internet, and these new opportunities for offending would disappear.

Third, the nature of the virtual environment, particularly with regard to the way in which it distanciates time and space (Giddens, 1990) by shifting the geosocial relationship between the two and also transfers economic value from physical property to ideas (Barlow, 1994), has engendered entirely new forms of (unbounded) harmful activity. Such activity includes the unauthorized appropriation of imagery, software tools, music products, and the like. Indeed, at the extreme end of this third category, the transjurisdictional, contestable, and private nature of some of the harms, particularly with regard to the appropriation of intellectual properties, falls outside the jurisdiction and experience of the criminal justice process. See, for example, the examples of virtual rape (Mackinnon, 1997) and virtual vandalism (Williams, 2003). See also the ongoing battle between the music industry and the prosecution of those who download MP3 as an example of this level of cybercrime (Carey & Wall, 2001; Marshall, 2002, p. 1).

The preceding categorizations begin to stratify cybercrimes into (a) offending that exploits communications technology, (b) crimes that focus on the content of computers, and (c) crimes that focus on the "products" of IT. Although the practical demarcations may be blurred, each of the three levels has different implications for investigation and enforcement, but also methodologically, when designing research to further our knowledge of cybercrime. For example, there is a clearer and more common understanding of which agencies are responsible for offending behaviors that fall under the first two categories than for those that fall under the third category. Indeed, not only is the subject matter of the first two levels covered by the public policing mandates of most countries insofar as there tends to be clear public support for policing agencies to intervene, but any problems that arise tend to relate to matters of transjurisdictional procedure rather than substantive law. This contrasts with the third level, where the responsibilities are not so clearcut. What is required now, however, is more understanding of the behaviors themselves.

Impacts on Criminal Behavior

On the *x* axis of the cybercrime matrix are the different types or groupings of crime. The many specific offenses reported in the media, by the police, by Internet service providers (ISPs), and by other agencies fall into one of three basic offense groups: offending related to the integrity of the computer and its network, offending related to the computer itself, or offending related to the content of the messages sent from the computer (Walden, 2003, p. 295). Each offense invokes different policy responses and requires quite different bodies of understanding. The offenses

include trespass (integrity), theft (computer related), obscenity, and violence (content), and each group illustrates a range of behaviors rather than actual offenses, reflecting not only bodies of law but also specific courses of public debate.

Computer Integrity-Related Offenses

Cyber-trespass, or hacking/cracking, is the unauthorized access of the boundaries of computer systems into spaces where rights of ownership or title have already been established. The distinction is increasingly being made between principled trespassers (hackers) and unprincipled trespassers (crackers) (Taylor, 2001, p. 61). In its least harmful form, cyber-trespass is an intellectual challenge that results in a harmless trespass. When most harmful, it is full-blown information warfare between social groups or even nation-states. Somewhere between these positions fall cyber-vandals, cyber-spies, and cyber-terrorists. Integrity-related offenses are also precursors to other types of cybercrime.

Computer-Related Offenses

Cyber-deceptions/thefts describe the different types of acquisitive harm that can take place within cyberspace. At a basic level are the more traditional patterns of theft such as the fraudulent use of credit cards and appropriation of cyber-cash. Of particular concern is the increasing potential for raiding online bank accounts, and there have already been incidents of this activity.[5] At a higher level are those acts that will cause us to reconsider our understanding of property and, therefore, the act of theft such as cyber-piracy, that is, the appropriation of intellectual properties. Interestingly, because of increases in the relative security of the Internet as a medium for exchanging information, there has been a noticeable increase in reported cases of identity theft as a precursor to economic crime.

Content-Related Offenses

There are two key broad areas of concern over content-related cybercrimes: obscenities and violent behavior. Cyber-obscenity is the trading of sexually expressive materials within cyberspace. The cyber-pornography/obscenity debate is very complex because pornography is not necessarily illegal. The test in the United Kingdom and other jurisdictions is whether or not the materials are obscene and deprave its viewers, but there are considerable legal and moral differences regarding the criteria that enable law enforcers to establish obscenity and depravation (Chatterjee, 2001, p. 78). In Britain, for example, individuals daily view risqué images through the various facets of the mass media. These same images might be legally obscene in some Islamic societies, yet they are deemed perfectly acceptable in more permissive countries.

Cyber-violence/harm describes the violent impact of the cyber-activities of another on an individual or a social or political group. Although such activities do not require a direct physical expression, the victim nevertheless will *feel* the violence of the act and may bear long-term psychological scars as a consequence. The activities referred to here may include cyber-stalking, hate speech, and "tech talk" (a term that describes the circulation of the technical aspects of cybercrime, usually through newsgroups, such as how to make weapons or reprogram smart cards) (Wall, 2000). In this category, one could also include the physical violence inflicted in the creation of child pornographic images for distribution over the Internet.

By analyzing cybercrimes in terms of a matrix of different levels of opportunity and types of impact, it is demonstrated that cybercrimes are a very heterogeneous group of acts. Furthermore, the matrix illustrates that, perhaps with the exception of the extreme end of third level (new opportunities for new types of crime), understanding of the particular behaviors is not outside the current professional experience of the main justice agencies. It is also not outside the experience of the fields of academic or applied criminology and sociolegal studies. Finally, the interstices of the matrix allow criminological debates to focus more clearly on the specific policy or resource implications for policing, crime prevention, and crime control. What the matrix does not do, however, is enable us to get a feel for the prevalence of cybercrimes.

Producing Reliable Criminological Knowledge About Cybercrimes

Without some measure of quantity and impact, misplaced or exaggerated public demands for policy responses from criminal justice agencies may occur and the impacts of media sensationalization that misshape public opinion may remain unchallenged. But how feasible is it to create reliable data streams when the activities are so heterogeneous? Indeed, is it possible to create such data in the same way that it is with non-cybercrime? (However, let us not forget the long-standing doubts in traditional criminology about the accuracy of the so-called "reliable data" as the basis for the recording of criminal activity.) For a number of practical reasons, it might not be possible to gain an overall picture of the prevalence of cyber-crime; however, it is still important to know why this might not be achievable as well as whether the information, statistics, and data that are currently available have any value. Moreover, there are now many sources of information available that describe harmful Internet activity along with a growing genre of methodologies for conducting virtual research. To maximize these resources, it is essential to take into account, and then control for, a range of dynamics that impede the production of criminological knowledge about cybercrimes when generating or using data about the Internet (Wall, in press).

Media Sensationalization

At the current time, Internet stories are so newsworthy that a single dramatic case can shape public opinion and feed public anxiety (Grabosky & Smith, 1998), frequently resulting in demands for "instant" solutions to what are extremely complex situations. Once voiced, these demands cannot simply be ignored given the widespread fear of the consequences that they generate. The problem is that once risk assessments are confused with reality (Levi, 2001), the only perceivable way in which to combat cybercrime is to use hard law and stringent technological countermeasures. This tends to shift the debate toward the needs of the state and corporate interests and away from important principles such as liberty and freedom of expression.

Shifting Definitions of Cybercrime Within the Power Struggle for Control

The fluidity of public concern flows into the power struggle for control over cyberspace that itself actively shapes definitions of "good" and "bad" behavior. The increasing political and commercial power of the Internet encourages a new political economy of information capital and the forging of a new set of power relationships. Consequently, definitions of acceptable and deviant cyberbehavior are themselves shaped by this ongoing power play, or "intellectual land grab," that is currently taking place for (market) control (Boyle, 1996). Of great concern is the increasing level of intolerance that is now being demonstrated by "the new powerful" (i.e., dominant groups that have emerged out of the power struggle) toward certain "risk groups" that they perceive as a threat to their interests, for example, the recent debates over MP3s (Carey & Wall, 2001, p. 36; Marshall, 2002, p. 1).

Victims

There is much confusion over who are the victims of cybercrime and, in some cases, over the manner of their victimization and how much weight to give it from a law enforcement perspective. Not only can victims vary from individuals to social groups, but the harms done to them can range from the actual to the perceived. Moreover, as has been found with the reporting of white-collar crimes, it is likely that many victims of cybercrimes—be they primary victims or secondary victims, individuals or organizations—either might be unwilling to acknowledge that they have been victimized or, at least, might not realize that they have been victimized for some time. At a personal level, reluctance to report offenses could arise due to embarrassment, ignorance of what to do, or simply "chalking it up to experience." Alternatively, where victimization has been imputed by a third party on the basis of an ideological, political, moral, or commercial assessment of risk, the victims or victimized groups might simply be unaware that they have been victimized or might even believe that they have *not* been victimized, as is the case in some of the debates over pornography on the Internet. At a corporate level, fear of the (negative) commercial impact of adverse publicity greatly reduces firms' willingness to report their victimization to the police, with firms preferring to pursue a "private" model of justice rather than a "public" one, thereby furthering the corporate interest rather than the public interest.

The small amount of research into reporting practices, police recording procedures, and prosecutions reveals some startling information shortfalls. The various cybercrime surveys published by Experian, CSI/FBI (Computer Security Institute/Federal Bureau of Investigation), and the U.K. Department of Trade and Industry (DTI)—all using reputable methodologies—indicate a large volume of victimizations (in the tens of thousands) each year. This contrasts sharply with empirical research conducted for the U.K. Home Office in 2002 that found that relatively few Internet-related offenses were reported to the police (Wall, 2002a). A detailed study of various police databases, followed up by interviews with reporting center staff members, revealed that only 120 to 150 Internet-related offenses per 1 million recorded crimes had been reported to the police and that most of these were reasonably minor fraud incidents for which no further action was taken. When extrapolated to the national figures, a statistic of somewhere between 1,500 and 2,000 Internet-related offenses per year throughout England and Wales was obtained (Wall, 2003, p. 132).

Another example of the information shortfall is found when the ballpark victimization figures are compared with actual prosecution statistics. The statistics produced by the various computer emergency response teams indicate numbers of system breaches each year in the high tens of thousands or possibly hundreds of thousands. These are offenses under the Computer Misuse Act of 1990 in the United Kingdom. Yet the victimization estimates contrast sharply with the actual prosecution figures. In England and Wales during the first decade (1991–2000) following the introduction of the Computer Misuse Act of 1990, a total of 53 offenders were cautioned under the act and a further 88 were prosecuted. Of the latter, 68 (77%) were convicted (Wall, 2003, p. 131). Because security breaches are a precursor to further offenses, it is probably the case that many breaches were eventually prosecuted under the more substantive offenses; however, as

with the reporting statistics, even if the true figures were 10 (or, for that matter, 100) times the number prosecuted, there would still be a considerable shortfall.

Offender Profiles

The relatively small number of prosecutions compared with the apparently large volume of offending restricts the profiling of offenders. The little factual knowledge that does exist about cyber-offenders suggests that they tend not to be burly folk devils of the streets; rather, they are more likely to display a much broader range of social characteristics. It is also the case that offender profiles vary according to the type of crime. However, the important point to emphasize here is that the Internet enables individuals to commit crimes that previously would have been beyond their means. As such, these individuals can become law enforcement's worst nightmare—empowered small agents.

Statistics

An immediate hindrance to those seeking to study cybercrimes is the lack of officially recorded statistics other than a number of reports and surveys that purport to estimate the extent of cybercrime, typically network abuse and commercial crime. The distributed environment in which cybercrime thrives renders impossible any attempts to obtain a full overview of victimization levels because information about reported victimization does not flow through a single portal, such as the police, in the same way as does information about traditional crimes. The only way in which reliable statistics about individual victimization can really be captured is through victimization surveys. A range of self-reporting victimization surveys do already exist and are run by organizations such as the U.S. National White-Collar Crime Center and the

SCI/FBI. The SCI/FBI annual computer security survey is currently one of the most often-cited sources of data that questions U.S. businesses about their victimizations. Similarly rigorous surveys are produced by companies such as Experian and KPMG. To this end, there are some signs of encouragement because from 2002 onward the British Crime Surveys have incorporated questions about individual Internet victimizations. Similarly, a number of victimization surveys in the United States have recently incorporated, or are in the process of incorporating, questions about victimization.

Public Sector Versus Private Sector Interests

A recurring theme throughout this discussion is the tension that exists between the public and private sectors, their respective interests, and their preferred routes to justice. The examples given earlier of relatively low levels of prosecutions for breaches of computer security and of low levels of recorded Internet-related fraud are poignant examples of this tension. Most breaches of security are clearly dealt with by the victims organizations themselves. The examples highlight the preference of corporate victims for pursuing private justice solutions instead of invoking public criminal justice processes that might expose their weaknesses to their commercial competitors (Wall, 2001, p. 174).

CRIMINOLOGICAL THEORY AND CYBERCRIMES

At this point, it is useful to take stock of what we do know about cybercrimes and to draw on the previous discussion to contrast traditional criminal activity with what we understand to be cyber-criminal activity. Broadly speaking, traditional criminal activity displays some fairly characteristic and commonly understood features (Braithwaite, 1992; Gottfredson & Hirschi, 1990). First, there is a degree of consensual or core values within a society as to what does and does not constitute a crime, and these shared values are usually based in criminal law. Second, criminal activities tend to take place in real time because their time frame is largely determined by the physical world, for example, having to take account of the speed of transport, the physical size of the haul, and the needs of the offenders involved. Third, the majority of offending and victimization tends to take place within a distinct geographic boundary. Fourth, the criminology of traditional crime tends to be offender based rather than victim or offense based. Fifth, serious fraud incidents notwithstanding, much of the debate over traditional crime has tended to focus on working-class subcultures.

In contrast, cybercrimes would appear to exhibit nearly the opposite characteristics. They are contentious in that there does not yet exist a core set of values about them. They appear to be largely free of a physical time frame; therefore, they are relatively, albeit not totally, instantaneous. Cybercrimes can also be transnational, transjurisdictional, and global, and if there is a topography of the Internet, it is expressed more in terms of levels of access to the Internet and language rather than in terms of physical geography. The discussion of cybercrimes has tended to be offense based rather than victim or offender based. Finally, Cybercrimes tend to cover a broad range of legal issues, many of which are the subject of civil law in addition to, or instead of, criminal law, demonstrating a resonance with the study of white-collar crime. It is the traditional model of crime, however, that tends to underpin the criminal justice paradigm and, therefore, informs our understanding, thereby highlighting the need to explore the maintenance of order and law on the Internet. Incidentally, the terms *order* and *law* are deliberately reversed here and elsewhere to break the conceptual link that has increasingly bound the two concepts since the late 1970s (see also Fowles, 1983, p. 116; Wall, 2001, p. 167).

What to Do About Cybercrimes

The preceding discussion introduces what appears to be a cyber-conundrum. If the Internet is apparently so criminogenic as the many media reports suggest, and it is not yet possible for us to measure absolute levels of cybercrime, how does online life continue to persist, thrive, and grow? Why are more cybercrimes against individuals not reported, and if they are not reported to the police or other responding organizations, why are they not reported to friends, family, and/or colleagues verbally, by e-mail, or by letter? If cybercrimes are so prevalent, surely traditional patterns of communication would carry the message across professional, friendship, and kinship networks; we would hear more about them by one means or another. The most likely answer to these questions is that we are not actually facing a cyber-conundrum but rather are facing two different scenarios running concurrently. In one scenario, the majority of cybercrimes are small-impact multiple victimizations in which the impact on individuals is fairly small, yet their collective impact on a business, an organization, or a society is often considerable (Wall, 2003). In another scenario, there are some quite serious crimes being committed against individuals by way of the Internet. But these is not street crimes, which is the common provenance of the police; rather, many are financial crimes, commonly referred to as white-collar crimes. These are resolved in a number of different ways, but mostly within a private framework of justice; therefore, they do not necessarily appear in the crime statistics.

What the parallel scenario theory strongly suggests is that, despite popular opinion, the Internet is not a lawless and disordered environment—a place where people go for a moral holiday[6]; rather, it is quite the contrary. The Internet is characterized by a sense of order resulting from a complex "assemblage" of governance that constantly shapes virtual behavior (Newman & Clarke, 2003, p. 160; Walker & Akdeniz, 1998a, p. 8; Wall, 1997, 2001, p. 171; 2002b, p. 192). The term *assemblage* (or *configuration*), with its neo-Foucaultian origins, is particularly useful in this context because it describes the relationship between heterogeneous contributors to governance that work together as a functional entity but do not necessarily have any other unity (Haggerty & Ericson, 2000, p. 605; Miller & Rose, 1990). In some of these relationships, there may be a consensus of interest in the approach taken; in others, the consensus may be in the outcomes or goals to be achieved. Consequently, a replication is found in the bifurcation of functions in terrestrial policing between the maintenance of order through the assemblage and the enforcement of law on the other to deal with the more serious crimes. By separating the two, some sense can be made of the rather conflicting messages that are emerging in debates over policing the Internet.

Maintaining Order on the Internet

There are currently six key constellations of active policing governance being effected within cyberspace. Each is composed of agencies, groupings, and/or organizations that are active responders and from whom assistance will be sought when disputes or grievances about online behavior arise.[7] They are described elsewhere in greater detail (Wall, in press), but they consist of the following.

Internet users and user groups combine to exert a very potent influence on online behavior, mainly through moral censure, although in more extreme cases the offending behavior will be reported to relevant authorities. The *network infrastructure providers,* such as ISPs, influence online behavior through the contractual governance arising from their contractual relationships with their clients. They are themselves also subject to contractual governance by their telecommunications providers, that is, organizations that provide the hardware and telecommunications links that make their Internet service delivery possible.[8] *Corporate security organizations* tend to use a variety of methods to impose governance over their own subjects so as to preserve their private interests, including contractual governance over direct clients, the threat (or actual removal) of privileges, and the threat of (and, in some cases, actual) prosecution failing remuneration of any loss. *Nongovernmental nonpolice organizations* include a number of hybrid arrangements and contribute directly to the governance assemblage by acting as gatekeepers to the other levels of governance but also contributing toward (cyber)crime prevention. Although most are private bodies, many perform a public function. *Governmental nonpolice organizations* use a combination of rules, charges, fines, and the threat of prosecution under the law. Not normally perceived as "police" (nor are they accorded that title), the

governmental nonpolice organizations include agencies such as customs and the postal service but also include a higher tier of agencies that oversee national Internet infrastructure protection policies or the enforcement of those protection policies. The *public police organizations* draw on the (usually) democratic mandate of government. Although they have a relatively small role (numerically) in the policing of crimes on the Internet, it is nevertheless a significant one because it ultimately imposes the formal sanction of the state on wrongdoers. Although the public police are located within nation-states, they are nevertheless joined by a tier of transnational policing organizations, such as Europol and Interpol, whose membership requires such formal status. A summary of these "constellations" of governance can be found in Table 4.2.

Cutting across the constellations of policing governance are a number of initiatives that seek to make their governance function more effective: international coalitions of organizations, multiagency cross-sectoral partnerships, and international coordination policies such as the Council of Europe's Convention on Cybercrime.

The significance of the parallel scenario theory is quite profound for our understanding of the way in which the Internet is

Table 4.2   Order Maintenance Entities

Level of Policing	*Population Served*	*Sanctions*
Internet users/User groups	All Internet users	Moral censure
Network infrastructure (ISPs)	Subscribing clients	Withdrawal of Internet service
Corporate security	Private clients	Withdrawal of service
Nongovernmental nonpolice hybrids	All Internet users	Withdrawal of participation/financial sanctions
State-funded nonpolice	All Internet users/business	Financial sanctions/prosecution (civil or criminal)
State-funded public police	All Internet users	Criminal prosecution

governed and our understanding of online risks and dangers because its starting point is one of order and compliance rather than disorder and resistance. Indeed, resistance must be understood within the compliance framework rather than outside it (Hermer & Hunt, 1996, p. 477). Furthermore, the assemblage model also has major implications for the framing of policy in that it is clear that the distributed nature of the Internet does not allow governments the privilege of monopoly control over either the Internet or user behavior. However, the assemblage itself, or parts thereof, can be the subject of international policy such as the European Commission's (1997) action plan for promoting safe use of the Internet. Better development and use of the existing assemblage could lay the foundations for a more effective, and more broadly democratic, structure of governance. But effecting this strategy requires a plural or multifaceted approach that combines a complex web of legal, regulatory, normative, and even technological measures.

Law Enforcement and the Internet

The governance assemblage described earlier effects a state of order—or, to be more accurate, various states of order—on the Internet. It does not contain some of the more extreme criminal behavior, but mechanisms for enforcing criminal law do exist within the constellations of assemblage. However, the Internet and communications-mediated technologies create some specific challenges for the criminal justice systems and component institutions—police, the prosecution process, and the courts. These challenges lie mainly in the capacity of organizations and their occupational cultures to deal with the new demands as well as the capacity of the professionals within those organizations. The focus here is on the police because the police, as key first responders to more serious offenses, subsequently shape the criminal justice response.

Broadly speaking, the public police in most Western countries are organized locally, but there also exist national/federal and even international police organizations (e.g., Interpol) to investigate crimes occurring across police forces as well as to collect intelligence and investigate organized crime. However, as established earlier, relatively few Internet-related crimes are reported to the police because most are dealt with elsewhere. Many of the larger local police forces/services possess the capability to respond to Internet-related complaints from the public and have local facilities to investigate computer crimes and conduct the forensic examination of computers. The investigations of an increasing number of traditional criminal code offenses now seek electronic evidence to establish motive or whereabouts, and much of this is located in computers, Internet traffic data, and mobile phone records. Some police forces set up their own units, whereas others enter into strategic alliances with other police forces to provide such services.

A common complaint made by police and law enforcement agencies is that they do not have the facilities to keep up with criminals, especially with regard to offenses that require what Brodeur (1983) termed a high policing response.[9] Revelations about police ineffectiveness make good news copy and ultimately reinforce the police-originated myth that criminals are ahead of the game. There may be some truth to this view. Because police agencies are largely responsive to public complaints, they tend to deal with routine matters and are subjected to tight budgetary constraints; this restricts the immediate allocation of major resources to emerging matters and, therefore, the responsive capability of the police. However, such complaints are by no means new. A century ago, for example, readers of the *Police Review* were told that police officers did not have the resources to obtain the latest technologies that would help them to respond to criminals more effectively. During those days, the police were seeking telephones, bicycles, and (later) automobiles.[10] Yet there is a tremendous irony here in the case of the Internet because the surveillant and "dataveillant" (Clarke, 1994) qualities of Internet technology—the same qualities that create new types of opportunity for crime—also provide police officers with new tools for investigation as well as new sources of evidence with which to secure prosecutions and convictions. The collection (and retention) of Internet traffic data is particularly significant because records of every Internet transaction that takes place can now exist, to the point where we are in danger of experiencing what was described earlier as the disappearance of disappearance (Haggerty & Ericson, 2000).

It is one thing to have the capabilities and another thing to be able to use them, and there are a number of obstacles and challenges to this task. At the broader level, the public police, like the other criminal justice agencies, are deeply conservative institutions that have been molded by the time-honored traditions; therefore, they do not readily respond to rapid change. Furthermore, part of this innate conservatism originates in the police also being symbolic expressions of state sovereignty. So, one way in which the police forces generally respond to new issues, while preserving their symbolic and organizational conservatism, is through the origination of specialist units into which officers with appropriate specializations are absorbed. Although this tactic constitutes an actual and visible response, it nevertheless runs the risk of marginalizing the issue and preventing the broader accumulation of organizational and professional experience across the force in dealing with the issue at hand. Ultimately, it is the presence of a relevant body of knowledge and expertise within a police force (and whether the other officers know about it) that can determine whether or not the

organizational and occupational response of the police to a new public concern is effective. The formation of "national" policing structures will greatly assist in strengthening police force capabilities, although the national structures tend to deal with national offending and not local offending.

At the police force level lie a series of challenges to addressing new policing concerns. They are fairly common across all independent police forces in neoliberal economies. Indeed, these challenges are not the sole provenance of the police organization given that the themes they embody are also found across the other criminal justice institutions and processes.

The first challenge is to obtain funding within an existing framework's resource allocation and management rules. Policing strategies are often reduced to decisions that are made at a very local level over the most efficient expenditure of finite resources (Goodman, 1997, p. 648), and because most cybercrimes are small-impact multiple victimizations, the "public interest"—a key criterion in releasing police resources for an investigation—is often hard to justify in individual cases.

The second challenge is that police forces are less likely to fund investigations when the offense, victimization, and impact of the offense span different jurisdictions. So, using the example of small-impact multiple victimizations, the aggregated loss from the many individual cybercrimes, although large, is spread across a range of jurisdictions and, therefore, does not warrant expenditure by local forces. Even if the national forces took over such investigations, local priorities might take precedence in the provision of assistance.

The third challenge is to respond to criminal activity that is "outside the box." Most public policing tends to be based on local and "routinized" practices that define occupational cultures and working patterns. Thus, investigative difficulties tend to arise when nonroutine events occur (Reiner, 2000; Wall, 1997, p. 223). In this case, nonroutine events, such as cross-border investigations and types of behavior not normally regarded as criminal by police officers, will arise due to the Internet.

The fourth challenge is the inadequacy of criminal procedures to deal effectively with interjurisdictional cases. On the one hand, if a case is clearly a criminal offense for which the investigation carries a strong public mandate, such as the investigation of child pornography, resourcing its investigation is fairly unproblematic from a police point of view. But on the other hand, resourcing is more problematic where there is not a strong mandate, for example, with cybercrimes other than child pornography. Of course, the other interjurisdictional problem is that some offenses may fall under civil laws in one jurisdiction and under criminal laws in another; an example is the theft of trade secrets, which is a criminal offense in the United States but only a civil offense in the United Kingdom. In the United Kingdom, only the manner by which the theft takes place can be criminal (Law Commission, 1997). But let us not forget police resourcefulness given that there are also situations where resourceful police officers and prosecutors can "forum shop" to use these differences to their advantage to achieve the most effective investigation and/or prosecution (Wall, 2002b). This was evident in *United States of America v. Robert A. Thomas and Carleen Thomas* (1996), where the prosecutors forum shopped to seek a site where they believed a conviction would best be secured. Tennessee, rather than California, was chosen due to the greater likelihood of conviction. In *R v Fellows* and *R v Arnold* (1996), the investigation was passed on from the U.S. police to the U.K. police because the former believed that the latter were more likely to gain a conviction.

A fifth challenge is the role of police occupational culture in resisting change. Despite long-standing concerns about corruption and impartial enforcement of law, occupational culture is also an important component of policing in applying the law (McBarnet, 1979) because, with safeguards, it enables officers to make sense of the world in which they must police and, without this cognitive map, officers would have no understanding of their environment. The culture relies on the accumulation of collective experience of police officers, but because cybercrimes are rather unique events for most officers, the culture does not assist them directly. It does, however, shape their response because they still tend to draw on the "cynical" application of conventional wisdom (Reiner, 2000) (recall the earlier vignette about the recurring century-old call for more technological resources to fight crime). So, it is understandable that street police officers will not tend to see the Internet in terms of its potential for the democratization of knowledge and growth in active citizenship (Walker & Akdeniz, 1998b) or the leveling of ethnic, social, or cultural boundaries. Rather, they are more likely to see it as a site characterized by risk, that is, as a place where criminals—notably pedophiles, Russian gangsters, and fraudsters—and other wrongdoers ply their trade (Shearing & Ericson, 1991, p. 500). Although great advances in police officer awareness of technology have taken place over the past decade or so, there still exists a cultural dissonance between traditional occupational police culture and the demands created by the Internet that allows the view to persist among many officers that cyberspace is "like a neighborhood without a police department" (Sussman, 1995).

Although this section has illustrated the challenges that networked technologies pose for criminal justice processes, it has also illustrated that public police involvement in the investigation of Internet crime is fairly minimal. Despite many impediments to potential policing responses, it would appear that there is little evidence to support the general police demand for a local capability to respond to cybercrimes. At this point in time, relatively few Internet offenses are reported directly to the police (as the first responders); the bulk of these tend to be related to credit cards, and complainants are frequently referred back to their banks, which are the actual victims. However, the main demand of police in the United Kingdom, European Union, and United States is the need to be able to search and seize computer hardware so as to conduct forensic examinations on its informational contents that might be evidence of wrongdoing with respect to non-cybercrime offenses. Such information might include e-mails indicating intentions, the acquisition of precursory materials, or data locating the suspect in a particular time and place. Anecdotal evidence from serving police officers, supported by news reports, suggests that the more serious cybercrimes are more likely to come to the attention of the national/federal police than to the attention of local forces.

Cybercrime Control and Cybercrime Prevention

As an adjunct to this discussion of policing cybercrimes, the role of crime prevention and crime control should not be overlooked. Following the principles of conventional crime prevention, four different approaches to cybercrime prevention are being taken.

The first strategy is to design crime out of new products and technologies. In the United Kingdom, the DTI's Foresight program has actively sought to identify the vulnerabilities in new technologies and to encourage industry to modify designs to reduce the opportunities for crime without compromising usability. The second strategy is to actively design crime control facilities into the technology. For example, during the mid-1990s, the U.S. government experienced mixed success in its attempts to "protect the interests of U.S. industry" (Reno,

1996) by introducing devices such as the V-chip technology, designed to filter out violence and/or pornography, and the "Clipper Chip," an "escrowed encryption system" that would have provided government with codes to unscramble encrypted files (Akdeniz, 1996; Post, 1995). Because the impact of many of these measures also curbs individual freedom of communication, it is not surprising that they failed at the policy stage and that much of the debate over Internet regulation has revolved around potential conflicts with the First Amendment of the U.S. Constitution. The third approach is to use technology to modify an environment, or "securitize" it, so as to reduce opportunities for crime. This typically involves the use of security software, spam filters, virus checkers, and encryption. A fourth approach is to proactively use "honeypots," or fake Web sites, that work rather like speed cameras, although some would argue entrapment. Currently, they are typically used by policing agencies against pedophiles. However, if a model that had a broader application were employed, users who access sites containing illegal images would find themselves facing a law enforcement message—a "gotcha"—with the data trail being traced back to the sender.

The downside of using technological solutions to achieve crime prevention goals is that an acceptable balance has to be reached between security and privacy. Furthermore, in the first three of the four approaches just mentioned, the key criticisms against situational crime prevention apply—namely, that although offending behavior is the provenance of comparatively few individuals, all users are affected by what is effectively an "anti-social criminology of everyday life" (Hughes, 2003). This is especially true with regard to the first and second approaches because many of the crimes being prevented have yet to fully materialize. Interestingly, the more intrusive proposals, along with those of recent years since the events of September 11, 2001, that suggested automated mass surveillance systems such as Total/Terrorism Information Awareness to "drain the swamp to catch the snake" (Levi & Wall, 2004) have largely failed due to legal challenges.

CONCLUSION

The discussion throughout this chapter has deconstructed and provided explanations for a range of contradictions and issues that have dogged our understanding of cybercrime. It highlighted the ways in which criminal behaviors have been transformed, and it demonstrated that cybercrimes are heterogeneous activities, before illustrating some of the problems that arise when seeking to produce reliable data about cybercrimes. One characteristic common to the cybercrime issue is the overall lack of critical assessment of data. Without systematically created knowledge about the substance and prevalence of cybercrimes and as well as about offenders and victims, the establishment of a corpus of knowledge is prevented. Such knowledge can counter the spin of media sensationalization, not just to salve the public brow but also to inform journalists, policymakers, and the cybercrime industry. The discussion then explored what can be done about cybercrime, blowing the myth that the criminal justice processes are woefully inefficient at bringing wrongdoers to justice and providing some plausible explanations for the low reporting and prosecution rates in the face of apparently high prevalence. Furthermore, the chapter queried the age-old police myth of being challenged by technological change, of being overrun by more technologically adept and equipped criminals, and of not having the resources to respond. Indeed, much of the challenge to police has been with regard to forensically processing computers in conventional crimes rather than in the pursuit of cyber-criminals. But this is not meant to downplay the problem; rather, it is to say that we have, for some intents and purposes, been looking at a new phenomenon through the wrong lens. By focusing on the transformative impacts of the Internet on deviant behavior and then applying the elimination test to imagine what behavior would remain if the Internet were to disappear, it is clear that it is most certainly a conduit for criminal activity. However, the chapter showed that the Internet is also conducive to the governance of behavior and that it also enables policing agencies to police cybercrimes.

NOTES

1. There are a number of very interesting texts that describe and theorize the origins and, importantly, the impact of the Internet. See also the work of Castells (1996–1999) as cited in Castells (2000), Webster (2002), Jordan (1999), Bell (2001), and Rheingold (1994).

2. The destructive gemeinschaft argument arises from the observation that in a society where personality transcends politics, individuals no longer become accustomed to doing things together or playing out public roles and, therefore, are unable to find community and the intimacy it gives. Virtual relationships neither contain the full panoply of social relationships nor include the expectations of gemeinschaft to which they give rise.

3. This extends Braverman's (1976) division of labor hypothesis to the construction of social life.

4. Retrieved March 8, 2004, from www.wordorigins.org.

5. In one example, some German students sent e-mails to people to register with them to win a $50,000 prize. On "registration," a cookie the students had developed searched for online banking programs, and if one was found, an invoice for $20 would automatically be mailed to the registree. The students collected a total of $640,000 before they were caught (Lorek, 1997).

6. See also Baron and Straus (1989, p. 132), who discussed the way in which vacationers sometimes believe themselves to be on a "moral holiday" that, to them, justifies their stealing hotel property and engaging in other illegal activities such as gambling, prostitution, fraud, and theft.

7. This is in contrast to passive responders (Newman & Clarke, 2003).

8. The role of the Internet Corporation for Assigned Names and Numbers (ICANN) is not discussed here.

9. See the debates over high and low policing in Brodeur (1983) and Sheptycki (2000, p. 11).

10. During the early years of the 20th century, the letters page of the *Police Review* contained much correspondence on the subject.

CASES

Godfrey v. Demon Internet Ltd., 4 All E.R. 342 (1999).

League Against Racism and Anti-Semitism and Union of French Jewish Students v. Yahoo Inc. and Yahoo France, Interim Court Order, County Court of Paris, RG: 00/05308 (2000, November 20).

R v. Fellows and R v. Arnold, Court of Appeal, Criminal Division, The Times (1996, October 3).

United States of America v. Robert A. Thomas and Carleen Thomas, 74 F.3d 701; U.S. App. Lexis 1069; Fed. App. 0032P (6th Cir.) (1996).

REFERENCES

Akdeniz, Y. (1996). Computer pornography: A comparative study of U.S. and U.K. obscenity laws and child pornography laws in relation to the Internet. *International Review of Law, Computers, and Technology, 10,* 235–261.

Barlow, J. P. (1994). The economy of ideas: A framework for rethinking patents and copyrights in the digital age (everything you know about intellectual property is wrong). *Wired, 2*(3), 84.

Baron, L., & Straus, M. (1989). *Four theories of rape in American society: A state-level analysis.* New Haven, CT: Yale University Press.

Bell, D. (2001). *An introduction to cybercultures.* London: Routledge.

Bottoms, A., & Wiles, P. (1996). Understanding crime prevention in late modern societies. In T. Bennett (Ed.), *Preventing crime and disorder: Targeting strategies and responsibilities.* Cambridge, UK: University of Cambridge.

Boyle, J. (1996). *Shamans, software, and spleens: Law and the construction of the information society.* Cambridge, MA: Harvard University Press.

Braithwaite, J. (1992). *Crime, shame, and reintegration.* Cambridge, UK: Cambridge University Press.

Braverman, H. (1976). *Labour and monopoly capital.* New York: Monthly Review Press.

Brenner, S. (2001). Is there such a thing as "virtual crime"? *California Criminal Law Review, 4*(1), 11.

Brodeur, J-P. (1983). High policing and low policing: Remarks about the policing of political activities. *Social Problems, 30,* 507–520.

Carey, M., & Wall, D. S. (2001). MP3: More beats to the byte. *International Review of Law, Computers, and Technology, 15,* 35–58.

Castells, M. (2000). Materials for an explanatory theory of the network society. *British Journal of Sociology, 51,* 5–24.

Chatterjee, B. (2001). Last of the Rainmacs? Thinking about pornography in cyberspace. In D. S. Wall (Ed.), *Crime and the Internet* (pp. 74–99). London: Routledge.

Clarke, R. (1994). Dataveillance: Delivering "1984." In L. Green & R. Guinery (Eds.), *Framing technology: Society, choice, and change.* Sydney, Australia: Allen & Unwin.

European Commission. (1997). *Action plan on promoting safe use of the Internet.* Retrieved June 5, 2004, from http://europa.eu.int/ispo/eif/internetpoliciessite/crime/publichearingpresentations/saferinternet.html

Fowles, A. J. (1983). Order and the law. In K. Jones, J. Brown, & J. Bradshaw (Eds.), *Issues in social policy.* London: Routledge and Kegan Paul.

Giddens, A. (1990). *The consequences of modernity.* London: Polity.

Goodman, M. (1997). Why the police don't care about computer crime. *Harvard Journal of Law and Technology, 10,* 645–694.

Gottfredson, G., & Hirschi, T. (1990). *A general theory of crime.* Stanford, CA: Stanford University Press.

Grabosky, P. N., & Smith, R. G. (1998). *Crime in the digital age: Controlling communications and cyberspace illegalities.* New Brunswick, NJ: Transaction Publishers.

Haggerty, K., & Ericson, R. (2000). The surveillant assemblage. *British Journal of Sociology, 51,* 605–622.

Hermer, J., & Hunt, A. (1996). Official graffiti of the everyday. *Law and Society Review, 30,* 455–480.

Hughes, G. (2003, August). *The future of crime reduction and the rise of the "new anti-social criminologies of everyday life": A sociological critique.* Paper presented at the meeting of the European Society of Criminology, Helsinki, Finland.

Jones, R. (2003). Review of *Crime in the Digital Age* by P. Grabosky and R. Smith. *International Journal of Law and Information Technology, 11,* 98.

Jordan, T. (1999). *Cyberpower: The culture and politics of cyberspace and the Internet.* London: Routledge.

Law Commission. (1997). *Legislating the criminal code: Misuse of trade secrets* (Consultation Paper 150). Retrieved March 8, 2004, from www.lawcom.gov.uk/library/lccp150/summary.htm

Levi, M. (2001). "Between the risk and the reality falls the shadow": Evidence and urban legends in computer fraud. In D. S. Wall (Ed.), *Crime and the Internet* (pp. 44–58). London: Routledge.

Levi, M., & Wall, D. S. (2004). Technologies, security, and privacy in the post-9/11 European Information Society. *Journal of Law and Society, 31,* 194–220.

Lorek, L. A. (1997, September 14). Outwitting cybercrime: No, you're not paranoid—Computer villains really are out to get you. *Sun-Sentinel of South Florida,* p. 1.

Mann, D., & Sutton, M. (1998). Netcrime: More change in the organisation of thieving. *British Journal of Criminology, 38,* 210–229.

Mackinnon, R. (1997). Virtual rape. *Journal of Computer Mediated Communication, 2*(4). Retrieved March 8, 2004, from www.ascusc.org/ jcmc/v012/ issue4/mackinnon.html

Marshall, L. (2002). Metallica and morality: The rhetorical battleground of the Napster wars. *Entertainment Law, 1*(1), 1.

McBarnet, D. (1979). Arrest: The legal context of policing. In S. Holdaway (Ed.), *The British police.* London: Arnold.

Miller, P., & Rose, N. (1990). Governing economic life. *Economy and Society, 1*(1), 1.

National Criminal Intelligence Service. (1999). *Project Trawler: Crime on the information highways.* London: Author.

Newman, G. R., & Clarke, R. V. (2003). *Superhighway robbery: Preventing e-commerce crime.* Cullompton, UK: Willan Publishing.

Pease. K. (2001). Crime futures and foresight: Challenging criminal behaviour in the information age. In D. S. Wall (Ed.), *Crime and the Internet* (pp. 18–28). London: Routledge.

Post, D. (1995, January–February). Encryption vs. the Alligator Clip: The feds worry that encoded messages are immune to wiretaps. *American Lawyer,* p. 111.

Reiner, R. (2000). *The Politics of the Police* (3rd ed.). Oxford, UK: Oxford University Press.

Rheingold, H. (1994). *The virtual community: Homesteading the electronic frontier.* New York: Harper Perennial.

Reno, J. (1996, June). *Law enforcement in cyberspace.* Address given to the Commonwealth Club of California, San Francisco.

Robertson, R. (1995). *Globalisation.* In M. Featherstone, S. Lash, & R. Robertson (Eds.), *Global modernities* (pp. 40–65). London: Sage.

Schneider, J. L. (2003). Hiding in plain sight: An exploration of the illegal(?) activities of a drugs newsgroup. *Howard Journal of Criminal Justice, 42,* 374–389.

Sennett, R. (1992). *The fall of public man.* New York: Norton.

Shearing, C., & Ericson, R. (1991). Culture as figurative action. *British Journal of Sociology, 42,* 481–506.

Sheptycki, J. (2000). Introduction. In J. E. Sheptycki (Ed.), *Issues in transnational policing* (pp. 1–20). London: Routledge.

Sussman, V. (1995, January 23). Policing cyberspace. *World Report,* p. 54.

Taylor, P. (2001). Hacktivism: In search of lost ethics? In D. S. Wall (Ed.), *Crime and the Internet* (pp. 59–73). London: Routledge.

Walden, I. (2003). Computer crime. In C. Reed & J. Angel (Eds.), *Computer law* (pp. 295–329). Oxford, UK: Oxford University Press.

Walker, C., & Akdeniz, Y. (1998a). The governance of the Internet in Europe with special reference to illegal and harmful content. *Criminal Law Review,* pp. 5–18. (Special issue on Crime, Criminal Justice, and the Internet)

Walker, C. P. & Akdeniz, Y. (1998b, Autumn). Virtual(e-) democracy. *Public Law,* pp. 489–506.

Wall, D. S. (1997). Policing the virtual community: The Internet, cyber-crimes, and the policing of cyberspace. In P. Francis, P. Davies, & V. Jupp (Eds.), *Policing futures* (pp. 208–236). London: Macmillan.

Wall, D. S. (1999). Cybercrimes: New wine, no bottles? In P. Davies, P. Francis, & V. Jupp (Eds.), *Invisible crimes: Their victims and their regulation* (pp. 105–139). London: Macmillan.

Wall, D. S. (2000). *The theft of electronic services: Telecommunications and teleservices.* Essay 1 on the CD-ROM annex to Department of Trade and Industry's *Turning the Corner.* London: DTI.

Wall, D.S. (2001). Maintaining order and law on the Internet. In D. S. Wall (Ed.), *Crime and the Internet* (pp. 167–183). London: Routledge.

Wall, D. S. (2002a). *DOT.CONS: Internet related frauds and deceptions upon individuals within the U.K.* Final report to the Home Office.

Wall, D. S. (2002b). Insecurity and the policing of cyberspace. In A. Crawford (Ed.), *Crime and insecurity* (pp. 186–210). Cullompton, UK: Willan Publishing.

Wall, D. S. (2003). Mapping out cybercrimes in a cyberspatial surveillant assemblage. In F. Webster & K. Ball (Eds.), *The intensification of surveillance: Crime, terrorism, and warfare in the information age* (pp. 112–136). London: Pluto.

Wall, D. S. (2004). Surveillant Internet technologies and the growth in information capitalism: Spams and public trust in the information society. In R. Ericson & K. Haggerty (Eds.), *The new politics of surveillance and visibility*. Toronto: University of Toronto Press.

Wall, D. S. (in press). *Cybercrime, deviance, and the Internet*. Cambridge, UK: Polity.

Webster, F. (2002). *Theories of the information society* (2nd ed.). London: Routledge.

Williams, M. (2003). *Virtually criminal: Deviance, harm, and regulation within an online community*. Ph.D. thesis, University of Cardiff, United Kingdom.

Section III

INFORMATION TECHNOLOGY AND CRIME REPORTING AND ANALYSIS

CHAPTER 5

The Impact of Information Technology on Crime Reporting

The NIBRS Process

Donald Faggiani and David Hirschel

I n this chapter, we examine the impact of information technology on official crime reporting. In particular, we focus on the development of national police crime reporting systems in the United States and their utility for producing empirically based crime policies at the local, state, and national levels. First, we outline the history of the Uniform Crime Reporting (UCR) system and discuss the limitations of that system for crime reporting and public policymaking in the United States. Second, we discuss the development of the more recent official reporting system, the National Incident-Based Reporting System (NIBRS). Third, we describe the technicalities associated with the NIBRS data collection process. We conclude with an example of how NIBRS information is being used to study the problem of domestic violence in the United States.

THE UNIFORM CRIME REPORTING SYSTEM

In January 1930, the International Association of Chiefs of Police (IACP) introduced the first nationwide system for reporting crime information. The UCR program was established to provide a standardized crime reporting system to aid law enforcement administration, operation, and management. The *Uniform Crime Bulletin* was the first publication containing the UCR data and included information from 400 cities in 23 states covering a population of more than 20 million. The original design of the UCR system was to report summary-level counts on seven major index crimes reported to law enforcement authorities: homicide, forcible rape, robbery, aggravated assault, burglary, larceny/theft, and motor vehicle theft.[1] The UCR system also reported basic arrest information for 21 additional crime categories.[2]

Following the release of the *Uniform Crime Bulletin,* the U.S. Congress enacted a code authorizing the attorney general of the United States to collect and report national crime information. The attorney general designated the Federal Bureau of Investigation (FBI) to serve as the national clearinghouse for this crime information. In September 1930, the IACP turned over responsibility for the UCR system to the FBI. The FBI has maintained that responsibility ever since.

The initial success of the UCR program was encouraging, but participation by law enforcement evolved slowly. Although the number of agencies submitting UCR data continued to grow, it was not until 1958—28 years from the introduction of the program—that the FBI had sufficient participation to provide aggregate crime totals for the United States. In 1958, the FBI first published *Crime in the United States* (*CIUS*). This publication changed the format previously used for reporting the UCR information and included estimates for a national crime rate (Maltz, 1999). Prior to *CIUS,* the FBI reported state- and local-level data in tables based on the size of the reporting jurisdiction.

CIUS is currently one of the most widely used sources for crime information in the United States, providing information for monitoring trends and fluctuations in crime nationwide as well as within states, counties, and cities. In 2002, *CIUS* reported data from more than 17,000 law enforcement agencies covering slightly more than 93% of the total U.S. population. In addition to the crime counts and trends discussed previously, *CIUS* includes data on crimes cleared, persons arrested (e.g., age, sex, race), and law enforcement personnel (e.g., the number of sworn officers killed or assaulted) as well as the characteristics of homicides (e.g., age, sex, and race of victims and offenders; victim–offender relationships; weapons used; circumstances surrounding the homicides).

With the introduction of *CIUS,* the UCR information was available to a wide audience that included policymakers, the news media, and academics and other researchers. However, as interest in the UCR system grew, so did criticisms of the system. Design and substantive limitations in the summary-based data system became a topic of much discussion in both academic and professional journals (Biderman & Lynch, 1991; Maltz, 1977, 1999). Two of the major criticisms, the use of hierarchical offense rules and the imputation of missing data, are discussed shortly; however, a full discussion of the many criticisms of the summary-based system is well beyond the scope of this chapter. Maltz (1999) provides an excellent summary of the criticisms of the summary-based UCR program.

The original design of the summary-based UCR program included a hierarchical structure for offenses, with only the most serious offense committed in an incident being counted. Criminal homicide was designated the most serious offense, followed in order by rape, robbery, aggravated assault, burglary, larceny, and motor vehicle theft. So, if an incident included both a burglary and an aggravated assault, only the aggravated assault would be counted. Over time, it became obvious that reporting only one offense per incident placed significant limitations on the utility of the UCR data for understanding the nature of some crimes. A classic example is provided by the work of Block and Block (1992). Using data from the city of Chicago, these researchers demonstrated that, in most instances, homicide is the fatal outcome of some other offense such as robbery or aggravated assault. Only by classifying the different types of homicide is it possible to define intervention strategies that might help to prevent these homicides from occurring.

Maltz (1999) notes that, because of variations in the number of agencies reporting UCR data from year to year as well as agencies reporting only partial data for a given year, there can be large amounts of missing information in the UCR reports. To compensate for the missing information and gaps in reporting, the FBI implemented a process to impute the missing information. Thus, the total number of crimes reported or arrests made during any given year is an imputed estimate of the total and not a precise number. The main criticism of the imputation process is that the reliability of the estimates is dependent on the total number of crimes reported. Thus, at the national level, with large numbers of crimes reported, the imputation is fairly reliable. However, at the state and county levels, where considerably fewer crimes are reported, the imputation might not be nearly as reliable. This can have a significant impact on research and funding decisions influenced by the number of crimes reported through the UCR program.

Two events that occurred during the late 1960s eventually affected the nature of crime reporting in the United States. First, several states, in an attempt to improve their crime reporting, began to serve as the central UCR repository for all jurisdictions within their state lines. With a state UCR repository submitting to the FBI the data from all state reporting agencies, this system eased the FBI's workload considerably and provided a useful model for all states participating in the UCR program. The second event was the introduction of the Law Enforcement Assistance Administration (LEAA), a federal funding program designed to improve law enforcement in the United States.[3]

The LEAA provided funding for two organizations that had an immediate impact on crime reporting in the United States and enabled the UCR system to become a truly national crime reporting system. First, funding was provided for centralized statewide UCR programs. Second, money was allocated to establish state criminal justice statistical analysis centers (SACs). The SACs were to serve as the central data repositories for the state UCR systems and to develop the reporting and analytic capabilities of the states. The SACs in many states were able to expand the FBI's reporting and use of state crime information.

There have been relatively few substantive changes to the UCR system since its original design during the late 1920s. The most significant change was the introduction of the incident-based Supplemental Homicide Report (SHR) in 1961. For the first time, demographic details of the victims and those arrested for homicide were reported at a national level. Essentially, the SHR is a separate report. The second significant change was the addition of arson to the list of reported index crimes in 1971.

THE NATIONAL INCIDENT-BASED REPORTING SYSTEM

The original design of the UCR system was as a summary-based reporting system. The data for each reporting jurisdiction were limited to counts of the seven (now eight) index crimes. The arrest data included summary-level counts of the demographics of persons arrested. Data collectors (police) and data users (everyone else) have long lamented the difficulty of collecting these data and their limited utility for solving crime and informing public policy. For example, basic information, such as the date and time of an incident, was not designed into the reporting process. Also, information on victims of crimes was not included in the original UCR design,[4] making it impossible to identify the characteristics of juvenile, elderly, and domestic violence victims or to assess the influence of drug or alcohol involvement on criminal activity. All of these were high-profile issues.

In September 1982, 52 years after the introduction of the UCR program, a special Bureau of Justice Statistics (BJS)–FBI task force undertook a study to review the FBI's crime reporting system and to make suggestions for improvement. After nearly 3 years of planning, meetings, and conferences, the BJS–FBI task force in 1985 issued the *Blueprint for the Future of the Uniform Crime Reporting Program* (Poggio, Kennedy, Chaiken, & Carlson, 1985).

To meet the informational needs of law enforcement, the *Blueprint* made three specific recommendations. First, offenses and arrests should be reported using an incident-based system. Second, a two-tiered reporting structure should be established. Tier 1 agencies would report incident-level details on the eight index crimes, whereas Tier 2 agencies would report incident-level details on all offenses. Third, a quality assurance program should be established to improve the overall quality of the data reported to the FBI.

During the years that followed, the FBI began a program to implement the NIBRS, with the expectation that it would eventually replace the summary-level UCR system as the primary information source for crime information in the United States. To accomplish the goals laid out in the *Blueprint,* the FBI proceeded in two directions. First, it used the services of an external contractor to revise and update offense definitions and to design and develop a database structure for maintaining and housing the new data. Second, while the contractor worked on the database structure and new data elements, the FBI began a review of all state systems to identify a state with an incident-based system in place that could be used as a test site for the new program.

The South Carolina Law Enforcement Division (SLED) had been using a statewide incident-based reporting system for several years and was chosen by the FBI as the test site for the new incident-based UCR program. With funding from the BJS, the SLED revised its existing incident-based system to meet the requirements developed by the FBI's contractor. The initial test of the FBI's new program was completed by the SLED in late 1987.

The results from the test were encouraging and provided the FBI with the information it required to proceed.

The FBI then brought together law enforcement executives from all over the country to Orange Beach, Alabama, to participate in a national conference on the new reporting system. Three recommendations came out of this conference. First, a national incident-based crime reporting system should be established. Second, the FBI should be responsible for the management of the new system. Third, an Advisory Policy Board (APB), composed of law enforcement executives from around the country, should be created to provide oversight for implementation of the new system.

Following the meeting in Alabama, the FBI and its consultant began to develop the documentation for implementing the new NIBRS. Three documents covering the data collection guidelines, data submission specifications, and error messages were produced and published by the FBI in 1988. The manuals were designed to assist state and local law enforcement in implementing systems for reporting NIBRS data to the FBI. The FBI announced that it would begin accepting NIBRS data in January 1989. The first NIBRS data submitted to the FBI came 2 years later in 1991.

The system implemented by the FBI is slightly different from the original design tested by the SLED. The FBI determined that implementing the NIBRS through a two-tiered system was not the most practical approach. Many departments indicated that submitting data for all offenses would not be a problem and that this was in fact preferable to Tier 1 participation, which was limited to providing data on the eight index offenses.

Structure of the NIBRS

The NIBRS addresses many of the limitations of the older summary-based UCR system. This is achieved by collecting data in which the criminal incident, rather than a combined group of incidents, is the basic unit of information. The FBI (1998) defines a criminal incident as "one or more offenses committed by the same offender, or group of offenders *acting in concert,* at the *same time and place*" (p. 17). The FBI notes that acting in concert

> requires that the offenders actually commit or assist in the commission of the crime(s). The offenders must be aware of, and consent to, the commission of the crime(s); or, even if nonconsenting, their actions assist in the commission of the offense(s). This is important because all of the offenders in an incident are considered to have committed all of the offenses in the incident. If one or more of the offenders did not act in concert, then there is more than one incident involved. (p. 17)

Although the stated intent of the NIBRS is to serve as a national crime report, its design and structure provide the basic foundation for a local law enforcement records management system (RMS). The result is a crime information tool with standardized data elements of utility for the local agency, allowing the possibility of true policy-relevant analysis at the local, state, and national levels.

When the FBI introduced the NIBRS to law enforcement, the new reporting system dramatically altered crime reporting in the United States. The NIBRS provides incident-level details on 22 different categories of crime (46 different offenses) that are reported to the police. The detailed information provided through the NIBRS can significantly improve our understanding of crime in the United States.

The FBI has defined two offense groupings for NIBRS reporting. Group A offenses are generally more serious offenses, and the FBI requires the reporting agencies to submit full incident reports with all applicable segments. Group B offenses are generally less serious offenses, and the FBI requires only that arrest reports be submitted. Table 5.1a lists all Group A offenses by offense category (person, property, and society), and Table 5.1b provides all Group B offenses by offense category.

An NIBRS Group A offense incident report consists of six different segments:

- Administrative
- Offense
- Property
- Victim
- Offender
- Arrestee

A Group A offense incident report can have only one administrative segment but can generate multiple records of the other five segments. The NIBRS allows up to 10 different offenses per incident report, with each offense triggering a separate offense segment record. The FBI's UCR offense hierarchy rule for selecting only the most serious offense in an incident is not used in the NIBRS. Each offense is recorded once per incident regardless of the number of victims or the number of perpetrators.

The victim data segment in a Group A offense incident report can contain up to 999 victim records, with each record providing detailed information on each victim. Similarly, the offender segment can contain up to 99 unique offender records, and the arrestee segment can contain up to 99 unique arrestee records. The property segment can contain up to 6 types of property loss, each of which is matched with a separate property segment record that can provide further details of the property. A Group B offense arrest report, which consists of only one data segment, can contain up to 99 separate arrestee segment records for a single Group B offense.

A key advantage of the NIBRS is its hierarchical structure. Essentially, the NIBRS

Table 5.1a   Group A Offenses

NIBRS Offense	Crime Category
Arson	Property
Assault offenses	
Aggravated assault	Person
Simple assault	Person
Intimidation	Person
Bribery	Property
Burglary/Breaking and entering	Property
Counterfeiting/Forgery	Property
Destruction/Damage/Vandalism of property	Property
Drug/Narcotic offenses	
Drug/Narcotic violations	Society
Drug equipment violations	Society
Embezzlement	Property
Extortion/Blackmail	Property
Fraud offenses	
False pretenses/Swindle/Confidence game	Property
Credit card/Automatic teller machine fraud	Property
Impersonation	Property
Welfare fraud	Property
Wire fraud	Property
Gambling offenses	
Betting/Wagering	Society
Operating/Promoting/Assisting gambling	Society
Gambling equipment violations	Society
Sports tampering	Society
Homicide offenses	
Murder and nonnegligent manslaughter	Person
Negligent manslaughter	Person
Justifiable homicide	Not a crime
Kidnapping/Abduction	Person
Larceny/Theft offenses	Property
Pocket picking	Property
Purse snatching	Property
Shoplifting	Property
Theft from building	Property
Theft from coin-operated machine or device	Property
Theft from motor vehicle	Property
Theft of motor vehicle parts or accessories	Property
All other larceny	Property
Motor vehicle theft	Property
Pornography/Obscene material	Society
Prostitution offenses	
Prostitution	Society
Assisting or promoting prostitution	Society
Robbery	Property
Sex offenses, forcible	
Forcible rape	Person
Forcible sodomy	Person
Sexual assault with an object	Person
Forcible fondling (child)	Person
Sex offenses, nonforcible	
Incest	Person
Statutory rape	Person
Stolen property offenses	Property
Weapon law violations	Society

Table 5.1b   Group B Offenses

NIBRS Offense	Crime Category
Bad checks	Property
Curfew/Loitering/Vagrancy violations	Society
Disorderly conduct	Society
Driving under the influence	Society
Drunkenness	Society
Family offenses, nonviolent	Person
Liquor law violations	Society
Peeping Tom	Society
Runaway	Not a crime
Trespass of real property	Society

functions as a relational database and, as such, permits linkages between segments. For instance, offenders can be linked with victims, and victims can be linked with details related to the offense segment, property segment, and so forth. These links are important for analyzing individual-level offenses as well as for providing far greater insights into the circumstances and nuances of criminal incidents.

There are 52 distinct data elements related to the different segments. Table 5.2 provides a list of the data elements by segment.

Quality Control and the NIBRS Certification Process

The NIBRS takes advantage of the reporting process established for the UCR program during the late 1960s. Local law enforcement agencies submit their data directly to the state's centralized UCR program. The state, in turn, submits to the FBI all data reported to its central repository. Although the FBI implemented a certification process for states reporting UCR data during the late 1960s, the certification criteria were fairly limited. With the introduction of the NIBRS, the FBI changed the rules considerably.

For the NIBRS, the FBI designed an extensive set of quality control standards to be applied throughout the data entry and submission processes to reduce the extent of missing information and data entry error in the database. Quality control is exerted at three stages in the data entry process. First, as part of the certification for a local department to qualify for submitting NIBRS data, the agency's RMS must meet certain data entry quality control requirements. Second, the local department must submit its data to a centralized state data repository that also must be certified to meet the FBI's quality control standards.[5] Finally, when the FBI receives the data from the state, the data are processed through more than 300 different quality control checks. Incidents not meeting the FBI's standards are rejected and returned to the locality for correction. The locality can resubmit the incidents once the missing details or errors are corrected. Unlike the UCR system, which does not allow for updates and corrections, the NIBRS allows for updates and corrections for up to 1 year beyond the end of the calendar year of the incidents. The FBI conducts audits of each state's data system to verify the resubmission of rejected incidents. Unfortunately, as the FBI admits, follow-up on resubmission of rejected incidents has lagged behind expectations. Still, the NIBRS data are by far the most comprehensive and best quality official law enforcement data available at the state and national levels.

Table 5.2   NIBRS Offense Group A Data Elements by Segment

Administrative Segment

Number	Data Element	Requirement	Occurrence(s)
1[a]	ORI number	Mandatory	Single
2[a]	Incident number	Mandatory	Single
3	Incident date/hour	Mandatory	Single
4	Cleared exceptionally	Mandatory	Single
5	Exceptional clearance date	Conditional	Single

Offense Segment

Number	Data Element	Requirement	Occurrence(s)
1[a]	ORI number	Mandatory	Single
2[a]	Incident number	Mandatory	Single
6	UCR offense code	Mandatory	Single
7	Offense attempted/completed	Mandatory	Single
8	Offender(s) suspected of using	Mandatory	Multiple
8[a]	Bias motivation	Mandatory	Single
9	Location type	Mandatory	Single
10	Number of premises entered	Conditional	Single
11	Method of entry	Conditional	Single
12	Type of criminal activity	Conditional	Multiple
13	Type of weapon/force involved	Conditional	Multiple

Property Segment

Number	Data Element	Requirement	Occurrence(s)
1[a]	ORI number	Mandatory	Single
2[a]	Incident number	Mandatory	Single
14	Type of property loss, etc.	Conditional	Single
15	Property description[b]	Conditional	Multiple
16	Value of property	Conditional	Single
17	Date recovered	Conditional	Single
18	Number of stolen motor vehicles	Conditional	Single
19	Number of recovered motor vehicles	Conditional	Single
20	Suspected drug type[c]	Conditional	Multiple
21	Estimated drug quantity	Conditional	Single
22	Type of drug measurement	Conditional	Single

Victim Segment

Number	Data Element	Requirement	Occurrence(s)
1[a]	ORI number	Mandatory	Single
2[a]	Incident number	Mandatory	Single
23	Victim (sequence) number	Mandatory	Single
24	Victim connected to UCR offense code(s)	Mandatory	Multiple
25	Type of victim	Mandatory	Single
26	Age (of victim)	Conditional	Single
27	Sex (of victim)	Conditional	Single
28	Race (of victim)	Conditional	Single

Number	Data Element	Requirement	Occurrence(s)
29	Ethnicity (of victim)	Conditional/Optional	Single
30	Resident status (of victim)	Conditional/Optional	Single
31	Aggravated assault/Homicide circumstances	Conditional	Multiple
32	Additional justifiable homicide circumstances	Conditional	Single
33	Type of injury	Conditional	Multiple
34	Offender number(s) to be related[d]	Conditional	Multiple
35	Relationship(s) of victim to offender(s)	Conditional	Single

Offender Segment

Number	Data Element	Requirement	Occurrence(s)
1[a]	ORI number	Mandatory	Single
2[a]	Incident number	Mandatory	Single
36	Offender (sequence) number	Mandatory	Single
37	Age (of offender)	Mandatory	Single
38	Sex (of offender)	Mandatory	Single
39	Race (of offender)	Mandatory	Single

Arrestee Segment

Number	Data Element	Requirement	Occurrence(s)
1[a]	ORI number	Mandatory	Single
2[a]	Incident number	Mandatory	Single
40	Arrestee (sequence) number	Mandatory	Single
41	Arrest (transaction) number	Mandatory	Single
42	Arrest date	Mandatory	Single
43	Type of arrest	Mandatory	Single
44	Multiple arrestee segments indicator	Mandatory	Single
45	UCR arrest offense code	Mandatory	Single
46	Arrestee was armed	Mandatory	Multiple
47	Age (of arrestee)	Mandatory	Single
48	Sex (of arrestee)	Mandatory	Single
49	Race (of arrestee)	Mandatory	Single
50	Ethnicity (of arrestee)	Optional	Single
51	Resident status (of arrestee)	Optional	Single
52	Disposition of arrestee under 18 years of age	Conditional	Single

a. Data elements 1 and 2 are repeated to allow links between all of the segments related to one incident.

b. Each property description category that is reported should also include a corresponding value of property for that category and the date the recovered property is entered.

c. Each reported drug type that is entered should also include an estimated quantity of the drug and the type of drug measurement used.

d. The offender sequence number identifies the connection between each offender and each victim in an incident. An offender can have only one offender–victim relationship recorded for each victim to which he or she is linked.

Implementation of the NIBRS

With the publication of the *Blueprint* in 1985 (Poggio et al., 1985), the FBI had the "blueprint" to begin implementing a reporting process that would require the voluntary cooperation and support of more than 17,000 federal, state, and local law enforcement agencies. The first step for the FBI was to develop the necessary data collection and reporting specifications. To achieve this, the FBI enlisted the cooperation of the potential submitters and users of the data: local and state law enforcement.

Despite publication of the first data collection and reporting specification manuals in 1988, submission of NIBRS data was still several years off. The first official NIBRS data were received by the FBI in January 1991. Between 1991 and 1996, the number of agencies reporting NIBRS data increased at a fairly slow rate, and most of the agencies reporting data during this period were small to medium-sized agencies.

In 1997, the BJS commissioned SEARCH, the National Consortium for Justice Information and Statistics, to conduct a study of large law enforcement agencies from around the United States to identify the impediments that were preventing these agencies from implementing the NIBRS. A second goal of the SEARCH project was to identify "promising and cost-effective approaches to encouraging wider adoption of NIBRS" (BJS, 1997, p. iii). SEARCH, through surveys and a series of focus group sessions, identified seven major impediments to the development of a NIBRS-compatible system by large law enforcement agencies. These impediments, in order of importance, are as follows:

1. Funding
2. Uncertainty of benefits
3. Policy concerns
4. Administrative issues
5. Federal and state reporting
6. Data elements
7. Education

The top two impediments, funding and uncertainty of benefits, have plagued the development of the NIBRS since the beginning. As with the UCR program, the NIBRS is a voluntary reporting system. State and local law enforcement agencies participate in the FBI's reporting program at their own discretion and, in many cases, at their own expense. For many large departments, the cost of modifying their existing systems or of purchasing new RMSs is significant. Without funding support or a better understanding of the benefits of using the NIBRS, there is little incentive for making the transition.

One technique used by a few states (e.g., Virginia, Tennessee, Idaho) was to mandate that for a law enforcement agency to qualify for state funding, the jurisdiction would be required to report NIBRS data by a set deadline. For these states, that was the impetus they needed to become NIBRS-certified states. But not all states are willing or able to make these types of demands.

NIBRS implementation received a major boost in 2001 when the BJS issued a solicitation for applications to receive funding for large law enforcement agencies to develop NIBRS-compatible systems. The BJS awarded slightly more than $13 million to qualified state UCR programs, with 95% of the funding going to large law enforcement agencies and 5% going to the states for program administration. A total of 26 state UCR programs received funding under the BJS program.[6]

Although the FBI is responsible for overall NIBRS development, the BJS has contributed a significant amount of funding for the implementation of NIBRS programs at the state and local levels. In addition to direct funding through the NIBRS Implementation Program, the BJS has provided funding to the Police

Executive Research Forum (PERF) to hold a national conference devoted solely to the NIBRS. In July 2001, the PERF held the first NIBRS Symposium in Baltimore, Maryland. The conference brought in presenters from local, state, and federal agencies to discuss the pros and cons of the NIBRS. The BJS has also provided funding to SEARCH to conduct focus group sessions with law enforcement around the country to discuss issues related to implementing the NIBRS.

Limitations of the NIBRS

One of the advantages that the NIBRS has over the summary-based UCR system is the introduction of an elaborate process for certifying state and local law enforcement. However, this is also one of the obstacles that is limiting participation by agencies. Many state and local agencies may have the data elements necessary to meet the NIBRS standards but might not have the more than 300 edit and error checks built into their RMSs to meet the data quality requirements specified by the FBI.

Like the UCR program, the NIBRS is a voluntary reporting system for local and state law enforcement. Unfortunately, this fact plays an important role in a state or local agency's decision to participate in the NIBRS. To meet the rigid NIBRS criteria, many law enforcement agencies might need to make significant alterations to their RMSs or purchase new RMSs. An agency's RMS might contain all of the required data elements, but if the RMS does not meet the error rate (3% error or less) or the statistical reasonableness criteria, the agency's data will not be accepted by the FBI. For many agencies, whether they be state or local, the cost associated with transitioning to the NIBRS can be significant. Without a strong reason for law enforcement agencies to comply, they generally will not make the move to the NIBRS. Consequently, over the first 13 years of the NIBRS, many

state and local agencies have been slow in transitioning to NIBRS-certified RMSs.[7]

In addition to concerns about cost and the difficulties of meeting quality control standards, there is another factor that may impede the movement toward nationwide adoption of the NIBRS. Police executives, aware that replacing the UCR system with the NIBRS is likely to produce an artificial increase in crime rates (especially as a result of elimination of the hierarchy rule), may be reluctant to adopt the NIBRS. They may fear that reports of increased crime rates may produce a backlash and that the public may believe that explanations suggesting that the increased crime rates are the result of changes in the crime reporting system are simply attempts by law enforcement officials to manipulate statistics and shift the responsibility for the perceived crime increase elsewhere. Therefore, prior to adopting the NIBRS, it is important to educate the press and the public about the very real increases in crime rates that a move to the NIBRS is likely to produce.

During the early years of its existence, the NIBRS was criticized as being slow to develop. A particular concern was that the submitted data were not representative of the nation as a whole because the only departments reporting data to the NIBRS were small to medium-sized agencies. However, since the introduction of the NIBRS, the number of agencies submitting incident-level data had risen to more than 4,000 in 21 states by 2001. As of December 2003, all but 5 states either were NIBRS certified or were developing their statewide programs toward certification. Although the agency size issue may have been valid during the first few years of reporting, recent funding by the BJS and a dedicated effort by the Criminal Justice Information Services (CJIS) division of the FBI have paid off, with many more large cities and counties participating in the program. In the 2001 NIBRS database, there were 180 agencies representing populations in excess of 100,000 and 53 agencies representing jurisdictions with populations in excess of 250,000.

As a database, the NIBRS is not without criticism. It contains official police data and, consequently, has limitations. Not all incidents are reported to the police, and some incidents to which the police respond are not recorded. The NIBRS, like the original UCR summary-based system, is dependent on the public to report all incidents and on the police to record all incidents to which they respond.

POLICY IMPLICATIONS

It is easy to say that a system like the NIBRS has significant potential. However, until law enforcement, policymakers, and researchers have begun to use the data, it is impossible to show how that potential can be realized. For research purposes, NIBRS data can unofficially be divided into two phases. Phase 1 of NIBRS data collection began in January 1991, when the FBI first received NIBRS data, and continued through the end of 1995, when many of the problems with the early reporting of NIBRS had been resolved.[8] Consequently, Phase 2 may be considered to have started in 1996.

With the array of information obtained on every incident reported to police, the NIBRS possesses significant potential to affect policy directives issued for individual jurisdictions, regions, states or groups of states, and the nation as a whole. Moreover, the NIBRS has the potential to exert influence not only on police policy but also on other segments of the criminal justice system, such as prosecutors' offices, court systems, and correctional systems, that receive cases from the police and whose levels of activity are influenced by police policy and practice.

The fact that the NIBRS gathers detailed information on the incident level means that a contributing police jurisdiction can conduct detailed analysis of any of the 46 types of criminal activity covered by the NIBRS to discern patterns in the commission of those offenses. For example, if a jurisdiction were concerned about the commission of burglary, a detailed examination of the relevant NIBRS data elements might be conducted. Depending on the outcome of analysis of factors such as the types of premise most commonly being burglarized, the modes of entry being employed, and the times of illegal entry, preventive measures involving target hardening and reallocation of patrol might be recommended. Most important, all policy initiatives would be based on the results of empirical research.

The NIBRS can also be used to examine the police response to any one of those 46 types of criminal activity. For example, there has historically been a concern that the victim–offender relationship has unduly influenced the police response to assaults, with offenders who are related to, or living with, their victims being less likely to be arrested than those who are not related to, or living with, their victims. In particular, husbands were perceived as getting away with abuse, with marriage licenses constituting "hitting licenses." Now, with the advent of pro-arrest and mandatory arrest policies, some argue that the pendulum has swung too far in the other direction. Using data from the NIBRS, it is possible to examine whether similar incidents involving husbands and wives are less likely, equally likely, or more likely to end up with the offender being arrested compared with incidents involving other types of victim–offender relationships. Depending on the outcome of analysis of the relevant NIBRS data and the goals sought by the policymakers, changes in police arrest policy may be made.

The NIBRS clearly provides sufficient data to conduct in-depth examination of police practices in a single jurisdiction. Because offenders move with ease from jurisdiction to jurisdiction, however, a crime problem is generally not confined to a single jurisdiction. The commonality of data elements in the NIBRS, the provision of an extensive set of quality control standards throughout the data entry and submission processes, and the thorough monitoring of those quality control standards exercised by the FBI ensure that comparable quality data can be obtained for a wide array of contributing jurisdictions. A regional approach, rather than a local approach, is required to combat the problems posed by illegal drug use. For example, Faggiani and McLaughlin (1999) use NIBRS data from Virginia to examine the possession and sale/distribution of drugs in three Virginia communities. Using data from three noncontiguous jurisdictions, this study demonstrates the potential strategic uses of the NIBRS for identifying drug incidents across jurisdictional boundaries and developing policy based on analysis of these incidents.

In another study, Faggiani, Bibel, and Brensilber (2001) build on the work of Faggiani and McLaughlin (1999) by using an enhanced version of the NIBRS to identify and map heroin-related drug incidents in Worcester, Massachusetts, and adjacent communities. Massachusetts is the first state to include street address details with the reporting of the NIBRS data. Faggiani and colleagues (2001) demonstrate that the addition of address details to the already rich NIBRS data structure takes the data to a higher tactical level. These authors use the data to graphically display and analyze individual heroin incidents within Worcester and the surrounding region without the need for specialized multijurisdictional agreements that had to be negotiated before the introduction of the NIBRS.[9] Their work demonstrates vividly how the NIBRS can promote true regional problem solving and policy analysis that heretofore was unavailable without specialized agreements.

As noted previously, in 2001, there were more than 4,000 jurisdictions in 21 states contributing to the NIBRS. Although there are some problems with the current representation of jurisdictions in the NIBRS, with large jurisdictions and western states still somewhat underrepresented in the database, the NIBRS database provides sufficiently large and diverse coverage of jurisdictions that analyses of crime patterns and the police response nationwide can be conducted. In the next section, we examine the issue of "dual arrest" in intimate partner violence cases and discuss how the NIBRS has been used to assess the extent of dual arrest nationwide and how policy recommendations can emerge from that assessment.

To date, we have focused on the use of the NIBRS as a sole data source. Clearly, the data from the NIBRS can be supplemented by data from a wide variety of sources, thereby enhancing their potential utility. The variety of possible units of analysis provided by the NIBRS (incident, offender, victim, arrestee, property, and jurisdiction) allows a wide range of additional information. For example, sociodemographic information on jurisdictions and case processing information on arrestees may be added to the NIBRS database. In the case study described in the next section, we observe how data obtained from analyses of state statutes were added to the NIBRS database to allow examination of the effect of legislative provisions on the police response to assault and intimidation cases.

CASE STUDY: USING THE NIBRS FOR DOMESTIC VIOLENCE RESEARCH

Since the 1970s, as a result of political pressure exerted by women's groups, lawsuits brought against police departments for negligence and failure to provide equal protection to female victims in intimate partner violence situations (see, e.g., *Bruno v. Codd,* 1979; *Scott v. Hart,* 1976; *Thurman et al. v. City of Torrington,* 1984), and the results of the Minneapolis Domestic Violence Experiment (Sherman & Berk, 1984a, 1984b), there has been a nationwide movement toward arrest as the preferred police response to domestic violence. As of January 1, 2002, 23 states had mandatory arrest laws, and 6 states had preferred arrest laws, for misdemeanor domestic violence cases. In addition, 33 states mandated arrest when responding officers had probable cause to believe that restraining orders had been violated (Hirschel & Buzawa, 2002, pp. 1451–1454).

As would be expected, research has indicated that the number of domestic violence arrests generally increased after the implementation of mandatory or pro-arrest laws and policies (see, e.g., Lawrenz, Lembo, & Schade, 1988; Municipality of Anchorage, Alaska, 2000, pp. 8–9; Office of the Attorney General, State of California, 1999; Wanless, 1996, pp. 558–559; Zorza & Woods, 1994, p. 12). Embedded in the general increase in arrests for domestic violence offenses was an increase in the number of cases in which the police arrested both the victim and the offender as mutual combatants, resulting in what are known as dual arrests (see, e.g., Epstein, 1987; Haviland, Frye, Rajah, Thukral, & Trinity, 2001; Martin, 1997; Saunders, 1995; Victim Services Agency, 1988; Zorza & Woods, 1994, pp. 17–18).

This increase in dual arrests has raised concerns. It is possible that these arrests of women are justified by the circumstances confronting the responding police officers. These women may be the aggressors, or the incidents may involve mutual acts of violence by the involved parties. It is also plausible, however, that these arrests are not justified. In cases of dual arrest, the police may be unable to determine a primary aggressor, and this may result in female victims being arrested along with their batterers. This may be especially likely in cases where there are minor injuries to both parties but there are no weapons or witnesses as well as no history of violence by either party. Same-sex relationships may be particularly vulnerable to dual arrests because the police may have increased difficulty in determining a primary aggressor due to similar physical strength. It is also possible that women are being arrested in circumstances where male batterers would not be arrested. In addition, there may be cases where the wrong party is arrested, that is, where defensive injuries are mistaken for offensive injuries (Hirschel & Buzawa, 2002, pp. 1449–1450).

To date, there has been little detailed research conducted on dual arrests. The research that has been performed has been piecemeal and limited to a single site or jurisdiction (see, e.g., Epstein, 1987; Martin, 1997; Saunders, 1995; Victim Services Agency, 1988; Zorza & Woods, 1994, pp. 17–18). It is unclear how broad a problem dual arrests constitute or what the prevalence rate of dual assaults is nationwide. Furthermore, it is unknown to what extent different rates of dual arrest are explained by differences in state legal structure (e.g., the existence of mandatory arrest and primary aggressor laws), differences in offender and victim characteristics (e.g., age, race, relationship), and differences in incident characteristics (e.g., injury, weapon).

A project funded by the National Institute of Justice is currently examining these issues.[10] As part of that project, the research team has been investigating the extent to which dual arrests occur nationwide both in nondomestic and domestic violence cases as well as the extent to which dual arrest prevalence rates vary in relation to the legal structure under which the police operate.

The best data source for examining the prevalence of dual arrest at the national level is the NIBRS because it provides incident-based information reported to the police in every jurisdiction that contributes to the NIBRS. Thus, researchers can examine the background characteristics of every reported incident and analyze the factors that result in the police arresting one of the involved parties, both of the involved parties (dual arrest), or none of the involved parties. As discussed previously, the data provide the information required for empirically based policy directives at the individual jurisdictional level. Despite its limitations in terms of underrepresentation of large and western jurisdictions, the NIBRS includes a sufficiently broad-based representation of jurisdictions throughout the United States to provide an indication of the situation nationwide.

Because the vast majority of domestic violence cases involve assault (see, e.g., Rennison, 2003; Greenfeld et al., 1998), the decision was made to limit the study to incidents in which the most serious offense reported to the police was aggravated assault, simple assault, or intimidation. The period chosen for the study was calendar year 2000.

The NIBRS database was supplemented by variables taken from analysis of state statutes. The key legal variable on which we focus in this chapter is the variable that represents the authority that state law gives police officers to make a warrantless arrest in a domestic violence case: whether under state law an officer *must* make an arrest if he or she finds probable cause to believe that an offense has been committed (mandatory arrest), whether state law instructs the responding officer that he or she *should* make an arrest (preferred arrest), or whether state law leaves the decision of whether to make an arrest up to the responding officer (discretionary arrest). In calendar year 2000, the year on which this study focuses, there were 23 states (including the District of Columbia) with mandatory arrest, and 6 states with preferred arrest, statutory provisions for officers responding to

the scene of a domestic violence incident.[11] In nondomestic cases, the law empowers, but does not generally mandate or indicate a preference for arrest, when an officer finds probable cause to believe that an offense has been committed.

A total of 2,821 police jurisdictions from 19 states contributed assault and intimidation cases to the NIBRS database used in this study. Of these 19 states, 8 had statutory provisions that mandated warrantless arrest in domestic violence cases,[12] 4 had preferred statutory provisions,[13] and 7 had discretionary arrest provisions.[14] For analytic purposes, the category of "domestic" is subdivided into "intimate partner" and "other domestic."[15] The "nondomestic" category is subdivided into "nondomestic but known to victim" and "stranger."[16]

As can be seen from Table 5.3, a total of 577,862 incidents of assault and intimidation were reported to these police jurisdictions in 2000. Of these incidents, 39.7% involved intimate partners, 14.2% involved other domestic situations, 36.7% involved nondomestic situations where the victim and offender knew each other, and 9.3% involved situations where the victim and offender were strangers. The majority (68.2%) of these incidents were cases of simple assault with either minor injury (42.0% of the cases) or no injury (53.8% of the cases) to the victim. Nondomestic cases were more likely than domestic cases to involve aggravated assault or intimidation and to result in serious physical injury (Tables 5.4 and 5.5).

The *police disposition* variable consists of three categories: (1) no arrest, (2) one or more offenders arrested, and (3) two or more parties, identified as both victims and offenders, arrested (dual arrest). A total arrest rate is obtained by adding categories 2 and 3.

Overall, 37.0% of the incidents resulted in the arrest of an offender.[17] Domestic cases were more likely than nondomestic cases to result in the arrest of an offender. Whereas

Table 5.3   Type of Victim–Offender Relationship

	Frequency	Percentage	Valid Percentage
Intimate partner	197,064	34.1	39.7
Other domestic	70,707	12.2	14.2
Nondomestic, known	182,448	31.6	36.7
Stranger	46,254	8.0	9.3
Missing	81,389	14.1	
	577,862	100.0	100.0

Table 5.4   Most Serious Offense by Victim–Offender Relationship

		Most Serious Offense Against the Victim			
		Aggravated Assault	Simple Assault	Intimidation	Total
Victim–Offender Relationship	Intimate partner	25,495 12.9%	150,758 76.5%	20,811 10.6%	197,064 100.0%
	Other domestic	11,068 15.7%	52,981 74.9%	6,658 9.4%	70,707 100.0%
	Nondomestic, known	33,506 18.4%	108,907 59.7%	40,035 21.9%	182,448 100.0%
	Stranger	12,311 26.6%	25,768 55.7%	8,175 17.7%	46,254 100.0%
Total		82,380	338,414	75,679	496,473

Table 5.5   Most Serious Victim Injury by Victim–Offender Relationship

		Most Serious Victim Injury			
		Serious Physical Injury	Apparent Minor Injury	No Injury	Total
Victim–Offender Relationship	Intimate partner	5,759 2.9%	94,819 48.1%	96,486 49.0%	197,064 100.0%
	Other domestic	2,365 3.3%	31,024 43.9%	37,318 52.8%	70,707 100.0%
	Nondomestic, known	9,415 5.2%	67,184 36.8%	105,849 58.0%	182,448 100.0%
	Stranger	3,212 6.9%	15,453 33.4%	27,589 59.6%	46,254 100.0%
Total		20,751 4.2%	208,480 42.0%	267,242 53.8%	496,473 100.0%

Table 5.6   Police Disposition of Incident by Victim–Offender Relationship

		Police Disposition			
		No Arrest	*One or More Arrests*	*Dual Arrest*	*Total*
Victim–Offender Relationship	Intimate partner	98,753	94,515	3,796	197,064
		50.1%	48.0%	1.9%	100.0%
	Other domestic	39,242	30,424	1,041	70,707
		55.5%	43.0%	1.5%	100.0%
	Nondomestic, known	129,277	51,344	1,827	182,448
		70.9%	28.1%	1.0%	100.0%
	Stranger	30,052	16,025	177	46,254
		65.0%	34.6%	0.4%	100.0%
Total		297,324	192,308	6,841	496,473
		59.9%	38.7%	1.4%	100.0%

49.9% of intimate partner cases and 44.5% of other domestic cases resulted in the arrest of at least one offender, only 35.0% of the cases in which the victim and offender were strangers and 29.1% of the nondomestic cases in which the victim and offender knew each other ended up with the arrest of at least one offender (Table 5.6). In terms of dual arrest, whereas 1.9% of intimate partner cases and 1.5% of other domestic cases resulted in the arrest of at least two parties who were both victims and offenders, 1.0% of nondomestic cases where the victim and offender knew each other and 0.4% of the cases where the victim and offender were strangers resulted in such a dual arrest (Table 5.6).

Of major interest to researchers, practitioners, and policymakers is the issue of whether arrest is more likely to occur in jurisdictions with mandatory, as opposed to preferred or discretionary, arrest statutes. Although these statutory provisions apply only to domestic violence cases, we examined the likelihood of arrest in all assault and intimidation cases to observe whether there might be any spillover effect on nondomestic cases.

Earlier, we reported that 37.0% of the incidents to which police responded resulted in the arrest of an offender. Whereas 32.3% of cases in jurisdictions with discretionary police arrest powers and 33% of the cases in states with preferred police arrest powers resulted in an arrest, 41.9% of the cases in states with mandatory arrest powers resulted in the arrest of an offender (Table 5.7). Higher dual arrest rates form part of the higher total arrest rate. Whereas 0.7% of cases in jurisdictions with discretionary police arrest powers and 0.6% of the cases in states with preferred police arrest powers resulted in a dual arrest, 1.9% of the cases in states with mandatory arrest powers resulted in a dual arrest (Table 5.7). These patterns were observed when we controlled for measures of seriousness of offense such as offense type, victim injury, and presence of weapon.[18]

When we examine police disposition by police warrantless arrest powers while controlling for victim–offender relationship, we see that regardless of the nature of the victim–offender relationship, cases in jurisdictions with mandatory arrest statutes are more likely to result in the arrest of an offender than are cases in discretionary or preferred jurisdictions. This is true with regard to single, dual, and total arrest rates (Table 5.8).

Table 5.7   Police Disposition by Police Warrantless Arrest Powers

		Police Disposition			
		No Arrest	One or More Arrests	Actual Dual Arrest	Total
Warrantless Arrest	Discretionary	118,158 67.7%	55,084 31.6%	1,235 0.7%	174,477 100.0%
	Preferred	88,062 67.0%	42,616 32.4%	838 0.6%	131,516 100.0%
	Mandatory	158,044 58.1%	108,670 40.0%	5,155 1.9%	271,869 100.0%
Total		364,264 63.0%	206,370 35.7%	7,228 1.3%	577,862 100.0%

Thus, although the mandatory arrest provisions apply only to domestic violence cases, there appears to be a spillover effect in mandatory arrest states, with officers in those states more likely than their counterparts in other states to arrest offenders in both domestic and nondomestic violence cases.

Removing officer discretion and requiring mandatory arrest in domestic violence cases may have implications with regard to the manner in which officers perceive their role in general. Mandatory arrest may lead officers to believe that there has been a shift both in their role and in their organizations' role, conforming more with Wilson's (1968) definition of a legalistic department. Officers may believe that it is inappropriate (or unacceptable) to exercise discretion, instead following a legalistic, somewhat mechanistic style in applying the law. This may have implications for police departments attempting to integrate domestic violence protocols into a community policing framework. They may find an inherent tension between attempting to problem solve and respond to specific individual and/or group needs and adhering to a generic mandated response to a broad range of diverse incidents.

Along with higher overall arrest rates, states with mandatory arrest statutes are producing higher dual arrest rates than are states with preferred or discretionary arrest statutes. Overall, the dual arrest rate is low at 1.3%. However, whereas the dual arrest rate is 0.7% in discretionary arrest states and 0.6% in preferred arrest states, it is 1.9% in mandatory arrest states. Although dual arrest rates are higher for domestic cases than for nondomestic cases, dual arrest rates are higher in mandatory arrest states regardless of the victim–offender relationship. Again, there would appear to be a spillover effect in operation. The circumstances associated with dual arrests remain to be more fully explored. Of more than passing interest is the fact that although 4.1% of the incidents to which police respond are identified as involving potential dual arrests, only 1.3% of the incidents—or 31.7% of the incidents identified as involving potential dual arrest situations—actually result in dual arrests (Hirschel, Buzawa, Faggiani, Reuland, & Pattavina, 2003). There are several possible explanations for this that need to be examined further. Evidentiary considerations, the behavior of the involved parties, and workload all may influence these decisions.

These preliminary results suggest that laws do have an effect on police operations and that

Table 5.8   Police Disposition by Police Warrantless Arrest Powers Controlling for Victim–Offender Relationship

Victim–Offender Relationship			Police Disposition			
			No Arrest	One or More Arrests	Actual Dual Arrest	Total
Intimate partner	Warrantless arrest	Discretionary	30,447	26,528	751	57,726
			52.7%	46.0%	1.3%	100.0%
		Preferred	26,161	20,755	563	47,479
			55.1%	43.7%	1.2%	100.0%
		Mandatory	42,145	47,232	2,482	91,859
			45.9%	51.4%	2.7%	100.0%
	Total		98,753	94,515	3,796	197,064
			50.1%	48.0%	1.9%	100.0%
Other domestic	Warrantless arrest	Discretionary	12,578	8,729	178	21,485
			58.5%	40.6%	0.8%	100.0%
		Preferred	8,498	6,556	130	15,184
			56.0%	43.2%	0.9%	100.0%
		Mandatory	18,166	15,139	733	34,038
			53.4%	44.5%	2.2%	100.0%
	Total		39,242	30,424	1,041	70,707
			55.5%	43.0%	1.5%	100.0%
Nondomestic, known	Warrantless arrest	Discretionary	43,619	12,813	254	56,686
			76.9%	22.6%	0.4%	100.0%
		Preferred	26,085	8,249	127	34,461
			75.7%	23.9%	0.4%	100.0%
		Mandatory	59,573	30,282	1,446	91,301
			65.2%	33.2%	1.6%	100.0%
	Total		129,277	51,344	1,827	182,448
			70.9%	28.1%	1.0%	100.0%
Stranger	Warrantless arrest	Discretionary	7,880	3,916	23	11,819
			66.7%	33.1%	0.2%	100.0%
		Preferred	6,605	3,119	7	9,731
			67.9%	32.1%	0.1%	100.0%
		Mandatory	15,567	8,990	147	24,704
			63.0%	36.4%	0.6%	100.0%
	Total		30,052	16,025	177	46,254
			65.0%	34.6%	0.4%	100.0%

the domestic violence laws influence a broader range of cases than is intended. For those interested in simply increasing overall arrest rates, the initial message appears clear: Adopt a mandatory arrest policy. At this stage, however, such a policy recommendation would constitute a case of proceeding too far on the basis of too little evidence. More detailed examination of the factors that lead to arrest (whether of one or both parties to the incident), and of what happens to cases after arrests have been made, is needed. For example, we need to examine the effect of mandatory arrest laws on specific subpopulations such as Blacks and same-sex couples. We need to examine the variation that exists both among and within states in arrest rates. Finally, we need to examine whether higher arrest rates are associated with increased victim safety or reduced reoffending.

CONCLUSION

The NIBRS, as discussed in this chapter, constitutes a substantial improvement over the UCR system and has the potential to provide policymakers at the local, state, and national levels with a powerful tool for analyzing crime and developing empirically based crime policy. Whereas the UCR system, for the most part, simply provided summary data on a limited number of crimes, the NIBRS has been designed to produce incident-based data on 46 different offenses. With a wide array of standardized data elements in the system and the rigorous quality control tests that the data have undergone, the NIBRS provides a sound database for public policy either on its own or, as demonstrated in the case study presented, in conjunction with other data sources.

However, jurisdictions are not required to adopt the NIBRS, and a number of factors may incline them not to adopt it. The costs of implementing and maintaining the NIBRS, difficulties in complying with the rigorous quality control standards, and concerns about possible political fallout as a result of increases in crime rates attributable to the move to using the NIBRS instead of the UCR system may impede a jurisdiction's decision to adopt the NIBRS until that jurisdiction is clearly convinced that the benefits of using the NIBRS outweigh the perceived costs. It is hoped that by conducting the types of single- and multijurisdictional studies discussed in this chapter and demonstrating the benefits of these studies, the utility of the NIBRS will become self-evident and even more jurisdictions will adopt the NIBRS. The case study examined in this chapter demonstrates that the NIBRS already includes a sufficient number of jurisdictions to conduct a meaningful analysis of police practice nationwide. However, the database will only be strengthened as more large police departments and more departments in underrepresented areas of the nation adopt the NIBRS.

NOTES

1. Arson was added to the list of reported index crimes in 1971.

2. For a full discussion of the UCR program, see Federal Bureau of Investigation (2002).

3. For a more detailed discussion of the impact of the LEAA and other changes in reporting, see Maltz (1999).

4. As discussed previously, the incident-level details provided through the SHR, a later addition, includes basic demographic information on homicide victims and persons arrested in the incidents.

5. The FBI (2002) states,

> In order for a state UCR Program to be certified for NIBRS data submission, the Program must be approved by the NIBRS Certification Board. . . . The Board is required to review and approve particular elements of the state Program including system description/compatibility, error rates, statistical reasonableness, and the updating capability and responsiveness of the submitting state. In order to further ensure the statistical reasonableness of all test data being submitted for certification purposes, the Board has elected to employ the national UCR Program's Quality Assurance Review (QAR) team to assist in this check. In general, the mission of the QAR is to assess the validity of the reported data through the review of local agency case reports. (p. 7)

6. The BJS has a list of the award amounts, the goals for each of the state awards, and the jurisdictions participating on its website (www.ojp.usdoj.gov/bjs/nibrsawd.htm).

7. The NIBRS certification and reporting process is extensive and well beyond the scope of this chapter. For a full explanation and description for reporting the NIBRS, refer to the FBI's NIBRS website (www.fbi.gov/ucr/ucr.htm) or contact the FBI's Criminal Justice Information Systems (CJIS) division for hard copies of the manuals.

8. For several reasons, data reported to the FBI during the Phase 1 time frame are sketchy, incomplete, and somewhat unreliable. For example, after reviewing the data from Alabama, one of the first contributors of NIBRS data, the FBI questioned why all of the incidents in that state reported only one offense per incident given that the NIBRS was intentionally designed to collect data on all offenses committed during an incident. It was discovered that the UCR program in Alabama had set up its NIBRS system to conform to the UCR offense hierarchical rule and was reporting only the most serious offense for each incident. After much discussion between the FBI's CJIS division and the UCR program officials in Alabama, it was decided that the FBI could not use Alabama's data, and this decision led to Alabama withdrawing from participation in the NIBRS.

9. For a discussion of the technical, logistical, and political obstacles that must be overcome before a regional crime analysis and problem-solving effort can occur, see Eck (2000).

10. This project is supported by Grant 2001-WT-BX-0501 awarded by the National Institute of Justice, Office of Justice Programs, U.S. Department of Justice. Points of view in this chapter are those of the authors and do not necessarily represent the official position or policies of the U.S. Department of Justice.

11. It is acknowledged that some subjectivity is involved in classifying states as having "mandatory," "preferred," or "discretionary" arrest provisions. In general, the states themselves do not explicitly designate the classification of their arrest provisions but rather indicate the nature of the provisions through their terminology. Thus, in general, terms such as "shall," "will," and "must" signify a mandatory provision, whereas terms such as "may" and "can" signify a discretionary provision. Occasionally, a state may give the appearance of having a mandatory arrest provision but then dilute it so as to make it, in essence, a discretionary provision. For example, the Illinois statutory provision states, "Whenever a law enforcement officer has reason to believe that a person has been abused by a family or household member, the officer shall immediately use all reasonable means to prevent further abuse, including (1) arresting the abusing party, where appropriate." For more detailed discussion of this issue, see Hirschel, Buzawa, Faggiani, Reuland, & Pattavina (2003).

12. These eight states are Colorado, Connecticut, Iowa, Ohio, South Carolina, South Dakota, Utah, and Virginia.

13. These four states are Arkansas, Massachusetts, North Dakota, and Tennessee.

14. These seven states are Idaho, Kentucky, Michigan, Nebraska, Texas, Vermont, and West Virginia.

15. "Intimate partners" include spouses, common law spouses, ex-spouses, homosexual relationships, and boyfriends/girlfriends. "Other domestics" include parents–children, children–parents, siblings, grandparents, grandchildren, and in-laws.

16. Included as "nondomestic but known to victim" are relationships categorized as involving acquaintances, friends, neighbors, employers/employees, or babysitters.

17. This percentage includes cases in which the victim–offender relationship is unknown (Table 5.7). Not surprisingly, cases in which the victim–offender relationship was unknown were less likely to result in arrest. Thus, when police disposition is examined by victim–offender relationship and cases with victim–offender information are omitted, the percentage of cases in which an arrest is made rises to 40.1% (Table 5.6).

18. For details of these findings, see Hirschel and colleagues (2003).

REFERENCES

Biderman, A. D., & Lynch, J. (1991). *Understanding crime incidence statistics: Why the UCR diverges from the NCS*. New York: Springer-Verlag.

Block, R., & Block, C. R. (1992). Homicide syndromes and vulnerability: Violence in Chicago's community areas over 25 years. *Studies on Crime and Crime Prevention, 1*, 61–87.

Bruno v. Codd, 396 N.Y.S. 2d 974 (Sup. Ct. 1977), rev'd, 64 A.D. 2d 582 (N.Y. App. Div. 1978), aff'd, 393 N.E. 2d 976 (N.Y. 1979).

Bureau of Justice Statistics. (1997). *Implementing the National Incident-Based Reporting System: A project status report* (NCJ-165581). Washington, DC: U.S. Department of Justice.

Eck, J. E. (2000, January). *Crossing the borders of crime: Factors influencing the utility and practicality of inter-jurisdictional crime mapping*. Paper presented at the Crime Mapping Research Center Conference Series, Washington, DC.

Epstein, S. D. (1987). *The problem of dual arrest in family violence cases*. Meriden: Connecticut Coalition Against Domestic Violence.

Faggiani, D., Bibel, D., & Brensilber, D. (2001). Regional problem-solving using the National Incident-Based Reporting System. In M. Reuland, C. Sole Brito, & L. Carroll (Eds.), *Solving crime and disorder problems*. Washington, DC: Police Executive Research Forum.

Faggiani, D., & McLaughlin, C. L. (1999). Using the National Incident-Based Reporting System for strategic crime analysis. *Journal of Quantitative Criminology, 15*, 181–191.

Federal Bureau of Investigation. (1998). *National Incident-Based Reporting System, Vol. 1: Data collection guidelines*. Washington, DC: U.S. Department of Justice.

Federal Bureau of Investigation. (2002). *Crime in the United States 2002*. Washington, DC: U.S. Department of Justice.

Greenfeld, G. A., Rand, M. R., Craven, D., Klaus, P. A., Perkins, C. A., Ringel, C., Warchol, G., Maston, C., & Fox, J. A. (1998). *Violence by intimates: Analysis of data on crimes by current or former spouses, boyfriends, and girlfriends*. Washington, DC: Bureau of Justice Statistics.

Haviland, M., Frye, V., Rajah, V., Thukral, J., & Trinity, M. (2001). *The Family Protection and Domestic Violence Act of 1995: Examining the effects of mandatory arrest in New York City*. New York: Urban Justice Center.

Hirschel, J. D., & Buzawa, E. (2002). Understanding the context of dual arrest with directions for future research. *Violence Against Women, 8*, 1449–1473.

Hirschel, J. D., Buzawa, E., Faggiani, D., Reuland, M., & Pattavina, A. (2003, July). *Victim–offender relationship and the likelihood of arrest in assault cases: Using NIBRS to provide the answer.* Paper presented at the National Institute of Justice Annual Conference on Criminal Justice Research and Evaluation, Washington, DC.

Lawrenz, F., Lembo, R., & Schade, S. (1988). Time series analysis of the effect of a domestic violence directive on the number of arrests per day. *Journal of Criminal Justice, 16,* 493–498.

Maltz, M. D. (1977). Crime statistics: A historical perspective. *Crime & Delinquency, 23,* 32–40.

Maltz, M. D. (1999). *Bridging gaps in police crime data* (NCJ 176365). Washington, DC: Bureau of Justice Statistics.

Martin, M. (1997). Double your trouble: Dual arrest in family violence. *Journal of Family Violence, 12,* 139–157.

Municipality of Anchorage, Alaska. (2000). *Analysis of police action and characteristics of reported domestic violence in Anchorage, Alaska: Ten year study, 1989–1998.* Anchorage, AK: Author.

Office of the Attorney General, State of California. (1999). *Report on arrests for domestic violence in California, 1998.* Sacramento, CA: Author.

Poggio, E. C., Kennedy, S. D., Chaiken, J. M., & Carlson, K. E. (1985). *Blueprint for the future of the Uniform Crime Reporting program.* Washington, DC: U.S. Department of Justice.

Rennison, C. M. (2003). *Intimate partner violence 1993–2001.* Washington, DC: Bureau of Justice Statistics.

Saunders, D. G. (1995). The tendency to arrest victims of domestic violence. *Journal of Interpersonal Violence, 10,* 147–158.

Scott v. Hart, No. 6–76–2395, N.D. Cal. (1976).

Sherman, L. W., & Berk, R. A. (1984a). *The Minneapolis Domestic Violence Experiment.* Washington, DC: Police Foundation.

Sherman, L. W., & Berk, R. A. (1984b). The specific deterrent effects of arrest for domestic assault. *American Sociological Review, 49,* 261–272.

Thurman et al. v. City of Torrington, 595 F. Supp. 1521 (D. Conn. 1984).

Victim Services Agency. (1988). *The law enforcement response to family violence: A state by state guide to family violence legislation.* New York: Author.

Wanless, M. (1996). Mandatory arrest: A step towards eradicating domestic violence, but is it enough? *University of Illinois Law Review, 2,* 533–587.

Wilson, J. Q. (1968). *Varieties of police behavior: The management of law and order in eight communities.* Cambridge, MA: Harvard University Press.

Zorza, J., & Woods, L. (1994). *Mandatory arrest: Problems and possibilities.* Washington, DC: Center on Women and Family Law.

CHAPTER 6

Information Technology and Crime Analysis

PHYLLIS PARSHALL MCDONALD

This chapter is crucial to understanding the overall development of policing in 20th-century America. Since 1970, American policing has revolutionized itself in a manner that was barely perceptible as it was occurring. Looking back on the past three decades and examining the phases and steps along the way, one can see that some of the greatest advances in policing occurred in relationship to technology but not necessarily *because of* technology. The role that technology played was to provide an environment in which the best minds in policing were able to take advantage of common police wisdom and put it to new and innovative uses. The process by which policing was led to the full use of information technology (IT) is an interesting and complex story.

The details of this story are revealed in this chapter through exploring the following phenomena:

- The relationship between the development of IT and crime analysis

- The developmental stages of crime analysis in police agencies
- The impact of developing police theories as they relate to IT and crime analysis
- The impact of crime analysis on crime control and reduction
- Policy implications for these developments

For the purposes of this chapter, the following behavioral definition of *crime analysis* is offered:

Police crime analysis operations consist of three essential functions: 1) to assess the nature, extent, and distribution of crime in order to efficiently and effectively allocate resources and deploy personnel; 2) to identify crime–suspect correlations to assist in investigations; [and] 3) to identify the conditions that facilitate crime and incivility so that policy makers may make informed decisions about prevention approaches.[1]

A second conceptual definition, which was developed by Interpol and agreed to in

June 1992 by 12 European Interpol member countries, is as follows: "Criminal intelligence analysis [or "crime analysis"] is the identification of and the provision of insight into the relationship between crime data and other potentially relevant data with a view to police and/or judicial practice."[2]

THE RELATIONSHIP BETWEEN THE DEVELOPMENT OF IT AND CRIME ANALYSIS

Although other chapters in this volume fully explain the technical evolution of IT as it relates to criminal justice, suffice it to say here that major developments using IT did not occur in law enforcement until the advent of the personal computer during the late 1970s. Prior to that era, some departments had large mainframes that could be used to store data and compile records. They often were located at a central city site, and not necessarily in the police department, making data accessibility nearly impossible. But it was the personal computer, with microprocessors that contained memory, logic, and control circuits on a single chip, that revolutionized computer applications not only in policing but also in all segments of society.

Personal computers made data accessible and supported analysis of data, whereas the needs of policing led to the development of computerized crime mapping. Still, despite these advances, a considerable amount of time would pass until the true capacity of IT was recognized and applied in law enforcement (for a comprehensive topology of events, see Table 6.1).

There are many processes in law enforcement that computer technology enhances. The list includes conducting forensic science analysis, tracking data with the capacity to hold individuals and units accountable, conducting scientific analysis of data for effective strategy development and monitoring, recording and tracking calls for service, pinpointing the geographic location of police officers, allowing officers to receive call assignments and submit reports while in their vehicles, providing cumulative data at the end of the year for progress reviews, and providing a viable means to interface effectively with the community. This chapter is primarily concerned with the development and advancement of crime analysis processes as they intertwined with the development and advancement of IT.

The concepts of mapping and analysis were not developed as the result of IT. Crime analysis/mapping is a field that developed independent of automated ability to rapidly collect, synthesize, and analyze data. The advent of the personal computer had a major impact on popularizing the concept and application.

The French social ecologists Guerry and Qutelet were two of the earliest crime analysts, (working during the early 1830s) interested in explaining differences in community crime levels in terms of varying social conditions of the resident populations. These two theorists manually created early maps of population-based rates of crime, suicide, and alcoholism; population age structure; family structure; educational levels; and population diversity in 19th-century geographic areas in France.[3]

Research on policing and the police organization, as opposed to research in the fields of criminology and sociology, began in the United States during the early 1970s as a result of the availability of federal funding to support police officers' college educations. Universities responded with whole new departments of criminal justice, and departments of policing research soon followed. Research using data collected independent of sophisticated records management systems (RMSs) was conducted in police agencies and in combination with data then being collected by police departments. These early studies would not have been possible if agencies had not begun to collect crime data, however primitive these data may have been. The first major police study was the Kansas City

Table 6.1   Chronology of Events

	IT Developments	IT Use in Policing	Police Strategy Development	Crime Mapping
1920		Police teletype Polygraph prototype	Traditional Professional model	Chicago School Crime mapping
1960	Mainframe IBM 360/65	National Crime Information Center (NCIC)/Federal Bureau of Investigation (FBI) 9-1-1 system (AT&T)	President's Advisory Committee on Civil Disorder	Census tracks plotted on computers Howard University crime maps (SYMAP)
1970		Computerization of police agencies Automated Fingerprint Identification System (AFISC)	COP/POP conceptualized research in policing	New York City manual crime mapping Geocoding (McEwen)
1980	Personal computers Graphic user interface	CAD RMSs Crime analysis	COP/POP experiments Hot spots policing conceptualized	Concept of spatial distribution of crime Manual pin maps
1990	MS Windows User-friendly GIS Development of mainstream IP-based communication systems	Crime mapping DNA reliability Computerized polygraph Handheld computers	Widespread use of COP/POP CompStat developed Widespread use of CompStat	CAD/RMSs programmed to input crime mapping and analysis Automated pin maps
2000	Mainframe on the desktop	Regional/State/Federal data sharing Interoperability	Integrated operations management COP/POP/CompStat data driven	Statistical application to crime mapping and analysis

NOTE: IT = information technology; COP = community-oriented policing; POP = problem-oriented policing; CAD = computer-aided dispatch; RMS = records management system; GIS = geographic information systems; IP = Internet Protocol.

Preventive Patrol Experiment. This study established experimental and control areas to determine the impact of random patrol on crime rates and concluded that random patrol essentially had no impact. National data explained these findings in that, typically, only 2 of every 8 hours is spent on nondirected cruising through a beat area. It would be surprising if this limited random activity would have an impact on crime rates.[4]

The San Diego Field Interrogation Experiment followed, using more sophisticated approaches and demonstrating that an active police presence made a dramatic difference in crime rates. That study, conducted in 1973, tested the differences across three areas of San Diego using varying intensities of "stop and question" activities. The most interesting finding was that when field interrogations were withdrawn, crime increased dramatically, and when field interrogations were reinstituted, crime dropped dramatically.[5]

During the 1990s, a prominent research study that continued to building on the notion of the applicability of crime data and analysis was Lawrence Sherman's Minneapolis Repeat Call Address Policing. Sherman had analyzed data to determine that 3% of Minneapolis's 115,000 residential and commercial addresses accounted for 50% of police calls for service and that 5% of the addresses generated 64% of calls. Minneapolis formed a special unit to use problem-oriented policing (POP) techniques with 125 residential addresses and 125 commercial addresses. After 6 months, the target addresses had 15% fewer calls for service. These gains were erased after 1 year, and Sherman concluded that target rotation was the most effective police strategy for dealing with problematic residential and commercial addresses.[6]

The concept of analyzing crime data, born in France in 1833 and continuing in the United States from the 1920s onward, generally consisted of isolated research studies rather than routine data analysis to affect policing on a daily basis. Ultimately, by 2003, increasing numbers of police agencies were using crime data produced on a daily basis to understand problems and issues in their neighborhoods, to determine when and where resources needed to be deployed, to monitor and track progress, and to hold members accountable. However, there are several stages through which police agencies traverse before arriving at an advanced mode of using IT in the management of police operations. These stages are outlined in what follows.

THE DEVELOPMENTAL STAGES OF CRIME ANALYSIS

Stage 1

The earliest or most primitive operations performed by police agencies as they begin to use IT in data analysis is to collect crime data and use them primarily for cumulative data reports.[7] For example, crime data can be used for end-of-year summaries of crime events in a jurisdiction and can be prepared for use by a police department or submitted to decision makers and policymakers in local government (e.g., mayor, city manager) as a "report card" on police performance. Reports may be generated more frequently (e.g., bimonthly, quarterly, semiannually) and distributed more broadly in the law enforcement agency (e.g., budget officer, all patrol commanders). Stage 1 represents movement toward understanding department performance as a totality, for example, the numbers of robberies occurring in the city annually or the closure rates of homicides. A separate crime category may be singled out for review (e.g., homicides, business center burglaries) for a very low level of accountability. A department functioning at Stage 1 usually is required to report cumulative data at the end of a year to its supervising government unit for budget accountability purposes. More often than not, when a department fails to reach a target, the consequence is not severe; new targets are established for the next budget year, and the cycle repeats itself. A police agency functioning at this level typically does not have a crime analysis unit as such, although one or two persons in the research/planning unit may be responsible for collecting and reporting data.

Stage 2

During Stage 2, a police agency prepares cumulative reports as described for Stage 1. The department may prepare reports at a greater frequency (e.g., monthly, weekly) and distribute them to a broader audience (e.g., all commanders in the police agency, community groups). Serious crime categories may be tracked, monitored, and compared with performance of the previous year and/or displayed on bar charts or other graphic presentations. Selected members of a research/planning unit may be organized to serve as an official crime analysis unit.

Stage 3

Advances during Stage 3 often are intertwined with a community policing program. At this juncture, crime data are analyzed and reported regularly (e.g., monthly, weekly, daily). Data usually are directed to beat areas and individual police officers to help identify "hot spots" or patterns and to be able to report to community groups. Data may be available directly to neighborhood residents. The Chicago Police Department during the late 1980s is a prime example of this level of functioning and further illustrates how technology and theory operate together and influence each other (see the case study on Chicago later in this chapter).

Stage 4

During Stage 4, police agencies recognize that preferred operations management is based on sound, accessible, and accurate data and that effective strategic decisions cannot be based on intuition, convenience, or a complaining government leader. In other words, a scientific approach to policing is instituted. Stage 4 departments, particularly larger ones, tend to have a centralized crime analysis unit and crime analysts at district levels. Crime mapping is used to enhance crime analysis capacity.

A Stage 4 department uses crime data to identify hot spots and crime patterns within districts and across the jurisdiction, to track progress and ensure that problems and issues are being mitigated, to hold members accountable for progress, and to understand new issues that may arise indigenous to a jurisdiction, district, or neighborhood. For example, the New York Police Department (NYPD) became aware of a rise in thefts of air bags from cars through crime mapping and data analysis, and the department immediately instituted a tactic to counter the mini "crime wave" by prosecuting car repair facilities if they installed stolen air bags in cars. Similarly, the NYPD used this same data analysis system to chart citizens' complaints against officers and to track progress in complaint reduction by precinct.

Stage 5

The original outline of stages of crime analysis ended at Stage 4, yet more recent developments suggest that there may be a fifth stage of development. Newer uses of data are being developed every day, and a police agency at Stage 5 may be one that has nearly every conceivable application programmed into its management process with an integrated approach to operations management. Some police agencies, even those implementing CompStat, may still view their agencies as a narrow and traditional mix of isolated functions. (CompStat is a comprehensive system to manage police operations. It consists of holding patrol commanders accountable for all problems and issues in their respective geographic areas, meeting regularly with top command to develop strategies and tactics to address problems, implementing the strategies rapidly and convincingly, and following up to determine whether or not the new strategies were effective.) For example, the canine unit may have drug-sniffing dogs to which only the drug enforcement unit has access. It might not occur to the operations manager that these same dogs could provide assistance in special circumstances for the patrol unit. Similarly, a juvenile unit may function separately from the domestic violence unit and/or sex offenders unit, although cases frequently may be interrelated or overlapping.

Stage 5 departments would be those that are experimental and continuously seek to find new applications for technology and new combinations of traditional functions. For example, racial profiling has given rise to a new era of data collection and analysis. In Montgomery County, Maryland, operating under a consent degree, the police chief and union together purchased handheld computers to enable police officer reporting of traffic stop data directly to the crime analysis unit for analysis as an easier method of collecting required data. The police agency in Stage 5 may have a wide range of data functions, including continuous and automatic data analysis programmed to sound an alert when a crime pattern or hot spot appears, data analysis to identify potential terrorists or other threats to homeland security, automatic location of police officers through the use of their cell phones and global positioning system (GPS) tracking capability (a step beyond tracking their vehicles), and automated management of criminal investigation processes.

The bolder departments may make headway in unresolved discussions such as that for a standard for the ratio of police officers to citizens. For example, Salt Lake City, Utah, has a 4.1 to 1,000 ratio, whereas San Diego, California, has a 1.5 to 1,000 ratio. Cities cannot gauge the numbers of police officers needed for their jurisdictions by comparing their ratios to those of other cities. The critical difference in police effectiveness is the sophistication level of their data analysis and strategic management, coupled with numbers of calls for service and numbers of felonies, that should ultimately dictate numbers of officers needed. Stage 5 departments would share data regionally and engage in regional strategies and tactics to control crime. They might also function similarly at the state and/or federal levels.

Describing the developmental stages of crime analysis is somewhat of a conundrum

because police agencies experience varying developmental patterns. On the one hand, a police agency may begin at the beginning with Stage 1 and proceed through all of the other stages described until reaching the advanced and sophisticated stage of full operations management. On the other hand, a police agency may be at Stage 1 when a new chief arrives with a high level of technical competency and may thrust the agency straight to the highest level of development without having proceeded through the intermediary stages. Furthermore, a department may begin at the most rudimentary stage and never advance beyond that stage due to a lack of competency and/or a demand on the part of the department's executive ranks or as a result of primitive communications technology that prohibits advancement.

There are no clear guidelines or police agency characteristics that delineate the progress from one stage to another. The confusion is better demonstrated by reviewing the findings from a study of crime analysis conducted by the Center for Public Policy at the University of South Alabama.[8] The Alabama researchers used both phone and mail surveys to contact all U.S. police agencies with 100 or more sworn officers, and they used a mail survey to contact a sample of agencies with fewer than 100 sworn officers. Their findings conclude the following:

- Size of the department is a weak predictor of crime analysis capacity. It does have a significant effect on operations. The larger departments appear to engage in a wider variety of crime analysis operations than do their smaller counterparts.
- Crime does not matter. The amount of crime has no bearing on hardware/software, quality and use of data, training, statistical methods, and type of analytic operations in which departments engage.
- The amount of resources that are devoted to police operations does affect the quality of hardware/software inventory; otherwise,

it has no effect on any other crime analysis dimension.

- Whether or not a department has adopted community policing practices seems to be only minimally related to how well it analyzes crime.
- When managers demand sophisticated levels of crime analysis output, the quality tends to follow accordingly.
- The degree to which targets appreciate crime analysis output is also a strong predictor of the quality of crime analysis operations.
- Crime analysis across dimensions is superior in departments that designate a specialized crime analyst position.

The topology that follows is a general description of developmental stages of crime analysis in police agencies.

POLICE STRATEGIES AND THEIR RELATIONSHIP TO CRIME ANALYSIS AND IT

Most Americans are no doubt unaware of the processes in law enforcement over the past three decades or so that transformed, and are still transforming, the police function from a cottage industry to a technologically sophisticated systems approach to crime management. In what ways did the police industry develop to result in agencies that are highly effective, technologically advanced, and managing operations with a totally different approach than are less able departments? This evolutionary process has already taken 30-plus years and is a complex process to understand.

Policing is a constantly changing profession, despite judgments by some that police agencies never change or that they change very slowly as a result of responding to criticisms, charges of inadequacy and/or corruption, and national or local events. According to Jack Greene,[9] much of American government has been in the throes of critique and reform since the early 19th century, experiencing continuing political, social, and economic reforms as a result of significant immigration to urban centers. Greene maintains, "Such transformation has invariably involved questions of justice and the role of the state in shaping and controlling everyday life. Moreover, as the police are the most visible element of government in civil society, they have often become both the symbolic and substantive lightning rod for civic reform" (p. 304).

Change can be promulgated by academic research and teaching. Raising community-oriented policing (COP) to a level of theory and "approach" was as much due to academic forces as it was due to police experience and experimentation. In contrast, CompStat implementation occurred from police chiefs meeting and discussing the new method of operations management and traveling to New York City to observe the process in action. David Weisburd's[10] research on CompStat documents the rapid and wide adoption of the process nationally.

Events during the late 1960s led to the conceptualization of community policing. Influencing this movement was the President's National Advisory Commission on Civil Disorder in 1968.[11] This commission severely indicted the police for their lack of parity and lack of effective techniques to work with neighborhoods. Well-known educated and progressive police chiefs responded by boldly experimenting in their departments. Early examples included Lee Brown in Houston, Texas (neighborhood-oriented policing [NOP]), 1982; Neil Behan in Baltimore, Maryland (COP), 1984; and Darryl Stevens in Newport News, Virginia (POP), 1984.

These initial COP and POP projects were not fully embraced by departments nationally until 1993, when the Clinton administration provided significant support to community policing through legislation, the Violent Crime Control and Law Enforcement Act of 1994.

This legislation established the Community-Oriented Policing Services (COPS) office and provided support to police agencies in the implementation of COP through vast amounts of funding. In addition, the COPS office awarded $1 billion for technology support to state and local agencies during this same time period.[12]

COP and POP were intimately related to technology innovations in policing but was not dependent on them. COP and POP took advantage of technology where available but could function effectively without formal data analysis. In community policing, the emphasis usually was on increasing crime prevention, improving relations with neighborhoods, improving police response to neighborhood perception of problems, and working with neighborhoods and other government agencies to solve problems, essentially capacity building within communities through support, partnership, and relationships. Throughout this same time period, it was hypothesized that because police were making efforts to improve their relationships with communities, command and control of officers should be decentralized (i.e., not supervised) so as to model open and free-flowing relationships between police and citizens. Theorists advocated that departments should be decentralized and flattened and that performance evaluation should be abandoned. The results were that COP officers were generally not supervised (except through citizens' complaints) or held accountable. One of the greatest disadvantages was that beat officers did not have access to police department resources because they were directed to use neighborhood and city resources to solve problems. (This approach is comparable to NASA telling astronauts to go ahead and build their own space vehicle and launch themselves into space. It connotes trust and respect, but it is, in fact, a recipe for failure.) Many of these "progressive" management practices derived from organizational development

experts such as Tom Peters[13] and Peter Senge.[14] It should be noted that the preceding actions were generated as the best intuitive thinking of police chiefs and theorists and in good faith that it would improve relationships between police and communities. However, although many subscribe to these administrative practices, these practices remain in the realm of theory because research to support and prove that they make a difference in achieving desired outcomes has not yet been conducted in policing or private industry.

Although some theorists described the process as officers being "encouraged to systematically scan police data, analyze [them] to discover problems and their causes, design responses, and assess the responses,"[15] this was not necessarily the reality. According to the Alabama crime analysis study, nearly 50% of departments surveyed did not use outside data, putting police officers at a decided disadvantage. Others were skeptical not only as to whether officers actually used data as theorized but also as to whether it was even prudent to do so. Heather MacDonald,[16] in an article supporting the CompStat movement in New York City, quotes then New York Police Commissioner William Bratton's view as follows:

> Though dedicated to problem solving, Bratton explicitly rejected the idea that the beat cop should be the main neighborhood problem solver. No green recruit could take on the problems of a complex Gotham neighborhood, he said. Bratton's problem solvers were the savvy, experienced precinct commanders, whom he unflaggingly held accountable for results. He also discarded the promise of a cop on every block, instead concentrating patrolmen on commercial avenues and at transportation hubs, where crime actually happened.
>
> Finally, he rejected the standard rhetoric of the community partnering with the police to solve crime, at least violent crime.

The citizen's role is to provide information to the cops, help set priorities, and obey the rules, though the police do have continuous contacts with their constituents. But New York never created a formal apparatus of citywide citizen crime-solving meetings, as have other cities. "If your crime problem is big and violent," says Northwestern University political science professor Wesley Skogan, the nation's foremost academic expert in community policing, "citizens should stay home." Citizens are "good at clean-up," he says, such as nuisance abatement and beautification. But for coming up with tactics to take out a drug gang, that's for the police.

Early forms of POP contained some elements of the future CompStat in that problems were targeted, and creative strategies and tactics were devised to solve the problems. In POP, similar to COP, officers were expected to function independently, that is, to create and apply the solution through their own inventiveness and discretion.

Most change occurs *in reaction to* something. In the case of CompStat, change occurred due to the fact that a formula for success for the most vexing problem of policing, such as serious crime, had been developed and tested, and other police chiefs quietly began to replicate the process in their own jurisdictions. Even so, the initial prototype in the New York Transit Police Department had been instigated by chief executive officer demands.

Simultaneously, another strategy was developing, initially in the New York Transit Police Department before later being institutionalized in the NYPD. The setting and environment in the Transit Police Department in 1990 was one that demanded action. Serious crime on the subway system was at an all-time high, a new chief was hired, and a new president of the New York Transit Authority (parent company to the police department) was in place. The new chief,

Bratton, knew that he had to reduce robbery, fare evasion, and the presence of disorderly persons on the subway if he wanted to retain his position as chief of the sixth largest police agency in the nation. The targets were clear: robbery, fare evasion, and disorderly persons. The technology was in place; the New York City Transit Police Department had a crime analysis unit that produced crime data, describing hot spots and patterns, every day by 7 a.m. for every commander in the department. What remained was the development of effective strategies and tactics.

Bratton alerted his district commanders that they would be judged by their ability to curtail robbery, fare evasion, and disorderly persons in their respective districts. Commander performance was tracked informally, and those who did not respond were transferred to other positions. In addition, the Crime Analysis Unit met every 2 weeks with all commanders of patrol units, the criminal investigations unit, and other specialized units to develop and plot strategies to manage hot spots and crime patterns. As a result, specialized units and the criminal investigations unit were thrust into a position of providing support to patrol commanders. Strategies and tactics for serious and nonserious crime were generated quickly, especially by patrol district commanders.

Bratton demanded a position for himself in the Transit Authority as a vice president to enable him to work with other units in the Transit Authority as his "community" for community policing. Thus, the rudiments of what was later to become the NYPD's CompStat were in place.

All crime on the New York City subways was reduced by 62% over a 4-year period, with felony crime decreasing by 75%. The police department had the reputation of being "Robocops," that is, of being everywhere, unpredictable, and active. This developing reputation contributed to crime reduction. The reaction of police chiefs and researchers to the remarkable crime reduction on the subways was that it was an aberration that was not to be taken too seriously. Some reminded Bratton that the strategy being examined and experimented with nationally was community policing, intimating that he too should get on board.

When CompStat was inaugurated into the NYPD by Bratton and Jack Maple, former transit lieutenant and deputy chief for crime control, they faced initial and serious challenges. NYPD crime data were published quarterly at best and largely represented cumulative data reports; the department was suspicious of the newcomers from the Transit Police Department, considered to be amateurish compared with the NYPD. Moreover, the NYPD had not been accustomed to strict demands for productivity. Few police agencies at that time were held accountable for controlling crime, and even fewer police commanders concerned themselves with crime data and crime control strategies. Most patrol commanders conceived of their jobs as being responsible for processing personnel issues, reports, overtime approval, and so forth. Persistence and sound leadership tactics, recognition of the application of police wisdom, and "proof in the pudding" in terms of crime reduction gradually won over the rank-and-file of the NYPD.

Soon, crime reduction rates in New York City were as significant as they had been on the subways, and the NYPD began to welcome visitors from across the country, as well as from foreign nations, to observe the CompStat process. In 1996, the NYPD held its first annual CompStat conference to showcase the new methods and thinking.

Major city departments began to duplicate the process, some with more success than others. The Major Cities Chiefs Association took a poll of its membership, and by 1997 CompStat was being applied in two thirds of major cities. Mid-sized departments, such as that in Lowell, Massachusetts, began to experiment with the process and were well satisfied with the results.

Initially, prominent researchers such as Herman Goldstein, the initiator of POP, criticized the new process in a *Law Enforcement News* interview, proclaiming that it was anathema to community policing and that the two strategies could not exist in one department and still maintain positive relations with neighborhoods. Al Blumstein[17] doubts the claims of police agencies that they can affect crime levels, maintaining that crime reduction occurs as a result of arrests of major drug dealers, a gradually diminishing youth population, high employment rates, and (to some extent) the blatant manipulation of data and crime reporting. Blumstein generally echoes the view that was perpetuated by 1970s research in policing, which concluded that random patrol did not affect crime and that criminal investigators did not solve crimes. Police research during the 1970s was extremely limited, partially because there was limited use of IT and naive crime control strategies.

There was another movement that paralleled that of CompStat. For some it was called "hot spots" policing, and for others it was called "situational" policing. It is difficult to determine who developed these concepts, but two names most closely associated with hot spots and situational policing are Lawrence Sherman, currently director of the Jerry Lee Center for Criminology at the University of Pennsylvania, and Ronald Clark of Rutgers University. The idea began innocently enough during the late 1960s and early 1970s, when enterprising researchers Glen Pitre, Susan Sparr, and Leboran Briggs in the Boston Police Department analyzed the number of calls for service from the same residential and commercial addresses and discovered that approximately 60% of all calls were generated by 15% of the addresses.

Sherman researched this phenomenon further in Minneapolis in 1988 and obtained similar findings (e.g., 3% of the city's 115,000 addresses accounted for 50% of police service calls). The study included the selection of a small cadre of officers to focus on those addresses and use POP techniques.[18] The hot spots policing concept continued to develop and has become embedded in crime analysis and crime mapping. A recent Police Foundation report found that 7 of 10 departments with more than 100 sworn officers reported using crime mapping to identify hot spots.[19] Hot spots policing branched and developed into situational policing, spurred primarily by Clark.[20]

There is yet another underlying theme associated with the development of CompStat. This silent but significant movement could not have occurred without the availability and use of IT. The focus on outcomes management was popularized in the literature by David Osborne[21] and was adapted to policing with the Government Performance and Results Act (GPRA) of 1993. This federal reform movement evolved in tandem with CompStat.

In policing, outcomes management was a natural phenomenon instigated by the president of the New York Transit Authority, who knew clearly what he wanted his new police chief to achieve. The focus on "outcomes" management is a superior method of accountability compared with "output" management. For years, managers had made assumptions that output connoted success. Police had engaged in output management for years (e.g., numbers of arrests, numbers of traffic stops, numbers of pounds of cocaine seized) without ever realizing that output statistics are an expression of productivity and not indicators of problem solutions or results. Many public agencies have begun to move in the direction of outcomes management not only as a way in which to justify their budgets and existence to taxpayers but

also as a means to motivate workers and ensure substantive impact. The City of Baltimore combined the outcomes management concept with CompStat to create CitiStat. One of the unexpected outcomes was a decrease in sick leave for public service workers as their jobs began to take on new meaning given that results management highlighted their contribution to quality of life in the city.[22] Gradually, through experimentation and creativity, competent police chiefs began to demonstrate that the most effective policing occurred when all three strategies—COP, POP, and CompStat—were integrated and applied systematically and scientifically. Recently, the Division of Public Safety Leadership at Johns Hopkins University conducted a study of model patrol commanders and found that essentially the "best and brightest" patrol commanders functioned similarly. These commanders consistently used data for decision making and integrated all three strategies (CompStat, COP, and POP) without concern for labels or whether or not the approaches were compatible with one another.[23] Other common characteristics of model patrol commanders were that they tended to identify problems using data analysis and then used teams of officers to attack the problems rather than relying solely on an "enforcement" approach; model patrol commanders spent long hours at work and clearly had a passion for the work. (An enforcement approach may mean that any number of officers are assigned to an area and told to make arrests for a specific violation. This is "silo" patrol or parallel functioning, where each officer is performing the same function but not necessarily working together with other officers strategically.) This keen interest in every aspect of patrol meant that the commanders made themselves consistently accessible and appeared to be effective in working with those in their commands because their high level of interest meant that they were aware of many details about the work and could relate to their personnel at an in-depth level rather than at a superficial or social level. The study was able to conclude that effective application of crime analysis requires a committed and talented commander.

In reviewing and interpreting history, there often are events that represent the beginning points of significant changes. Perhaps that moment in law enforcement occurred at a juncture where two critical forces came together: (a) a serious and rising violent crime problem in the United States and (b) the realization that computer-aided dispatch (CAD) systems and RMSs could generate data that could be used to understand the dynamics of crime in a geographic area. For example, the connection may have been made when an enterprising detective was mapping crime using a manual system (e.g., cardboard pin maps with colored plastic pins) to plot serious crimes and realized that the data in the CAD system could be plotted automatically. Automatic plotting could eliminate tedious labor and could support more effective problem solving as well as improved relations with the community. It is unknown exactly when these events may have occurred and whether the events occurred in the United States or in Europe, but these are important moments in history to be captured and understood because ultimately they dramatically changed the face of law enforcement.

The Impact of Crime Analysis on Crime Control/Reduction

One remaining issue is how and to what extent did IT and crime analysis, in combination, effect significant changes in policing. As stated earlier, COP did not depend on crime analysis but did use it to enhance relationships, particularly with the community. CompStat and POP could not have occurred, or might not even have been conceptualized, without needed advances in IT and crime

analysis theory and application. The fact that crime data were available every day for all commanders in the New York Transit Police Department supported accountability through tracking and monitoring. Because highly detailed information was available (e.g., descriptions of perpetrators involved in crime patterns, situational descriptions of hot spots), police managers found that they could analyze and strategize to greater depths. In departments where the technology did not support daily reporting or daily comparisons with the same day, week, or month during the previous year, but where the police chief was committed to using CompStat, funding was rapidly generated and the departments would be advanced to a technology level sufficient to support the new strategy.

POLICY IMPLICATIONS AND ISSUES

If one were to survey the American policing landscape today, one would see highly varied investments in the three major strategies and within each investment would see varying levels of competency for implementation of the selected process. In some departments, one would detect all three strategies operating harmoniously. At the same time, one would also see that levels of sophistication and complexity of IT and crime analysis are highly varied in terms of levels of competency and effectiveness and that the goals of policing may range from good community relations to an absence of serious crime. What does this mean for those with concerns about the effectiveness of American policing, particularly during these times of homeland security concerns? These important policy issues are iterated in what follows.

Vast Array of Competency Levels

There is a serious problem in modern policing due to the vast array of competency levels among police chiefs. Some departments function at high levels of competency and technical complexity, whereas others appear almost to be throw-backs to the 1950s. Many hiring authorities in jurisdictions are generally unaware of the differences in technical capabilities of police chief applicants, and some applicants are equally unaware. A city manager or mayor may select a chief based on personality and past experiences rather than on the ability to manage police operations. Some cities strive to meet a goal of repairing relationships with any disenfranchised segments of their communities, whereas others want corruption routed out or, at least, want the appearance of corruption removed. Few cities are concerned with crime control and reduction to a degree sufficient to measure and monitor and to hold their new chiefs accountable for public safety in respective jurisdictions. In general, hiring authorities do not know what experiences or skills a police chief applicant must possess to achieve the greatest potential for a jurisdiction. Programs are needed to educate government hiring authorities so that they may assist in the development of the police discipline to its fullest potential in the 21st century. One may suggest that it is lack of motivation and/or knowledge to adopt and adapt that slows law enforcement and that once a decision is made, changes can occur rapidly. The question remains as to who or what force can facilitate movement toward modern, technologically driven, strategic policing.

Lack of Standardization

CompStat is not replicated consistently across the many departments implementing it, and the crime analysis capabilities do not always meet police departments' needs. For example, one agency on the East Coast can produce crime data daily, but it consists of only cumulative data and the district crime analyst is responsible for in-depth analysis. If a department has a crime analyst who is sufficiently talented, he or she will actually analyze the data for the commander. On the other hand, if the crime analyst simply supplies a list of events from the previous day and the patrol commander has to conduct the analysis himself or herself, the commander is at a serious and time-consuming disadvantage. Some agencies today have parts of an IT system in place and are working on other parts. When the Prince George's County (Maryland) Police Department implemented CompStat, it had no automated means to transmit crime information to the crime analysis unit. The problem initially was solved by having police officers fax reports of serious crime incidents to the crime analysis unit as soon as possible to enable crime analysts to conduct their analysis of serious crimes. The appropriate IT was eventually obtained.[24]

So, although many departments have central crime analysis units and district-level crime analysts, this does not necessarily mean that police management is effective given that analysts and commanders operate at various levels of competency. It will be left to the next generation of police managers to describe standards and find ways in which to ensure that all or most departments meet these standards.

A Philosophically Integrated Approach to Police Operations

This chapter has suggested that there are police leaders who espouse one theory of policing, whereas there are those who espouse another. The chapter has also suggested that the three prominent theories—COP, POP, and CompStat—are not incompatible and that when they are applied in concert, they achieve noticeable success. Perhaps police theorists should be seeking a "unified" theory of policing much like the "unified field theory" sought by Albert Einstein and others.[25]

Language, Descriptors, and the Gap Between Researchers and Practitioners

In 1995, soon after the COPS office was so significantly supported through federal legislation, significant funding was transferred from the COPS office to the National Institute of Justice (NIJ) for research pertaining to COP. Because IT and data availability was thought to be an important part of COP, the NIJ not only funded research in the area of crime mapping but also established a national center for crime mapping.

The objectives of the new center were to fund research in crime mapping, hold conferences, and develop training. Principles of the crime mapping center referred to the "GIS Revolution"[26] (where GIS refers to geographic information systems). Although research in the area of crime mapping and mapping for ecological and medical purposes had been continuous, the NIJ became a prime motivator for researchers to attend fully to research in crime mapping.

The problem that became apparent was that there was an ever-widening gap between researchers and practitioners for two reasons. First, researchers developed obtuse and abstract jargon to explain crime mapping concepts. Second, researchers viewed crime mapping and analysis as a statistical process, whereas practitioners viewed it as more of a simplistic process that would lead to effective tactics. In many respects, the technical language of crime mapping is a severe barrier to practitioners' ability to understand research. Abstract research jargon no doubt serves researchers well, but it motivates police practitioners to avoid researchers and research reports. Crime mapping researchers need to find a way in which to simplify communications if they have any hope that practitioners will heed their findings and use them to improve police crime mapping.

In the Alabama study[27] mentioned earlier, when the larger departments were asked to estimate the extent to which statistical packages were used for crime analysis, 80% responded "no" and 20% responded "yes." Similarly, a series of questions pertaining to the use of individual statistics was asked, and departments responded as follows:

- Use of frequencies: 18% never, approximately 82% sometimes to very often
- Use of mean, median, and mode: 36% never, approximately 64% sometimes to very often
- Use of standard deviation: 51% never, approximately 49% sometimes to very often
- Use of crosstabs: 60% never, approximately 35% sometimes to very often
- Use of correlation: 42% never, approximately 57% sometimes to very often
- Use of regression: 64% never, approximately 37% sometimes to very often

In his evidence-based policing article, Sherman[28] recommends broad-based evaluation research to test the effectiveness of police practice. Sherman reasons that the missing link in policing is basic research on what works best when implemented properly under controlled conditions and ongoing research on the results that each unit is actually achieving by applying basic research practice. Clearly, this is the application of the scientific method to police practice as a means to improvement.

Sherman's approach raises the second issue pertaining to data, technology, and police practice: the conflict between the goal of researchers and the goal of police. Researchers are convinced that statistical applications and the scientific method applied to broad-based data collections will enlighten police as to what is effective and what is not. The police, conversely, are functioning primarily at a tactical level, seeking to eliminate hot spots or patterns in the interest of crime control. The difference is also illustrated by the fact that researchers are committed to understanding substantive causative factors related to criminal events, whereas the police only have time to be concerned with removing conditions in hot spots that attract criminals or with catching perpetrators who are producing crime patterns. Law enforcement agencies engage in different levels of complexity and sophistication to obtain these results.

The solution to these problems is discussion, observation, experience in policing (on the part of researchers), and knowledge of research (on the part of practitioners) so that the two groups will arrive at some level of understanding and mutual goals that will ultimately benefit the American public.

One researcher, Urban Nulden,[29] began with the "right" question: What are the characteristics of police work in the field, and how can we design IT to support this work? His research study began the process of identifying police practices and identifying meaningful language to make these processes explicit. Nulden describes three dimensions at the outset:

♦ *Central authority versus local autonomy,* for example, a concern with whether a centralized unit uses data to control police units or whether the police unit can use crime analysis to do its own planning
♦ *Reactive intervention versus reactive work,* for example, a concern with whether crime analysis is used to develop an effective interruption of the problem at hand or whether it is used as "busy work" or an output measure
♦ *Control versus support,* an issue that is similar to the first one in that the author is questioning whether the primary concern is predicting behavior or encouraging innovative strategies and tactics development

Nulden then describes the extent to which technology can support these functions. As an example, he describes "awareness technology" as being related to the difference between a friendly situation and a hostile one

and to the varying needs of the police officers. In this dimension, the use of GPS can enable the police officers to know, for example, where their partners or backups are when encountering a hostile situation. This approach is understandable to police practitioners because it begins with the language and concepts used by police. More researchers should follow Nulden's lead.

Structuring Databases

One potentially serious issue in policing that may serve as an obstacle to production of creative strategies is the structure of current police databases. For the most part, current databases are derived from, and designed to accommodate, police reports. The structure of police reports, probably derived from the 19th century, contains basic data for prosecution. As social ecology invades policing, it is apparent that data captured for one case may be usable for another case but tend not to be captured. Even if the data are captured, they tend to be retained in the original file and not transferred to a second unit where they may have further use. For example, if police officers responding to a domestic violence incident recorded the names of children in the home (who may or may not have been present at the time of the violence), not only are these children useful to the prosecution as witnesses, but their names also should be forwarded to the juvenile division. The juvenile division could then enter them into case follow-up to determine whether these same children have other criminal justice or school issues and/or need further attention and care.

Standardized Equipment, Processes, and Training

There is no one police agency in the United States in our system of autonomous police agencies that is in a position to advocate standardized crime mapping/analysis equipment, processes, or training. In addition, given the operation of the free enterprise system and numerous vendors entering the crime mapping/ data analysis field, police agencies are sometimes at a loss to know what equipment they need or even what their data needs might be. Vendors seek only to sell the most expensive version of their wares and are not in the business of advising police and other criminal justice agencies as to what the most cost-effective and beneficial package would be. To some extent, there is a severe need for an "honest broker," that is, an agency that would advise police agencies and assist them in selecting those products that truly meet their particular needs. All of this must occur before there can be any real hope of standardization. Currently, police agencies engage in widely varying techniques, administrative structures, quality of crime analysts, and expected results. This situation also mitigates against Sherman's recommendations for broad-based evaluation given that databases and processes are often incompatible with each other.

Homeland Security Needs

In the post-9/11 homeland security era in the United States, several data and technology issues have become highly pronounced as they inhibit security work and development toward homeland security. In a recent survey of police chiefs of major cities,[30] when asked to describe the impediments to homeland security, one of the most frequent responses was "interoperability." The respondents focused not only on the hardware and software incompatibilities but also on provincial attitudes of police agencies at the local, state, and federal levels. They also described the need for standardized training for intelligence and crime analysts. The need for compatibility of communications systems regionally and vertically (e.g., among police, fire, and emergency medical responders as well as

among law enforcement agencies) across the spectrum was also identified as being a serious need.

Integrated Philosophical and Operational Approach to Policing

The adversity among the COP, POP, and CompStat approaches has been described, alluded to, and criticized throughout this chapter. Suffice it to say that these three systems are not viewed as incompatible by all police executives, researchers, and other ranking officials. Some use all three successfully. They are seen as a panacea for public safety when the skilled police chief is able to understand the need for integration of philosophy and approach. Furthermore, CompStat exposed a second serious flaw in police operations: the separation of patrol services from all other specialized units. CompStat also demonstrated the power of the police agency when it understood the true relationships among these units and how they could better serve each other and, thus, better serve the community.

CASE STUDIES

This section contains three case studies designed to illustrate the interrelationships among crime analysis, crime mapping, and police theory or strategy and to illustrate the serendipitous nature of change and progress as the increasing needs, creativity, and tools interface.

Case Study 1: Chicago Police Department

A rising crime rate during the mid-1980s motivated many communities to seek means to protect their own neighborhoods. Many police agencies were not yet heavily involved in community policing and were perceived by citizens as being uninterested in conditions in individual neighborhoods.

This set the stage for the developments in the City of Chicago and the Chicago Police Department (CPD). It is important to note that the CPD was considered an early user of automated information systems. In 1962, the CPD was the first police agency to install the IBM 1401 model mainframe. By the 1970s, the CPD was one of the many users of the City of Chicago's IBM 370 mainframe.

The Chicago Alliance for Neighborhoods (CANS), seeking solutions and assistance, approached Northwestern University with its dilemma and an idea that maps that graphically displayed crime and its effects in specific locations could be obtained from the City of Chicago. Previously the CANS organization had been using maps to illustrate how community development investments varied from community to community in terms of effectiveness. A transfer to the concept of using maps for crime data was an easy leap.

The CANS organization consulted the mayor of Chicago, Harold Washington, to find an acceptable approach to the police department for the purposes of receiving permission for the community organization to procure tapes from the mainframe that would include basic offense data. Even though the data were usually a month old by the time the tapes could be generated, the community organization found useful applications for the data.

The CANS organization then translated the data to maps depicting the location of crimes with the integration of other data such as the locations of abandoned buildings, schools, and parks. Crime patterns became evident very quickly.

This series of activities was followed by an appeal to academics seeking funding to support an evaluation of the crime mapping project, a very advanced consideration given the time frame. In the course of the evaluation project, a single police district was identified to serve as the experimental site. The patrol commander of the district intuitively knew, almost immediately, that month-old data were nearly useless in planning immediate responses to crime patterns. He instituted a system whereby his officers would enter Uniform Crime Reporting (UCR) Part I offenses from the previous day into a computer every morning by hand for his own use in deploying resources.

Much of the remainder of this story is well known to police and research professionals. In 1993, the CPD launched a major and full-scale citywide COP project titled Chicago Alternative Policing Strategy (CAPS). This initiation was soon followed by a crime mapping program, Information Collection for Automated Mapping (ICAM), with a goal of providing community members with up-to-date statistical information to help them identify and target problems.[31] Chicago communities were already used to working with crime maps and viewed them as essential to planning.

Many reviewing the Chicago experience no doubt assume that the program to supply crime mapping data to neighborhoods had been initiated by the police department, congruent with their best thinking about COP. These individuals are unaware of the precedent set by the CANS organization in working with universities and academics to bring relief to neighborhoods from the crisis engendered by rising crime and violence to neighborhoods.

Communities received crime data regularly and used them to understand events in their neighborhoods; however, it has been noted that even though police officers serving these areas had access to data, they usually did not use the data. Most officers simply printed maps of their beat areas and passed them on to residents. This situation illustrates a serious problem with the proliferation of technical and contemporary police methods, and it raises several questions. Did beat officers not use crime mapping and data because the data were not useful to them in their daily patrol routines? Did the officers not use the tools available to them because they had not been trained to use the data in a meaningful way? Or did the officers not use the tools because crime mapping data were limited and ineffective for a single patrol officer on a beat?

It is interesting to note that the CPD eventually recognized that although beat area crime mapping was satisfying to residents, it did not tell the whole story given that criminals do not necessarily confine their activities to accommodate certain beat areas. The CPD began to have its sergeants review data for their respective sectors to identify crime patterns that logically crossed beat lines. Ultimately, lieutenants were assembled to review entire districts for the same reasons. In the year 2000, Terrence Hillard, the police chief, instituted a full-scale CompStat program to fully institute a process that had been, in some senses, inaugurated by concerned citizens but had been applied only piecemeal by beat officers, sergeants, and district-level lieutenants over the years.

Case Study 2: U.S. Housing and Urban Development

In 1998, U.S. Housing and Urban Development (HUD) researchers began a process of experimenting with crime mapping to measure crime in and around public housing. At the time, there were few attempts to understand the dynamics of crime in public housing projects, although some believed that it might *not* be the same as the dynamics of crime in other areas of cities and that appropriate information could serve to improve police services to these communities. HUD researchers became intrigued with two factors. First, given all of the progress being made in cities as a result of CompStat, perhaps they too could find ways in

which to improve crime control in housing projects. Second, as a result of learning about crime mapping and crime analysis, perhaps these tools could be equally useful to HUD policymakers.[32]

HUD researchers began their study by exploring the feasibility of using GIS as a tool for comparing crime rates in public housing developments with those in adjacent neighborhoods and with those in the respective municipality.[33] Although on the surface this exercise appears to be simple, in actuality there were many issues to be resolved to complete the analytic process. First, crime data for public housing areas were resident in city police agencies. These agencies first had to agree to provide HUD with specified data. Second, data in police agencies were configured by beat area and sector, whereas housing projects may span more than one beat area or be located across two sectors. Even when municipal police agencies agreed to provide the requested data, there was the matter of providing overtime pay so that analysts could gather data for the HUD project outside of regular duty hours. Finally, there was an issue of configuring data to differentiate between crime occurring in public housing and crime occurring in surrounding areas.

The second phase of the 1998 study sought to focus on crime victims in and around the developments to determine principally whether crime victims are visitors to, or residents of, public housing developments given that the association between public housing units and drug markets was discussed so continuously. The results of the study are surprising.

HUD researchers hypothesized that female residents of public housing are at greater risk for aggravated assaults than are women living elsewhere. Victimization studies by the U.S. Bureau of Justice Statistics and others had suggested that poor and urban dwellers are at higher risk for personal violence and that three of four incidents of criminal violence against women take place in or near the victims' homes.

HUD researchers selected two experimental sites: one consisting of high-rise buildings located close to a downtown commercial district and one consisting of garden-style dwellings scattered throughout the jurisdiction. In 1998, the aggravated assault rate in U.S. metropolitan areas was 3.9 per 1,000 population. In the garden-style site, the assault rate was 5.3 per 1,000 population, only slightly higher than the national average; however, in the high-rise complex, the assault rate was an astonishing 21.2 per 1,000. When the researchers compared the study results with data pertaining to male assaults, it was clear that African American female residents in high-rise public housing units suffered disproportionately high rates of aggravated assaults. Further analysis yielded that the preponderance of assaults occurred in private spaces rather than in public spaces.

When principles of situational crime prevention were applied to the results of this study, it was clear that the physical structure of public housing projects contributed significantly to assault rates. The garden-style structure provided less privacy and more awareness by neighbors of activities in adjacent areas, whereas high-rise buildings contributed to anonymity of activity and assaults.

The implications of the study results were clear. HUD had to reconsider the physical structure of public housing units, generate police strategies specifically tailored to curtail assaults, and provide training and orientation to women in public housing units for their self-protection.

Case Study 3: Washington (D.C.) Metropolitan Police

In 2001, Patrol Commander Catherine Lanier of the Washington (D.C.) Metropolitan Police Department (MPD) was enrolled in the Police Executive Leadership Program (PELP) at Johns Hopkins University. In a research and evaluation class, she opted to do a research paper on "hot spots" policing. The information she gleaned, coupled with rising crime in her district, motivated her to develop a new patrol strategy to reduce crime in hot spots in her district.

Lanier designed and launched a "precision patrol team" strategy after careful and meticulous preparation. She began the process with highly detailed crime maps available only through the central crime analysis unit. She subsequently used these data to select target areas for the strategy and later to evaluate the impact of the strategy. She then selected a team of patrol officers and extracted a strong commitment to follow the program as planned. She organized data by target area to share with the new patrol team and requested that the central crime analysis unit select peak time periods for crime in each target area. She also requested that the central crime analysis unit select comparable areas in the jurisdiction to serve as control sites. Target areas were approximately six blocks in length and were the sites of 32% of all crimes, and 15% of homicides, in her district.

The new strategy had three objectives: (a) to keep uniformed officers on the street, (b) to ensure that officers on the street are highly visible in the neighborhood area to reduce fear, and (c) to prevent crime to the extent that the overall number of crimes in the city decreases rather than increases. Lanier operated from the following hypothesis:

> The more precisely patrol presence is concentrated at the "hot spots" during "hot times" and directed at specific criminal activity, there will be less crimes in those places during those times. Simply stated, because hot spots of crime are themselves clustered, if crime at these few places can be substantially reduced, overall crime in the district will be substantially reduced.

She extracted her hypothesis from the writings of John Eck and David Weisburd's book, *Crime and Place*.[34,35]

The ideas for this program derived from Lanier's study of hot spots in combination with the acquisition of highly detailed crime maps that allowed her to easily identify the hot spot situation. Also, she took to heart complaints from citizens in her district that they never saw patrol cars. When Lanier herself was on the street, after extremely close scrutiny, she recognized that patrol cars were so much a part of the landscape that citizens no longer even noticed them, hence their impression that the police were not really out there.

Initially, precision patrol teams were to park at a designated location, or hot spot, "with their lights on" for 15 minutes of each hour during the targeted time period. A second phase would require that the precision team officers distribute crime prevention information. The third phase would require them to engage in directed patrol activities in the targeted area.

As crime analysis data became available, Lanier searched for three indicators of success: (a) reduction in crime in targeted areas, (b) displacement and diffusion effects, and (c) reduction in fear levels in the community.

Two months following the initiation of the project, UCR Part I crimes were reduced in target areas from 1% to 20%, with an overall reduction of 10%. These reductions were achieved through the application of activities during the first phase only. Lanier further concluded from crime mapping data that displacement did occur in some areas, but never at the same high rate as before to the strategy implementation.

The new patrol strategy and its effects were noted almost immediately by the police chief (Charles Ramsey) and the mayor (Anthony Williams), both of whom advocated that the strategy be implemented citywide immediately. Lanier had the following suggestions if replications were to be successful.

First, district commanders' ability to focus their attention on selecting appropriate target areas is crucial. Along with this endeavor, there is a need for enhanced crime analysis and computer mapping capabilities that *must* be carried out in-house (i.e., within the district) because the data must be recent and must not depend on the central crime analysis unit to produce them. Second, district commanders must spend concentrated amounts of time with the precision patrol team officers to ensure not only that they understand the concept but also that they are given opportunities to provide feedback for modifications on a daily basis throughout the program; this process tended to motivate officers to perform well. Third, district commanders must demonstrate their commitment to the program through daily interactions with team members during roll call *and* on the street in target areas.

Discussion

These three case studies were selected to illustrate the widely varying dynamics that lead to change and innovations in police agencies related to technology. The common thread is crime mapping and crime analysis. The CPD is an example of a bottom-up community movement that ultimately paved the way to highly significant changes in the way in which the CPD normally conducts business. Crime mapping and crime analysis, a core part of the project, forced expansion in thinking and approaches to crime control in neighborhoods and ultimately moved the CPD toward comprehensive and integrated approaches to managing police operations. The HUD study is an illustration of academically oriented individuals whose interest is piqued by something they saw or read about crime mapping coupled with severe crime issues surrounding public housing and a desire to make a difference. The initial application of the crime mapping tool ultimately led to an understanding of crime dynamics, in this case assaults against women, opening the way to new applications of principles of physical structures applied to public housing as well as to police strategies for patrol and preparing women living in public housing projects to take action to protect themselves and others. The third case study is an example of a thoughtful and enterprising patrol commander with a strong desire to improve quality of life in her patrol district for residents. It applies learning, presented to her through her academic pursuits, to her job. Her actions and creativity ultimately influenced the entire police agency.

Although all of these projects are to be applauded in that they demonstrate the power of motivated people with access to proper tools, in this case crime mapping, while illustrating the difficulty in policing today of an evenly progressing change process, which now appears to be nearly haphazard and left to random chance. It is the latter situation that police leaders must consider, and they must find means to promulgate and stimulate effective and creative ideas to bring law enforcement to a greater potential in ensuring public safety.

NOTES

1. Timothy O'Shea and Keith Nicols, *Crime Analysis in America* (Washington, DC: U.S. Department of Justice, 2002), p. 12.

2. Interpol, *Criminal Intelligence Analysis: Frequently Asked Questions.* Available: www.interpol.int/public/cia/ciafaq.asp

3. Luc Anselin, Jacqueline Cohen, David Cook, Wilpen Gorr, and George Tita, "Spatial Analysis of Crime," in *Criminal Justice 2000: Policies, Processes, and Decisions of the Criminal Justice System* (Washington, DC: U.S. Department of Justice, 2000), pp. 213–262.

4. G. L. Kelling, T. Pate, D. Dieckman, and C. E. Brown, *The Kansas City Preventive Patrol Experiment: A Technical Report* (Washington, DC: Police Foundation, 1974).

5. J. E. Boydstun, *San Diego Field Interrogation: Final Report* (Washington, DC: Police Foundation, 1975).

6. L. W. Sherman, "Police Crackdowns: Initial and Residual Deterrence," in *Crime and Delinquency Justice: A Review of Research,* edited by M. Tonry and N. Morris (Chicago: University of Chicago Press, 1990).

7. Phyllis Parshall McDonald, *Managing Police Operations: Implementing the New York Crime Control Model–CompStat* (Belmont, CA: Wadsworth, 2002).

8. O'Shea and Nicols, *Crime Analysis in America,* pp. 34–35.

9. Jack Greene, "Community Policing in America: Changing the Nature, Structure, and Function of the Police," in *Criminal Justice 2000: Policies, Processes, and Decisions of the Criminal Justice System* (Washington, DC: U.S. Department of Justice, 2000), pp. 299–370.

10. David Weisburd, Stephen Mastrofski, Roseanne Greenspan, and Anne Marie McNally, *CompStat and Organizational Change: A National Assessment* (Washington, DC: U.S. Department of Justice, 2003).

11. *President's National Advisory Commission on Civil Disorder* (Washington, DC: Government Printing Office, 1968).

12. O'Shea and Nicols, *Crime Analysis in America.*

13. Tom Peters and R. H. Waterman, Jr., *In Search of Excellence: Lessons from America's Best-Run Companies* (New York: Harper & Row, 1982).

14. Peter Senge, Art Kleiner, Charlotte Roberts, Rick Ross, and Bryan Smith, *The Fifth Discipline Fieldbook: Strategies and Tools for Building a Learning Organization* (London: Nicholas Brealey, 1994).

15. Ibid., pp. 3–4.

16. Heather MacDonald, "America's Best Urban Police Force," *City Journal* (vol. 10, Summer, 2000), pp. 14–31. (New York: Manhattan Institute)

17. Al Blumstein, "Why Is Crime Falling—Or Is It? in *Perspectives on Crime and Justice: 2000–2001 Lecture Series* (Washington, DC: U.S. Department of Justice, 2002), pp. 1–34.

18. Sherman, "Police Crackdowns."

19. Anthony A. Braga, *Systemic Review of the Effects of Hot Spots Policing on Crime*. Review protocol submitted to the Campbell Collaboration Crime and Justice Group and the Smith Richardson Foundation Testbed Review of Randomized Controlled Trials, draft copy, 2003.

20. Ronald V. Clark, *Situational Crime Prevention* (Orem, UT: William Fowlke Associates, 2002).

21. David Osborne and Ted Gaebler, *Re-inventing Government: How the Entrepreneurial Spirit Is Transforming the Public Sector* (New York: Plume, 1993).

22. Conversation between the author and Peter O'Malley, deputy mayor and Citi-Stat manager for the City of Baltimore, October 2000.

23. Phyllis McDonald and Barbara Boland, *Final Report to the Governor's Commission on Crime Control and Prevention (State of Maryland): A study of Patrol Effectiveness and Implications for Hot Spot Policing*. Unpublished report, 2003.

24. Interview with Cynthia Lum, crime analyst for the Prince George's County Police Department, and Phyllis McDonald, October 1997. (Lum is now on the faculty of Northeastern University.)

25. The unified field theory in the field of physics seeks to understand the dynamics and interrelationships of electromagnetism and gravitation.

26. Nancy La Vigne and Cynthia Mamalian, "Mapping Crime and Geographic Information Systems," in *Mapping Crime: Principle and Practice* (Washington, DC: U.S. Department of Justice, 1999).

27. O'Shea and Nicols, *Crime Analysis in America*, pp. 34–35.

28. Lawrence Sherman, "Evidence-Based Policing," in *Ideas in American Policing* (Washington, DC: Police Foundation, 1998).

29. Urban Nulden, *Police Practice and Information Technology*. Paper presented at the Viktoria Institute, Goteborg, Sweden.

30. Thomas Frazier and Phyllis McDonald, *Impediments to Homeland Security* (Columbia, MD: Division of Public Safety Leadership, 2002).

31. Marc Busik and Michael Maltz, "Power to the People: Mapping and Information Sharing," in *Crime Mapping and Crime Prevention,* Crime Prevention Studies, vol. 8, edited by David Weisburd and Tom McEwen. (Monsey, NY: Criminal Justice Press, 1997), pp. 113–130.

32. H. R. Holzman, R. B. Hyatt, and Joseph M. Dempster, "Patterns of Aggravated Assault in Public Housing," *Violence Against Women* (vol. 1, no. 6, 2001), 662–684.

33. H. R. Holzman, R. A. Hyatt, and T. R. Kudrick, "Capable Guardians," in *Dangerous Spaces: A Geographic Information Systems (GIS) Analysis of Crime in Public Housing*. Paper presented at the annual meeting of the American Society of Criminology, Toronto.

34. Catherine Lanier, *Precision Patrol Team: Initial Summary Report*. Unpublished report, Washington (D.C.) Metropolitan Police Department, 2002, p. 7.

35. Eck and Weisburd, *Crime and Place*.

CHAPTER 7

Geographic Information Systems and Crime Mapping in Criminal Justice Agencies

APRIL PATTAVINA

Crime mapping is not a new analytic tool. For centuries, researchers have observed the link between environmental conditions and social problems. Weisburd and McEwen (1998) describe an early use of mapping during the 1800s to detect the source of a cholera outbreak in London that had killed hundreds of people. Working on the assumption that contaminated water causes cholera, an astute doctor mapped the incidents of cholera in the city and noticed that they were clustered near a particular water pump. The handle of the pump was removed and the outbreak was contained.

The mapping process in this case was simple: Locate and mark the instances of a phenomenon on a paper map and visually scan for patterns. In fact, this continues to be a popular method of studying crime patterns. What has changed is the technology that can be used to examine geographic patterns of criminal activity. Advances in computer hardware and software during the past 20 years or so have made it cheaper, faster, and easier

to map significant amounts of information and have resulted in the development and application of more sophisticated spatial analytic techniques that can be used by researchers and practitioners to study criminal activity patterns.

Crime mapping today is considered to be part of a group of computer applications that belong to geographic information systems (GIS) technology. Because many disciplines use GIS and hardware and software capabilities are constantly evolving, an exact list of all GIS components and capabilities is difficult to explicate. In general terms, however, a basic GIS consists of computer hardware, individual- and/or area level-data with geographic identifiers, computerized maps, and software that has the capacity to store, manipulate, analyze, display, and query geographic data for the purpose of generating maps and reports (Leipnik & Albert, 2003a). Some off-the-shelf commercial mapping software packages used by criminal justice agencies include MapInfo and ArcView. Other packages, such as CrimeStat (developed by

Ned Levine and Associates), were created specifically for crime analysis.

Mapping technology has been adopted by many criminal justice agencies. Police departments are the most common users of mapping technology. Using information from the Law Enforcement Management and Administrative Statistics (LEMAS) survey, it was reported that 32% of police departments used crime mapping in 1999, including a large majority of those serving 100,000 or more residents (Hickman & Reaves, 2001). Courts, corrections, and other social services agencies are also becoming aware of the many benefits of mapping and are incorporating its use for a variety of agency functions.

Indeed, some users of mapping technology in the criminal justice field have been quite innovative in using mapping in creative and useful ways that examine crime in a geographic context (Casady, 2003; La Vigne & Wartell, 1998, 2000). Recognizing the potential benefits of mapping technology, the federal government has sponsored the development of several agencies to support those interested in the technology. In 1997, the National Institute of Justice (NIJ) established the Mapping and Analysis for Public Safety (MAPS) program, formerly known as the Crime Mapping Research Center. This program is designed to serve as a centralized source of GIS information for the criminal justice community. The objectives are to promote research, evaluation, development, and dissemination of GIS technology.

The NIJ has also sponsored agencies to provide technical assistance to agencies planning to implement GIS technology. The Crime Mapping and Analysis Program (CMAP), under the direction of the National Law Enforcement and Corrections Technology Center, provides technical assistance and both introductory and advanced GIS training to agencies. GIS support is available for mapping criminal activity and monitoring offenders in the community.

However, even though the adoption of GIS technology has made the mapping process easier, there are many challenges involved in the implementation and application of mapping technology. Some of the challenges deal with the technical aspects of using mapping software for crime analysis, and others involve organizational issues involved in incorporating new technology into agencies. In addition, there are legal issues and responsibilities that go along with the use of information technology (IT) and that require data about individuals who are involved in the criminal justice system and/or the location of criminal activity.

There are several purposes of this chapter. The first is to describe the theoretical and philosophical movements in the criminal justice field that served to promote the use of mapping technology during the past few decades. The second is to describe how the technology is currently being used to study the geographic context of crime. The third is to identify the technical and organizational challenges that confront the adoption and use of mapping technology by criminal justice. These sections are followed by a discussion of the legal implications of mapping technology.

THEORETICAL AND PHILOSOPHICAL SUPPORT FOR GIS DEVELOPMENT IN CRIMINAL JUSTICE

The development and adoption of GIS technology in the field of criminal justice was, and continues to be, bolstered by trends in the field that place an increasing emphasis on crime and the environmental context in which it occurs. Two important movements are central to this claim. First has been the growing interest among academics in environmental criminology over the past few decades. Second has been the shift in policing philosophy to a more community- or problem-oriented approach. Together, these forces have created an abundance of opportunities to use the latest mapping technology in powerful ways to assist those interested in addressing crime in local communities.

During the 1980s, there was a renewed theoretical interest among researchers in the relationship between community characteristics and criminal behavior. Much of this research was grounded in social disorganization theory. This theory was initially developed by Shaw and McKay (1969). They mapped the residences of delinquent boys in Cook County, Illinois, from 1900 to 1966. What they discovered was that certain neighborhoods had consistently higher delinquency rates than did others. They also found that neighborhoods with high crime levels also had high levels of poverty, mobility, and ethnic heterogeneity. These characteristics were described as indicators of social disorganization, a condition that has come to be understood as the inability of residents to engage in informal social control of behavior occurring in their neighborhoods.

Summaries of research in this area have consistently shown that social and economic conditions of neighborhoods are related to offending and victimization rates in ways that are consistent with social disorganization theory (for reviews, see Bursik, 1988; Bursik & Grasmick, 1993; Sampson & Lauritsen, 1994). The initial work by Shaw and McKay provided an important foundation on which academics have advanced our understanding of the relationship between communities and crime.

Mapping technology has facilitated developments in these areas due to the increasing ease with which large data sources containing geographic identifiers can be analyzed. Even data sets that were initially developed for administrative purposes are being used for research. For example, Warner and Pierce (1993) were able to examine the relationship

between social disorganization and police calls for service in Boston neighborhoods. For their study, thousands of calls for service geocoded by police were aggregated to the neighborhood level. Using social disorganization indicators taken from the U.S. census, they found that poverty, heterogeneity, family disruption, and structural density were important predictors of neighborhood crime.

The physical condition of neighborhoods and their relationship to crime was also becoming a focus in criminology. According to the broken windows theory of Wilson and Kelling (1982), criminals take cues from the environment. An area that is in the process of physical decay conveys a message that there is a lack of social control in the area. Out of fear, residents withdraw from community life, and the cycle of decline intensifies until the area becomes attractive to criminals from both inside and outside the area.

Other theories during this time were advancing the importance of place characteristics and criminal opportunity to the explanation of criminal events (Rossmo, 2000). Some theories, such as routine activity theory and crime pattern theory (Brantingham & Brantingham, 1993), emphasize how certain factors contribute to the location of criminal activity. These factors may include offenders' spatial awareness, their daily routine activities, and the physical environment.

Routine activity theory attempts to explain why offenders may act in certain neighborhoods and/or places and not in others. According to this theory, crime opportunities are maximized when there is a convergence in time and space of a suitable target (the victim) and a motivated offender in the absence of capable guardianship (Cohen & Felson, 1979). Crime victimization will be more concentrated in areas where these elements are likely to converge. Studies in this tradition that have focused on small areas have shown that crime victimization is more frequent in areas that provide ample criminal opportunities such as bars (Roncek & Maier, 1991) and shopping malls (Ouimet, 2000).

Crime pattern theory attempts to describe how criminal opportunities come to the attention of offenders (Brantingham & Brantingham, 1993). Offenders may come into contact with criminal opportunities through their daily activities and awareness space, which may center around work, shopping, and/or entertainment. This theory suggests that there may be environmental features in a neighborhood that may draw criminals who do not live in the immediate area but who may otherwise be familiar with or frequent the area. For example, research by Block and Block (1995) suggests that some high-crime areas have the potential of drawing criminals to their locations due to accessibility by way of transit stops.

Together, these theories belong to a growing body of work defined as environmental criminology. Bottoms and Wiles (1997) define environmental criminology as the "study of crime, criminality, and victimization as they relate, first, to particular places and, secondly, to the way individuals and organizations shape their activities spatially and in doing so are in turn influenced by place based or spatial factors" (p. 305). This perspective emphasizes the location of criminal events in space and time. Crime event patterns may be associated with places, defined by Block and Block (2000) as small areas where events take place (e.g., bars, train stops, parks) and spaces that are larger areas that contain many places and events.

Supporting these areas of investigation are spatial analytic techniques that can easily identify crime "hot spots." Crime hot spots are places or spaces that experience high concentrations of criminal activity. There are various analytic tools available to determine hot spot activity (Anselin, Cohen, Cook, Gorr, & Tita, 2000), and some are already programmed into existing mapping software.

Changes in policing philosophy were also emerging during this time. There was a growing shift away from a reactive model of policing and toward a community- or problem-oriented approach to dealing with crime. This policing philosophy emphasizes the importance of resident involvement in identifying and solving crime problems as well as the need for police accountability. Central to both of these objectives is the ability of police to analyze local crime problems. Computer mapping has proved to be a valuable tool for this purpose due to the capabilities it offers for analyzing and visually displaying large amounts of information.

Police departments may have crime analysts who are responsible for preparing maps and other forms of crime analysis. Maps have become an important component of CompStat programs that involve the use of computer-driven crime statistics to manage police operations (McDonald, 2002). In her research on the New York CompStat model, McDonald (2002) describes the program as "enhanced leadership and management that focuses on a restructuring and integration of police operations driven by scientific analysis of data" (p. 29). Some of the many objectives of this model include crime control, problem solving, and accountability.

Computer mapping also serves an important community policing function that involves communication and involvement with residents. A major tenet of modern community policing is that residents and the police are coproducers of public safety (Buslik & Maltz, 1998). This implies that members of the community need information about what is happening in their neighborhoods. If community residents have knowledge about where and when crime is occurring, they can provide police with information regarding the context of the criminal activity and work with the police to determine solutions.

Maps support the coproduction model because they are often easy to interpret visually.

Crime patterns are determined from observing the data in map form, and interpretation can be open for discussion among the police and residents. The intended result is a more cooperative approach to problem solving.

Computer mapping is also gaining popularity in courts and corrections agencies. Indeed, there are a variety of computer mapping applications that can benefit many criminal justice agencies. The ultimate utility of any GIS technology, however, will depend on the data sources that serve as the basis for geographic analysis, how mapping technology is implemented in an organization, and how it is applied to relevant issues.

MAPPING THE GEOGRAPHIC CONTEXT OF CRIME

There are many approaches one can take to examine the geographic context of criminal activity. The approach taken will depend on the type of questions to be addressed and the type of information available for analysis. For example, the focus of an inquiry may be on the location of criminal activity. Some examples of crime data sources that serve this approach include police calls for service, crime incidents reported by police, and crime victimization surveys.

Other questions may require locating criminal offenders. Data sources available for this purpose may include persons arrested, gang intelligence, and offenders returning from jail or prison. Additional sources include possible crime targets, crime victims, and resources available to address the needs of communities dealing with high levels of criminality.

Mapping the Location of Criminal Activity

Using GIS to describe the spatial distribution of criminal activity is a common mapping technique used by many police departments.

The goal of this approach is to identify patterns with recent crime incident data. Pattern identification involves searching for common characteristics, such as crime type, weapon, and location, among a series of offenses.

According to Canter (2000), two types of mapping are useful for pattern identification: descriptive and analytic. Descriptive (or thematic) mapping is intended to show the geographic distribution of crime and related information. This type of map may show, for example, a point display of crime incidents and related attributes such as the location of burglaries in a city shaded by time of day. These same burglaries may then be aggregated to the neighborhood level with the counts displayed on a map of all neighborhoods across a city. The number of burglaries in each neighborhood may be further standardized by population or number of housing units in each area to map burglary rates. Information from other sources may also be included for descriptive purposes. School locations or transportation stops may be layered onto maps to explore possible relationships.

Descriptive mapping can be a powerful tool for identifying patterns. The interpretation of such maps is often based on visual inspection and subjective interpretation. Analytic mapping involves the application of statistical methods to identify patterns. In this type of mapping, observed crime distributions are compared with hypothetical random distributions to statistically test for unique patterns. Perhaps one of the more familiar applications of analytic mapping involves the identification of hot spots of criminal activity. Hot spots are often used to define places where greater than expected numbers of crimes occur (Sherman, Gartin, & Buerger, 1989).

Analytic mapping techniques are developing rapidly and often involve advanced training to use them appropriately. For example, there are several statistical methods available for hot spot analysis, but there is no consensus on which method is best. It has also been found that different techniques do not always yield the same results (Ratcliff, 2002). In addition to hot spot analysis, there have been a variety of techniques designed to support crime forecasting that involves predicting where crime is likely to occur in the future (Groff & La Vigne, 2002). Many of these techniques are still in their development phases, and their utility in predicting crime has yet to be determined.

Identification of crime patterns can assist police in allocating resources to high-crime areas (Neese, 2000) and may help to determine other factors that explain criminal events (Canter, 2000). The use of pattern detection and analyses for tactical and strategic planning has become routine for many police departments. In a survey of police departments, Mamalian and La Vigne (1999) found that among those departments that use mapping, 94% use it to inform officers and investigators of crime incident locations, 56% to make resource allocation decisions, 49% to evaluate interventions, 47% to inform residents about crime activity and changes in their community, and 44% to identify repeat calls for service.

One function of crime analysis units involves the use of crime maps as a tool for communication within the departments. Maps support the communication process and can facilitate discussion among staff members that focuses on possible reasons for any observed crime patterns. These discussions may result in suggestions for further analyses of a particular problem or development of problem-solving strategies.

To facilitate a relationship with community residents, many departments have made neighborhood-level crime maps available to the public on the Web. Some community groups have even developed their own mapping capabilities. Using crime data provided by the police in Hartford, Connecticut, citizen-based problem-solving groups were able to create their own maps to contribute to the problem-solving process (Rich, 2001).

Mapping the Location of Criminals

A major goal of mapping and pattern identification is that the process generates enough information to apprehend those responsible for committing crimes. Methods have been developed that use GIS and sophisticated spatial modeling techniques to determine an offender's residence. This process is called geographic profiling and is used in police investigations of serial crimes such as murder, rape, and arson. The technique applies a geographic focus to the spatial behavior of the offender that led to the location of the crime (Rossmo, 2000).

Geographic profiling is based on the theoretical principles of environmental criminology. To determine the most probable area of an offender's residence, this spatial analytic technique takes into account findings from "journey to crime" research that have revealed that crimes occur in close proximity to the home of the offender and that crime trips follow a distance decay function, with the number of crimes decreasing with the distance from the offender's residence. The distance that an offender will travel to commit crimes also varies by type of crime, with violent offenses occurring closer to the offender's residence than is the case with property crimes (Rossmo, 2000).

In Gore and Pattavina's (in press) investigation of neighborhood-based journey to crime patterns, they found that some high-crime neighborhoods draw clusters of offenders from neighboring communities. These observed patterns may be the result of environmental factors that bring the target neighborhoods into the awareness space of offenders living near each other. The neighborhood connection may be physical in nature (e.g., T-stops, other transportation sources), or it may be social in nature (e.g., a gang operation).

During recent years, the location of offenders has become increasingly important to courts and correctional agencies. These agencies have become responsible for providing the public with information on dangerous offenders. An example is the sex offender registry. As of February 2001, there were 386,000 convicted sex offenders registered in 49 states and the District of Columbia (Adams, 2002). Sex offender registries may be operated by police, courts, or correctional agencies. Mapping can be used to locate the addresses of dangerous offenders as well as places in close proximity to offender residences, such as schools and parks, that may be cause for community concern.

There are many other mapping applications that may be used in courts and corrections agencies. For example, some probation departments assign officers to small community areas so that they have closer contact with probationers and other community resources such as police. Some mapping software can be used to draw assigned districts based on the distribution of caseloads (Harries, 1999). Mapping applications may also be used to support prisoner reentry programs. For example, Cadora (2003) used community-level mapping to show the relationship between neighborhood incarceration levels and other government services in efforts to bolster the argument for better resource planning for incarcerated offenders when they return to communities.

Other applications in the probation and parole field might include mapping dangerous areas where probation or parole officers should be accompanied by police officers and/or mapping areas that offenders are to avoid (Harries, 1999). In this context, mapping can also facilitate greater cooperation across agencies. For example, the ability to locate the home addresses of parolees and probationers along with methods of operation

information enables law enforcement to quickly identify potential perpetrators of particular crimes occurring in a neighborhood. For example, using information on parolees provided by the Tennessee Board of Parolees, the Knoxville police were able to arrest a serial rapist by matching the addresses of parolees in conjunction with the locations of rape incidents (Hubbs, 1998).

Some programs have integrated global positioning systems (GPS) with crime mapping. GPS is a technology that uses satellite communication to identify geographic location. Offenders carry tracking devices that communicate their locations at given time intervals. In Florida, the Department of Law Enforcement, the Department of Corrections, and the Tallahassee Police Department collaborated to create the CrimeTrax system. CrimeTrax uses GPS offender tracking data and combines them with crime data extracted from law enforcement agencies. The tracked offender movements are then examined in relation to locations and times of reported crime incidents (Frost, 2002). This program demonstrates the capabilities of combined geo-based technologies along with cross-agency and cross-jurisdictional collaboration in dealing with crime problems.

Mapping has also proved to be useful in court trials. It was used for courtroom presentation at a murder trial in Lowell, Massachusetts. The evidence in the case was spread out over a large geographic area. The district attorney used a map to show the path that the offender took after the murder. The maps were referenced throughout the trial by both the prosecution and the defense (Cook, 1998).

Mapping the Location of Resources

Mapping is also increasingly being used to locate social services for offenders and victims. This process requires that additional information about services be made available for mapping. Stoe (2003) documents several applications of crime mapping for this purpose. She argues that by integrating multiple-source data, such as funding information from a variety of government agencies that sponsor victim service providers under the Victims of Crime Act (VOCA), administrators can analyze victim services in-depth.

In Stoe's (2003) report, she demonstrates a potential use of this information for delivering services to elderly victims. Using law enforcement crime reports and calls for service information, VOCA administrators can determine areas where many incidents occur and overlay this information with the locations and use rates of existing victim resources, senior housing, senior citizen centers, "meals on wheels," and other relevant services. VOCA administrators can then use this information to work with agencies to identify needed services and evaluate service need and delivery over time.

Harris, Huenke, and O'Connell (1998) used a more localized approach. They examined the proximity of recently released inmates to social services, including unemployment offices, mental health services, and substance abuse treatment centers. They found that offenders living in rural areas had limited access to these facilities, and This information was used to justify the need for drug rehabilitation services for offenders as they reintegrate into their communities.

GIS applications can also assist in identifying suitable locations for prison, jail, and halfway house facilities. This type of location or siting analysis is a specialized application of GIS and has been in use for some time (Harries, 1998). The basic approach involves using mapping to locate developable land as potential sites for a building facility. These sites may then be filtered through a series of factors that eliminate them from consideration, including prohibited land uses, lack of utilities, and lack of adequate transportation

links. The resulting sites may then be further reviewed and prioritized using additional criteria or field investigation.

Strategic Crime Mapping

Strategic crime analysis involves the study of crime data along with information collected from a variety of additional sources collected over a period of years. This approach is often used to identify factors that may be contributing to observed crime patterns. The process relies on the ability to add physical, social, and economic dimensions to crime maps. The inclusion of theoretically relevant environmental data to GIS offers significant potential for a much more comprehensive understanding of problems confronting communities.

The physical features of environments, such as the locations of schools, parks, abandoned buildings, bars, and transportation outlets, are important because they help to define the landscape of communities. As mentioned earlier, the physical environment may contribute to criminal activity by serving to concentrate criminal opportunities in space or by providing easy or familiar access to places for motivated offenders. Observed relationships may serve as the basis for testing theories or designing intervention strategies. In Cincinnati, Ohio, analysis of crime maps revealed that a rash of property crime was due to a set of unguarded steps connecting several streets. These steps gave outsiders direct access to the areas being victimized. The steps were removed, and the area was fenced off. The removal of the steps and the creation of a neighborhood watch program were credited with the subsequent decrease in crime (Neumann & Ball, 2000).

Social and economic neighborhood indicators are important because they present opportunities to study neighborhood-based crime patterns, conduct neighborhood needs assessment, and design and evaluate crime prevention and control programs. Prior research on communities and crime has consistently revealed that some neighborhoods have higher crime rates than do others, regardless of whether hot spots are present. By examining crime levels over time, one may find relationships with theoretically relevant social and economic factors that might be missed if examining address-level data exclusively. Moreover, neighborhood-level information may be used to support hot spot and place-based analysis by providing a social context with which to examine point patterns.

A report by Greene, Rich, and Ward (1999) notes the importance of linking criminal justice information with that of other government agencies: "If community oriented policing is meant to mobilize the community, and problem solving is meant to address persistent community crime and disorder problems, then linkage with other agencies and interventions is a central need of police agencies shifting from traditional to [problem-oriented policing]" (p. 150). Recognizing that comprehensive community-based profiles can assist community policing and inform the design of crime prevention and control programs, the federal government has sponsored several projects that adapt information from a variety of agency sources to enhance GIS analytic capabilities. These projects include the NIJ-sponsored Strategic Approaches to Community Safety Initiative (SACSI) and the Computer Mapping, Planning, and Analysis of Safety Strategies (COMPASS) project. These and similar projects are being developed in several cities and emphasize a "multi-agency collaboration to data-driven problem solving" (Groff, 2001, p. 1).

It may be easy for a criminal justice agency to develop or access information sources that are useful for defining the physical landscape of a community such as the locations of schools, hospitals, and vacant lots. Indeed, these are important community factors to consider for problem solving and planning. However, information about individuals living in communities is also important for understanding problems. Getting information about persons at the individual level introduces a new set of issues, particularly those associated with confidentiality.

Government agencies have traditionally been reluctant to share information, and until recently, paper files kept in file cabinets somewhere on some floor made it easy for agencies to avoid sharing large amounts of information. Now that most government agencies have become automated, requests for information are easier to fill and more difficult to deny. The government has recognized this issue, and most local agencies, state governments, and the federal government have tried to put in place information policies to protect the privacy of individuals. These laws make it difficult to access agency-based information with personal identifiers (e.g., names, addresses), especially for vulnerable groups such as crime victims, minors, and those receiving health services.

In cases where individual-level data are unavailable, there are some data-sharing projects that avoid having to deal with privacy concerns because they focus specifically on the development of neighborhood-level indicators intended for public use in analyses of social problems. The Urban Institute has sponsored the development of the National Neighborhood Indicators Project (NNIP), whose goal is to provide operational and development support to projects in major cities that merge agency data from many sources to create neighborhood-level social and economic indicator databases (Kingsley & Petit, 2000; Pattavina, Pierce, & Saiz, 2002).

These "ready-made" databases, developed at universities and research organizations, are available in more than a dozen cities. They are very useful for area-based crime analysis because they are comprehensive in content and cover communities for entire cities over long periods of time. Moreover, neither the police nor any other participating agency is solely responsible for the considerable effort needed to build, maintain, and distribute such databases. Because the data are provided to the public in aggregate form, confidentiality issues are not problematic in most cases. Small neighborhood units such as block groups offer some flexibility in constructing neighborhood boundaries.

There are a variety of federal, state, and local agencies that make available to the public information that may be used to develop area-level indicators of social, economic, and physical conditions (Coulton & Hollister, 1998; Pattavina et al., 2002). Perhaps the most widely used data source for this purpose is the U.S. Census of Housing and Population. Conducted once every 10 years by the U.S. Bureau of the Census, the census provides comprehensive information on housing stock and population for the entire country. The census also provides this information for small geographic units such as census block groups and census tracts. Government agencies and researchers commonly use these geographic units to determine neighborhood boundaries. The census bureau also provides computerized maps. Base maps available from the census include street maps, census blocks, tracts, and many other map products.

Other federal agencies provide information that reflects their respective missions. These data are usually collected for administrative purposes, but they also offer potential for community-level analysis. For example, the U.S. Department of Housing and Urban Development collects and maintains information about public and subsidized housing units. These data are available for census tracts and individual housing projects. The Federal Reserve Board, under mandate from the Home Mortgage Disclosure Act, requires lending institutions to provide information about the home purchase and improvement loan applications they receive. Demographic information about the applicants, as well as the status of the loan applications, is available. These data sources can be used to create indicators of social and economic stability of neighborhoods.

State agencies also maintain information sources that may be used to create community-level indicators. State departments of liquor control are responsible for granting permits to sell and distribute alcoholic beverages. These permits are public records and contain information on the locations of the permits and the types of outlet (e.g., liquor store, bar) (Coulton & Hollister, 1998). The number of outlets per community may be created with this information and compared with the level of crime in neighborhoods. Vital records are also maintained by state agencies and made available to the public. Information on births and deaths may be used to develop public health indicators. For example, the Massachusetts Department of Public Health provides information on births such as birthweight, health scores, and quality of prenatal care (Pattavina et al., 2002).

Local agencies also provide a wealth of information that can be useful for community-level analysis. Local property assessors' offices provide information on property for taxation purposes. Contained in these data are property addresses, descriptions of land use (e.g., residential, commercial), property condition, and assessed value of land and buildings. School departments collect information on students, including their addresses, subsidized lunch status, special education enrollment, days absent, dropout status, and test scores.

Private agencies, such as yellow pages and other business directories, maintain data on local businesses. Information collected may include street address, type of business or organization, sales volume, and number of employees. From these data, the numbers and types of businesses in local communities can be determined. Other public safety sources include resident surveys. According to Smith and Hayeslip (1998), city surveys are a way in which to obtain information about citizens' concerns such as attitudes toward police and the perception of crime issues confronting their communities.

How useful agency data sources will be depends on the availability and quality of the data. Table 7.1 summarizes some of the important data quality issues. Positional accuracy refers to precision in assigning geographic coordinates or geocoding. Geocoding a file with addresses may be subject to a variety of errors. Addresses may fail to be assigned geographic coordinates due to inaccurate address information from the person who enters the address. Sources of error may include inaccurate street spellings, inconsistent abbreviations for streets, multiple streets with the same name, and even wrong street numbers. The computerized street maps also may be outdated or inaccurate (for further discussion of geocoding issues, see Powell & Clifton, 1999; Ratcliff, 2002).

Although most geocoding software routines have procedures that filter out problem addresses and even suggest corrections, analysts must pay careful attention to the percentage of records that get assigned coordinates. Mapping a data set where a significant percentage of records were not geocoded can result in an invalid analysis.

Attribute accuracy pertains to how attributes or indicators are measured. Specific issues include data collection methods and indicator measurement. Data collection problems can result in reporting bias and error. One example involves school dropouts. Often at the end of the year, the number of official dropouts is tabulated. However, there are instances in which children just stop coming to school and do not officially withdraw. These are considered unofficial

dropouts and are not counted at the end of the year. A dropout figure based on the end-of-year official dropout tabulation would be underestimated, and the degree of this type of error may differ across schools and communities in an unknown way. Another issue is how specific categories should be. A race or ethnicity variable with too few categories may mask important variations in racial composition of communities that might have relevance for understanding problems. Data entry errors also affect the accuracy of attributes.

Logical consistency involves the degree to which there are contradictory relations in the underlying database. An example is that some calls for service are geocoded to the places where the crimes took place, whereas others are geocoded to the places where the calls originated. Completeness of data sources is another data quality issue. Missing data is a common problem, especially where agency data sources are collected for administrative purposes. The extent of missing data may compromise the usefulness of a particular database (e.g., a database where less than half of the addresses were entered). Even if the database has an acceptable number of cases, particular attributes may have a significant number of missing values. For example, residents who agree to provide addresses might be unwilling to answer specific questions about police performance in their neighborhood.

A final data quality issue involves the lineage or availability of data sources over time. Some data sources, such as the U.S. census, are conducted every 10 years. Although between census estimates are provided, they are available only for select groups of demographics. This is problematic when the goal of a mapping project is to examine trends over time or to evaluate a particular program.

Changes in reporting practices over time may compromise time series analysis. For example, consider the recent change in official crime reporting from the Uniform

Table 7.1   Categories of Data Quality

Category	Definition	Examples
Positional accuracy	Degree of accuracy in assigning geographic coordinates (geocoding)	Updated and accurate computerized maps must be available. Locational information in criminal justice databases must be accurate.
Attribute accuracy	Degree of error associated with the way in which attributes are measured and categorized	Broad crime categories such as "gang crime" may be misleading. "High school dropouts" may include only those who have officially withdrawn and not those who simply failed to show.
Logical consistency	Degree to which there may be contradictory relations in the underlying database	Some calls for service are geocoded to the places where the crimes took place, whereas others are located where the calls originated.
Completeness	Degree to which data are missing and method of handling missing data	The ability to estimate crime rates for specific areas may be compromised if data for those areas are missing.
Lineage	Degree to which there is a chronological set of similar data developed using the modeling and processing methods	Changes in reporting practices or technology development over time will compromise forecasting techniques and time series analysis. Population estimates might not be available for all years but may be estimated using different techniques and data sources.

SOURCE: Adapted from O'Looney, J. (1997). *Beyond maps: GIS and decision making in local government.* Washington, DC: International City/County Management.

Crime Reporting (UCR) system to the National Incident-Based Reporting system (NIBRS) that many police agencies have undergone. There is a major difference in the way in which crime incidents are recorded. The UCR system uses the hierarchy rule, whereby only the most serious offense per incident is reported. The NIBRS system requires that all offenses related to an incident be reported. Such changes in reporting practices would affect a longitudinal study of crime trends if the study time period spanned the reporting system change because the number of crimes would be counted differently depending on the reporting system used.

Related to data quality problems are technical issues that arise when sharing information across agencies. Data may come in a variety of database formats that require translation to a common format. Agencies that do geocoding may have different geocoding rates. The result may be the loss of important data.

Eck (2002) describes factors that further influence the utility of interjurisdictional crime mapping for police. Across jurisdictions, agencies may experience different citizen reporting practices. For example, one jurisdiction may be involved in a campaign to increase awareness and reporting of domestic violence. The result may be a higher level of reported domestic violence incidents in that jurisdiction compared with the levels in adjacent areas. Agencies may also vary in how crimes are recorded and classified. Although there are federal standards to reduce discrepancies, variations in how minor crimes and incivilities are recorded may persist. Some agencies may provide more descriptive information about crime events than do others. All of these factors affect the validity and reliability of the data.

When using aggregate information, there is potential for error because relationships observed at one level of aggregation might not hold at other levels of aggregation. The probability of error increases as the level of aggregation becomes greater (O'Looney, 1997). Thus, it is often desirable to use the lowest level of aggregation possible. Interpretation of maps at aggregate levels may also fall victim to the ecological fallacy, whereby assumptions about individuals are made based on the examination of aggregate data.

The importance of data quality to GIS applications should not be underestimated. The validity of any geographic analysis using crime and related data will depend on a variety of factors associated with collection, entry, geocoding and attribute creation. Therefore, quality assurance is an important responsibility of any agency that uses information from, or provides information to, a GIS.

ORGANIZATIONAL ISSUES

The successful implementation of any new IT requires considerable organizational support and commitment. Some agencies have been more successful than others in making the most of a GIS. O'Looney (1997) describes three phases of GIS implementation and the typical structure of operations at each level.

First is the beginning phase. At this point, there is usually a single user such as a crime analyst assigned within the agency to collect and enter the relevant data into a GIS. This person often has limited training and little time to develop skills. Without organized access to essential skill building, most GIS users during this phase are limited to basic inventory functions and descriptive mapping. Agencies here have yet to combine criminal justice experience with GIS expertise in ways that lead to more advanced analysis of data.

Second is the intermediate phase. At this point, many of the technical issues involved with GIS have been addressed, including the specification of standards for entering data and plans to eliminate duplication of data collected within the department. All map layers (e.g., street maps, district maps, census maps) have been standardized, and there is some sharing of departmental databases and map layers. There is sufficient access to training and more criminal justice expertise among the GIS users. The result is more productive exploration of data.

Last is the advanced phase. This phase is characterized by greater data sharing across agencies and with the public. Access to GIS, data, and maps is provided by way of a central repository. The GIS becomes a major function of a skilled team that has analysis capabilities, has knowledge of a full range of data sources, is able to use a variety of GIS technologies, and can produce a variety of data analysis projects. Criminal justice area expertise or access to such expertise is organized across departments where GIS is used.

La Vigne and Wartell (2001) offer case studies of several regional crime analysis programs that would fall in the advanced category. One example is the Regional Crime Analysis Geographic Information System (RCAGIS) serving the Baltimore (Maryland) Metropolitan Area. During the early 1990s, the Baltimore Police Department and the Baltimore County Police Department began to share information on a series of robberies being committed by an organized group of offenders. Based on information contributed by both agencies, the robbers were apprehended. The success of that operation was used to garner support for the development of a program specifically designed for regional sharing of information. The RCAGIS was the resulting program. A major objective of the RCAGIS was to standardize the technical aspects of how crime data are presented on maps as well as the analytic tools and procedures that crime analysts and managers would use on a routine basis.

Successful GIS development and implementation is a multistep process that involves both organizational and technical considerations (O'Looney, 1997). Initially, it involves establishing a project team. Members of this team should include, but should not be limited to, those members of the organization who are interested in using GIS outputs as well as those who will be responsible for managing the implementation of the system. Individuals from other agencies who have recently implemented GIS capabilities might also prove to be useful to the team (Leipnik & Albert, 2003b).

The project team would then be responsible for conducting a needs assessment for the agency. This would involve determining what specific tasks the GIS would be used for and who in the organization would likely use the GIS. This would be followed by the implementation plan. This plan focuses on many of the technical aspects that the organization must address based on the needs assessment. Questions about system functionality are particularly important. For example, Leipnik and Albert (2003b) argue that a functional requirement study is useful here because it would help the organization to identify key issues such as whether the GIS system would need to interface with other data systems or would exist as a stand-alone system. Also relevant are the types of spatial analysis that the organization wishes to conduct using the GIS (e.g., hot spot analysis,

geographic profiling), staff training needs, and technical documentation. The answers to such questions are important because they guide the selection of hardware and software and determine the level of support necessary for the GIS to meet organizational needs.

Mazerolle, Bellucci, and Gajewski (1998) argue that the processes involved in purchasing, installing, customizing, and using crime mapping systems can be complicated because there are many possible configurations for a GIS. A GIS may be simple and consist of a single copy of an off-the-shelf desktop mapping program installed on a stand-alone PC, or it may be a customized integrated system specifically designed for an organization by a third-party software vendor. Given the wide range for possible system configurations, identifying key GIS tasks and users becomes essential. Without an understanding of who in the organization is going to use the system and for what purposes, efforts to implement crime mapping technology can become misguided, and the result may be a system design that fails to meet expectations.

Once the specific GIS functionality has been determined, the implementation process must be managed by the organization. Individuals from the organization who are involved in the implementation plan and the end users must communicate with software vendors during the system configuration, especially in cases where software must be customized to meet organizational needs. This is important because the role of the vendor can be quite influential in how agencies are informed about crime mapping.

In a study of police departments in New Jersey, Chamard (2003) found that 44% of police chiefs reported that they had learned about crime mapping from computer hardware and software vendors. Without key organizational input at this stage, many technical decisions will be left to vendors that often have little experience in criminal justice or little knowledge of how criminal justice agencies operate. Systems designed by vendors with little organization input are often underused. The final installation should involve hands-on training for all users as well as the provision of training documentation appropriate for beginning and more advanced users along with documentation to support relevant system functions.

Even if a GIS is effectively installed in an agency from a technical standpoint, this does not guarantee a systemwide adoption and planned use of the technology. Manning (2001) argues that, in addition to the technical constraints facing GIS implementation in organizations, there may be cultural issues supported by long-standing traditions that might not be consistent with the new work processes and objectives imposed by new ITs. For example, Manning acknowledges the potential of crime mapping as a means to support the preventive and problem-solving aspects of the community policing philosophy, but he argues that the nature of this technology is contradictory to the still dominant operational functions of the police as a responsive, demand-driven situational force. He further argues that the agencies will more likely adapt the technologies to support traditional work patterns rather than adapt to the technologies and embrace the new opportunities for work presented by innovation.

This concern has been echoed in other agencies as well. In a meeting summary of the NIJ-sponsored Mapping in Corrections Resource Group Meeting, a major factor impeding the adoption and use of mapping technology was the reluctance of corrections personnel to change the ideology of corrections from one that is institution or "fortress" based to one that is more community based and willing to take advantage of mapping technologies (Crime Mapping Research Center, 1999).

As described earlier in the chapter, sharing crime information with the public has its advantages. Just how organizations share maps and spatial data with the public has

become an important public concern, especially as advances in Web-based technology make it easier to provide information to the public. Internet mapping may involve posting pregenerated maps in standard graphic formats (e.g., .jpg, .gif), or it may be interactive, thereby allowing users some choices in the information to be mapped. The latter is more sophisticated and involves the use of specialized software.

Wartell and McEwen (2001) argue that there are several major issues related to the sharing of spatial data with the community. The first involves reaching a balance between citizens' right to know about crime in their community and victims' right to privacy. Victims may be averse to having the locations of their residences or locations of the offenses indicated on a map planned for public release. They may experience fear that they will be viewed as easy targets in the future. Victims might not cooperate with investigations and prosecutions if they believe that offenders will be able to locate them on a public map. If future victimizations do occur, some victims may be reluctant to report the incidents to the police due to the publicity that may be generated through a released crime map.

A related issue involves the release of geocoded information to researchers. Most researchers abide by confidentiality requirements applying to collection and use of sensitive information, but those requirements have not been formally addressed with geocoded data (Wartell & McEwen, 2001). In this case, the balance is between privacy and the advancement of the criminal justice field through research.

Standards and guidelines for criminal justice information sharing are increasingly becoming the subject of local, state, and federal policies. For Web-based mapping, security becomes an additional concern because the underlying data supporting the programs may be vulnerable to modification by intruders, even if security features are built in to prevent access to sensitive information.

There are also potential social and economic ramifications of releasing maps to the public. Although to date there have been no systematic studies of the negative consequences of publicly available crime maps, researchers and policymakers warn that the maps may be used in ways that should be of concern. Wartell and McEwen (2001) argue that crime maps may be used for controversial commercial purposes such as the aggressive advertising of security systems in high-crime areas or even to those who have been crime victims.

The economic health of communities may be affected by crime maps. For example, real estate values may decrease and insurance premiums may increase (or insurance may be denied altogether) in areas shown to have crime problems. Businesses may choose not to locate in these areas. Individuals might not want to work or seek recreation in these areas. Ratcliff (2002) argues that these outcomes result from spatial labeling, whereby communities become undesirable due to the publicizing of problems.

CONCLUSION

The integration of GIS technology into the field of criminal justice has helped to move criminal justice policy and research in a direction that places increasing emphasis on the relationship between crime and the environmental context in which it occurs. As discussed throughout this chapter, there are an abundance of opportunities to use the latest mapping technology in powerful ways to assist those interested in addressing public safety issues in local communities. The successful application of crime mapping technology will rely heavily on the software capabilities, knowledge of theory, and creativity of the analysts generating the map products (Manning, 2001; Ratcliff, 2002).

There are many potential users of GIS technology in criminal justice. In cases where individual-level data are unavailable or the focus of an analysis is on neighborhoods, users may include agency administrators, line staff members, researchers, and members of the public. In the rush to adopt new technology, however, there are important issues associated with GIS implementation, organizational culture, data quality, and information privacy that must be carefully considered for the responsible development and use of GIS technology. It is important to learn from past mistakes and be willing to share experiences so that we can continue to assess how GIS technology is changing the operation of the criminal justice system.

REFERENCES

Adams, D. (2002). *Summary of state offender registries, 2001*. Washington, DC: U.S. Department of Justice.

Anselin, L., Cohen, J., Cook, D., Gorr, W., & Tita, G. (2000). Spatial analysis of crime. In *Criminal justice 2000* (pp. 213–262). Washington, DC: U.S. Department of Justice.

Block, R. L., & Block, C. R. (1995). Space, place, and crime: Hotspot areas and hot places of liquor related crime. In J. Eck & D. Weisburd (Eds.), *Crime and place* (pp. 145–184). Monsey, NY: Criminal Justice Press.

Block, R. L., & Block, C. R. (2000). The Bronx and Chicago: Street robbery in the environs of rapid transit stations. In V. Goldsmith, P. McGuire, J. H. Mollenkopf, & T. Ross (Eds.), *Analyzing crime patterns: Frontiers of practice* (pp. 137–152). Thousand Oaks, CA: Sage.

Bottoms, A. E., & Wiles, P. (1997). Environmental criminology. In M. Maguire, R. Morgan, & R. Reiner (Eds.), *The Oxford handbook of criminology.* Oxford, UK: Clarendon.

Brantingham, P. L., & Brantingham, P. J. (1993). Environment, routine, and situation: Toward a pattern theory of crime. In R. V. Clark & M. Felson (Eds.), *Advances in criminological theory,* Vol. 5: *Routine activity and rational choice* (pp. 259–294). New Brunswick, NJ: Transaction Publishers.

Bursik, R. J. (1988). Social disorganization and theories of crime and delinquency: Problems and prospects. *Criminology, 26,* 519–551.

Bursik, R. J., & Grasmick, H. G. (1993). *Neighborhoods and crime.* New York: Lexington Books.

Buslik, M., & Maltz, M. D. (1998). Power to the people: Mapping and information sharing in the Chicago Police Department. In D. Weisburd & T. McEwen (Eds.), *Crime prevention studies,* Vol. 8: *Crime mapping and crime prevention* (pp. 113–130). Monsey, NY: Criminal Justice Press.

Cadora, E. (2003). Criminal justice and health and human services: An exploration of overlapping needs, resources, and interests in Brooklyn neighborhoods. In J. Travis & M. Waul (Eds.), *Prisoners once removed* (pp. 285–312). Washington, DC: Urban Institute.

Canter, P. (2000). Using a geographic information system for tactical crime analysis. In V. Goldsmith, P. McGuire, J. H. Mollenkopf, & T. Ross (Eds.), *Analyzing crime patterns: Frontiers of practice* (pp. 3–10). Thousand Oaks, CA: Sage.

Casady, T. (2003). Specific examples of GIS successes. In M. R. Leipnik & D. P. Albert (Eds.), *GIS in law enforcement* (pp. 113–126). New York: Taylor & Francis.

Chamard, S. (2003, November). *Police chiefs' exposure to information about computerized crime mapping and their opinions about the innovation.* Paper presented at the annual meeting of the American Society of Criminology, Denver, CO.

Cohen, L. E., & Felson, M. (1979). Social change and crime rate trends: A routine activity approach. *American Sociological Review, 44,* 588–608.

Cook, P. (1998). Mapping a murderer's path. In N. La Vigne & J. Wartell (Eds.), *Crime mapping case studies: Successes in the field* (Vol. 1, pp. 123–128). Washington, DC: Police Executive Research Forum.

Coulton, C., & Hollister, R. (1998). Measuring comprehensive community initiative outcomes using data available for small areas. In K. Fulbright-Anderson, A. C. Kubisch, & J. P. Connell (Eds.), *New approaches to evaluating community initiatives,* Vol. 2: *Theory, measurement, and analysis.* Washington, DC: Aspen Institute.

Crime Mapping Research Center. (1999). *National Institute of Justice Mapping in Corrections Resource Group Meeting.* New York: Author.

Eck, J. (2002). *Crossing the borders of crime: Factors influencing the utility and practicality of interjurisdictional crime mapping.* Washington, DC: Police Foundation.

Frost, G. (2002). Florida's innovative use of GPS for community corrections. *Journal of Offender Monitoring, 15*(2), 6–8.

Gore, R., & Pattavina, A. (in press). Applications for examining the journey to crime using incident-based offender residence probability surfaces. *Police Quarterly.*

Green, J., Rich, T., & Ward, S. (1999). *Police Department Information Systems Technology Enhancement Project: Cross-site report* (report to the Office of Community-Oriented Policing Services). Cambridge, MA: Abt Associates.

Groff, E. R. (2001). *Strategic Approaches to Community Safety Initiative (SACSI): Enhancing the analytic capacity of a local problem solving effort.* Washington, DC: U.S. Department of Justice.

Groff, E. R., & La Vigne, N. G. (2002). Forecasting the future of predictive crime mapping. In N. Tilley (Ed.), *Analysis for crime prevention* (pp. 29–58). Monsey, NY: Criminal Justice Press.

Harries, K. (1999). *Mapping crime: Principle and practice.* Washington, DC: U.S. Department of Justice.

Harris, R., Huenke, C., & O'Connell, J. P. (1998). Using mapping to increase released offenders' access to services. In N. La Vigne & J. Wartell (Eds.), *Crime mapping case studies: Successes in the field* (Vol. 1, pp. 61–68). Washington, DC: Police Executive Research Forum.

Hickman, M., & Reaves, B. (2001). *Local police departments, 1999.* Washington, DC: U.S. Department of Justice.

Hubbs, R. (1998). The Greenway rapist case: Matching repeat offenders with crime locations. In N. La Vigne & J. Wartell (Eds.), *Crime mapping case studies: Successes in the field* (Vol. 1, pp. 93–98). Washington, DC: Police Executive Research Forum.

Kingsley, T. G., & Petit, K. L. S. (2000, October). Getting to know neighborhoods, 2000. *National Institute of Justice Journal,* pp. 10–17.

La Vigne, N. G., & Wartell, J. (Eds.). (1998). *Crime mapping case studies: Successes in the field* (Vol. 1). Washington, DC: Police Executive Research Forum.

La Vigne, N. G., & Wartell, J. (Eds.). (2000). *Crime mapping case studies: Successes in the field* (Vol. 2). Washington, DC: Police Executive Research Forum.

La Vigne, N. G., & Wartell, J. (2001). *Mapping across boundaries.* Washington, DC: Police Executive Research Forum.

Leipnik, M. R., & Albert, D. P. (2003a). How law enforcement agencies can make geographic information technologies work for them. In M. R. Leipnik & D. P. Albert (Eds.), *GIS in law enforcement* (pp. 1–8). New York: Taylor & Francis.

Leipnik, M. R., & Albert, D. P. (2003b). Overview of implementation issues. In M. R. Leipnik & D. P. Albert (Eds.), *GIS in law enforcement* (pp. 9–46). New York: Taylor & Francis.

Mamalian, C. A., & La Vigne, N. G. (1999). *The use of crime mapping by law enforcement: Survey results.* Washington, DC: U.S. Department of Justice.

Manning, P. (2001). Technology's ways: Information technology, crime analysis, and the rationalizing of policing. *Criminal Justice, 1,* 83–103.

Mazerolle, L. G., Bellucci, C., & Gajewski, F. (1998). Crime mapping in police departments: The challenges of building a mapping system. In D. Weisburd & T. McEwen (Eds.), *Crime prevention studies,* Vol. 8: *Crime mapping and crime prevention* (pp. 131–156). Monsey, NY: Criminal Justice Press.

McDonald, P. P. (2002). *Managing police operations: Implementing the New York crime control model–CompStat.* Belmont, CA: Wadsworth.

Neese, A. (2000). Using GIS for police redistricting. In N. G. La Vigne & J. Wartell (Eds.), *Crime mapping case studies: Successes in the field* (Vol. 2, pp. 109–116). Washington, DC: Police Executive Research Forum.

Neumann, M., & Ball, A. (2000). Guiding environmental design and neighborhood problem solving. In N. G. La Vigne & J. Wartell (Eds.), *Crime mapping case studies: Successes in the field* (Vol. 2, pp. 37–41). Washington, DC: Police Executive Research Forum.

O'Looney, J. (1997). *Beyond maps: GIS and decision making in local government.* Washington, DC: International City/County Management Association.

Ouimet, M. (2000). Aggregation bias in ecological research: How social disorganization and criminal opportunities shape the spatial distribution of juvenile delinquency in Montreal. *Canadian Journal of Criminology, 42,* 135–156.

Pattavina, A., Pierce, G., & Saiz, A. (2002). Urban neighborhood information systems: Crime prevention and control applications. *Journal of Urban Technology, 9*(2), 37–56.

Powell, E., & Clifton, M. (1999). *Address based geocoding: Final report.* Washington, DC: U.S. Department of Justice.

Ratcliffe, J. H. (2002). Damned if you don't, damned if you do: Crime mapping and its implications in the real world. *Policing and Society, 12,* 211–225.

Rich, T. (2001). *Crime mapping and analysis by community organizations in Hartford, Connecticut.* Washington, DC: U.S. Department of Justice.

Roncek, D. W., & Maier, P. A. (1991). Bars, blocks, and crimes revisited: Linking the theory of routine activities to the empiricism of "hot spots." *Criminology, 29,* 725–754.

Rossmo, D. K. (2000). *Geographic profiling.* Boca Raton, FL: CRC Press.

Sampson, R. J., & Lauritsen, J. L. (1994). Violent victimization and offending: Individual-, situational-, and community-level risk factors. In A. J. Reiss & J. A. Roth (Eds.), *Understanding and preventing violence,* Vol. 3: *Social influences* (pp. 1–114). Washington, DC: National Academy Press.

Shaw, C., & McKay, H. (1969). *Juvenile delinquency and urban areas* (rev. ed.). Chicago: University of Chicago Press.

Sherman, L. W., Gartin, P. R., & Buerger, M. E. (1989). Hotspots of predatory crime: Routine activities and the criminology of place. *Criminology, 27,* 27–55.

Smith, S. K., & Hayeslip, D. W. (1998, October). Using city-level surveys to better understand community policing. *National Institute of Justice Journal.*

Stoe, D. A. (2003). *Using geographic information systems to map crime victim services.* Washington, DC: U.S. Department of Justice.

Warner, B. D., & Pierce, G. L. (1993). Reexamining social disorganization theory using calls to the police as a measure of crime. *Criminology, 31,* 493–513.

Wartell, J., & McEwen, T. (2001). *Privacy in the information age: A guide for sharing crime maps and spatial data.* Washington, DC: National Institute of Justice.

Weisburd, D., & McEwen, T. (1998). Introduction: Crime mapping and crime prevention. In D. Weisburd & T. McEwen (Eds.), *Crime prevention studies,* Vol. 8: *Crime mapping and crime prevention* (pp. 1–25). Monsey, NY: Criminal Justice Press.

Wilson, J. Q., & Kelling, G. L. (1982, March). Broken windows. *Atlantic Monthly,* pp. 29–38.

Section IV

INFORMATION TECHNOLOGY ISSUES IN CRIMINAL JUSTICE AGENCIES

CHAPTER 8

Comprehensive Planning of Criminal Justice Information and Intelligence Systems

ATF's Experience in Implementing Firearms Tracing in the United States

GLENN PIERCE AND ROBERTA E. GRIFFITH

In 2002, there were 9,369 firearms-related homicides in the United States, and of these, 3,651 involved victims under 25 years of age. In terms of aggravated assault and robbery, 19.0% of the 894,348 aggravated assaults and 42.1% of the 420,637 robberies reported by the Uniform Crime Reporting (UCR) program in 2000 involved firearms (Federal Bureau of Investigation [FBI], 2003).

Firearms violence in the United States has been linked to the operation of illegal gun markets (Blumstein & Cook, 1996). Importantly, because two of the most frequent groups of firearms offenders in the United States—criminal offenders and juveniles—are legally prohibited from purchasing handguns nearly everywhere in the nation, such individuals are likely to turn to illegal markets to obtain firearms. Equally important, research suggests that if the supply of guns could be stopped or severely disrupted, gun violence could be hindered. Research by Braga, Cook, Kennedy, and Moore (2002) shows that "illegal gun markets consist of both 'point sources'—ongoing diversions through scofflaw dealers, trafficking rings, and gun thieves—and 'diffuse sources'—acquisitions through direct theft and informal voluntary sales" (p. 337). This research suggests that a better understanding of the illegal firearms markets is a necessary step toward a more comprehensive understanding of violent firearms crime.

AUTHORS' NOTE: The authors thank Terry Austin, chief of the National Tracing Center for the Bureau of Alcohol, Tobacco, Firearms, and Explosives; Susan Ginsburg, former Senior Advisor to the Department of Treasury's Office of the Under Secretary for Enforcement; Anthony Braga, John F. Kennedy School of Government, Harvard University; John Freeman of the Crime Gun Analysis Branch, Bureau of Alcohol, Tobacco, Firearms, and Explosives; Lois Mock, program manager for the National Institute of Justice; and Alan Saiz of Northeastern University for their highly valuable comments and insights.

Research also indicates that there is significant regional variability in the character of illegal firearms markets (Pierce, Braga, Hyatt, & Koper, 2004). This type of complexity presents challenges to law enforcement officials interested in disrupting the illegal supply of guns to criminal offenders and other prohibited persons because it suggests that there may be no single best strategic and/or tactical approach to disrupting the illegal supply of guns across different jurisdictions in the United States (Pierce et al., 2004). Given this variability, jurisdictions engaged in disrupting illegal gun markets and reducing gun violence need ready access to accurate and comprehensive information on the character of illegal firearms markets within their respective communities.

Such information can help to provide a basis for improving our strategic and tactical understanding of local and regional firearms trafficking, and this in turn provides the potential for better focusing and coordinating law enforcement resources and intervention initiatives. A major source of this type of information is potentially available through analyses of traced firearms recovered by law enforcement from criminal offenders, juveniles, other prohibited persons, and/or criminal circumstances.

The Bureau of Alcohol, Tobacco, Firearms, and Explosives (ATF) is the agency responsible for tracing firearms, which is the systematic tracking of the movement of firearms recovered by law enforcement. Ideally, ATF will trace a firearm from the manufacturer or importer through the distribution chain (i.e., wholesalers and retailers) to the first retail purchaser or to a point where all other possibilities of identifying the original purchaser have been thoroughly exhausted. There are two primary components in the tracing process: (a) the systematic collection of information on crime-related firearms from law enforcement units that confiscated or found these weapons and (b) the tracing of the commercial transactions of the crime-related firearms recovered by law enforcement.

A FRAMEWORK FOR COMPREHENSIVE INFORMATION AND INTELLIGENCE SYSTEM PLANNING

The objective of this chapter is to examine the information management, crime analysis, and intelligence capabilities developed by ATF over the past decade so as to use crime gun trace data to investigate firearms trafficking and help reduce firearms crime. In addition, the chapter examines the context within which ATF developed firearms tracing information systems and crime analysis/intelligence systems so as to help formulate improved guidelines for designing and implementing complex applications for the criminal justice system.

The challenge of developing this type of capability goes well beyond information technology (IT)-related issues. The structure and geographic organization of criminal justice has had profound effects on the evolution of information systems. The American criminal justice system operates at the local, county, metropolitan, state, and federal levels of government. At each level of government, agencies are further divided along functional lines (e.g., police, courts, prosecution and defense, corrections, probation and parole). In addition, various state and local jurisdictions operate under different legal and regulatory systems. Finally, variations in the character of violent crime across jurisdictions can result in different regional law enforcement priorities and the concurrent need for different types of intelligence and crime analysis. The results are organizational disjunctures that present significant potential barriers to developing integrated information systems but also represent a major rationale for developing such systems.

Beyond geographic, functional, and legal factors, organizational disunity and communication problems are increased when multiple agencies have responsibility for implementing and managing a given policy or set of policies. Peters (1996) notes that for multiagency policy implementation/management, "the problems of organizational disunity and communication become exaggerated when the individuals involved are not bound even by a presumed loyalty to a single organization but have competing loyalties to different organizations, not all of which may be interested in the effective implementation of a particular program" (p. 120).

The current analysis examines the legal, organizational, and technical contexts that shape ATF's ability to acquire, analyze, and ultimately use information on illegal firearms markets for the purpose of controlling firearms crime. A review of these factors suggests a set of questions or issues that provide a framework for examining ATF's efforts in this arena. Importantly, the analysis also provides a more general framework for assessing IT systems and intelligence projects in the criminal justice system.

The specific research questions/issues incorporated in the framework include the following:

1. How does the legal context of ATF affect the agency's ability to (a) collect, manage, and disseminate firearms trace data from law enforcement agencies and (b) use these data to identify patterns (and specific instances) of illegal firearms trafficking?

2. How does the organizational context of ATF affect the agency's ability to (a) collect, manage, and disseminate firearms trace data from law enforcement agencies and (b) use these data to identify patterns (and specific instances) of illegal firearms trafficking?

3. How has ATF's communication and information systems infrastructure evolved

to support the agency's ability to collect and manage information on crime-related firearms recovered by law enforcement agencies?

4. Can firearms trace information be used to identify patterns of firearms trafficking and specific instances of firearms trafficking?

5. Can intelligence derived from firearms trace data be effectively disseminated to appropriate law enforcement personnel?

6. How does the organizational context of a law enforcement agency that potentially wishes to use firearms trace information affect the agency's ability to use this information to help focus, prioritize, and coordinate its activities, initiatives, and programs?

7. What are the policies and crime control implications of using an intelligence/knowledge-based system to reduce firearms trafficking and violence in the case of ATF or to meet a criminal justice agency's goals more generally?

The proposed framework is intended to provide a set of questions to help guide analyses of the design, implementation, and use of information and intelligence systems within specific legal and organizational contexts. In particular, we are interested in how information collected and managed in such systems is ultimately used by an organization for strategic and tactical purposes. Questions 1 to 5 focus on the development and implementation of systems to acquire, manage, analyze, and distribute criminal justice-related information and knowledge. Questions 4 and 5 have been examined in three studies funded by the National Institute of Justice (NIJ) and ATF conducted by Northeastern University, Abt Associates, and RAND Criminal Justice. Questions 6 and 7 focus on the capacity and readiness of an agency to use this type of data and on the utility of such information to the agencies. This chapter focuses primarily on Questions

1 to 5 outlined in the framework. In the case of ATF, Questions 6 and 7 are beginning to be addressed,[1] but these efforts involve agencies and law enforcement partnerships across the country and are beyond the scope of this analysis.

FIREARMS TRACING AND ATF

Legal and Regulatory Contexts of Firearms Tracing

Context

ATF regulates the firearms industry and enforces civil penalties and criminal laws relating to firearms production, import (not export), sales, transport, use, carrying, and possession. It collects, maintains, and uses firearms-related information for six purposes: (a) as directly specified by statute; (b) to assist in agency management; (c) to support firearms-related education and compliance measures, regulation, and enforcement; (d) to inform the public; (e) to respond to executive branch oversight bodies, Congress, and others seeking information about, evaluating, or doing research associated with ATF activities; and (f) to protect the public and reduce violence.

The primary legislative foundation for ATF's authority is the Gun Control Act of 1968 (GCA), which established a set of requirements that allowed for the "chain of commerce" of any given firearm to be traced from its manufacture or import to its first sale by a retail dealer. Following passage of the act, ATF began conducting traces recovered by law enforcement. The GCA mandated that each new firearm, whether manufactured in the United States or imported, must be marked with a unique serial number.[2] In addition, the GCA requires all federally licensed firearms dealers (FFLs), including manufacturers, importers, distributors, and retail dealers, to maintain records of all firearms transactions, including whole/retail sales and shipments received. In response to a request for trace information, the GCA also requires FFLs to provide information from transaction records (i.e., acquisition and disposition logs) to ATF and to report multiple handgun sales[3] and information on firearms stolen from dealers to ATF. ATF can perform an audit of an FFL's transaction records once during a 12-month period to ensure compliance with record-keeping requirements of the GCA. Finally, when an FFL goes out of business, the GCA requires the FFL to transfer its transaction records to ATF, which stores them for the purpose of tracing. In essence, the GCA created enhanced record-keeping procedures, thereby establishing a paper trail for gun transactions that can be followed by ATF agents.[4]

The submission of ATF traces by any law enforcement agency remains voluntary. However, in 1994, Congress recognized tracing as an essential tool for firearms law enforcement by requiring firearms manufacturers and FFLs to cooperate with ATF in providing information to complete a firearms trace within 24 hours.

Congress has also passed legislative mandates that place restrictions on the collection and management of firearms trace information. During the late 1970s, Congress passed a restriction prohibiting ATF from consolidating or centralizing records of receipt and disposition of firearms maintained by FFLs. Specifically, ATF's fiscal year 1979 appropriation provided that

> no funds appropriated herein shall be available for administrative expenses in connection with consolidating or centralizing within the Department of the Treasury the records of receipt and disposition of firearms maintained by Federal firearms licensees or for issuing or carrying out provisions of the proposed rules of the Department of

the Treasury, Bureau of Alcohol, Tobacco, and Firearms, on Firearms Regulations, as published in the *Federal Register,* volume 43, number 55, of March 21, 1978.

Congress has passed similar restrictions in ATF appropriation since then.

Implications

The information that ATF collects and maintains closely mirrors the agency's statutory authority. ATF's legal and regulatory mandates give it the authority to follow the commercial chain of transactions of a crime-related firearm to at least its first retail purchase. Importantly, for many crime-related guns, the ability to trace firearms to a first-time retail sale provides potentially valuable information regarding possible sources of trafficking.[5] Perhaps more importantly, analysis of ATF investigations indicates that firearms trace data have been a useful tool in many trafficking investigations (ATF, 2000a). In an analysis of 1,530 firearms trafficking investigations initiated during the period from July 1996 to December 1998,

almost 30 percent of investigations (448 of 1,530) were initiated through the innovative investigative methods of information analysis— analysis of firearms trace data, multiple sales records, or both. After initiation of the investigations, tracing was used as an investigative tool to gain information on recovered crime guns in 60 percent of the investigations (918 of 1,530). (ATF, 2000b, p. x)

ATF legal and regulatory mandates, however, also place important restrictions on how and what firearms-related data the agency can use for tracing or other purposes. An important legal and regulatory limitation on tracing is that ATF cannot easily trace firearms beyond the point of first retail purchase to firearms that are resold or otherwise transferred by the original purchaser (in a private transaction) or are resold by a retail dealer as a secondhand gun (in a retail transaction). Firearms can be traced past the point of a first-time retail sale through a time-consuming, often unsuccessful process of ATF agent interviews of subsequent gun possessors (i.e., "investigative traces"). Important exceptions potentially exist where a state requires the registration of firearms and/or records of all firearms purchases and sale data (for a list of states that have such systems, see Vernick & Hepburn, 2003). In such circumstances, it is potentially possible to trace a firearm to the last known retail sale (or, in some states, to the last reported retail and/or private sale) by cross-referencing the traced firearm with a state's firearms registration or purchase and sale data. Information on such transactions, especially for pawnshops, is also sometimes available through ATF's Out-of-Business Records Repository. Finally, ATF is capturing this information on selected FFLs that are subject to additional reporting requirements through the administrative mechanism of "demand letters" issued in response to non-compliance with rules regarding cooperation with tracing.

The absence of legislation can also be a factor in an agency's ability to collect data. In ATF's case, there is no federal legal or regulatory mandate for police departments to submit crime-related firearms to ATF for tracing. ATF is not unique in this regard; for example, the Federal Bureau of Investigation's (FBI) Uniform Crime Reporting (UCR) program does not have such a mandate.

Finally, the prohibition on ATF against consolidating or centralizing the records of receipt and disposition of firearms maintained by FFLs has practical implications for the management of the firearms tracing process.

Administrative and Interorganizational Context of Firearms Tracing

Examination of an agency's legislative and regulatory context is a necessary starting point for any analysis of its information systems, crime analysis, and intelligence capabilities. However, a comprehensive examination of an agency's organizational and administrative environment is an equally important component of this type of analysis. Within complex organizational and administrative environments, data definitions must be developed, data collection procedures and systems must be established, and information management systems must be implemented to collect data and information that an organization deems important or is mandated to collect.

This is an especially complex set of tasks in the case of ATF. Within the agency, the National Tracing Center (NTC) has the responsibility to accurately and efficiently conduct firearms traces for all levels of law enforcement for the purpose of providing investigative leads. During fiscal year 2003, the NTC received more than 280,000 firearms trace requests. In April 2004, the NTC employed 66 full-time ATF employees and 350 contractors at its facilities in Falling Waters and Martinsburg, West Virginia (personal communication with T. Austin, NTC, April 2004).

The tracing process begins with a law enforcement agency's submission of a trace request to the NTC. The requestor must submit one of two forms before a trace can be initiated: ATF F 3312.1 NTC trace request or ATF F 3312.2 NTC obliterated serial number trace request. Each form requires information regarding the firearm type (e.g., pistol, revolver, shotgun, rifle); the manufacturer, caliber, serial number, and importer (if the gun is of foreign manufacture); the location of the recovery; the criminal offense associated with the recovery;

and the name and date of birth of the firearm possessor.

Each firearm trace request is assigned to an NTC firearms program specialist (or a "firearms tracer"). The information is first checked against an index of manufacturers and firearms serial numbers contained in the records of out-of-business FFLs that are stored by ATF and in the records of multiple handgun purchases reported on an ongoing basis by FFLs as well as in records reported stolen by FFLs and demand letter records supplied by selected FFLs. If the firearm does not appear in these databases, the tracer contacts the manufacturer or importer and tracks the recovered crime gun through the distribution chain (i.e., wholesaler and retailer) to the first retail sale dealer. If the dealer, wholesaler, or manufacturer is still in business, the dealer is asked to examine its records to determine the identity of the first retail purchaser.[6] Importantly, on completion of each step during the tracing process, the tracer enters the data he or she has acquired into the Firearms Tracing System (FTS). Table 8.1 presents a simplified flowchart of the tracing process.

For traces where a dealer does not respond to NTC requests within the mandated 24-hour period, the tracer selects the "letter" option on the FTS workflow screen to generate a certified mail disposition letter to send to the retail dealer documenting an instance of noncompliance. If the trace is more than 12 days old, the tracer selects the "call" option on the FTS workflow screen to generate a dealer call worksheet that is routed to the retail trace section. Finally, if the tracer is unable to resolve the trace using standard procedures, the tracer selects the "research" option on the FTS workflow screen to print a research worksheet that is routed to the trace research section. At this point, another tracer rechecks the trace information.

This basic description of the tracing process does not adequately describe the magnitude

Table 8.1   Simplified Flowchart of the Firearms Tracing Process

1. A law enforcement agency recovers crime-related firearm.

    ↓

2. The law enforcement agency submits information to the NTC on firearm, recovery location, and firearm possessor.

    ↓

3. The NTC sends information on firearm to the manufacturer (unless information is not available in out-of-business or multiple gun sale records).

    ↓

4. The manufacturer sends information to the NTC regarding the dealer to which it sold the firearm.

    ↓

5. The NTC requests information from the dealer regarding the sale of the firearm and regarding the purchaser of the firearm. This process can proceed through a series of transactions between dealers (e.g., wholesale dealer to retail dealer) before a gun is sold to a private citizen in a retail sale.

    ↓

6. The dealer sends the date of sale and the purchaser of the firearm information to the NTC.

    ↓

7. The NTC integrates information on the (a) firearm, (b) firearm possessor, (c) crime-related circumstances, (d) firearm recovery location, (e) firearm dealer, and (f) retail purchaser of the firearm into the FTS, where it is stored for possible retrieval. Results of the trace are sent to the requesting agency.

NOTE: NTC = National Tracing Center; FTS = Federal Tracing System.

and complexity of the task of collecting firearms trace information. In 2003, ATF processed approximately 280,000 trace requests on crime-related firearms recovered by law enforcement agencies. In the course of conducting these firearms traces, the NTC communicated with approximately 700 different firearms manufacturers, 46,023 separate retail and wholesale firearms dealers, and 6,543 individual law enforcement agencies or units. Of these, approximately 60% were successfully traced to the first retail purchasers. In addition, information was collected on 203,933 crime gun possessors and on 46,588 associates of crime gun possessors.[7] Finally, the NTC received data on 232,926 multiple sale guns, with 80,671 unique purchasers being identified with these sales. Significantly, the tracing process necessitates that the NTC communicate with thousands of different

organizations across the nation from both the private and public sectors as well as from the federal, state, and local levels of government. The average time to complete a trace varies with this workload, ranging from 12 to 17 days for routine traces in recent years (personal communication with T. Austin, NTC, April 2004).

The number and diversity of parties potentially involved in the firearms tracing process creates a variety of possible problems in tracing a firearm. As the analysis of the tracing process indicates, successful traces depend on the actions of a set of actors. For example, (a) firearms manufacturers or importers (of foreign-manufactured firearms) must correctly stamp or mark guns with serial numbers; (b) manufacturers, importers, or wholesalers must record the next step in the chain of commerce; (c) retailers must create and maintain accurate transaction records; (d) law enforcement agencies must submit complete and accurate trace requests to ATF; (e) the NTC must find guns' retail destinations and submit the trace requests to FFLs; and (f) out-of-business FFLs need to have sent ATF their out-of-business firearms records. Any break in this sequence can potentially render traces unsuccessful and less valuable to law enforcement.

Technological/Information Systems Infrastructure

The legal, regulatory, and organizational contexts of the firearms tracing process have created a complex environment for the collection and management of firearms trace data.[8] The challenge for ATF of administering the firearms tracing process can be viewed, in part, as a problem of managing or reducing the costs associated with the acquisition, management, quality control oversight, and dissemination of firearms trace data. This has become particularly important as the number of firearms trace requests has continued to increase over the past decade or so, with the number of trace requests rising from approximately 40,000 per year during the early 1990s to 280,000 in 2003 (personal communication with T. Austin, NTC, April 2004). In addition, there has been a corresponding demand for more complete and accurate firearms trace data and for a quicker turnaround time on trace requests. To meet these demands, ATF has developed, and continues to develop, a technological and information systems infrastructure to support and manage the firearms tracing process so as to reduce human labor requirements (both within ATF and for all other law enforcement and private sector participants in the process) and to improve the quality and completeness of trace data.

This section examines the information infrastructure that ATF has developed to support and manage (a) the acquisition of firearms trace and related information from law enforcement agencies, firearms dealers, firearms wholesalers, and manufacturers; (b) the management and storage of firearms trace and related information; and (c) information quality control. It also examines the potential impact of ATF's developing IT infrastructure on the firearms tracing process.

IT to Support the Acquisition of Firearms Trace Data

Currently, the NTC provides three methods for law enforcement agencies to submit trace requests electronically: the batch downloading of trace requests; the Electronic Trace Submission System (ETSS); and eTrace, an Internet-based firearms trace submission and analysis system (law enforcement agencies also use conventional methods of submitting trace requests such as via fax and mail). In addition, ATF has developed an IT application, Access 2000, to support the acquisition of "chain of commerce"-related information on firearms submitted for tracing by law enforcement. ATF began the development and testing of batch downloading and ETSS during the mid-1990s and began to deploy the eTrace system in 2004.

Batch Downloading Trace Requests. To use the batch downloading process, law enforcement agencies must currently have accurate and uniform information stored in a database with gun description, possessor, and recovery location. Law enforcement agencies with this type of information management capacity can, with a software application supplied by the NTC, routinely download or send batches of crime gun trace request information from their information systems directly to the NTC by way of the Internet and/or phone lines. Batch downloading was the first electronic trace submission method to provide submitting agencies with a lower cost and less labor-intensive alternative to manual trace request submission. In addition, it was implemented to decrease the turnaround time for routine traces and to reduce the number of errors. This approach is used by larger law enforcement agencies.

ETSS Submission of Trace Requests. ETSS enables law enforcement agencies to submit and retrieve trace request information data with the NTC by way of a graphical user interface (GUI) using simple icons, checklists, and data entry screens to simplify and standardize the submission of data on crime guns. ETSS can be implemented as a standalone computer system or as part of a network. Data are exported from ETSS and then are sent, by way of a dial-up modem or the Internet, to the NTC for processing. ETSS is currently available to all ATF field offices and police departments.

eTrace Submission of Trace Requests. The eTrace system is an Internet-based application that provides agencies with the ability to electronically submit firearms trace requests, monitor the progress of trace requests, and efficiently retrieve the completed trace results in a real-time environment. The focus of the eTrace application is to enhance current trace protocols for user efficiency in a Web-based environment and to provide for the secure exchange of firearms trace-related information between users and the NTC.

The data submission functionality available through the eTrace application includes the following capabilities:

- Enter, validate, and submit comprehensive firearms trace request data
- View a summary listing of recently submitted traces
- View the status of a trace (e.g., in progress, completed, delayed)
- View, print, and download detailed trace request and trace result information

- Perform a quick search or a detailed multilayer search for traces
- Submit urgent trace requests for processing
- Generate analytic reports (e.g., number of traces, top firearms traced, time-to-crime rates,[9] age of possessors)

ATF expects the eTrace application to supersede other more conventional methods of submitting trace requests (e.g., fax, mail) by providing the following:

- A significant decrease in the turnaround time required to process a trace request
- An increase in the overall number of crime guns traced due to a user-friendly interface for entering trace data
- Improved data quality of trace-related information due to real-time data validation

Finally, a key advantage of eTrace is that the only infrastructure needed to use this application is a personal computer and access to the Internet. Thus, unlike the ETSS application, the eTrace system does not require law enforcement agencies to install client application software on their computers. This capability is particularly important for law enforcement agencies that lack adequate computer expertise and gives virtually all agencies the capacity to comprehensively trace their crime-related firearms.

Access 2000 Support for Acquisition of Commercial Transaction Trace-Related Data. ATF developed Access 2000 to allow larger manufacturers, importers, and wholesalers to download a subset of those companies' data regarding the distribution or sale of their weapons into stand-alone personal computers that are managed by the respective companies. ATF tracers can then dial up and conduct a query on a specific serial number to find out the dealer or wholesaler to which a specific weapon has been transferred. Access 2000 allows 24-hour access to manufacturer, importer, and wholesaler records and, therefore, is particularly useful for urgent traces. The system speeds the trace process by eliminating the step of calling or faxing the manufacturer, importer, or wholesaler and waiting for the results of a crime gun's disposition while also reducing firearms industry trace-related costs. This in effect reduces the labor costs associated with fulfilling firearms trace reporting requirements.

The Access 2000 system does not contain names of individuals or any information about individual purchasers, nor does it allow the NTC to examine all of the distribution records of a participant at once. It limits ATF personnel to conducting single queries about individual crime guns, and only ATF employees who are assigned to the NTC can use this system.

Management and Storage of Firearms Trace Information

The NTC maintains the FTS database, which consists of all prior firearms trace requests, multiple sale records, and firearms reported stolen from FFLs. The NTC is also the repository for all FFL out-of-business records. In 1998, the FTS application and its submodules (e.g., Trace, Multiple Sales, Suspect Gun, FFL Theft, Interstate Theft) were transitioned from an IBM mainframe configuration to a UNIX-based client/server platform. The database chosen to support this platform, as well as NTC applications, was Oracle. The software used to develop the FTS application was Oracle Forms. By combining the Oracle database and application design software, the resulting automated system provided a GUI similar to the Microsoft Windows software that has become an industry standard. This computing environment provides faster system response time and a lower user learning curve. The client/server computer platform also eliminated the requirement for large expensive computer rooms with their required temperature- and humidity-controlled environments.

Structured Query Language (SQL) functionality is also provided with the Oracle software suite. This software allows ad hoc querying of the database for reporting and statistical purposes, and it provides a tool to increase the integrity of the data within the many database tables. The FTS online application is enhanced with a batch system called the Trace Operations, Workflow, and Reporting System (TOWRS). The TOWRS module provides an automated business process capability that eliminates many of the redundant and mundane tasks that were required of tracing personnel using the earlier system. These features have allowed the NTC to perform a constantly increasing workload (from 197,000 traces in 1998 to nearly 280,000 traces in 2003) without proportional staffing increases (personal communication with T. Austin, NTC, April 2004).

The Firearms Tracing System. The FTS contains information relating to all firearms traced by the NTC since 1989. There are several subsystems that make up the FTS: Firearms Crime Gun Traces, Multiple Sales, Suspect Gun, FFL Theft, and Interstate Theft.

The Firearms Crime Gun Traces subsystem organizes data by individual and dealer. Authorized personnel are allowed to enter a new trace and to retrieve, view, reopen, and update an existing record. It can be searched by serial number, country, manufacturer, firearm type, caliber, model, and FTS identification number (i.e., a unique number associated with every firearm trace submission).

The Suspect Gun subsystem stores information on firearms that have not been recovered by law enforcement but are suspected of being used in criminal activity. There are several conditions making firearms suspect guns: (a) individuals (not importers) purchasing large quantities of firearms, (b) firearms suspected of being involved in trafficking, (c) dealers with improper record keeping, and (d) individuals suspected of being straw purchasers (i.e., legally entitled purchasers buying at least one gun for a prohibited person). Suspect gun submissions by law enforcement agencies are accepted by an ATF office only on a preformatted submission form that may be faxed, mailed, or e-mailed to the NTC. Once a request has been reviewed for all required information, it is entered into the Suspect Gun subsystem.

Firearms trace information is entered into the FFL Theft subsystem when an FFL reports to ATF that there was a theft of a firearm or reports a firearm missing from its inventory. Beginning in 1994, with the enactment of the Brady Handgun Violence Prevention Act (or Brady Act), all FFLs are required by law to report theft or loss of firearms from their inventories or collections to local authorities and to ATF. This includes personal firearms lost or stolen from the licensees' places of business. Once ATF has been contacted, theft report numbers are issued and must be recorded in the disposition portions of their records.

Firearms trace information is entered into the Interstate Theft subsystem when a firearm has been stolen in transit from one dealer to another dealer or from a dealer to an individual. Interstate theft occurs when firearms physically move in interstate commerce by means of a commercial carrier or the U.S. Postal Service. The U.S. Postal Service does not have rigid reporting procedures for gun theft or loss to ATF. Interstate theft reports are voluntary, unlike thefts from licensees that are required to report thefts and losses. When a firearm is reported as a licensee theft or an interstate theft to ATF, a brief description of the firearm, including its serial number, is entered into the National Crime Information Center (NCIC). Firearms that are reported as missing from inventory are not entered into the NCIC. All reported thefts and losses become part of a database managed by the NTC Stolen Firearms Program (SFP) subsystem.

One important limitation of the theft/loss program is that many individuals do not know, or fail to record, their firearms' serial numbers. When these firearms are lost or stolen, they cannot be entered into the system and their loss cannot be formally documented. In addition, the locations of thefts are often difficult to determine. The shipping routes may also have included multiple transfers and several states. In general, thefts are revealed only when the firearms fail to arrive at their intended destinations.

Finally, FFLs are required by law to report multiple sales transactions of handguns (i.e., two or more handguns within 5 business days) and to forward those records to the NTC. FFLs are required to complete (by the close of business on the day of the multiple sale) a multiple sales report (ATF Form 3310.4) that contains information about the firearms involved in the transaction and the individual who acquired them. The purpose of the multiple sales reporting requirement is to enable ATF to monitor and deter illegal commerce in handguns and to increase the speed of crime gun tracing.

An important function of these subsystems is that when law enforcement agencies submit firearms requests, the subsystems can be searched first to determine whether the firearms in question are associated with any crime gun firearms trace requests. Thus, if the serial number and manufacturer of a crime-related firearm submitted for tracing matches a serial number and manufacturer in the Multiple Sales subsystem, the crime gun trace request can be closed immediately with the multiple sales purchaser information without time-consuming telephone calls to FFLs. This also helps ATF to determine whether multiple sales or thefts are a potentially important source of trafficked firearms in a region or city.

Out-of-Business Records Repository. The GCA authorizes the treasury secretary to send letters to licensees demanding the submission of all records information required to be kept by law. The Out-of-Business Records Repository (OBR) records are located at the NTC, which receives all firearms transactions completed by FFLs that have discontinued business or other forms deemed necessary by ATF to conduct tracing.

OBR records can be identified and retrieved manually by a tracing specialist by way of the Microfilm Retrieval System (MRS). The MRS contains indexes of weapon serial numbers, manufacturers, and firearms dealers. Once the index(es) has been queried, the results indicate which roll of microfilm and frame contains the requested information. As of March 2004, 380 million firearms records had been indexed; more than 1 million records were in the process of being indexed monthly and, therefore, were accessed for crime gun tracing purposes by manual searches. System security is provided by requiring a user identification and password.

Quality Control of Firearms Trace Information

ATF has developed an extensive training program and has deployed contract staff members to the field to enhance the quality and volume of firearms trace data. In parallel with ATF's training program, the agency has implemented a range of IT applications to improve the quality of firearms trace data. These range from workflow support applications for the FTS, to Internet-based applications that can assist agencies' submitting trace requests, to applications designed to enhance the quality of geographic firearms trace data. In what follows, we outline the major quality control applications currently employed by ATF.

The firearms tracing process conducted by the NTC is monitored by the TOWRS application. After every step in the process, a tracer is required to either close out a trace or send it to the next step in the tracing process. The TOWRS application provides functionality to support the workflow of a trace through automated generation of trace worksheets, disposition request letters to FFL dealers as necessary for ongoing traces, selected lead referrals to ATF field offices (e.g., indicating recent multiple sales), trace volume and performance statistics, and a microfilm firearms match report. In addition, the Smart Close-out module performs a series of automated closeouts, thereby reducing trace workload. Using the TOWRS application, trace workflow is primarily paper driven through output from the TOWRS by generating output appropriate to the next task in the workflow.

For data submitted by way of the batch downloading system, ATF developed the Error Correction Module (ECM) application. The ECM application provides users with the capability to query, view, edit, report, and research possible hit traces on retained batch downloaded traces. ECM security is implemented by controlling user access by way of a user identification and password.

To check for potential duplicate trace submissions once a trace has been reviewed, corrected, coded, and entered into the FTS, data entry personnel first check whether the serial number already exists in the FTS with a matching manufacturer, weapon type, model, and caliber, indicating that the firearm already exists in the FTS. A match could occur for a duplicate request, a reopened request, a multiple sale, a suspect gun, or a theft entry. The trace can be closed in data entry for a number of reasons, including a duplicate request, a stolen firearm already in the system, an obliterated serial number, and omission of a serial number or manufacturer from the requestor. This type of checking is critical in a system that involves so many different participants. Without this type of checking, the FTS system would have an unknown but significant number of duplicate firearms traces.

The eTrace application also provides online support designed to enhance the quality of data submitted. Specifically, eTrace provides an agency with the ability to accomplish the following:

- Update a trace (user may update only a trace he or she submitted)
- Reopen a trace based on the provision of previously missing or invalid data
- Use the online help and frequently asked questions bulletin board
- Access the Firearms Identification Guide, which is a guide for local law enforcement agencies

However, several factors that can affect the quality of data acquired during the tracing process are external to ATF. First, as noted previously, current legislation restricts ATF's ability to ensure the accuracy of an FFL's records by limiting inspections.[10] In addition, inspections can be made to be more difficult by a deliberate falsification of dealer records, especially given that there is no audit trail of firearms shipped to a dealer. Some of the problems presented by such factors can be partially addressed by examining patterns of crime gun traces to a dealer. For example, if a set of firearm wholesalers show a consistent pattern of sales of traced crime guns to a particular retail dealer FFL, and this dealer reports no record of having received such firearms from the wholesalers, this can provide the basis for a more intensive scrutiny of the retail enterprise.

ATF's organizational context is another important factor that can affect the quality of trace information that the agency collects. Significant problems can arise from variability in how local agencies report related crime gun data. These issues can be thought of as falling under the broad heading of data standardization and accuracy that arise when a large and diverse range of actors are involved in collecting, managing, and exchanging data. This, of course, also represents a problem for many criminal justice agencies. For the tracing process, data quality problems can range from

issues relating to proper identification of firearms serial numbers, to provision of recovery locations, to possessor names, to the crimes associated with the recovery of firearms. In addition to ATF training programs, the agency is developing programs to produce more standardized information. The eTrace application and ATF's prototype Universal Geocoding Repository (UGR) both are examples of this effort. The UGR application will provide a major enhancement to ATF's capacity to geocode geographic location information (e.g., recovery location, possessor address, FFL business location) in trace data, and the eTrace application provides features to improve the quality of submitted trace information by law enforcement agencies.

Some improvements in the quality of firearms trace data will need to wait on the development of common data definitions across the criminal justice system and an improvement in the overall quality of criminal justice data. Fortunately, the issue of developing interoperable data standards is a growing concern in many sectors of the economy. For example, see Accredited Standards Committee X12 (n.d.), where this committee is "the U.S. standards body for the cross-industry development, maintenance, and publication of electronic data exchange standards." In the financial services industry, there is concern about developing common data standards for the purpose of reducing costs and improving productivity ("FundSERV and XML," 2000). Another example of this difficult process is the development of standards for health information under the Health Insurance Portability and Accountability Act of 1996 (HIPAA). As data become more standard and interoperable within the criminal justice system, this will be especially helpful to agencies, like ATF, that must exchange information with many different organizational entities.

The collection of trace data by ATF should also benefit from emerging improvements in accurately identifying criminal offenders and arrestees. This is occurring because arrestee identification is increasingly crosschecked using fingerprints. This trend will help to reduce problems associated with the purposely or mistakenly inaccurate identification of individuals.

Implications of ATF's IT Infrastructure for Firearms Tracing

From the perspective of information economics, the evolution of ATF's IT infrastructure to support firearms tracing can be viewed as an effort to reduce the transaction costs of acquiring and managing firearms trace data and of disseminating firearms trace information and intelligence to appropriate law enforcement organizations. Coase (1960) first advanced the concept of transaction costs in his seminal article, "The Problem of Social Costs." Transaction costs have been defined as the costs of exchange or the costs of using the marketplace, and they can be categorized into three types: search costs, bargaining costs, and enforcement costs (Cooter & Ulen, 1997). In the case of ATF, a public sector organization, transaction costs are highly related to the human labor costs associated with providing and managing firearms trace data. If these costs become too high due to time requirements and/or the complexity of the task, it becomes difficult to maintain or increase participation in the system (by law enforcement agencies) and difficult to improve data quality.

From a technology perspective, ATF is taking advantage of Internet-based technologies to increase the efficiency of the firearms tracing process. In addition, ATF has engaged in an ongoing effort to help standardize data definitions regarding traced firearms and associated information. As noted previously, data standardization for some tracing system attributes will depend on broader trends within the criminal justice system. For other attributes (e.g., firearm manufacturer and dealer information, crime gun-related information,

recovery date information), ATF is helping to establish data standards that, in effect, represent a set of de facto XML-like[11] data definitions in this arena. This is important to ATF due to the efficiencies that these activities can introduce to the tracing process. More generally, it is potentially useful to the criminal justice system as an example of the importance of data standardization for the integration and coordination of criminal justice programs.

From a legal perspective, ATF's legal mandate not only shapes what information can be collected but also shapes how these data are stored and managed. To some extent, the tracing process and the supporting information systems are made more complicated by the fact that ATF is prohibited from compiling and using data in any way, so that this may be construed as a central national registration system. This creates some data management inefficiencies in accessing firearm-related trace information in the FTS or the out-of-business record databases.

ATF's efforts, over the past decade or so, to develop an IT infrastructure to facilitate and expand the firearms tracing process have produced significant progress in managing the tracing process. As noted previously, over this period, ATF has increased the number of requests for firearms traces more than five-fold (from approximately 40,000 during the early 1990s to 280,000 in 2004), and this occurred during a period of significant decline in firearms crime in the United States. In addition and equally important, ATF has improved the quality and completeness of firearms trace data. Between 1996 and 1999, the percentage of firearms trace requests traced to retail purchasers rose from 37.3% to 52.1% (as noted previously, this figure then rose to approximately 60% by 2003) and the percentage of traces with recovery date information provided rose from 65.4% to 96.4% (Pierce et al., 2003). In effect, ATF significantly increased both the quantity and quality of firearms traces over the past decade or so. This would not have been possible without the broad information infrastructure that the agency has implemented.

Development of Firearms Trace Intelligence and Database Mining

For most organizations, IT was used mainly for accounting and record-keeping duties. Data collected by an organization were "*rarely* collected for the mining of knowledge, but *usually* as a by-product of other tasks" (Fayyad, Piatetsky-Shapiro, Smyth, & Uthurusamy, 1996, p. vii). In this regard, ATF is not any different from most private or public sector organizations.

Originally, following the enactment of the GCA in 1968, there was probably little or no expectation that ATF would use tracing data to identify patterns of firearms trafficking or to initiate investigations.[12] As noted previously, ATF began the collection of trace information on firearms records by law enforcement agencies primarily to conform to statutory requirements. However, as firearms trace information began to be collected more systematically (by the NTC and in selected cities), ATF investigators started to use firearms trace information for the purpose of conducting and initiating firearms trafficking investigations.[13] In this process, ATF investigators began to accumulate significant amounts of tacit knowledge concerning potential indicators of firearms trafficking available in trace data.

As investigative experience accumulated, a major question began to emerge concerning whether firearms trace information could be used to identify patterns of firearms trafficking rather than simply to support individual investigations. A parallel, and perhaps unstated, question was whether firearms trace data could be transformed or codified into explicit knowledge that is relevant and accessible to a broad range of law enforcement investigations and analysts and not just the most innovative or technically proficient investigators. In addition,

once the data have been transformed into explicit knowledge, is it then possible to disseminate this knowledge to ATF and other law enforcement agencies?

The process of extracting this type of intelligence or these types of patterns from existing databases is often referred to as database mining or knowledge discovery in databases (KDD). KDD has been defined as "the nontrivial process of identifying valid, novel, potentially useful, and ultimately understandable patterns in data" (Fayyad et al., 1996, p. 6). As it became apparent that firearms trace data could potentially provide this type of information or knowledge, ATF undertook took two major approaches to database mining of its trace data resources. First, the agency systematically began to identify insights derived from the best practices of expert ATF investigators and crime gun analysts in using firearms trace data for investigative purposes. More specifically, what types of patterns did expert investigators find in trace data that were useful for identifying patterns of trafficking and initiating investigations? This process could be thought of as developing rules-based models for identifying potential patterns and/ or leads based on the field experience of expert investigators.

Second, by the early 1990s, "some ATF field offices were developing methods of analyzing trace information to detect patterns in the local supply of crime guns" (ATF, 2000b; Kennedy, Piehl, & Braga, 1996). According to ATF (2000b), the systematic analysis of firearms trace data to identify patterns of firearms trafficking on a national basis "began with a joint Northeastern University–ATF study published in 1995. The study's goals were to develop potential crime gun trafficking indictors." This study concluded that a very small percentage of licensees were associated with a high volume of total crime gun traces, and it affirmed time-to-crime as a potential indicator of trafficking (Pierce, Briggs, & Carlson, 1995). Since that time, ATF, in collaboration

Table 8.2 Distribution of Traces Among Current Retail Dealers, 1999

	Dealers		Traces	
Number of Traces to a Dealer	Percentage	Number	Percentage	Number
0 or more	100.0	80,523	—	—
1 or more	14.5	11,684	100.0	51,640
2 or more	7.4	5,959	88.9	45,915
5 or more	2.7	2,184	69.8	36,036
10 or more	1.2	964	54.6	28,201
25 or more	0.4	296	35.8	18,498
50 or more	0.2	124	24.7	12,752

with research partners and the NIJ, has initiated statistical analyses of firearms trace data that are designed, in part, to identify potential patterns of trafficking, including three NIJ/ATF-funded studies conducted by Northeastern University, Abt Associates, and RAND Criminal Justice (for examples of this research, see Pierce et al., 2003, 2004; Wintemute, Cook, & Wright, 2004). Using these two approaches, ATF has made, and continues to make, a consistent effort to mine firearms trace data so as to identify potential patterns of firearms trafficking and other useful investigative leads.

To date, this effort appears to have provided useful strategic and tactical information to law enforcement investigators, analysts, and policy planners. Table 8.2 provides one example of this type of analysis (Pierce et al., 2003). The table examines the distribution of firearms traces recovered by law enforcement in 1999 and retail dealers that sold these firearms to purchasers. The analysis is restricted to dealers that were in business during 1999. The analysis shows that a relatively small number of dealers were associated with a relatively high proportion of firearms traces. For example, dealers with 10 or more traces represented 1.2% of all active retail dealers in 1999 and were associated with 54.2% of the traces to active dealers. This does not mean that these dealers are engaged in illegal activity, but it could represent one avenue by which to help focus ATF regulatory

resources. ATF uses this type of analysis with the restriction that it examines only short time-to-crime firearms traced to dealers for the agency's Demand Letter 2 program.

Analyses of firearms trace data have also identified significant cross-jurisdiction variability in potential illegal firearms markets and indicators of firearms trafficking in local or regional markets (ATF, 2002). For example, in New York City, 17.4% of the firearms recovered by law enforcement in 1999 were traced to in-state retail dealers and purchasers. In contrast, in Philadelphia, 70.4% were traced to in-state dealers for firearms recovered by law enforcement (Pierce et al., 2004).

ATF's efforts to analyze trace data and examine the best practices of expert investigators have helped to identify a range of potential patterns in firearms trafficking. This is critical because the existence of regularities or patterns in firearms trace data can significantly enhance the value of these data to investigators, policy analysts, and/or administrators. Under these conditions, it is possible to use trace information or intelligence derived from trace data to examine how illegal firearms markets operate across regions and to use trace data to help identify diffuse and/or point sources of trafficking within a specific region.

The type of information derived from ATF's database mining efforts can be used to support supply side-oriented tactics and strategies to reduce firearms trafficking and crime. In effect, these efforts have potentially produced a set of new products or resources from trace data in the form of crime gun analyses and intelligence. These new resources represent an added benefit from trace data that goes beyond the more traditional uses of these data to provide supplementary or corroborating information to ongoing individual investigations.

ATF's experience also demonstrates that database mining/knowledge management initiatives operate best as an interactive activity among administrators, analysts, investigators, and IT experts. This type of process allows ongoing input and reviews from top-level investigators and analysts concerning the design, implementation, and operation of decision support/intelligence systems and procedures. In addition, because the character of threats facing law enforcement is continually changing, and because sources of potentially useful information continue to evolve, database mining and knowledge discovery need to be ongoing activities. In a sense, this type of development is similar to policy implementation and evaluation processes described by Browne and Wildavsky (1979) as follows: "In many ways, implementation and evaluation are completely interactive in practice, although necessarily remaining distinctive in concept" (p. 205).

Although ATF's initiatives to identify potential patterns of trafficking in trace data information are an essential step in the development of the agency's crime analysis/intelligence capabilities, they are not sufficient without complementary investigations in all components of this process. More specifically, if information is acquired and managed effectively, and there are policy- or investigation-relevant regularities in the data, the next logical question is how to disseminate or communicate such information and/or intelligence to appropriate law enforcement personnel and, in some cases, to the public. A parallel question is how ATF trace data can be effectively disseminated to other law enforcement data resources. The next section addresses the issue of data dissemination.

Disseminating Firearms Trace Investigative Leads, Analysis, and Intelligence

The utility of firearms trace data to law enforcement investigators depends not only on the trafficking-related knowledge theoretically available in these data systems but also on the ability of law enforcement to access such information at reasonably low costs (in terms of funds and/or time) to individuals and agencies. Currently, ATF can provide agency-specific firearms trace data back to law enforcement agencies that originate the trace requests, and it can provide regional firearms trace information to law enforcement partnerships of the type established by the Project Safe Neighborhoods (PSN) program.

This section examines the initiatives that ATF has developed to facilitate access to firearms trace data by collaborating with law enforcement agencies and partnerships. In addition, it discusses a combination of support services and IT applications developed by ATF to facilitate the access to firearms trace data by law enforcement agencies. The major ATF initiatives to facilitate the dissemination of firearms trace-related information and analyses include support to law enforcement in the field by crime gun analysts and a growing complement of software applications to make direct access to trace data and potential indicators of firearms trafficking less technical and time intensive. Specific types of support are discussed in the following subsections.

Crime Gun Analysis Branch

ATF established the Crime Gun Analysis Branch (CGAB) in 1997 to support regulatory and criminal investigations of illegal trafficking activity and armed criminals using analysis of crime gun traces, multiple sale and stolen gun reports, and other information. CGAB analysts are involved with suspect guns and suspect persons (by name), interstate theft, common carriers, and obliterated serial numbers, and they are responsible for Online Lead software. They are the primary users of the FTS for investigative purposes. CGAB analysts send out leads and firearms trace reports to investigators in the field.

Online Lead

Online Lead is a software application that allows ATF special agents and inspectors in the field to have access to firearms trace data that have been updated daily from the FTS. This software can be used to analyze individual trace records, analyze links among traces, and find repeat sellers and buyers of crime guns. The basic purpose of Online Lead is to help agents generate investigative leads. In November 1999, ATF extended access to Online Lead to all ATF field offices (via the ATF intranet), where federal, state, and local agencies can also use the system. This program provides field investigators with important leads regarding firearms trafficking patterns. The Online Lead application runs from a mirrored version of the FTS system and is refreshed on a nightly basis because data entry/editing applications and data mining applications need to be indexed differently for maximum performance. Currently, users have nationwide access to all firearms traces and multiple sales records. Online Lead can be used to make very specific queries on a particular piece of information (e.g., a person's name) or to make broader queries.

eTrace

The eTrace application provides an additional new feature that gives police agencies immediate access to the online database comprised of all trace requests submitted by the agencies. This tool provides agencies with the ability to perform detailed search functions and customized analyses of firearms trace information within their jurisdiction. The eTrace application also provides agencies with the ability to perform analyses of their own trace data using a broad search utility. A search for traces can be initiated on virtually any data field captured or combination thereof, including an individual name, a recovery location address, a type of crime, or a date of recovery. Finally, eTrace provides users with the ability to generate analytic reports using a selected set of trafficking indicators, including number of traces submitted over time, the most frequently traced, time-to-crime rates, and ages of possessors.

Geographic Information Systems Capabilities of the NTC

Currently, the NTC and ATF's regional crime gun centers use an extraction of FTS data that is imported into a mapping application. The extraction is done at the NTC for CGAB analysts, and an on-site support specialist does a weekly extraction of FTS data for Los Angeles and New York City as well as a monthly extraction of data for Chicago and Washington, D.C. The extracted data are then downloaded to computers at the centers, where the data are geocoded using ArcGIS 8.2 software and StreetMap USA. Currently, the CGAB and gun centers also have ArcView 3.2 and StreetMap 2000 as well as a spatial analyst for ArcView and ArcGIS.

The extraction process is time-consuming for staff members and affects the timeliness of the data available to analysts. Once the address information has been geocoded and another update is received, it is still necessary to recode all of the addresses again, including the ones completed the previous week or the previous month, as the case may be.

The prototype UGR that ATF has developed will allow analysts to run a query in

Oracle Discoverer, or use the application directly against the geocoded data warehouse, with either an online mapping application or the desktop ArcGIS. This will give real-time information to the end users and will save time both on the extraction process and on the end users having to recode addresses that are already completed.

Firearms Trace
Decision Support System

To further enhance the value of tracing information to law enforcement investigators, ATF, in collaboration with academic partners, has developed a prototype analysis application called the Firearms Trace Decision Support (FTDS) system.[14] The purpose of the FTDS application is to codify or organize patterns of firearms trafficking found in firearms trace data into a form that is more accessible to investigators and analysts. As Davenport and Prusak (1998) note, "The aim of codification is to put organizational knowledge into a form that makes it accessible to those who need it. It literally turns knowledge into a code to make it as organized, explicit, portable, and easy to understand as possible" (p. 68).

The FTDS application is intended to address two important needs of law enforcement: (a) to provide timely and targeted intelligence on firearms trafficking and (b) to minimize the training and technical expertise required to obtain this type of intelligence. The combination of expert knowledge and Internet access to this knowledge is intended to allow less experienced investigators or analysts to quickly identify patterns of firearms trafficking in local regions and communities without the need for customized programming or database queries. This is potentially important because the training that investigators need to conduct database analyses using complex computer query methods can be prohibitive both in terms of the financial

costs to agencies and in terms of investigator time.

The FTDS system provides investigators and analysts with the ability to perform custom cross-attribute queries on selected criteria (e.g., on whether a gun was recovered during a short time period following its original sale) with a minimum of training and technical skills. The query functions built into the FTDS system have been derived from the analysis of the best practices of expert investigators and statistical analyses trace data. Using simple drop-down menus, the FTDS application allows users to select trafficking indicators, individually or in combinations, to produce reports on potential sources of trafficking. Firearms trafficking reports can be generated for FFLs, regions (e.g., out-of-state sources), communities, gun purchasers, and gun possessors. Figure 8.1 provides a graphical representation of the major types of relationships in trace data for which indicators are available in the FTDS application. In the future, an operational Internet-based version of the FTDS application will provide decision support capabilities to law enforcement agencies without the need to manage a client/server application. Once the prototype FTDS system is tested, ATF will evaluate how best to deploy this type of system to the field.

ATF continues to develop methods and applications to disseminate firearms trace information and analyses. The process is complicated by the complexity of collecting, managing, mining tracing data for relevant information, and disseminating this information and/or analyses to appropriate law enforcement investigators and units. For example, sharing firearms trace information across jurisdictions generally needs to be accomplished with the concurrence of local and regional law enforcement authorities. The sharing of firearms trace data and information on a regional basis is beginning to be implemented through law enforcement

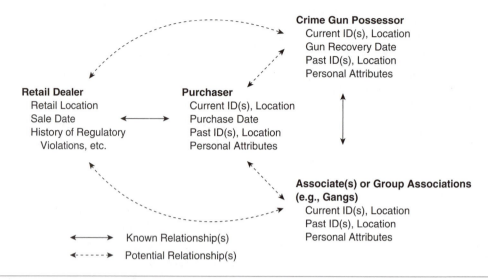

Figure 8.1 Known and Potential Trafficking Relationships Available From Firearms Trace Data

NOTE: ID = identification.

partnerships established under the auspices of the PSN program.

Integrating Firearms Trace Analysis Into Law Enforcement Tactics and Strategies

How firearms trace information and analyses are being incorporated into the local and regional law enforcement tactics, strategies, and planning is an ongoing process in a fairly early stage of development and is beyond the scope of this chapter. However, it is possible to review the use of firearms trace information by ATF investigators and managers. As noted previously, trace data were an important element in the majority of 1,530 firearms trafficking cases reviewed in the ATF (2000b) study, *Following the Gun.* ATF also provides strategic analyses of illegal firearms markets and trace data to more than 50 police departments that have committed to comprehensively tracing all crime-related firearms they recover. This information is being provided to law enforcement agencies through ATF's Crime Gun Trace Reports (ATF, 2002). In addition, an NIJ/ATF-funded study conducted

by RAND Criminal Justice is testing the utility of using firearms trace data in Los Angeles for the purpose of helping to develop more focused supply-side strategies and tactics.

Complementing ATF's use of trace data in trafficking investigations, the agency has also developed programs to facilitate the regulation of firearms dealers. These programs include the demand letter initiatives and the FFL eZ Check (personal communication with T. Austin, NTC, April 2004). The Demand Letter 1 initiative focuses on FFLs that had been uncooperative and/or unresponsive to requests for firearms trace information by the NTC. For these dealers, NTC requires the submission of all their firearms transaction records for the previous 3 years and requires them to submit monthly update reports of additional acquisitions. ATF seeks this information so that the NTC can quickly trace firearms sold by these dealers if they continue to be uncooperative. The issuance of Demand Letter 1 to uncooperative dealers has resulted in a dramatic increase in the compliance rates of previously uncooperative dealers; none of these dealers has failed to cooperate with a trace request since the issuance of the demand letter. The focus on this initiative also appears to provide an incentive for all dealers to comply with their legal obligation to respond to ATF trace requests in a timely manner.

The Demand Letter 2 initiative originally focused on FFLs that had 10 or more crime guns with a time-to-crime of 3 years or less traced to them during a calendar year. The letter required these dealers to provide ATF with the following information about the used guns they had acquired during the past year: the manufacturers or importers, the serial numbers, the models, and the calibers or gauges.[15] The dealers are also notified that, following their initial reports, they will be required to submit this information on a quarterly basis.

For calendar year 2001, the cutoff point was raised to 15 due to both staffing issues and the increased volume of crime gun traces that year. In 2001, there were 324 FFL retail dealers with 15 or more crime gun traces with a short time-to-crime of 3 years or less.[16] Volume of sales is not part of the demand criteria because ATF does not have the means to monitor the volume of sales by FFLs. However, particular attention is paid to instances where information exists that dealers are not high-volume firearms businesses and yet have enough guns traced back to meet the demand letter criteria. The demand letter does not infer that ATF assumes that such dealers are engaged in illegal behavior.

Finally, the FFL eZ Check system, which became operational in October 2000, was created to help the firearms industry prevent the fraudulent use of firearms licenses. Prior to a licensee's disposing of a firearm to another licensee, the former must verify the identity and licensed status of the person to whom the firearm will be transferred. This is generally accomplished by obtaining a certified copy of the license. To prevent fraud, licensees may now access ATF's eZ Check at www.atf.treas.gov. The eZ Check system allows a federal firearms licensee to verify the license prior to shipping or transferring a firearm to a licensee. There is also a phone number that licensees can call to determine the validity of an FFL.

Although ATF and other law enforcement agencies have only recently begun to use firearms trace information, it is possible to ask what this new type of resource can potentially provide law enforcement. Brynjolfsson and Hitt (2000) note that a major component of IT's value is its ability to enable complementary organizational investments or innovations. Ideally, such investment should "lead to productivity increases by reducing costs and, more importantly, by enabling firms to increase output quality in the form of new products or in improvements in intangible aspects of existing products like convenience, timeliness, quality, and variety" (p. 27). To date, ATF has shown how to use trace information to produce new approaches to firearms trafficking within its own organization. This process is still ongoing, and efforts are now under way to extend these capabilities to local and regional law enforcement agencies and partnerships.

CONCLUSION

Investigating criminal activity, implementing problem-oriented policing, processing court cases, and managing correctional facilities all are heavily dependent on information for their successful operation. Meeting this challenge requires a comprehensive and dynamic planning approach.

Comprehensive information systems planning, as the examination of the ATF experience demonstrates, first requires a detailed assessment of an agency's legal and organization context—Questions 1 and 2 of the framework. Examination of the legal and organizational context identifies key constraints on the design, implementation/management information, and intelligence systems.

Comprehensive planning also requires an assessment of how an organization's IT infrastructure can optimize support for the collection, management, and dissemination of relevant information and intelligence—Questions 3 and 5 of the framework. From the perspective of information economics, the evolution of ATF's IT infrastructure to support firearms tracing can be viewed as an effort to reduce or control the transaction costs of acquiring, managing, and disseminating firearms trace information to appropriate law enforcement organizations. To be successful, an information or intelligence system should reduce transaction costs across all aspects of collecting, managing, analyzing, and disseminating information. In effect, ATF has introduced technology designed, in part, to reduce the time that investigators and other law enforcement personnel spend in the data collection and management process. ATF's experience shows that this is a complex process that requires managing and coordinating multiple applications across different functional areas. ATF's experience also demonstrates that taking advantage of technology advancements can significantly reduce human transaction costs associated with the tracing process.

Comprehensive planning should include a systematic program on database mining and knowledge discovery. This is important because a major part of the value of any information system rests on the extent to which data contained in the system can identify patterns or activities of use to an organization's tactical and/or strategic goals. ATF's efforts to analyze trace data and examine the best practices of expert investigators have helped to identify a range of potential patterns in firearms trafficking. In effect, these efforts have produced a potential set of new products and resources from trace data in the form of crime gun analyses and intelligence. Without such a systematic data mining program, significant amounts of valuable knowledge may remain unavailable to operational, investigative, and administrative personnel as well as to policymakers.

ATF's experience in developing the agency's firearms trace information and analysis capacity indicates that the planning and implementation of such systems should often be an interactive process that involves researching, prototyping, and reassessing components of the overall system. This type of approach can be especially important in large and/or multiple organization contexts. Such contexts are typically too complex for single-effort implementations. As Bidgoli (1998) observes, "Throughout the information systems history, we have learned that by building small models or prototypes and testing them, the problems, as well as the solutions, become more understandable" (p. 36). In the case of ATF, the prototyping and assessment of systems and system components has helped the agency to assess alternative approaches to developing its information systems and analysis capabilities.

The process of integrating information and/or intelligence into organizations' tactical and strategic planning presents its own unique set of substantive issues. However, issues concerning the acquisition, management, and dissemination of information, as well as issues related to information quality control and knowledge discovery, are an important set of precursors to the question of how organizations ultimately use this potential new resource.

NOTES

1. Strategic Disruption of Firearms Markets (an NIJ/ATF-funded project to RAND Criminal Justice) and Project Safe Neighborhoods (PSN) are examples of such efforts. Project Safe Neighborhoods is a U.S. Department of Justice nationwide

program committed to reducing "gun crime in America by networking existing local programs that target gun crime and providing those programs with additional tools necessary to be successful" (www.psn.gov/about.asp).

2. "Licensed importers and licensed manufacturers shall identify, by means of a serial number engraved or cast on the receiver or frame of the weapon, in such manner as the Secretary shall by regulations prescribe, each firearm imported or manufactured by such importer or manufacturer. The serial number of any semiautomatic assault weapon manufactured after the date of the enactment of this sentence shall clearly show the date on which the weapon was manufactured. A large capacity ammunition feeding device manufactured after the date of the enactment of this sentence shall be identified by a serial number that clearly shows that the device was manufactured or imported after the effective date of this subsection, and such other identification as the Secretary may by regulation prescribe" (GCA, 18 U.S.C. sec. 923 (i)).

3. FFLs must forward transaction data when an unlicensed person purchases two or more handguns at once or within 5 consecutive business days. Data must be forwarded by the close of business on the day of the multiple sale. ATF originated this practice by regulation in 1975. Congress codified it in the Firearms Owners' Protection Act of 1986 (FOPA).

4. Prior to the GCA of 1968, the National Firearms Act of 1934 required certain firearms to be federally registered. Registration consists of providing personal identification information (including a full set of fingerprints, a photograph, and certification of permission to possess from a local law enforcement official) and paying a $200 tax for each item registered. Congress's purpose was to reduce crimes committed with guns used by gangsters—machine guns (fully automatic weapons), sawed-off shotguns, sawed-off rifles, silencers, and destructive devices (e.g., explosives, grenades, poison gas, any ammunition greater than a half inch).

5. For example, see research on Maryland handgun trace requests that were cross-referenced with the first and last known retail sales in Maryland using 15 years of the state's handgun registration database. More than 75% of crime gun trace requests were associated with the first retail sales, and no other sales were recorded in Maryland's handgun registration system (Pierce et al., 2003).

6. By law, FFLs in the United States are required to respond to trace requests from ATF within 24 hours.

7. An associate of a crime gun possessor is any person "who can be linked to the possessor of the crime gun at the time of its recovery by law enforcement" (ATF, 2002, p. A3).

8. Unless a specific cite has been referenced, all information contained in this section was derived from interviews with individuals from ATF's NTC in April 2004.

9. Time-to-crime is "the period of time from a firearm's acquisition by an unlicensed person from a retail licensee and law enforcement's recovery of that firearm during use, or suspected use, in a crime. A short time-to-crime suggests the firearm will be easier to trace. This measure can be an important indicator of illegal firearms trafficking" (ATF, 2002, Appendix A-6).

10. "[The ATF] Secretary may inspect or examine the inventory and records of a licensed importer, licensed manufacturer, or licensed dealer without such reasonable cause or warrant—for ensuring compliance with the record keeping requirements of this chapter [GCA]—not more than once during any 12-month period" (18 U.S.C. Sec. 923 (g)(1)(B)(ii)(I)).

11. XML (eXtensible Markup Language) is "a widely used standard from the World Wide Web Consortium (W3C) that facilitates the interchange of data between computer applications" (www.rlg.org/redlightgreen/glessary.html)

12. ATF is not unique in collecting data for one purpose and finding that the information is useful for another purpose. For example, when scanners were first

introduced into supermarkets, their primary purpose was to reduce grocery checkout time. Today, information collected from this process is a key element in supermarkets' inventory control and management.

13. For information on how firearms trace information is used by ATF investigators, see the agency's *Following the Gun* (ATF, 2000b).

14. The FTDS prototype application has been developed under two NIJ/ATF-funded studies conducted by Northeastern University and RAND Criminal Justice. It is being field-tested in Los Angeles under the RAND study.

15. These FFLs were not required to submit any identifying information on the individuals who had transferred the guns to them or on individuals who subsequently purchased the firearms.

16. When the NTC receives demand letter records, the demand letter group at the NTC enters selected information from the records into an FTS Demand Letter subsystem that was created as part of this program. Information on firearms purchasers contained in Demand Letter 1 records is not placed into the FTS. All demand letter data information is locked and secured at the end of each day. Each demand letter data packet must be quality controlled by another demand data letter entry person at the NTC.

LEGISLATION

Brady Handgun Violence Prevention Act P.L. 103-159, 18 U.S.C. sec. 922 (1994).

Firearms Owners' Protection Act, P.L. 99-308, 100 Stat. 449, 458 (codified at 18 U.S.C. sec. 924) (1986).

Firearms Regulations, 43 Federal Register, No. 55 (proposed March 21, 1978).

Gun Control Act, P.L. 90-351, 82 Stat. 225 (codified as 18 U.S.C. chap. 44 §§ 921–929) (1968).

Health Insurance Portability and Accountability Act, P.L. 104-191 (1996).

REFERENCES

Accredited Standards Committee X12. (n.d.). *ASCX12 vision and mission.* Retrieved February 9, 2004, from www.x12.org/x120rg/about/visionmission.cfm

Bidgoli, H. (1998). *Intelligent management support systems.* Westport, CT: Quorum Books.

Blumstein, A., & Cook, D. (1996). Linking gun availability to youth gun violence. *Law and Contemporary Problems, 59,* 5–24.

Braga, A. A., Cook, P. J., Kennedy, D. M., & Moore, M. H. (2002). The illegal supply of firearms. *Crime and Justice, 29,* 319–352.

Browne, A., & Wildavsky, A. (1979). Implementation as mutual adaptation. In J. L. Pressman & A. Wildavsky (Eds.), *Implementation.* Berkeley: University of California Press.

Brynjolfsson, E., & Hitt, L. M. (2000). Beyond computation: Information technology, organizational transformation, and business performance. *Journal of Economic Perspectives, 14,* 23–48.

Bureau of Alcohol, Tobacco, Firearms, and Explosives. (2000a). *Commerce in firearms in the United States.* Washington, DC: U.S. Department of the Treasury.

Bureau of Alcohol, Tobacco, Firearms, and Explosives. (2000b). *Following the gun: Enforcing federal laws against firearms traffickers.* Washington, DC: U.S. Department of the Treasury.

Bureau of Alcohol, Tobacco, Firearms, and Explosives. (2002). *Crime gun trace reports (2000): National report.* Washington, DC: U.S. Department of the Treasury.

Coase, R. (1960). The problem of social costs. *Journal of Law and Economics, 6,* 1–44.

Cooter, R., & Ulen, T. (1997). *Law and economics* (2nd ed.). Reading, MA: Addison–Wesley.

Davenport, T. H., & Prusak, L. (1998). *Working knowledge.* Boston: Harvard Business School Press.

Fayyad, U. M., Piatetsky-Shapiro, G., Smyth, P., & Uthurusamy, R. (Eds.). (1996). *Advances in knowledge discovery and data mining.* Menlo Park, CA: AAAI Press.

Federal Bureau of Investigation. (2003). *Crime in the United States 2002: Uniform Crime Report.* Washington, DC: U.S. Department of Justice.

FundSERV and XML: The next generation of standards. (2000, November 22). Retrieved February 9, 2004, from http://standards.fundserv.com

Kennedy, D. M., Piehl, A. M., & Braga, A. A. (1996). Youth violence in Boston: Gun markets, serious youth offenders, and a use-reduction strategy. *Law and Contemporary Problems, 59,* 169–180.

Peters, B. G. (1996). *American public policy: Promise and performance* (4th ed.). Chatham, NJ: Chatham House.

Pierce, G., Briggs, L., & Carlson, D. (1995). *The identification of patterns in firearms trafficking: Implications for focused enforcement strategy.* Unpublished manuscript (commissioned by Bureau of Alcohol, Tobacco, Firearms, and Explosives), College of Criminal Justice, Northeastern University.

Pierce, G., Braga, A. A., Hyatt, R., & Koper, C. (2004). The characteristics and dynamics of illegal firearms markets: Implications for a supply-side enforcement strategy. *Justice Quarterly, 21*(2), 391–422.

Pierce, G., Braga, A. A., Koper, C., McDevitt, J., Carlson, D., Roth, J., Saiz, A., Hyatt, R., & Griffith, R. (2003). *The characteristics and dynamics of crime gun markets.* Unpublished manuscript (final report to the National Institute of Justice and the Bureau of Alcohol, Tobacco, Firearms, and Explosives), College of Criminal Justice, Northeastern University.

Vernick, J. S., & Hepburn, L. M. (2003). State and federal gun laws: Trends for 1970 to 1999. In J. Ludwig & P. Cook (Eds.), *Evaluating gun policy* (pp. 345–411). Washington, DC: Brookings Institution.

Wintemute, G. J., Cook, P. J., & Wright, M. A. (2004). *Predicting handgun retailers' sales of guns that are used in crime.* Unpublished manuscript, Violence Prevention Research Program, University of California, Davis.

CHAPTER 9

Offender-Based Information Sharing

Using a Consent-Driven System to Promote Integrated Service Delivery

KATHLEEN R. SNAVELY, FAYE S. TAXMAN, AND STUART GORDON

During recent years, there has been a growing need to provide integrated and timely information concerning criminal offenders. Desirable information includes all phases of the criminal justice system as well as involvement in services from a variety of community providers. This is a horizontal process that follows the offender flow through the various phases of the criminal justice system (i.e., from arrest through reentry) instead of emphasizing the organizational boundaries that affect data on offender status.

The success of this comprehensive offender process tracking depends on a management information system that allows data from various systems to be integrated in a process that follows the offender flow and also provides the ability to share real-time information across agencies. Recent advances in technology, both hardware and software, have fostered the ability for data from multiple agencies to reside in one database structure, yet the degree to which the data are integrated varies depending on the horizontal needs of the system. An integrated approach produces improved tracking and coordination of services, more precise reporting and evaluation, and an enhanced ability to protect public safety.[1]

With the field of criminal justice demanding a more preventative proactive approach to serving offenders,[2] a major challenge involves monitoring offenders in real-time fashion. This requires direct access to information as well as the ability to prioritize caseloads and services delivered, to identify and prioritize offender needs, to determine the services available, and to make referrals in a timely fashion. It also requires timely access to information about offender status, timely information on offender compliance, and quality information about offender outcomes that can be used to determine program effectiveness. In this new world, the exchange of offender information is paramount in the delivery of comprehensive services. The system and users must be able to access intraagency communications in a timely manner and must be able to share that information without creating an undue threat to offenders' privacy rights.

The purpose of this chapter is to describe how an integrated consent-driven system monitors offender flow. Essentially, the integrated consent-driven system allows multilayering multiagency programs (e.g., drug courts, intensive supervision, diversion to treatment) to collect data in a uniform manner. Second, the chapter discusses the current models of information sharing, followed by a discussion of the benefits of an integrated system. Third, it provides an in-depth focus on the legal issues associated with information gathering, dissemination, and research. Finally, the chapter provides a case study of the University of Maryland Automated Tracking System (HATS). HATS is an integrated, consent-driven, automated management information system that is used to track offenders by the Maryland Division of Probation and Parole, drug courts, community-based treatment programs, and other agencies serving offenders in Maryland. Two examples of how HATS is being used in Maryland are discussed.

OFFENDER-BASED INFORMATION SYSTEMS

As criminal justice agencies begin to think about how to approach information sharing, it is important to identify what data should be captured, who captures the data, and whether the data should be shared with other agencies. Also, it is important to determine whether the information is captured on a case basis, where information is captured and associated with each case as it is processed through the system. Alternatively, the information can be captured on an individual basis, where information is captured on an individual and where cases and events are associated with each individual. The American Probation and Parole Association (APPA,

2003) recommends that information be "individual-based rather than case-based."

The ultimate management information system will yield the most benefits with the least amount of duplicate data entry. This ultimate system will be coordinated, where one agency is responsible for initiating the case and all other functions build on the initial client record and are entered by the appropriate agency, thereby ensuring a collaborative electronic client record with the highest level of data quality.

The development of an automated system should be based on modeling the business practices of the agencies involved and should adhere to the laws and policies governing offender information. The APPA (2003) outlines six primary functions in case processing: (a) case initiation, (b) case planning, (c) scheduling, (d) monitoring and compliance, (e) document generation, and (f) the case close function. The APPA also identifies two management functions: (a) management and statistical reporting and (b) security and data integration. Criminal justice agencies will be challenged to work through the basic flow of information according to the existing business practices and case and information flow to identify where the information is currently captured (i.e., in one place or multiple places). The next challenge involves identifying the entity or agency responsible for entering and maintaining the data in the electronic system.

Current Models of Information Sharing

Common platforms include closed systems, open systems, and integrated consent-driven systems. A closed system is a single-unit system with one point of entry and a limited ability to exchange information electronically. An open system is a single-unit system with the ability to exchange information through the uploading and downloading of data from one system to another. An integrated consent-driven system is a multiorganization system with the ability to electronically access and exchange information at the client, management, and system levels.

Traditionally, closed and open applications were the mainstay of information systems, where each agency had its own automated information system and tracked the progress of offenders within each agency, communicating only electronically with agency components. However, these systems are somewhat limited. Closed systems do not share information electronically with other agencies, and they are often limited in their flexibility. Special procedures are required to share information through uploading or downloading computer files; information is usually stored at the client level and is used only by that particular agency, with little management performance information being available to facilitate program evaluation.

Open systems linked through a network offer a bit more flexibility. Each staff member has access to data all of the time and has the ability to build on a client record maintained within an agency with an open system. Open systems also offer enhanced case management and reporting capabilities not offered by closed systems. However, open systems are still limited when one is trying to share information about a client electronically across agencies.

Agencies make decisions about offenders and cases, as well as about staff members and program/agency performance, through intraagency communications. Automation should allow timely access to client information, reduced duplication of data entry, increased agency efficiency, increased agency accountability, and improved agency decision-making capabilities. Also important is the "ability to institutionalize case management practices into the daily routine" of criminal justice practitioners (APPA, 2003). No matter what type of automated information system is developed or purchased, the needs of each agency must be identified to ensure maximum intraagency communication and efficiency in administration, client tracking, reporting, and information exchange protocols.

The Benefits of Integrated Systems

Agencies share information externally through a variety of means, including court orders, consent forms, interagency agreements, and written releases. However, information can be slow in getting from one agency to another by way of traditional means such as mail, fax, and courier. Automation offers the opportunity to expedite this process exponentially. According to SEARCH (2000), the National Consortium for Justice Information and Statistics,

> Integrated systems improve the quality of information, and thereby the quality of decisions, by eliminating error-prone redundant data entry. In addition, by exchanging data between systems (programs), integration typically improves the timely access to information, a critical factor at many decision points. Moreover, integration enables the exchange of crucial information without regard to time or space; multiple users can access the same record simultaneously from remote locations around the clock.

Automated management information systems, specifically integrated systems, offer an effective means to bridge the information gap between criminal justice agencies. Integrated systems allow a higher level of coordination between agencies to provide appropriate supervision and services to individuals. Integration permits the electronic access to, and the exchange of, critical information at key decision points without the need for data manipulation processes (e.g., uploading, downloading, or merging documents) or manual or paper requests (APPA, 2003).

The benefits of an integrated system lie in its ability to facilitate decision making at three levels: client (services), management (efficiency), and system (effectiveness). Data systems that function at the client, management, and system levels benefit all end users. At the client level, the goal is to improve client outcomes by providing the appropriate level and type of services. To do this, it is important to have valid and reliable information about the client from various perspectives, not just the typical self-assessment provided by the client. The information must be historical and multiagency to ensure a whole and accurate picture of the client and his or her needs. At the management level, the goal is to see that system services contribute to outcomes and planning for new services. Management's concerns relate to program development, service delivery, quality assurance, and performance evaluation. Finally, at the system level, the goals are to facilitate the measurement of societal outcomes, make recommendations for future resource allocations, and ensure public accountability.

Through integration, agencies are equipped to determine the types of services necessary and to coordinate their efforts. Integrated information sharing can improve decision making and feedback concerning offenders. This can lead to a reduction in the service redundancy that is often overwhelming to offenders trying to meet the requirements of several agencies simultaneously. Greater agency cooperation also creates increased offender accountability, reducing the amount of time that the client is under supervision and treatment. This reduced time may, in turn, reduce client recidivism.

Legal Issues Affecting the Sharing of Information

The sharing of information both within and across agencies is governed by a series of legal requirements that influence practice. Federal, state, and local laws regulate the sharing of electronic information. Federal statutes and regulations will generally preempt state and local statutes and regulations, except where federal laws specifically require that stricter or more stringent state or local laws prevail. Although most federal laws restrict access to electronic information, there are laws that broaden access. It is beyond the scope of this chapter to explicate all of the federal, state, and local laws pertaining to electronic information sharing, but the chapter provides an overview of the important legal requirements. This section highlights portions of regulations put forth according to the Code of Federal Regulations (CFR).

28 CFR Part 23: Criminal Justice History Information

Regulations adopted by the U.S. Department of Justice, Office of Justice Programs, govern criminal intelligence systems operated under the Omnibus Crime Control and Safe Streets Act of 1968. These are systems designed to receive, store, and disseminate information on individuals or organizations based on a reasonable suspicion of criminal activity (28 CFR § 23.3(b)). The regulations note the importance of being able to expose ongoing networks of criminal activity by pooling information about such activities, but they also note that information pooling poses a potential threat to the privacy interests of the individuals described in the pooled data. For this reason, policy standards that attempt to safeguard privacy rights are developed (28 CFR § 23.2).

The basic principle under the regulations is that an "intelligence project"—single agency or multijurisdictional—may collect and maintain information on an individual only if there is a reasonable suspicion that the individual is involved in criminal conduct or activity and the information is relevant to that activity. An intelligence project may not collect or maintain criminal intelligence information about political, religious, or social views, associations, or activities unless the information relates directly to criminal conduct or activity. The determination of reasonable suspicion of involvement in criminal conduct is based on whether there are sufficient facts to believe that the individual is involved in a definable criminal activity or enterprise (28 CFR § 23.20(a)–(c)).

Dissemination of Information. A project may disseminate information collected only when there is a need to know and a right to know in the performance of a law enforcement activity (28 CFR § 22.20(g)). Recipient law enforcement authorities must agree to follow procedures consistent with the outlined principles and must establish "need to know" and "right to know" standards.

Maintenance of Records—Security Requirements. A project must ensure that administrative, technical, and physical safeguards, including audit trails, are adopted to prevent unauthorized access and intentional or unintentional damage to records. The project must maintain a record of who has been given information, the reason for the disclosure, and the date of dissemination. Information must be labeled to indicate levels of sensitivity and confidence as well as the identity of the submitting agency or official.

28 CFR Part 22: Confidentiality of Identifiable Research and Statistical Information

U.S. Department of Justice regulations govern the confidentiality of identifiable research and statistical information obtained, collected, or produced by the Bureau of Justice Assistance (BJA), Office of Juvenile Justice and Delinquency Prevention (OJJDP), Bureau of Justice Statistics (BJS), National Institute of Justice (NIJ), or Office of Justice Programs (OJP) (28 CFR § 22.20(a)). These agencies fund and oversee criminal justice projects. The regulations are intended to protect the privacy of research subjects by restricting the use of research subject-identifiable information that is obtained in a research program to the intended research use only (28 CFR § 22.1).

The regulations specify information as identifiable (and thus protected) if it is labeled by name or other personal identifiers or if it can, by virtue of sample size or other factors, be reasonably interpreted to refer to a particular individual (28 CFR § 22.2(e)). The regulations also prohibit admitting identifiable information as evidence or using it for any purpose in a judicial or administrative proceeding without the consent of the person that the information identifies. Where consent is obtained, it must be obtained at the time the information is sought for the proceedings. The consent must set out the specific purposes for which information will be used and must specify the scope of the information to be used (28 CFR §§ 22.1 and 22.28). Four significant exceptions should be noted: The regulations do not apply to (a) information gained regarding future criminal conduct, (b) records from which identifiable research or statistical information was originally obtained, (c) records designated as public under existing statutes, and (d) information extracted from records designated as public.

Where information is requested by a person other than one of the controlling agencies, the request must describe the general objectives of the project for which the information is requested and must specifically justify the need for the information. The request also must show that the requestor's conduct will not, either directly or indirectly, cause legal, economic, physical, or social harm to individuals whose identities are revealed.[3]

42 CFR Part 2: Sharing Substance Abuse Treatment Information

Section 408 of the federal Drug Abuse Prevention, Treatment, and Rehabilitation Act of 1972 and Section 333 of the Comprehensive Alcohol Abuse and Alcoholism Prevention, Treatment, and Rehabilitation Act of 1970 restrict the disclosure and use of substance abuse treatment records maintained as part of a federally assisted alcohol and drug abuse program. These laws are intended to ensure that a patient in a federally assisted treatment program is not made more vulnerable by the existence of his or her patient records than is an individual who has not sought treatment (42 CFR § 2.3(b)(2)).

The application of the regulations is broad because they apply to records maintained by any federally assisted drug and alcohol abuse treatment program and, for the most part, have defined the norm in the substance abuse field. A treatment program is considered to be federally assisted if it is carried out by a federal agency in whole or in part; under a license, certification, or registration granted by a federal agency; by a Medicare-certified provider; by a provider authorized to conduct methadone maintenance treatment; by an entity registered to dispense a dangerous controlled substance; by a recipient of federal financial assistance in any form; by a state or local government unit that receives federal funds; or by an entity that uses federal income tax deductions for contributions to the program or that is granted federal tax-exempt status.

Under these laws and the regulations that implement them, patient records obtained for the purpose of diagnosis, treatment, or referral may not be disclosed and may not be used to initiate or substantiate any criminal charges against a patient or to conduct an investigation of a patient. Disclosure is permitted where there is written authorization by the patient or under a court order.

The regulations make clear that use or disclosure of the information is prohibited not only in criminal proceedings but also in civil, administrative, or legislative proceedings conducted by any federal, state, or local authority. The prohibition against use for prosecutorial investigation continues after the patient ceases to be a patient and includes information obtained by an undercover agent or informant placed in the program, even if the agent or informant was placed in the program under a court order. An entity to which information is disclosed may not further disclose that information.

Patient Notification Under the Substance Abuse Treatment Regulations. At the time of admission, or as soon as the patient is capable of rational communication, a treatment program covered under the substance abuse treatment regulations must provide the patient with a notice of his or her rights under the regulations, the exceptions to those rights, and the sanctions provided for violations of the regulations. That is, the patient must agree to share treatment-related information specifically identifying the type of information that can be shared, the person or agency/agencies that can receive the information, and the length of time that the sharing of information is permissible. These conditions define the sharing of information and provide a framework for ensuring the adherence to privacy issues regarding sensitive treatment-related information.

Disclosure to Referring Entities in the Criminal Justice System. The substance abuse patient records regulations allow a program or facility to disclose information about a patient to entities within the criminal justice system that have made participation in the program a condition of the disposition of any criminal proceedings or of the patient's parole or release from custody. However, the patient still must sign a written consent to the disclosure, and the disclosure may be made only to those individuals within the system who have a need for the information in connection with their duty to monitor the patient (42 CFR § 2.35(a)). The written consent must state the period during which it remains in effect, and the period must be reasonable, taking into account the anticipated length of treatment, the type of criminal proceeding involved, the need for the information in final disposition, and when the disposition will occur. Finally, the written consent must state that it is revocable on a specified passage of time or on the occurrence of an ascertainable event. The time or occurrence must be no later than the final disposition of the conditional release or other action in connection with which consent is given.

Other Exceptions. Also particularly relevant to our review is that disclosure or use of a diagnosis is not prohibited if the diagnosis was made solely for the purpose of providing evidence. Nor is disclosure or use of a diagnosis of drug overdose or alcohol intoxication prohibited if the diagnosis shows clearly that the individual was not an alcohol or drug abuser.

Patient-identifiable records also may be disclosed without the patient's permission (a) to medical personnel in a bona fide medical emergency; (b) in a deidentified form to persons conducting scientific research, management audits, financial audits, or program evaluation; or (c) by order of a court of competent jurisdiction, only after the court has weighed the public interest in disclosure against the injury to the patient, to the physician–patient relationship, and to treatment services.

A court order cannot mandate disclosure; it can only authorize disclosure. An additional subpoena or other legal mandate must be sought to compel disclosure. Furthermore, a court may order disclosure only if (a) it is necessary to protect against an existing threat to life or of serious bodily injury, (b) the

disclosure is necessary in connection with the investigation or prosecution of an extremely serious crime, or (c) the disclosure is in connection with litigation or an administrative proceeding in which the patient offers testimony or other evidence relating to the content of the confidential communication.

Criminal Court Orders Authorizing Disclosure. A court may authorize the disclosure and use of information to criminally investigate or prosecute a patient only if (a) the crime involved is extremely serious, (b) there is a reasonable likelihood that the records will disclose information of substantial value to the investigation or prosecution, (c) other ways of obtaining the information are not available or would be ineffective, and (d) the public interest in the need for disclosure outweighs the potential injury from the disclosure to the patient, to the patient–physician relationship, and to the ability of the program to provide services to its patients. Disclosure and use must be limited to those parts of the patient's record that are necessary to fulfill the objective of the order and to those law enforcement or prosecutorial officials who are responsible for, or are conducting, the investigation or prosecution.

Security: Written Versus Electronic Records. Written records that are subject to the law and regulations must be maintained in a secure room, locked file cabinet, safe, or similar container. If a program discontinues operations or is taken over or acquired, it must purge patient-identifying information unless the patient gives his or her written consent for a transfer or there is a requirement that the records be kept for a period of time specified by law. If the records must be retained by law, the regulations require that the records be kept in sealed envelopes or containers that are labeled with a disposal date.

The privacy provisions of the Health Insurance Portability and Accountability Act of 1996 (HIPAA), the law governing disclosure of patient-identifiable electronic health care information maintained by providers, governs information also covered under the law governing substance abuse treatment information. An entity covered under the HIPAA must reasonably safeguard protected health information from any intentional or unintentional use or disclosure, and the entity must reasonably safeguard protected information to limit incidental uses or disclosures.

In a National Drug Court Institute publication, *Federal Confidentiality Laws and How They Affect Drug Court Practitioners*, Tauber and Weinstein (1999) address the application of the substance abuse treatment confidentiality provisions on records retention to electronic records by stating,

> Procedures involving computers should conform to the spirit of the regulations through the use of safeguards built into procedures, software, and hardware. With hard drives, diskettes, and similar storage vessels, this could be fairly simple. Records covered by Section 290dd-2 should be password-protected, and the password should be guarded in the same manner as the key to a file cabinet. . . . Networked computers can be managed in a similar fashion. One danger that may be more significant on a network than on a single computer is the alteration of data. For such concerns, the court should consult computer specialists. . . . The regulations accompanying Section 290dd-2 expressly permit disclosures to qualified service organizations to the extent necessary to obtain services (although it might be possible to obtain assistance from computer consultants without disclosing confidential information). Finally, all storage systems should include procedures for limiting access to records after the participant's consent expires or is revoked. . . . Records on computers can be sealed by changing the password or other access authorization, either manually or with programs designed

to perform that function at the appropriate time. (p. 18)

45 CFR Parts 160 and 164: The Privacy of Health Information

By enacting the HIPAA, Congress recognized that advances in electronic technology could erode the privacy of health information.[4] The law required the U.S. Department of Health and Human Services (HHS) to adopt privacy protections for individually identifiable health information. The HIPAA privacy regulations do not replace other federal or state laws that grant individuals even greater privacy protections, and covered entities are free to retain or adopt more protective policies or practices.

There are no restrictions on the use or disclosure of information that neither identifies an individual nor provides a reasonable basis to identify the individual. However, to deidentify information, the regulations require the removal of all of the following identifiers of the individual as well as those of every relative, employer, and household member of the individual:

- Name
- Geographic subdivisions smaller than a state, including street address, city, county, precinct, and zip code
- All elements of dates (except year) directly related to an individual, including birth date, admission date, discharge date, date of death, and any indicator that an individual is 89 years of age or over
- Telephone and fax numbers
- E-mail addresses
- Social security number
- Medical record numbers
- Health plan beneficiary numbers
- Account numbers
- Certificate or license numbers
- Vehicle identifiers and serial numbers, including license plate numbers
- Device identifiers and serial numbers
- Internet Universal Resource Locators (URLs)
- Internet Protocol (IP) address numbers

- Biometric identifiers, including fingerprints and voice prints
- Full-face photographic images or any comparable images
- Any other unique identifying numbers, characteristics, or codes not previously identified

An entity covered by the regulations is permitted, but not required, to use and disclose patient-identifiable health information (a) to the individual; (b) for treatment, payment, and health care operations; (c) for public interest and benefit activities; and (d) in limited data sets for research, public health, or health care operations.

Public interest and benefit activities that permit disclosure without authorization include the following:

- Those required by law
- Those in which public health authorities collect or receive information to prevent and control disease, injury, disability, or consumer product or workplace injuries
- Disclosures to government authorities about abuse, neglect, or domestic violence
- Activities such as audits and investigations necessary for the oversight of health care systems and government benefit programs
- Court orders of disclosure in judicial and administrative proceedings
- Provision of information to funeral directors about decedents
- Provision of information to facilitate organ or tissue donations
- Research approved by an institutional review privacy board
- Serious and imminent threats to health and safety of a person or the public
- Essential special government functions such as national security activities, the separation or discharge of military personnel, protective services for high government officials, and medical suitability determinations for security clearances or mandatory military service

- Information related to workers' compensation for injuries and illnesses
- Law enforcement activities

The final category of authorized disclosures is the one that has the greatest impact on the ability of criminal justice information systems to collect and maintain patient information. Under this exception, information may be disclosed to law enforcement officials for law enforcement purposes under six circumstances:

1. As required by law under court order, warrant, subpoena, or administrative request

2. To identify or locate a suspect, fugitive, material witness, or missing person

3. In response to a law enforcement official's request for information about a crime victim or suspected crime victim

4. To alert law enforcement personnel of a person's death if the covered entity believes that criminal activity caused the death

5. When a covered entity believes that protected health information is evidence of a crime that occurred on its premises

6. In a medical emergency not occurring on the premises of the covered entity when necessary to inform law enforcement authorities about the commission, nature, or location of a crime, crime victim, or perpetrator (45 CFR § 164.512(f))

Other law enforcement-related disclosures that do not fall directly under the law enforcement category, but that fall under one of the other categories of permitted disclosures, are permitted.

Notices of Privacy Practices for Protected Health Information. In general, a patient has the right to receive adequate notice, in plain language and sufficient detail, of permitted uses and disclosures of protected health information by the covered entity as well as the patient's rights and the covered entity's legal duties with respect to the protected information. The HIPAA regulations detail what the privacy notice must contain.

Authorization of Disclosures. A covered entity must obtain the individual's written authorization for any use or disclosure of protected health information that is made for reasons other than treatment, payment, or health care operations or reasons otherwise permitted. The authorization must be written in plain language and must contain specific descriptions of the information to be disclosed or used as well as the persons disclosing and receiving the information, the purpose for each restricted use or disclosure, an expiration date or event, and the dated signature of the authorizing individual. It also must note the individual's right to revoke the authorization and a description of revocation procedures. The authorizing individual must be provided with a copy of the authorization.

Required Safeguards. Covered entities must have in place appropriate administrative, technical, and physical safeguards to protect the privacy of protected information. They must reasonably safeguard protected health information from any intentional or unintentional use of disclosure in violation of the standards and must reasonably limit incidental uses or disclosures.

Laws Broadening Access and Opportunity for Information Sharing

U.S.A. Patriot Act

The U.S.A. Patriot Act, enacted in 2001 to track terrorists, expands information gathering and information sharing to assist federal authorities in investigating terrorist conspiracies and activities or in prosecuting terrorist activities. The act expands the authority of federal intelligence officers to obtain records in electronic networks if those records contain information that relates to terrorist conspiracies or activities. Unlike the federal laws discussed previously, which restrict access to information that is important to case management, the Patriot Act may open access to information retained within a case management database to federal officers alleging involvement of a client, or known associates of a client, in terrorist conspiracies or activities.

Jacob Wetterling Crimes Against Children and Sexually Violent Offender Registration Act

The federal law authorizing states to register convicted child molesters, the Jacob Wetterling Crimes Against Children and Sexually Violent Offender Registration Act, provides ready access to information about those offenders, and requires the offenders themselves to ensure that the information is up-to-date. The law provides no privacy protections to registrants. The law authorizes the U.S. attorney general to allow states to require that a person convicted of a criminal offense against a minor victim register his or her current address for 10 years. Registration can be for life if the person has two or more convictions or if the crime was considered to be aggravated. A person who is a sexually violent predator can be required to register his or her current address for life. The law defines a "sexually violent predator" as an individual convicted of a sexually violent offense who suffers from a congenital or acquired mental abnormality that predisposes the individual to predatory sexually violent offenses.

Developing an Information-Sharing System

Having explored the various legal restrictions relevant to creating an integrated criminal justice information system, the legal framework does not preclude the sharing of information. Instead, it defines the conditions and premise for the sharing of information, and CFR 42 defines the parameters for how that information can be shared. To develop an information system that incorporates the core principles of protecting privacy concerns but also provides for real-time sharing to facilitate public safety goals, the development of the tools should be pursued through a process that requires strategic planning, collaboration, and the identification of functional needs as well as a plan for implementation and maintenance.

Traditionally, the development of a collaborative system is often met by internal resistance that often creates artificial barriers. Resisters often will cite one or more of the following difficulties:

- The costs associated with planning and implementation
- The time and expense of training
- Fear of new technology (commonly referred to as "techno-phobia" or "techno-terror")
- Internal issues (e.g., an agency may have an existing system or may be getting a new system)
- The perceived violation of confidentiality of client-level information
- A lack of knowledge about key concepts underlying an integrated information system
- Technical incompatibilities between component systems (e.g., different data definitions, incompatible systems)
- The cost of sustaining the system after the initial start-up funding runs out

An information system can be developed and implemented smoothly if all potential barriers and the impact they may have are identified and strategies are implemented to overcome those barriers early in the development process. We recommend envisioning the development or purchase of an integrated information system as a three-pronged process: planning, implementation, and maintenance. A key element is to have the stakeholders in the room to assist with key decision making and to address the organizational issues that often affect the ability to share information. Other key areas of success

are to (a) contract with or hire competent technology staff members who share the agency's or jurisdiction's best interests, (b) purchase or develop a system that is flexible and easily adjustable to meeting the dynamic needs of the agency or jurisdiction, and (c) develop a maintenance plan to sustain the system after it has been implemented. Putting these strategies in place should address most of the barriers that an agency or a jurisdiction will encounter and should ensure a functional and manageable system.

PHASE 1: PLANNING

Identifying Stakeholders

Information sharing is not an issue of one agency instructing another agency about the type of information that is permissible to share. Instead, it is a joint activity that requires mutual agreement among all of the parties. The best way in which to facilitate the sharing of information is to have all of the parties be part of the partnership to develop and implement the system. The system's stakeholders—those who have a vested interest in the program and its successes—need to be involved in the decisions about the development of an integrated information system because they know what variables need to be addressed. Each agency or jurisdiction should convene a committee of stakeholders to guide the development and implementation of the information system. Representatives from every agency participating in the criminal justice system, as well as those from non-criminal justice agencies (e.g., courts, supervision providers, treatment providers, law enforcement representatives, public health providers) and local information system experts, should be present. Stakeholders should be involved in, and should monitor, all aspects of information system planning, design, and implementation.

Defining the Goals and Objectives of the System

Before tackling the design of an integrated criminal justice information system, each jurisdiction's stakeholder team should define the goals and objectives of the intended system. These goals and objectives must be in conjunction with the goals of the collaborating criminal justice and non-criminal justice agencies, and they should guide the planning, design, and implementation.

In identifying goals and objectives, planners also need to identify the sources to be used to create the common pool of information (e.g., police, corrections, prosecution, courts, supervision, social services), and planners should determine which agencies want to share what information and with whom. It is important to determine who maintains the necessary data and can enter the data into the system at the earliest point in time. Usually, the goals to be addressed by an integrated criminal justice information system include at least ensuring the timely entry and transmittal of information, providing support for operational decision making, facilitating the collection of data early in the criminal justice process, ensuring ease of use, integrating with other systems, ensuring easy system modification, maintaining data security and complying with client privacy laws, and meeting the needs of the entire criminal justice system.

Defining Data Elements

In a multiagency information system, the business process that includes offender flow should drive the data elements that are included in the system. The stakeholder committee should oversee the compilation and inventory of all necessary information. Stakeholders determining the key data elements should make sure they include the following:

- List common categories of useful data
- Create a matrix showing where that information is traditionally originated and maintained (e.g., treatment provider, supervision agency, laboratory, school, workplace)
- Identify variations in definitions for crucial commonly used terms so that a data dictionary can be developed to enable all users to use the data in the same manner
- Identify reporting requirements imposed by other (usually federal) agencies
- Identify the needs and reporting requirements of state and local officials
- Identify end users of each data component

Identifying System Evaluation and Reporting Requirements

An information system can provide data at three levels: the client level, the program/service level, and the system level. Reports are usually needed at all three levels. Client reports are generated to monitor client progress and to provide individual client information such as supervision contacts, court hearings, drug testing results, and treatment progress. Management reports track staff caseloads and caseload progress as well as agency or program outcome information. System reports reflect progress and outcome information for the entire criminal justice system.

The stakeholder committee should lay the groundwork for the structure of automated reports, generated by and from the information system, at each of the three data-reporting levels. Because data will no longer have to be collated manually, these automated reports will save considerable staff time. The stakeholder committee should identify what types of report designs and features will be most beneficial to the system. The reports generated should reflect the different reporting requirements of the various local, state, and federal lawmakers and agencies.

Building in Security

It is important to ensure that the new integrated information system adheres to all intra- and interagency security protocols and requirements imposed under federal, state, and local laws and regulations, as described earlier in this chapter. Implementing a system that is able to set permissions and restrictions at the user level and set securities at the client level will alleviate some potential issues. Critical security issues pertain to the following.

Intraagency Setup

The information system should be flexible enough to accommodate all types of users at each level. It should be able to assign a user type to each user; for example, an "inquiry" user would have read-only access to information, whereas a "general" user could read, enter, and edit information. An administrator should have the authority to dole out administrative permissions to specific users as needed. The system should be capable of allowing users to access some agency units while restricting their access to others. Finally, the system should be able to grant or deny individual users permission to access each screen or report available in the system.

It also is important to make decisions about system access such as the following:

- Log-in parameters and the characteristics of passwords
- Who will be responsible for establishing log-ins and passwords
- Whether to incorporate double authentication
- How often passwords should be reset and how to handle their resetting
- The types of firewalls needed for database security
- Which users should be able to query the system
- At what point the system should automatically terminate the sessions of idle users

Establishing Interagency Protocols

The electronic management of the release of information between agencies should be built into every aspect of the integrated information system. The system should allow the sharing of information between agencies through a consent authorization process. Where an agency is still required to obtain written or electronic consent from a client, information in the system should be released in a fashion that mirrors the consent process for hard copy. Once consent has been obtained, the automated system should be enabled to manage and enforce the rules for releasing client information. There should be a component that ensures that the receiving agency verifies the receipt of consent electronically before reviewing client information.

If the agency that receives the client wants to require that all consents be verified before the information is released, the agency should be able to verify directly from the incoming referral management screen. Any office outside the original agency that has not received the client's consent should be restricted from seeing the same set of client data. The client data can be further protected with the use of selective data-sharing options and the timed expiration of consent-authorized permission.

Finally, the technical staff members for the system should be required to sign confidentiality forms that prevent them from disclosing any confidential information, particularly where they are providing technical assistance to end users at all levels and have access to client data.

Establishing System Procedures

Once these decisions have been made, policies and procedures should be developed to formalize the gathering and sharing of information in a secure environment (Slayton, 2000). Interagency agreements, consent policies, and written confidentiality waivers all must be developed. Policies and procedures should be well defined and written so that all types of users can understand them. The policies and procedures should specifically address the following:

- Where the database will be housed, how the database will be maintained, and issues of security and access
- Who or what agency will be responsible for administrative functions and procedures such as agency and user setup and technical assistance
- The processes and procedures for linking to other systems
- Data definitions
- Procedures for identifying the level of information (e.g., case level, department level, community level) accessed by each user
- Procedures for capturing and correcting the entry of inaccurate information
- Procedures for information modification
- Procedures for navigating each screen or module in the system

PHASE 2: IMPLEMENTATION

Preimplementation Activities

The stakeholder committee should choose a pilot site to beta-test the new software and identify any bugs before implementation. The implementation timeline should allow for the time it will take to administer the beta test and make necessary changes. In addition to testing the software, efforts should be made to engage all employees in the change process. Employees asked to work in new ways—with new business processes and new technologies—are often concerned that they will be less competent with the new methods. This perceived level of competence would be directly related to the level of employee job satisfaction. Failing to address these concerns (whether spoken or unspoken) may result in resistance behavior.

Full implementation should begin only at the appropriate time, that is, when comfort levels have been reached and training has been completed. The agency or jurisdiction should strategize as to the most efficient and effective implementation plan, that is, whether to implement in one phase through a phase-in process and whether to implement all functions of the system at once or through the phase-in of modules. Addressing the pros and cons of these issues and clearly identifying the best implementation plan for all users will help to reduce the initial bumps and bruises.

Training and Technical Assistance

Management information systems are useful tools, but they can fail without the proper user training and support. If training needs are underestimated, the utility of the system is reduced. End users may enter the required data, but the data in the system might not be used to improve client, agency, or system outcomes. The stakeholder committee should identify training and technical assistance needs. Areas that should be covered include system access, administrative procedures, navigation, security and confidentiality measures, operational procedures for handling data, system functional modules, and report generating.

The training curriculum should address not only the functional aspects of the system but also the business practices of each user type and each agency. Building the training around the duties and job responsibilities of users greatly enhances system utility. Training sessions should be held as close as possible to the time that the users are expected to use the system, thereby reducing the need for repeat training. Some consideration also should be given to the question of whether to include the entry of live data in the training program.

PHASE 3: MAINTENANCE

Too often, the system's "go live" date is perceived as the end, rather than the beginning, of the system implementation process, and thus long-term strategies are not implemented. The ongoing need for maintenance and support to ensure smooth system operations is often overlooked. The agency or jurisdiction should ensure that the software vendor or implementation consultants have established a maintenance plan. Ongoing system evaluation should be in place to catch any new bugs as they come along. If the system is dynamic and will be enhanced or modified, there should be an established procedure for testing system enhancements on an ongoing basis.

Finally, a system for notifying users and securing data should be in place for the times when the system goes down. A disaster recovery plan should be in place to protect the data in the database or in multiple databases during and after natural or other disasters. For example, planners should decide whether there will be a backup database at a separate location and whether backup tapes will be removed every evening.

HATS: An Illustrative Case Study

In 1996, the University of Maryland, with demonstration grant funding through the Office of National Drug Control Policy (ONDCP), developed an integrated database system that is currently in operation in the state of Maryland as well as in some jurisdictions in Virginia, Missouri, Georgia, and Florida. Some agencies in the District of Columbia also use HATS. HATS is an integrated management information system where multiple agencies maintain information in one database (for a description of the HATS application, see Taxman & Sherman, 1998a, 1998b). The management information system is maintained by the University of Maryland. In 2002, more than 3,500 HATS users and more than 900 organizations in Maryland used HATS, including criminal justice, juvenile justice, substance abuse treatment, mental health, family service, social services, and public schools. HATS is most widely used in Maryland; the Maryland Alcohol and Drug Abuse Administration (ADAA) has mandated that all certified treatment agencies report their data through HATS, the Maryland Drug Treatment Court Commission has recommended that all drug courts in Maryland use HATS to track client and program progress, and the Maryland Division of Probation and Parole (DPP) also uses HATS to track client progress. HATS will soon be used by reentry programs to track clients' progress as the clients move from jail or prison back into the community and by faith-based organizations to track clients in transitional housing. All of these are examples of agencies that use the system to facilitate the ease of exchanging information across agencies.

The benefit of all these agencies using HATS, where data are stored in one database, is that the agencies can electronically share information with each other in a timely fashion. There is no more waiting for faxes to come through or for the mail to arrive. If an offender is released from prison today and is transferred to transitional housing, his or her record can be referred today and the transitional housing staff members can review the client records electronically and prepare in advance for the client's arrival. There are no more lost files or misplaced information. Staff members will know whether the offender poses a danger to himself/herself or others, what medications the client needs, the client's history of substance abuse and choice of drugs, and any peculiar behaviors of the client. This ensures staff and client safety and a smooth transition as the client tries to reintegrate back into the community.

The HATS Application

HATS is a consent-driven, integrated management information system that functions at the client (services), management (efficiency), and system (effectiveness) levels, where performance measures can be generated at every level (for more information, refer to the website for the University of Maryland's Bureau of Government Research: www.bgr. umd. edu). It was originally geared toward the case management needs of criminal justice and treatment providers, incorporating the functional needs of both service areas. However, as a dynamic system, it has expanded its scope to public schools, social services, family services, and mental health.

HATS was developed in Visual Basic 6.0 to maximize flexibility for use in a variety of settings. Seagate Crystal Reports are used to create formatted reports that allow flexibility and options regarding the dates for which the reports will be generated, the staff members and units that will be generating the reports, and the case types (preadmission, active, or closed) to be reported. Connecting through SQL Server 7 to a Windows NT 4.0 server operating system, HATS is network server-based computer software designed to allow the entry and sharing of offender and client information across various organizational networks while maintaining all of the federal protections for confidentiality.

HATS mimics the paper world and business practices of its agencies. Using HATS, agencies can perform and record all of their internal operations, including intake, case management and supervision, drug testing, treatment events and progress notes, sanctions management, client needs and service referrals, reporting of services received, billing for services, and state and federal automated data reporting.

Case information can be shared as permitted by the participating agencies. The electronic management of the release of information between agencies is built into every aspect of the HATS application. Information entered into HATS, including drug testing results, client sanctions, attendance, and assessments, can be shared between agencies using standard procedures consistent with federal and state laws governing client confidentiality. As shown in Figure 9.1, the HATS system has a built-in control to grant access to specific information across agencies. CFR 42 provided the platform for HATS with each offender granting access to information, the agency that can receive the information, and the duration of time that the information can be shared. The system ensures that information is available

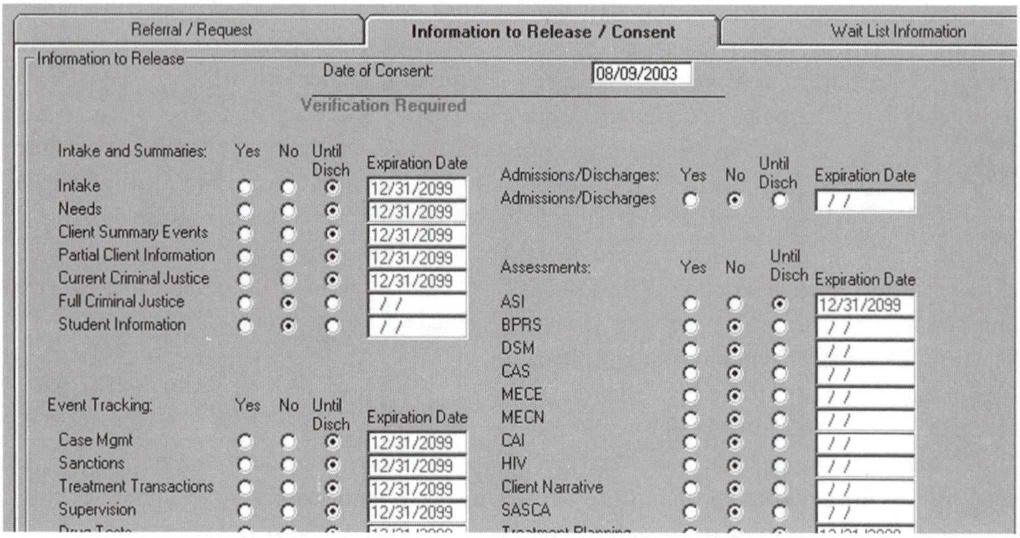

Figure 9.1   HATS Consent

only through the consent process. The consent process can be set up to be agency to agency or within agency (e.g., program to program).

The system uses a unique HATS client numerical identifier. This identifier is then used to track the client's progress through the

Client Intake	Basic information—name, date of birth, social security number, race, ethnicity, marital status, employment status, and contact information. Includes aliases and additional numerical identifiers (e.g., driver's license, sheriff's identification number, FBI number).
Assessments	Standard tools that are used to capture information that aids in identifying client needs and connecting offenders to the appropriate services such as Addiction Severity Index (ASI), the Client Assessment Instrument (CAI), the Human Immunodeficiency Virus Assessment, the Brief Psychiatric Rating Scale, and the criteria established by the *Diagnostic and Statistical Manual of Mental Disorders* (DSM) to codify substance abuse severity problems. Other assessment information tools are available through the system.
Criminal Justice History	Documents criminal activity (arrests and court dispositions) and provides an overview of a client's past criminal behavior (juvenile and adult arrests and convictions).
Criminal Supervision	Identifies the type and frequency of contacts between a supervision agent and a client.
Drug Testing	Schedules drug testing appointments, monitors drug testing attendance, and records drug test results. Chain of custody is also monitored.
Graduated Sanctions	Track noncompliance with supervision and treatment plans and the consequences resulting from those behaviors.
Case Management	Records participation in indirect services identified in client's supervision or treatment plan. The case management function also can be used to document interventions and to track whether the client is receiving the appropriate care in the appropriate setting.
Treatment Modules	Record the type and level of treatment services provided as well as their duration and outcome. Clinicians can track progress notes and excused absence notes for each service. It has a treatment planning module, where clinicians can identify client problem behaviors and goals, objectives, and strategies.
Referrals/Appointments	Referral screen assists in making referrals to, and scheduling appointments with, agencies and service providers that will best serve the needs of the client.
Consent	Two types of consent to establish the electronic sharing of information: (1) an agency can schedule an appointment with another agency using the consent process or (2) an agency can request records from another agency. The agency receiving the referral or request for records must verify receiving a copy of the consent form signed by the client before accessing the client information.

Figure 9.2   HATS Core Modules

treatment and criminal justice systems. The system also has a validation feature that enables staff members to determine whether an identifier has already been assigned. The identifier is keyed to each of the modules. Figure 9.2 illustrates some of the key modules of HATS.

HATS provides users with two main summary screens. The first is the Caseload Summary screen, which provides an overview of each staff member's caseload and the most recent activity dates for certain events (e.g., drug testing, treatment, graduated sanctions) for each client. The Client Summary screen provides a more detailed overview of the activities for a particular client. Figure 9.3 shows an example of the Client Summary screen.

HATS is equipped to generate various reports for each module in the system as well as to generate management reports and reports to fulfill federal, state, and local reporting requirements. The HATS report feature permits data to be extracted from the database into a written report format. These reports can be used to view summary and detailed information for each client, staff caseload, or agency caseload. In addition to the programmed canned reports, HATS allows users to export their data into a Microsoft Access database so that they can present their data in a different format.

Electronic Drug Test Results in Maryland's Division of Probation and Parole

HATS includes drug testing management software that can be installed at drug testing laboratories, where drug test results can be posted automatically and uploaded so that the appropriate agency in HATS can review the results. This software tracks the chain of custody of each urine sample from the collection site to the lab. Currently, several agencies receive drug testing results electronically through the drug testing lab, including the Maryland DPP. The DPP operates its own drug testing lab, where all specimens collected from offenders under supervision are tested and results are generated electronically through HATS.

This automated drug testing process through HATS has saved tremendous time and effort among DPP staff members. Not only can the chain of custody be tracked electronically, but also staff members can receive an offender's drug test results in a timely fashion (within an hour of the test being taken) and then respond appropriately to test results. This decreases the general lag in time between behavior (use) and response. For offenders who are also in substance abuse treatment as a condition of their probation, with the proper consents to share client information in place, the treatment agency also sees these test results and can address positive tests and "no shows" at the next treatment session, thereby providing a more collaborative and timely approach to client services. In addition, if the drug testing agency is testing the offender, the supervising agency can also view the test results from the treatment system.

An example of the process is provided in Figure 9.4. Agent S can log into HATS each morning and generate a report that will identify all offenders on her caseload who tested positive or failed to appear for drug testing appointments. This allows Agent S to immediately identify those clients who she must contact immediately to address their behavior for potential violations of their probation contracts. For each offender, Agent S can also electronically review the offender's treatment progress and any progress notes entered by the treatment provider as well as any drug test results captured at the treatment agency. Agent S identified that offender Betty Boop tested positive for cocaine yesterday, although her drug of choice is primarily marijuana.

With this knowledge, Agent S then clicks in HATS to review Betty's progress in treatment. This allows the agent to learn whether the offender has been attending her counseling

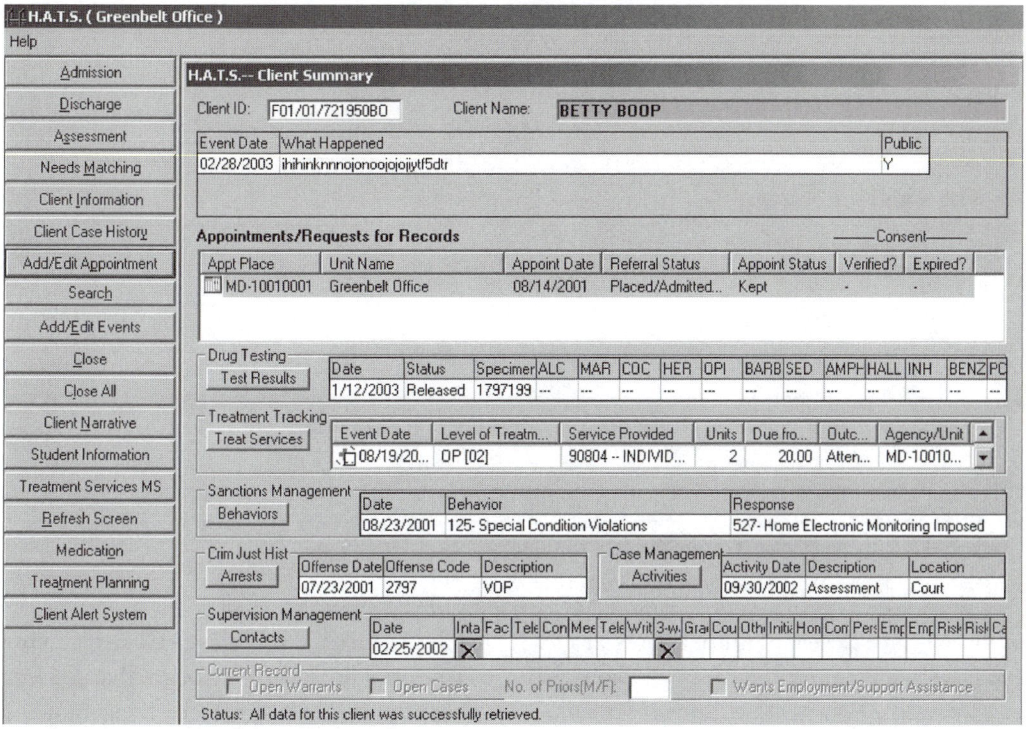

Figure 9.3   HATS Client Summary Screen

sessions as well as whether any progress has been made. In this case, the agent learns that Betty has experienced a stress factor with her mother being diagnosed with cancer last week. The clinician also indicated that Betty might be a danger to herself. Equipped with this knowledge, Agent S can then determine the appropriate action such as a home visit to assess Betty's situation. After talking with Betty, Agent S can remind the offender of the importance of her commitment to meeting the conditions of her probation and also make a referral to a therapist to help Betty better cope with the situation. The information allows the agent to respond to the offender swiftly and to be aware of any case-related factors. It reduces the reliance on the offender having to repeat information or provide explanations.

In addition to client information, the DPP can track drug test result information for its agency or comparison across units within the agency to ensure that test results are being tested and documented appropriately. For example, the DPP director might want to know how many drug tests were administered in March and what percentage of those were positive. By looking at the report for each site, the director is able to determine that 29.8% of specimens tested at the Mondawmin office are positive, compared with only 11.8% at the Guilford office (Figure 9.5). The director may use this information to then query staff caseloads and resources at each site to determine whether additional resources or staff members are needed to better monitor client supervision. The information can also be used to examine the performance of a particular unit.

HATS in Maryland Drug Courts

In Maryland, the drug courts are using HATS to track client and program progress and

Print date: 4/9/2004 Page 2 of 3

Appointment Listing, With Test Results, by Client Name

Showina Appointments Scheduled bv Reported Aaencv/Units

Agency: MD-100100 Generic Agency A, Unit: ALL

Staff: Snavely, Kathleen (2788), Client: ALL, Cases: Active

March 9-April 9, 2004

Appt Date *Place* *Data Entry* *Staff* *Appt Status* *Remarks*

Intake Unit: Second SDU - test [02]

Client Name/ID: BOOP, BETTY - F01/01/721951BO

Agency: MD-100100 Generic Agency A

Unit: 01 Greenbelt Office

4/8/2004 MD-10010001 ksnavely ksnavely Released

ALC	AMPH	BARB	BENZO	COC	CREAT	HALL	HER	INH	MAR	METH	OPI	PCP	SED	THC20
N	---	---	---	POS	---	---	N	---	N	---	N	---	---	---

Client Name/ID: PIG, PETUNIA - F06/01/621962PI

Agency: MD-100100 Generic Agency A

Unit: 01 Greenbelt Office

4/8/2004 MD-10010001 ksnavely ksnavely Released

ALC	AMPH	BARB	BENZO	COC	CREAT	HALL	HER	INH	MAR	METH	OPI	PCP	SED	THC20
N	---	---	---	POS	---	---	N	---	N	---	N	---	---	---

Figure 9.4 Client Drug Testing Results for Hypothetical Offender

so serve as an excellent example of how HATS functions in an integrated manner and how the consent process works. Drug courts are collaborative programs that provide a comprehensive array of services to drug-involved offenders, often including substance abuse and mental health treatment, employment assistance, education services, health services, and life skills and parenting skills training, among other services. Successful offenders are usually offered reduced sentences and/or dismissal of charges.

Each drug court has developed a process for implementing HATS. In one jurisdiction, when a hypothetical client (Penelope Pitstop) is referred to drug court, the drug court coordinator initiates her case in HATS and enters the client information—Penelope's intake information, arrest information, employment status, and drug court beginning and end dates. The coordinator then refers Penelope to the Maryland DPP and to the County Health Department (CHD). The DPP accepts the referral in HATS through a consent verification process, and the information entered by each agency is then shared by both agencies. The DPP then enters drug testing information, probation contacts, and graduated sanctions that can be viewed by the drug court agency. The CHD also accepts the referral in HATS through the consent verification process. The CHD then conducts client substance abuse and psychosocial assessments, develops a treatment plan, and tracks treatment contacts. If the client is in need of treatment services that cannot be provided by the CHD, a referral is made to another treatment provider who will track client treatment progress in that clinic. All of this is done electronically without the offender actually needing to be reassessed or recertified to be eligible for services. This process can save up to three intake appointments that are more likely to be the norm in a typical agency.

Each agency can review and track client progress in HATS by viewing the screen or generating reports. For example, the treatment provider might want to track the client's progress in treatment, or the DPP might want to track the client's compliance with supervision. Numerous reports are available in HATS to generate this information. The DPP could generate a daily report listing those offenders who tested positive or failed to appear for their drug testing appointments, or it could generate a report listing compliance

General Drug Testing Output Summary Report
For Realeased Specimens Collected During
Period From: 03/01/2004 To: 03/31/2004

MD-200100 - MD Parole & Probation
20 - Mondawmin

	Client Individuals	Specimens No.	%	Assays No.	%	Average No.	%
Count	1096	3842	100.0	19245	100.0	17.6	
Positive		1139	29.6	1526	7.9	1.4	8.0
Negative		2710	70.4	17708	92.0	16.2	92.0
Unable to Determine		0	0.0	11	0.1		
Results Pending				0	0.0		

23 - Guilford

	Client Individuals	Specimens No.	%	Assays No.	%	Average No.	%
Count	2387	9390	100.0	46950	100.0	19.7	
Positive		1112	11.8	1446	3.1	0.6	3.0
Negative		8278	88.2	45486	96.9	19.1	97.0
Unable to Determine		0	0.0	18	0.0		
Results Pending				0	0.0		

Figure 9.5   Agency Drug Testing Summary Report

with treatment. As such, the DPP agent has all of the necessary information and does not rely on the client to self-report or for the treatment provider to fax the information. All of the information is in one place—HATS.

As part of drug court, each client must attend a court hearing periodically depending on the requirements set out in his or her drug court contract. During the first few phases of the drug court, offenders usually must attend a review hearing every 2 weeks. Prior to the review hearing, the drug court team reviews each case and makes a decision regarding how to respond to the client. To assist in making these decisions, the drug court coordinator generates a report in HATS, the Client Progress Report, which provides a summary of the offender's compliance across all involved agencies—drug testing results, treatment attendance, supervision attendance, graduated sanctions, and summary progress notes. The judge reviews this report, and the team uses this information to make a decision about the client.

In reviewing Penelope's Client Progress Report (Figure 9.6), we can quickly see that the client has been attending her treatment sessions and supervision contacts but that

during the past week she tested positive for cocaine and failed to appear for another drug test. The case manager recommends that Penelope's support group sessions be increased from two per week to five per week and that Penelope find another sponsor. The drug court team then makes a decision, based on this report, to follow the advice of the case manager and increase Penelope's support groups to five per week and request that she find another sponsor who will be more supportive. However, the judge also believes that although Penelope has a part-time job, she really does not like her job and should be looking for full-time employment. The judge believes that Penelope could benefit from career counseling and adds that to her drug court requirements. The drug court team worked together collaboratively and used the information to provide the best services to Penelope based on information in HATS.

At another level, the program director/ supervisor can use HATS to review staff case-loads (e.g., how many cases are assigned to each staff member), review whether or not staff members are entering client information in a timely fashion, and generate reports indicating program progress. Programs can also export data, through the HATS export process, to Microsoft Access, where additional reports can be generated specific to each program. In addition, programs can export data to the Maryland Drug Court Commission, which monitors all drug courts in Maryland. HATS provides a valuable tool for drug courts and assists greatly in the comprehensive and collaborative approach to serving drug court offenders in Maryland.

CONCLUSIONS AND LESSONS LEARNED FROM THE FIELD

Planning, designing, and implementing an integrated criminal justice information system requires a significant amount of organization and collaboration. One of the first steps is realizing that creating an integrated system involves changing the traditional way in which each agency's information is managed. Under an integrated system, information will be managed electronically—without paper—and collaboratively. An agency will no longer rely totally on its own staff members for data input. Instead, each agency will be responsible for entering its own information, and that information will be shared within the collaboration, limited only by the constraints of federal, state, and local confidentiality laws and regulations. This chapter has provided an example of one system that has built-in safeguards to protect privacy rights but also provides for sharing information across organizational boundaries.

Client Progress Report
July 23, 2003 Through July 31, 2003

Agency:	Baltimore City Drug Court		MD-20032001	
Client Name:	Penelope Pitstop		Case Number:	C12331
Address:	1234 BB Way		HATS ID:	F05/23/19789999PI
	Baltimore City, MD 21218			
Student:	Yes		Grade Level:	11th
Phase:	Phase I	Started: 06/01/2003	Employed:	Yes

Treatment Attendance:

July 25, 2002	Attended	Support Group (AA/NA)	Kathleen Snavely	
July 27, 2002	Attended	Support Group (AA/NA)	Kathleen Snavely	
July 26, 2002	Attended	Group Counseling	Kathleen Snavely	BC Health Dept
July 29, 2002	Attended	Individual Counseling	Kathleen Snavely	BC Health Dept
July 29, 2002	Attended	Group Counseling	Kathleen Snavely	BC Health Dept

Drug Tests Results: Last Positive Drug Test Result: 07/25/2003

| July 25, 2002 | Attended | Positive | Cocaine, Marijuana |
| July 31, 2002 | FTA | | |

Graduated Sanctions:

| **Behavior:** | | **Sanction:** | |
| July 25, 2002 | Positive 1st Urine | July 31, 2002 | Increased Treatment Sessions |

Supervision Contacts:

| July 25, 2002 | Attended | Home Contact | Steven Gray |
| July 29, 2002 | Attended | Face to Face Contact | Steven Gray |

Case Management Contacts:

| July 27, 2002 | Attended | Case Review |

Case Management Summary Note:

July 31, 2002   *Requirements:*   Court hearings every week; drug testing twice a week, individual counseling once a week, group counseling twice a week; AA/NA meetings twice per week

Penelope is still employed at Salon Roi in Baltimore City, part time. Penelope has been generally compliant in attending supervision, however she has missed one drug testing appointment since her last court appearance. She has also tested positive for cocaine and marijuana, however her marijuana levels have dropped). I recommend increasing Penelope's AA/NA requirements from 2 per week to 5 per week in response to her FTAs and her positive drug tests for cocaine. She may also need a new sponsor to help her along in this process. [Signed July 31, 2002 4:32pm by Kathleen R. Snavely, MS].

Figure 9.6   Client Progress Report

Criminal justice systems need to be aware of the political climate of each agency and its effect on system implementation. Politics plays an important role in the way in which business is conducted, and simply mandating the use of a new system will not work. Agency readiness for system integration should be established through an ongoing rapport and collaboration. It is important to empower each agency as an equal partner in the process, working within the confines of the agency's political environment. The blanket approach of treating each agency in the same way, without recognizing each agency's specific needs, will serve only to reinforce territorial issues. Although the needs of the various agencies may be more similar than different, each agency must come to this conclusion on its own if it is to buy into the integrated system.

In the same light, the information system should have built-in flexibility to grow and change as each agency grows and changes. Criminal justice agencies often have leaders who are appointed by, and serve at the pleasure of, elected officials. This means a constant change in administration. These administrative changes, and the constant change in federal, state, and local laws and procedures governing the use and disclosure of client information, dictate that the business practices of each agency will be constantly in flux. The system must be capable of meeting these changes without being costly or cumbersome.

The most critical things learned in implementing HATS were the importance of training, technical assistance, and the need to incorporate a change process into the implementation plan. Limiting training to software training alone will not lead to an effective and efficient use of the system. Users and agencies will benefit more from a series of training sessions rather than a one-shot training approach. Integrated criminal justice information systems should provide training that is based on the business practices of each agency and, when appropriate, is designed for each user type (e.g., data entry staff, intake staff, supervision staff, law enforcement officers).

Maintaining the information system at several levels is also of great importance, as is constantly looking for more efficient ways in which to make the software run smoothly. New technologies are constantly being developed to increase the capabilities of existing software.[5] It also may be advantageous to have an outside agency—a neutral party—maintain the system on behalf of the participating agencies to avoid agency disputes.

Overall, an integrated criminal justice information system should make criminal justice agencies more efficient and effective in processing offenders and providing client services. There should no longer be a duplication of services draining system resources. Agencies should have vital information available at their fingertips, providing the tools they need for federal, state, and local reporting. Staff members should spend less time in data entry and more time in making better informed decisions about clients. If approached correctly, an integrated criminal justice information system should benefit the clients, the agency, and the criminal justice system. In addition, it should assist with some of the more difficult parts of the process such as managing compliance as offenders participate in different programmatic units and assisting offenders in meeting targeted public safety goals.

APPENDIX: JUVENILE HEALTH CARE RECORDS

Health Insurance Portability and Accountability Act

The HIPAA privacy regulations specifically address authorizations for the release of identifiable health information about minors. A parent or guardian who has the authority to act on behalf of an unemancipated minor in making health care decisions also may act as a personal representative of the minor with respect to the disclosure of protected health information.

Drug Abuse Prevention, Treatment, and Rehabilitation Act

Similarly, the regulations adopted under the federal substance abuse treatment laws provide that if a state law grants a minor the legal capacity to seek and obtain treatment on his or her own, written consent for disclosure can be provided only by the minor. The federal regulations define "minor" as a person who has not attained the age of majority specified in the applicable state law. If the state law does not specify an age of majority, it is deemed to be 18 years.

State Laws

The state laws governing the capacity of an adolescent to consent to health care (and thus, under the HIPAA and the Drug Abuse Prevention, Treatment, and Rehabilitation Act, to the release of identifiable health care information) are "a patchwork of rights and limitations." A teenage mother may be able to consent to her baby being treated but might not be able to consent to her own health care. A married 16-year-old will be considered emancipated and able to consent to his or her own health care decisions, whereas an unmarried 16-year-old might not (Oberman, 1996).

NOTES

1. Although the need for integration confronts all criminal justice agencies, drug courts serve as a good example of the collaboration that is necessary to effect adequate client monitoring and services. Throughout this chapter, examples of how automation works in drug courts are referenced because drug courts represent how criminal justice and non-criminal justice agencies are working together to coordinate services for individual offenders and are either using or not using automation to their advantage.

2. This chapter refers to both *offenders* and *clients*. The two terms are used interchangeably.

3. 28 CFR § 22.26.

4. For a discussion of health care regulations pertaining specifically to juveniles, see the appendix.

5. When HATS was first developed, it was not accessible by way of the Web and users could access the system only by way of a telephone or cable dial-up connection. With Citrix NFuse software, users can now access HATS over the Web, even though HATS itself is not Web-based software.

REFERENCES

American Probation and Parole Association. (2003). *Functional standards development for automated case management systems for probation.* Washington, DC: U.S. Department of Justice.

Oberman, M. (1996). Minor rights and wrongs. *Journal of Law, Medicine, & Ethics, 24,* 127–138.

SEARCH. (2000). *Planning the integration of justice information systems: Developing justice information exchange points* (Cooperative Agreement 98-DD-BX-0066). Sacramento, CA: Author.

Slayton, J. (2000). Establishing and maintaining interagency information sharing. *JAIBG Bulletin.* (Washington, DC: U.S. Department of Justice, Juvenile Accountability Incentive Block Grant)

Tauber, J., & Weinstein, S. (1999). *Federal confidentiality laws and how they affect drug court practitioners.* Alexandria, VA: National Drug Court Institute.

Taxman, F., & Sherman, S. (1998a). Seamless systems of care: Using automation to improve outcomes. In L. Moriarty & D. Carter (Eds.), *Criminal justice technology in the 21st century.* Springfield, IL: Charles C Thomas.

Taxman, F. S., & Sherman, S. (1998b). What is the status of my client? Automation in a seamless case management system for substance abusing offenders. *Journal of Offender Monitoring, 2*(4), 25–31.

CHAPTER 10

Environment, Technology, and Organizational Change

Notes From the Police World

Peter K. Manning

lthough the authors of many articles yearn to demonstrate dramatic and directly visible change as a result of introducing new information technologies (ITs), little research evidence supports this claim (Orlikowski, 1992, 1996, 2000; Orlikowski & Tyre, 1994; Thomas, 1994; Weick, 1977). ITs do not inevitably produce the positive, expected organizational change in the direction of efficiency (Roberts & Grabowski, 1996). IT, as a type of technology or a means of accomplishing work, is perhaps the most difficult technology to evaluate because the input and output both are symbolic, and it reverberates and affects social relationships subtly as well as altering structures by way of feedback loops (Orlikowski, 1992; Poster, 1990). This ambiguity of cause and effect is perhaps not remarkable given the great flexibility and adaptability of formal organizations and the ambiguity that surrounds the very plastic concept of "technology." Technology has independent effects in that it creates structures and processes, but it also is dependent on the organizational context within which it is embedded.

These generalizations hold for studies of policing technologies (Abt Associates, 2000; Dunworth, 2000; Greene, 2000; Manning, 1992, 2004). Although Chan's (1999, 2003) work on the New South Wales police is suggestive, she found that use is patterned by age and rank, such that younger officers are predisposed to using technologies well rather than learning to use them on the job, and that the primary valued uses are the already trusted ones concerning records, number plates, and warrants. The perceived virtue of the IT was not that it expanded vision or imagination but rather that it was faster.

AUTHOR'S NOTE: Portions of the final sections of this chapter were given as a talk in the College of Criminal Justice at Northeastern University in September 2003 and as a talk at the University of Montreal in October 2003. I have benefited from the detailed comments from April Pattavina on previous drafts.

If we are to anticipate the future of the police organization and its responses to change induced by technologies, it is important to envision the current organization—its capacities and predilections—and to anticipate what resistance might be stimulated by introduction of a technology (Manning, 2004, pp. 144–174). What is needed is a comparative framework within which policing is analyzed as a type of organization with features that vary empirically. In such a framework, the relative contribution of technologies to goals or objectives can be assessed.

The chapter begins with a critique of Crank's (2003) broad characterization of policing-as-an-organization. This sets the stage for a version of the police organization as a formal interactional system. The chapter then focuses on ITs in policing and their potential for transforming the organization. Here, an ethnographically grounded example of police IT, specifically crime analysis and mapping in the context of general meetings, is used to suggest the limits of technologically driven change in policing.

CONCEPTIONS OF THE POLICE ORGANIZATION AND ITS TECHNOLOGIES

Crank (2003, pp. 187–188) sketched policing in its organizational environment, following the ideas of Meyer and Rowan (1977). Meyer and Rowan argue that organizations without a refined effective technology that can affect and influence an environment—"institutionalized organizations"—are characterized by a strong ideology, an unexamined myth of effectiveness, and buffered or loosely coupled relations to an environment. Examples include schools, public service agencies (e.g., police, probation), and social welfare organizations. The myth protects them against criticism and aligns them with powerful quasi-sacred forces such as safety, morality,

and the state. These organizations must argue for effectiveness because they cannot reshape their market, their environment (they have local service bases), or their clientele as can market-based organizations. Whatever differentiation of structure and roles is present is not technologically based, in their view. Finally, such organizations are loosely coupled with the environment. Loose coupling is a metaphor indicating that the organizations are linked to the environment symbolically rather than directly and that the organizations manipulate symbols and rhetoric to sustain their legitimacy rather than to produce something (e.g., goods, services, products).[1]

Crank (2003), following Meyer and Rowan (1977), claims that police are institutionalized organizations. Crank, translating the ideas of Meyer and Rowan, avers that this condition in policing results from three identifiable features of institutionalized organizations: how they cope with *complexity in the environment,* how they manifest *loose coupling,* and how they demonstrate *good faith* (reflecting the values of those they serve, in effect, their publics). His position is that police organizations resolve complexity by being responsive to their constituents, that loose coupling enables lower participants to carry out the job, and that good faith—belief in what one is doing—sustains high morale in the face of criticism. I believe that several of Crank's fundamental definitions are misleading or wrong, I do not think that the term *institutionalized organizations* is helpful because it implies technological determinism, and I find several of his empirical claims to be unsubstantiated. Let us consider the argument in order.

The Question of Environmental Complexity

Clearly, the complexity of the environment in which an organization operates has consequences, but this formulation begs the question of what complexity means and how it is processed (Jervis, 1997). Modern organizations, using multiple, rapid, and disembodied communications that are sent and received in "disembedded" space and time (the cyber world), face complex uncertain environments. Organizations seek to manage uncertainty *internally* (with respect to supervision, production, and deployment of resources) and *externally* (with respect to controlling the flow of information, competition with other organizations for resources, and impact on their targeted populations). As a result, organizations produce accounts, or rationalizations, for why things that were done must have been done and will have been done.[2]

It is often argued that IT adds complexity, and thus adds uncertainty, to organizational operations (Weick, 2001). Policing, like other organizations, responds to and encodes information, makes sense of it, and enacts responses to the environment that it has encoded. Although it is easy to mistake imagery and reality, IT at best is a way of envisioning the external world and shaping it, but it is nearly impossible for a system to encode data for which it is unprepared (or for which it possesses no codes) (Luhmann, 1998). In Luhmann's (1998) terms, the encoding and decoding processes of an organization permit it to manage external uncertainty and to define itself to itself rather than in terms of the external world. Thus, IT stands midway between stabilizing the organization and creating new information that may be destabilizing. Modern organizations are means to minimize and reduce such contingencies.

Policing is no more or less subject to external complexity than is any other organization. It sustains feedback and reflection mechanisms that stabilize and reenact its responses to the environment. Its technology is a mixture of many kinds of tools (material or mechanical); human skills, techniques, and practices; and tacit knowledge (Chan,

2003). It is clear, however, that embedded organizations that serve a locale, such as state, county, and local police, cannot relocate and must cope with the current demands for service (Thompson, 1967). When one takes into account policing as a generic not restricted to the public police (Johnston & Shearing, 2003), the claim of vulnerability is less sustainable because additional resources can be allocated more easily within private organizations. Meyer and Rowan (1977) state an important point, that is, that rationalities based on sheer technical power no longer suffice to legitimate organizations. This suggests as a corollary that additional technology will not augment legitimacy or expand the occupational mandate.

More precisely, one can ask the question: How do the police respond to and manage external demands from their publics?[3] Bear in mind that these publics include those who are served directly by responses, those who are served indirectly through externalities of public trust and order that are attributed to the police, and those who are pursued, investigated, arrested, and even detained by police. This issue often leads to the false and misleading equation of responsiveness to calls for service with the quality of such response, and it collapses one strategy (response to calls) with others that are quite distinctive (random patrol and investigation of allegations). It also ignores the following:

♦ The powerful screening process (of calls at every level, from operators to officers in the street, that reduces calls processed by more than 50%)
♦ Demand management modalities (the informal allocation of time to serious crime allegations and investigations)
♦ Differential responses to certain crimes such as domestic violence and hate crimes
♦ The fact that the greater the contact with police, the lower the level of trust of the citizens
♦ The increasing demand of cell phone calls that, because they do not emanate from a

place, cannot be tied directly to a caller, a place, a problem, or even a demand for service

In addition, many large departments, such as the Boston Police Department, have worked at reducing calls by problem solving, investigating locations from which calls originate, seeking alternative processing modes for seven-digit numbers, adding 3-1-1 systems (Mazerolle, Rogan, Frank, Famega, & Eck, 2002), and handling cell phone calls under innovative procedures. As this suggests, police organizations buffer themselves against uncertainty and complexity by slack resources and are positioned to scan the environment in the interest of detecting and responding to rare and unusual events as well as to the routine (J. Thompson, 1967; V. Thompson, 1961). Thus, while police are poised between routine and emergency, they strive to reduce uncertainty to routines. As a public service organization, the police maintain a striking sensitivity to both that which might happen and that which happens repeatedly.[4] Police organizations isolate themselves from other agencies as the "law enforcement" aspect of their mandate become salient, perhaps as insulation against influences that might alter or taint their claim to objectivity and justice.

The Question of Loose Coupling

Meyer and Rowan and Crank draw on Weick's idea of loose coupling. It is important to note that Weick does not see loose coupling as unique to a particular type of organization, and loose coupling is not a unique feature of policing. Crank's argument that loose coupling causes or sustains some organizational forms is a mistake at several levels of abstraction (Manning, 1990, pp. 48–50, 53–54; Weick, 2001, pp. 43–44). First, organizations do not couple action with formal behavior as Crank (2003, p. 188) claims.

Weick (2001), in fact, argues that two kinds of organizing or sensemaking take place in organizations simultaneously: making sense of microinteractional processes and relating such processes to the rules and metaphors that actors believe animate their environments. These two sometimes conflicting obligations occur in all organizations, not just in "institutionalized" ones. Therefore, loose coupling cannot be an explanation for the shape, structure, or processes of any type of organization or a given organization. Second, the environment is constructed cognitively and rehearsed within the organization (Manning, 2004, chap. 2). Meyer and Rowan's (1977) argument is rejected explicitly by Weick; complexity inheres in organizational processes, not the "environment." Third, the environment itself is enacted in the sense that the organization processes messages to create meaning for organizational action. The process of responding to the environments does not vary across organizations in the way that Crank suggests. The process, and not the demand or the complexity, produces organized response.

The Question of Good Faith

Consider further the idea of good faith advanced by Crank (an idea from Sartre that refers to the extent to which a person believes in what he or she is doing). The evidence is that police sustain a very negative view of the general public. They demean the public (Young, 1991); they divide the world into a blurred Manichean concatenation of good and evil (Young, 1991); they consider middle and top management to be capricious, irrelevant, and even malevolent (Manning, 1977; Reuss-Ianni, 1983), and they elevate themselves as a bulwark against the erosive evil of others.[5] This combination of cognitive sensemaking mechanisms ensures that the police view themselves as ennobled by their battle against "the others." This embattled yet responsible role, given that the police are directed to assess the truth of others' statements as officers of the court, means that they elevate and dramatize their truthfulness, not their authenticity or emotional good faith. This claim, when validated, raises their status in the eyes of the public. They assert and dramatize their role as truth tellers, even though the work is predicated on dissembling, dissimulating, and lying. Because police treasure their claim that they tell the truth, they feel compelled to reaffirm this in fellow officers in court, in the media, and with the public. It is this shared epistemological status, as truth tellers rather than shared values, that weaves together the occupational web.

The Question of Technology

Technologies work in a context, and until recently the attitude of modern society has been to accept the technological conceit and to minimize the negative, destructive, dirty, and blameworthy aspects of modern technologies.[6] Although the police have not accepted this dogma, they have elevated science and communications technologies as one of their primary presentational strategies. However, many heavily weighed and mutually reinforcing factors root the police in the past, in tradition, and in a conservatism altered only by legal change (if the law changes, they are under pressure to change their enforcement practices). These themes in policing are not recent manifestations, a product of the professionalism movement, or illustrations of "neo-institutionalism" (Meyer & Scott, 1992; Powell & DiMaggio, 1991). It is true that they rely rather heavily on presentational strategies, especially rhetoric about their work as "law enforcement officers," fluctuations in crime, official crime rates, and fear of crime, when claiming their mandate. Police use complex, human-based "technologies" because their obligation is to solve the vexing, unremitting human problems presented to them. These create demand conditions for intervention, whether they be crime or loss of income, health, or family stability. Perhaps the opacity of the demand arises because the dominant technology is actually interpersonal skills, including the use of the body, language, good judgment, respect, and civility (Mastrofski, Reisig, & McCluskey, 2002) rather than weapons, means of mobility, and scientific equipment.

Technology has a negligible effect in shaping internal differentiation (Manning, 2003). As Meyer and Scott (1992, pp. 8–9) also argue, complexity does not produce further complexity. The lack of meaningful differentiation in police departments is further supported by recent work on the 200 largest U.S. police departments by Maguire (2002). His findings do not demonstrate dependency; rather, they demonstrate a rather striking *independence* of the internal structure of police organizations from their environments. Only age and secondarily size (probably a function of the large urban forces in Maguire's sample) are correlated with structural differentiation, and they in fact do not much shape internal task structures. This research, unlike the arguments noted previously, suggests that police are quite independent of their environment and that this is not because they are institutionalized. They have always been sacred, protected, buffered, and embedded in the moral sentiment of Anglo-American society.

There is also the nagging suspicion that police organizations are different and that they are different for identifiable historical reasons (Manning, 1977, 2003, 2004; Reiss, 1992). These include their links to violence, the state, and past associations with chivalry. Bittner (1972) argues that the police are a tainted and traditional occupation with links to honor, violence, and ultimately the glorification of mannered violence called chivalry.

They stand for and represent the sacred, mysterious, inexplicable, and distant, and they connect these sentiments to the law and absolutist morality. They are set aside not only because they are anachronistic, violent, and dangerous but also because they symbolize these very things. Police are ritualized, sacred, and cloaked in myth, but not because they are resource dependent or institutionalized. It is possible that resource dependency may lead to conflict within and that this in turn leads to their inability to function "efficiently" in that environment and puts them at risk for organizational death. But this correlation begs the question of causation or at least directionality. Does dependency lead to conflict, or does the internal conflict increase dependency and reduce autonomy?

ORGANIZATIONS AND CHANGE

Organizations are fluid, meanings-generating, and meanings-based systems. Formal organizations are authoritatively coordinated systems of interaction in which the density of interaction is greater within organizations than between members and other organizations, and they typically occupy an identified spatial–ecological niche. The center of an organization is sensemaking or the ongoing, social, plausible extraction of cues that order experience and serve to enact a sensible environment (Weick, 1995, p. 17). Work within such bureaucracies is embedded in processes of moral exchange and reciprocity that are disturbed but not effaced by technological innovations (Gouldner, 1961; Thomas, 1994).

Technologies are multifaceted or speak with many voices. So, as Weick (1995) states, "Running the technology is an art form" (p. 171). He means that responses to events cannot be fully predicted, that new responses emerge from crises, that events must be connected to formal goals and rules, and that the more complex and covert the

workings of a technology, the more creative the working must be. Think of this in another fashion: Events can be routine, easily assessed, and carried out using conventional, learned, and standard techniques; they are enhanced by the "reliability imperative" (Roberts & Grabowski, 1996, p. 412) or the pressure to standardize and not to vary from the accepted modes and the unexpected events that require innovation or departure from the script (metaphorically).

Departures, common in every organization except a high-reliability one, require imagination. Departures from routine events, and responses to them, are particularly indicative in IT because they induce what might be called the invisibility paradox. As work is more shaped and structured by technologies, especially ITs, what is done is out of sight and what is required is to orient practices to *abstract concepts*. As Weick (2001, p. 157) notes, two invisible processes are at work: one beneath the surface of the machine and one beneath the surface of the human actor (body and mind). This implies, of course, that all work is collective, social, and in some sense rooted in sentiments and practices that must be displayed. The meaning of technologies within this framework takes its contours through the vocabularies of talk used in the work—ideologies, work talk, and specific machine talk (Suchman, 1991; Weick, 1995, p. 107). What is not seen (e.g., what is indicated by error messages and failures of computer-based machinery) must be imputed (Suchman, 1991, pp. 121–163).

IT reduces the time available for deciding and reflection. The greater the time constraints on action given ambiguity in technological human interaction, the greater the tendency for coping based on collective cues and signals (Janis, 1972; Janis & Mann, 1977). When the expert system or menu can predict only what is known to regularly happen, innovation is not "built into the system." Coping, even in high-reliability organizations, is a relative matter, not an absolute one. In effect, any software designed to reduce time and create shortcuts reduces complexity in the relationships it reflects but does not reduce their existence in the organizations' responses. For example, when a new software system is introduced—say, XP in a university system—the new system produces errors of its own, rough spots, bugs, and the like as it is adapted to the current hardware and software. Furthermore, the new technology must interface with the current system, for example, the drivers of all the printers that are set to interface with the master software and the particular printers on campus. The printers do not work. The error messages are ambiguous because they refer to the operating system, not the particular new attachments. As the surface features of computers have become simplified, iconic, and superficial in the most literal sense of the word, their interiors have become more complex.

Organizations shape their responses to technology. These responses suggest a continuing response, and it is likely that organizations shift modalities from crisis to routine and from logics of practice to rule-based definitions. Crisis and routine are fundamental conditions that are always implicit or shadowed, one by the other. Crises can arise internally as a result of a succession crisis in an organization (e.g., the naming of a new chief), or they can arise externally as a result of a fatal shooting, a car chase, an accident involving police in a car chase, and so forth. Logics of practice are dominant when internal stability obtains in the organization, but as Gouldner (1961) notes, rules are employed in rule-oriented organizations, such as the police, to punish, sanction, shame, and marginalize violators. There are *shifting modalities* within organizations, not single stable responses to a stable environment. The most important oscillation is between routine and emergency. In an emergency mode, organizations communicate internally quite differently

from how they communicate externally (Manning, 1990, p. 141); they communicate more quickly and with less reflection and anticipation of outcomes. In other words, from a rhetorical perspective, these are two different organizations.

RULES, PROCESSES, AND ROUTINES IN POLICE WORK

This chapter now examines the rules, processes, and routines that organize police work. They are malleable or subject to change and reorganization (Feldman & Pentland, 2003). The segments of the organization (e.g., top management, middle management, lower participants) tend to be loosely connected, one with the other, through routines that are occasioned. Although the technologies have a strong material constraint, technologies produce responses and counterresponses that are attempts by those in power to stabilize the organization. The time frame of the introduction of and response to new technologies will shape the organization's responses to and with technologies.

Organizational Rules

The rules in police organizations, perhaps more than the rules in other organizations because they are designed to reduce temptation and corruption and provide a basis for punishment, are complex, opaque, and seen as capricious in their application. Police organizations are "mock bureaucracies" designed to provide flexibility in sanctioning, not guidance (Gouldner, 1961). They are highly stratified, with very different notions of the scope of the work, success, promotion, and utility of technologies (Manning, 2003). The mode of organizations, whether crisis or noncrisis, will suggest their malleability.

Rules for organizing are bureaucratic until matters such as "exceptions" must be handled.

Exceptions fall to the top management to define and resolve; thus, what top management does is define into the routines those matters that are in fact outside of their control. Although it displays itself as militaristic, policing is an ecologically dispersed organization that is nearly 25% civilian, and supervisors sometimes have the political power to define exceptions resting with the lower participants, that is, the uniformed officers on the street. Thus, any technological innovation may come from the "top," but its success lies in the lower participants' responses to the innovation.

Organizational Processes

Capturing change empirically by studying organizational processes is difficult. Change echoes in social, political, and cultural dimensions. Studies that view change narrowly— for example, evaluating a new program, a short-term effort, or a task force—miss the contours of change over time. Organizations are echo chambers in which goals are proximal, tacit, and unrecognized (MacKenzie, 1993, p. 162; Weick, 2001, pp. 148–175); goals are unclear or in conflict (MacKenzie, 1993, p. 237); goals are made visible by routines rather than clear statements of purpose and accomplishment (Feldman & Pentland, 2003); and organizations, whatever their goals, are characterized by competing rationalities or sanctioned ways of getting things done (Espeland, 1998). As with rules, formal directives coming from the top are subverted, sabotaged, redefined, and redirected by those implementing them (Roy, 1952, 1954).

Routines and Tasks

Work is based on routines or sequences of tasks that cluster together and are repeated. These routines may produce outputs and may be organized around material objects, but such a view seizes on the superficial because the material aspects of technologies are a *foreground* for imagining. This is, of course, glaringly obvious in the case of ITs that work silently, invisibly, and magically. Work practices must be watched and displayed, shown and learned, and then repeated so that an imagery remains of the work, a sedimentation of how the thing (work) is done here. This demonstrable aspect is particularly powerful in policing because it is a cohort-based apprentice-like craft learned by watching and emulating and reinforced by storytelling (Shearing & Ericson, 1991). The lingering symbolic images of the craft, of good work, or stories that encapsulate what is done and why are important for sensemaking (Weick, 1995, p. 171). Warnings, cautionary tales, and "cock-ups" mark what is to be avoided, but their generality is always dubious. Tools of the trade shift in and out of importance and are reified in the oral culture of policing. Cars, weapons, communications equipment, strategies, and tactical lines (Bayley, 1986) vary in utility.

Consider, for example, the routine as a set of tasks called a traffic stop (Bayley, 1986). Making a traffic stop is taught, and it is shaped by the form of the stop (the code) and the content (the interactions); however, stylish variations on both code and content emerge as shared practices, developed by partners over time, and include how to deal with boisterous or obnoxious citizens, how to disguise and organize high-speed car chases, how to manage the radio, lights, and positioning of the car. As the mobile data terminal (MDT) and video camera become part of the repertoire of the stop, new action *choices* emerge. Consider a sequence of thoughts that officers might review as they are about to make a traffic stop:

♦ Has a new tape been inserted, is it recording images, and am I confident that it is functioning now?

♦ Are the camera and the microphone on or off? Shall I turn the camera or microphone on or off?

- Do I run the plate first before stopping the car?
- What is the stated reason communicated for the stop?
- Should I radio in my position, intention, and details of the car?
- Should I just click the microphone to inform other officers that I am out of the car?
- Should I turn off the microphone or camera at the stop? (Officers are often confused about whether the camera or microphone is on or off, and they turn it off as often as they turn it on when they leave the car to address a stopped driver.)
- How should I position the car? So that the camera cannot penetrate the darkness of the parked car? So that it captures my image clearly? So that it captures no images at all?

New data and reporting requirements, such as issues raised by the question of profiling, reshape practices. Is the "race" of the stopped party and/or passengers noted? Is the stop written down, or is evidence recorded in some fashion (e.g., written, aural, visual)? The routines that emerge face the reliability imperative brought on by external reviews of stops and practices (now mandated by law in many states). Although many of the routines are redundant or repeat known procedures, new equipment, if used properly, produces variety in the range of choices made and in the uses of technologies during the stop. In this sense, and based on ethnographic evidence, three things are ongoing: (a) routinization, (b) ritual or repeated actions, and (c) innovations and variety. Bateson's brilliant work on schismogenesis, or the ways in which minor variations are amplified over time in social interactions, suggests that variety in choice is geometric in consequence.[7]

It is perhaps excessive to comment on the irony of new technologies and their functioning. New ITs employed in police departments, such as Blackberries, handheld computer personal digital assistants (PDAs), and cameras with cell phones, are misleadingly named given that it is impossible to name devices that have up to 50 functions and 12 main menus and also can take calls, take and save photos, send text and voice messages, save memos and phone numbers, "hot sync" into a computer to download and upload data, send information by way of laser beam from one device to another, keep a calendar, and provide games and diversion—as well as accomplish work. Within these devices are both personal and work content, making them symbolically multifaceted. For example, police officers carry personal cell phones behind the sun visors of their cars to receive personal calls in addition to calls on their departmental phones. The proliferation of functions, devices, menus, and new channel modes increases the variety of channels that can be used, alters the options for going around any supervisory system, calls for playful experimentation, and produces new errors and what might be called "meta-errors," that is, errors that result from the interface between extant systems and new systems (e.g., cell phones and computer-assisted dispatch [CAD] systems).

DEFINING TECHNOLOGY: AN OVERVIEW OF THE MEANING OF TECHNOLOGIES IN POLICING

Most of the classic work in sociology sees technology as a *material thing*—only one aspect of its functioning—and extract its functioning from organizational routines, meanings, and roles, especially over time.[8] Of course, technologies occupy space and have density and weight, and these alter social relations. Technologies have an instrumental purpose in that they produce something—goods, services, or information. Technology also has a poetics or aesthetics—how it looks and feels, its shape and design—as well as a mechanics. What has been almost totally overlooked in studies of IT innovations in policing is the creative emergent effects of new technologies, their *playful* potential, and the new codes or ways of looking at the world that they precipitate (Barley, 1986). In new ITs where the workings are out of sight, the process of work, as well as the product, may be invisible or very abstract. We treat computers, copy machines, cell phones, and PDAs as magical devices, wondrous and amazing black boxes, so amazing that even when they malfunction we might not be aware of it. In summary, technology has a material space, instrumental purposes, a logic of production, and a playful and imaginative dimension. Each of these varies when organizations change.[9]

The Special Case of IT and Innovation

IT encompasses the means by which *data* (raw facts as recorded) are transformed into *information* (data placed in some context with a purpose), stored, analyzed, and retrieved. IT is a multiple-sided mirror. It ingests data, shapes and stores them, transforms them in myriad ways, and then produces the texts, screens, files, images, and sounds used to interpret its work and the nature of the "outside world." Thus, IT is reflexive; it is the primary way in which organizations see themselves, speak to themselves, and store their memories. Its very reflexivity is an enigma because although IT is a way in which organizations talk to themselves about themselves, it is also a conduit of information.

The current situation in policing must be characterized because a failure to properly describe the current situation means that one cannot imagine the imagining that is going on within organizations.[10] Fieldwork and interviews (Dunworth, 2000; Greene, 2000; Manning, 2003) in large North American departments suggest that although departments have acquired new ITs, and most departments typically possess many of them, these ITs remain unintegrated, are scarcely used beyond daily needs, and remain marginal to the core work as seen by officers. Consider the following features of modern information systems in policing:

◆ *Many nonlinked databases that are locally sourced* (e.g., CAD, jail booking systems, criminal records, other management data, fingerprints, visual images such as mug shots, records management systems [RMSs], geographical information systems [GIS] that chart data points spatially, many paper files). The range of these national accessible but nonlinked databases is large and growing. They include the basic managerial RMSs (budgets, personnel, workload, payroll, leaves, and holidays) and various investigative records (detectives' work, case records, statements, evidence, and court decisions that are kept in paper files or in separate databases). The latter are not integrated with patrol-generated data.

◆ *Other databases that are nominally national* (e.g., National Crime Information Center [NCIC], with wanted persons, warrants, and stolen vehicles and other property, including firearms; Uniform Crime Reporting [UCR]; National Incident-Based Reporting System [NIBRS]; National DNA Index System [NDIS], a DNA profile databank run by the Federal Bureau of Investigation [FBI]; National Incident Check System [NICS], for people disqualified from receiving firearms; Automated Fingerprint Identification System [AFIS]; Criminal History Record Information [CHRI] system). These are nominally national because not all states participate in submitting data to these databases, the quality of data varies, and the data are frequently redundant and contain useless or dated information (Morris & Geller, 1992). The stated capacity to gather and process data quickly, to store data in an accessible and orderly fashion, and to develop vast fact-based files of fingerprints, criminal records, lab reports, arrest documents, and cases is considerable.

♦ *Storage capacity and use that are not calibrated.* The growth in storage capacity absent access and use reveals the tendency within policing, and perhaps within other public agencies, to acquire systems without clear standards or stated purposes and without considering the complexity of creating usable and simple modes of interface, colocation, and analysis. At times, this burgeoning of tools and databases strains the memory capacity of departments, and so computers crash or lack functional memory for peak time operations (Greene, 2000).

♦ *Numerous software systems* (e.g., ArcView for geocoded material, PopTrak for monitoring problem solving, specialized programs for workload management, many spreadsheets for accounting and noncriminal records maintenance) *and workstations that are equipped with many kinds of word processing and software.* Research suggests that they are rarely used or poorly used (Abt Associates, 2000; Dunworth, 2000; Manning, 2003) and that data transfer is awkward and flawed. Large departments have diverse workstations running software of various generations (several versions of Microsoft) and a sprinkling of Macs and IBM clones that do not "speak" to each other.

♦ *Websites with descriptive materials, some data on calls for service or crime patterns, and hyperlinks to other websites.* These tend to be "taken-as-read" texts with no explication or guidance as to their significance.

♦ *Secrecy and nonlinked access points.* Although there are decentralized terminals allowing minimal data access to citizens in some neighborhood terminals and laptops to be taken home by some officers, few terminals permit direct access by officers or citizens to detailed maps, selected printout data, or online data. The databases that can be accessed are limited to recent CAD data, and questions of privacy limit access to many databases.

♦ *Multiple and incompatible channels of communication between the public and the police and within the police department.* These now include websites, e-mail, cell phones and land-based phones, "snail" mail, personal visits to stations, face-to-face encounters, networked communications by way of fiber-optic cables, paper documents, and e-files sent as attachments.[11] None is assembled or noted for overlap, inconsistency, validity, or utility. Departments are awash with facts and are starved for information.

♦ *Inconsistent user and backside technology interfaces* (e.g., several servers, diverse and uneven mainframe access). Perhaps as a result of the ad hoc accretion of these by way of purchasing, the influence of vendors, trends, and failed innovations, police have disparate IT clusters that are not additive or cumulative in their effects.

♦ *A tendency to use mapping information for short-term tactical interventions absent "problem solving" in areas such as Boston and New Orleans* (personal communication, Jack McDevitt, May 17, 2002). This is reported in publications on "CompStat." These deployments, in turn, are not assessed as to effect or consequence.

In summary, even the most advanced forms of communicative technologies have been backfitted to the extant structure and traditional processes of police organizations. By 2000, no research had reported that a single police department had refined a systematically integrated collection of technologies to facilitate problem solving, crime prevention, policy analysis, and community interfaces (Abt Associates, 2000, pp. 150–165). Dunworth's (2000) review suggests, in general, that none of these is operational in any police department and that the fundamental dimensions of community policing, interface with communities, interorganizational links, workgroup facilitation, environmental scanning, problem orientation, area-based accountability, and strategic management are not seen as well developed anywhere.

A CASE STUDY
OF POLICE USE OF IT

Three police sites developing crime analysis infrastructure were studied between 1998 and 2003 using interviews, observations, documents (drawn from departmental websites, obtained from the Internet, and gathered at the sites), and newspaper clippings. I focused on the development and deployment of crime analysis capacities and meetings. I use this case study as a vehicle for showing how and why organizational change takes place with respect to IT in the police.

Previous studies of crime analysis meetings (Henry, 2002; McDonald, 2002; Silverman, 2000; Weisbord, Mastrofski, McNally, Greenspan, & Willis, 2003) have generally been positive, uncritical, and excessively optimistic about the current and future capacity of these meetings to mobilize officers or, more generally, to control crime. These studies assume a single logical developmental paradigm (what might be called classic or Weberian rationality) in which problem solving or surfacing uncertainty, feedback, evaluation, and readjustment of means to ends govern the deciding process. Unfortunately, the logical chain that links the meetings, deployment, and action to crime reduction remains totally unexplicated. In addition, studies of CompStat meetings and related processes tend to see them, on the one hand, as thoroughly legitimated and used technology that is everywhere appreciated and, on the other, as a narrowly orchestrated set of

meetings using online data. No evidence showing that the information was the basis for deployment, and how that deployment over time reduced crime, has been provided. Because crime was reduced, it must have been a function of policing, with the single difference internally being CompStat meetings. The influence of other matters is unmeasured and unreported, permitting this police-based argument free rein in public discussion. Let us now turn to the Boston Police Department (BPD), my primary research site.

I attended the crime analysis meetings. I did not follow up on what was done with the information shared in these meetings. In the 2-hour (strictly observed) bimonthly crime analysis meetings held in the BPD, selected police personnel from two districts (uniform branch and detectives presented), civilian crime analysts, visitors, and invited guests sit in a large room on rows of chairs behind the primary audience, the top command. Top command members sit in front with their backs to the audience and facing a huge screen on which data, pictures, cartoons, and maps are projected. A crime analyst flashes PowerPoint sequences from a laptop on the front table and draws data with the specially developed software in use in the BPD. The meeting is opened by the commissioner or his representative. The format, or order of presentations, is constant and produces what I call a "format effect." Selected data for the department for the month may be presented in a PowerPoint mode by a crime analyst (e.g., UCR figures for the department for the previous month, gunshots fired, weapons arrests made), and then similar data are presented by representatives of the selected police districts (they are rehearsed and coached by crime analysis staff members the previous week) with the assistance of crime analysts at one or more laptops. Additional data or pictures can be requested from the online databanks accessed from the laptops, and the crime analysts are very skillful in changing menus, screens, and databases and in complying with requests to return to or find previous screens. At the end of each district report, a problem-solving exercise (5 minutes or so) is presented. Questions are asked frequently by the top command, and presenting speakers are often interrupted with questions or comments.

My aim here is not to present an example of crime analysis but rather to consider how it is possible. Consider that what is shown (a map, a table, a picture, a diagram, etc.) is a *representation* (an icon or miniature in some cases), not the thing itself. It is the map, not the territory. Both the representation and its symbols, and the areas and places to which they refer, must be imagined. By *imagined,* I mean that the signifier has to be connected to the signified (what is represented or pointed to) so as to form a full sign. This sign formation is done by bringing a perspective or point of view to it or by providing a context. A police officer who sees a crime map showing a cluster of crimes might think, "Let's saturate that area with cars" or, more broadly perhaps, "What's going on there?" In such expositions, the imaginative process is employed: What is needed to reduce, control, or manage X? Data about the outcomes or desired processes must be selectively identified and sorted. Some sense of the current capacities (material, human, and knowledge-based technologies) must be reviewed, and as such, a context is brought to the expressions shown.

The ecology, formatting of the discussion, and social factors made the objects of concern or the problems addressed visible. Observations of the meetings and interviews suggested that three *themes* shape the process of resolving uncertainty. These are, in shorthand terms, (a) constraints operate, (b) meetings are in the here and now, and (c) any questions that are asked should always be answered. Because the themes remain constant, they stabilize the discussion and make its path knowable.

♦ *First theme.* Several sets of *constraints,* some visible and some rather more subtle, operated. One set involved shaping the order of questioning, topic, depth of discussion, questions asked, and by whom. These reflected the dominance of, and deference to, the top command. A second set arose from the ecology of the room, gender and color dominance, and formatting. A third set concerned the topics discussed. Highly political matters of the city and the police (e.g., fatal shootings and chases, alleged police beatings, trials or police misconduct, union matters) were not mentioned. Crime scenes, bloody pictures, and victims were not shown. A fourth set of constraints involved silence about certain matters. Silence ruled on "deeper" questions that might reveal the taken-for-granted grounds that ordered the meeting. No one asked questions such as "Why would you ask that?" "What do you want to know?" and "Why look into that?"

♦ *Second theme.* The meetings were about the *here and now.* The meetings contained no evaluation, feedback, or assessment of the actions taken previously, nor did they contain discussion of how one would know whether such actions worked. The content of each meeting was ahistorical, and the actions taken were only modestly projected into the imagined future.

♦ *Third theme.* When questions were asked, they were *always answered.* Any questions about what to do were always met with answers in the event.

These themes made visible the invisible— the practices of police work. They are important for describing the process of what was done. What apparent rational ends or cluster of purposes were in action here, for example, to control crime? To produce accountability? To increase the quality of neighborhood life? To increase problem-solving dialogue across ranks and units? Given these modes of resolving uncertainty (what to do about any pattern queried, whether imagined or observed), I argue that no single form of rationality, or linking of ends to means, was operative. Instead, I found competing rationalities (Espeland, 1998) or "situated rationalities." The notion of situated rationalities, or ways of solving problems approximate to the case in the here and now and responding to the immediate context, is derived from Karl Mannheim's essays and was used in *Narcs' Game* (Manning, 2004). Three *situated rationalities* were observed repeatedly:

1. *Emergent rationality* was present when meetings used data, maps, and statistics in a short-term action-based fashion. Sometimes they were combined to create an ensemble of information. This was manifest most when resources enabled some shifting around of priorities, using overtime and "details" to respond to an identified problem. When actualized, these present the appearance of energetic order maintenance and crime control crackdowns. They simulate military-like short-term interventions. They appear to get things done, but the things done are undefined.

2. *Occasioned rationality* was present when talk and discussion were focused by the maps and information and when *new* unconventional avenues were opened for imagining the opportunities presented. This rationality was situated, local, and transitory (not transcendental), and it drew on the invisible power of the new forms of IT (e.g., it makes it possible to discuss whether multiple occupant dwellings are a loci of crime or illegal immigrants).

3. *Pragmatic rationality* hinged on the unstated notion that one must "reduce"

crime through direct police action of a visible, obvious, and conventional sort. If a "rash" of auto thefts breaks out, the solutions (typically) imagined are more overtime for police presence, more undercover officers, and increased surveillance in the area. There will be increased pressure to clear any crimes of this type reported. The problem is so apparent that it requires no discussion.

Two other forms of rationality that have been reported in other studies were not present. Boston crime analysis meetings do not display directly the most commonly seen "paramilitary" rationality in which command and control are based on formal orders given by superiors to inferiors and in which rules and regulations are used to sanction (positively or negatively) officers' actions. This is implicit in the meetings, although the effects of rank, deference, gender, and civilians versus warranted officers and other observers remain to be seen in the interaction. Because there is no feedback on results or systematic recording of outcomes reported back to the committee of the whole, accountability existed only in the meeting itself and was subtle and indirect. Another kind of rationality did not appear in the meetings but was a concern. This might be called damage control rationality. This arises when media interest becomes more than apparent. Damage control assumes that a problem exists without further discussion. The target is media intrusiveness and banal curiosity. As a result, concealing and distorting information, lying and avoiding direct answers, and distributing disinformation are acceptable. This rationality is especially associated with high-profile cases that may focus attention on police incompetence and/or failures. The fact that such matters were not talked about in the crime analysis meetings is an example of both an absent rationality and the constraints mentioned previously.

These rationalities provide a means to sustain in yet a new way the structuration of police work. That is, the meetings display the production and reproduction of a formal social system through members' use of rules and resources in interaction (Weick, 2001). By their choice of responses to rather abstract and abstracted events (maps, tables, figures, and diagrams), the meaning of which is dubious, they assert the validity of policing as done in spite of the overt change in setting and level of abstraction. In this case study, this new technology, crime mapping and crime analysis (insofar as they are linked here), mediates social relations within the organization and reflects the traditional structure of policing.

CONCLUDING REMARKS

Technology is a multifaceted matter and serves both to process information and material and to affect the roles and tasks used in the process. Metaphorically speaking, the introduction of a technology, especially an IT, may change the way in which an organization speaks to itself. The study of organizational resolution or management of uncertainty by police departments is somewhat challenging, even for field-workers, because although the new IT produces a potential for amplification of uncertainty, police organizations also seek to reduce it. Both are apparent. Although IT has the potential to disrupt and realign power and authority in a police organization, it is also a means to solve and routinize uncertainty. IT is, in effect, a two-edged sword.

It would appear from this fieldwork that IT, as applied in crime analysis meetings, spawns diverse, useful situated rationalities. It also stabilizes sanctioned practices that have long characterized police work. The fieldwork also suggests that in the BPD, crime analysis meetings were shaped by three themes that shaped and ordered the meetings. At least three sorts of emergent situated rationalities were seen frequently, whereas one type of situated rationality—traditional rank-based authority—was seen infrequently. It may be that the democratization of discourse is one of the most significant consequences of such meetings. It would appear that these meetings function to stabilize the organization internally in spite of emergent uncertainties and provide differentially useful institutional–organizational accounts for why one does "the thing that needs doing." In effect, this research supplies a warrant for deeper examination or a closer look at what is out of sight.

Turning to the broader questions of IT and policing, the playful aspects of the technology were present; cartoons and animated visuals would pop across the screen unexpectedly from time to time and always produced a (somewhat nervous) laugh. Perhaps the most significant dimensions affected by these meetings are not the material or logical ones, given that the logics of crime fighting and disorder reduction remained as before, but rather the social functions that are being modified. This occurs because people are seen as colleagues before the screens and do share views (there are dialogues, albeit dialogues skewed to top command), and they question options together. In my view, the notion of situated rationalities explains how the imaginative aspect of the technology firmly roots it in the past rhetoric and practices of policing in spite of the surface changes.

The hope for change in police organizations arises from several sources. Police research has been devoted to proscriptive and prescriptive research rather than to empirically querulous and penetrating research that reveals the deep contradictions between its current practices and current claims. Much of the current research on IT is intended to imagine the horizon for technology rather than to reveal and rectify the current fundamental infrastructural problems of training, skills, database merging, and software compatibility associated with transforming and rationalizing policing. Questions such as how to enhance the capacities needed to transform policing toward crime prevention and problem solving, how to develop links to the Internet and other agencies, how to design websites and public data access, and how to use problem solving in investigative work are scarcely discussed outside the world of police researchers and consultants.

The fantasy of more efficient and effective policing is, of course, a fundamental contradiction in a democratic society where values such as equality and justice have an ostensive place in rhetoric. Police organizations do not provide risk management services, police chiefs are not chief executive officers or "champions of industry," and the police serve not just a market but rather the entire society. Police remain wedded to the here and now. It is perhaps redundant to state that the focus of the police organization on responsiveness and demand management, a result of historically claiming a service mandate, makes the successful introduction of problem solving, complex crime analysis, and prevention into large urban departments unlikely.

NOTES

1. For further discussion of these ideas as applied to the police, see Manning (1990, 1997, 2004).

2. Consider the concept of uncertainty. Uncertainty characterizes modernity and is called "contingency" by Luhmann (1998). Luhmann defines contingency as follows: "Anything is contingent that is neither necessary nor impossible. The concept is therefore defined by the negation of necessity and impossibility" (p. 45). Organizations manage contingency, not complexity.

3. See reviews by Manning (1988, 1990, 1992, 2003).

4. It seems to me that the fire service is similarly poised, but the relatively more rare character of fires requiring equipment, personnel, and skills means that it is sensible for firefighters to stay put and wait, whereas the more routine human delicts considered police relevant are ongoing, current in some measure, and increasingly brought to police attention.

5. There is mixed evidence, of course, about whether schoolteachers, social workers, and police or corrections officers actually believe in what they do and, thus, act in good faith. Perhaps the idealism brought to the job is eroded, causing a toxic sediment. Perhaps the job is fundamentally destructive of positive views of human nature. Perhaps those recruits are frail and easily pessimistic, and it is true that police, when criticized from the outside, present a united front.

6. I borrow this phrase from Heidegger (1977).

7. My fieldwork suggests that many officers do not know or understand the workings of much of the basic equipment they handle, especially the computer and mobile terminals. It is not possible to study the innovation in use in practice because there is little descriptive work on the use of the equipment.

8. I consider here important works such as those of Ogburn, Cottrell, Woodward, and Perrow as well as variations on Marxist themes.

9. Perhaps the most difficult matter is disentangling the effects of technology in process from other changes. Although studies might see technology in the *foreground* in the analysis, for members of the organization, it is *background* unless it interrupts their routines and practices with a visible consequence.

10. Some of these points are made in Manning (2003, pp. 134–136).

11. In a recent interview (October 23, 2003) on *The Today Show,* a representative of the Transportation Security Administration (TSA), when asked about an e-mail sent to TSA concerning hidden box cutters and Play-Doh (explosive like in shape and density), said, "Our e-mail system is not set up to screen for these types of messages. ... We are developing a software to flag them." This is an example of bringing a technological solution to a human intelligence problem.

12. Chan's (1999) work in Queensland, Australia, suggests advances in learning and an acceptance of new electronic systems that is promising,. She found subtle changes in officers' use of time, skill levels among younger officers, and a positive attitude toward computer-based innovation.

REFERENCES

Abt Associates. (2000). *Police department information systems.* Washington, DC: Community Policing Services Agency.

Barley, S. (1986). Technology as an occasion for structuring. *Administrative Science Quarterly, 31,* 78–108.

Bayley, D. (1986). The tactical choices of police officers. *Journal of Criminal Justice, 14,* 329–348.

Bittner, E. (1972). *The function of police in modern society.* Washington, DC: National Institute of Mental Health.

Chan, J. (1999). *Report on uses of technology in police.* Unpublished manuscript, University of New South Wales.

Chan, J. (2003). Police and new technologies. In T. Newburn (Ed.), *The handbook of policing* (pp. 655–679). Cullompton, UK: Willan.

Crank, J. (2003). Institutional theory of police. *Policing, 26,* 186–207.

Dunworth, T. (2000). Criminal justice and the information technology revolution. In J. Horney (Ed.), *Criminal justice 2000* (Vol. 3). Washington, DC: U.S. Department of Justice.

Espeland, W. (1998). *The struggle for water.* Chicago: University of Chicago Press.

Feldman, M., & Pentland, B. (2003). Reconceptualizing organizational routines. *Administrative Science Quarterly, 48,* 94–118.

Gouldner, A. W. (1961). *Wildcat strike.* New York: Harper.

Greene, J. (2000). Community policing in America. In J. Horney (Ed.), *Criminal justice 2000* (Vol. 3). Washington, DC: U.S. Department of Justice.

Heidegger, M. (1977). *The question concerning technology and other essays.* New York: Colophon Books.

Henry, V. (2002). *The CompStat paradigm.* Flushing, NY: Loose Leaf Law Publications.

Janis, I. (1972). *Victims of groupthink.* Boston: Houghton Mifflin.

Janis, I., & Mann, L. (1977). *Decision-making.* New York: Free Press.

Jervis, R. (1997). *System effects.* Princeton, NJ: Princeton University Press.

Johnston, L., & Shearing, C. (2003). *Governing security.* London: Routledge.

Luhmann, N. (1998). *Observations on modernity.* Stanford, CA: Stanford University Press.

MacKenzie, D. (1993). *Inventing accuracy.* Cambridge, MA: MIT Press.

Maguire, E. (2002). *Organizational structure in American police agencies.* Albany: State University of New York Press.

Manning, P. K. (1977). *Police work.* Cambridge, MA: MIT Press.

Manning, P. K. (1988). *Symbolic communication.* Cambridge, MA: MIT Press.

Manning, P. K. (1990). *Organizational communication.* Hawthorne, NY: Aldine de Gruyter.

Manning, P. K. (1992). Police and information technology. In M. Tonry & N. Morris (Eds.), *Modern policing.* Chicago: University of Chicago Press.

Manning, P. K. (1997). *Police work* (2nd ed.). Prospect Heights, IL: Waveland.

Manning, P. K. (2003). *Policing contingencies.* Chicago: University of Chicago Press.

Manning, P. K. (2004). *Narcs' game* (2nd ed.). Prospect Heights, IL: Waveland.

Mastrofski, S., Reisig, M., & McCluskey, J. (2002). Police disrespect toward the public: An encounter based analysis. *Criminology, 40,* 519–551.

Mazerolle, L., Rogan, D., Frank, J., Famega, C., & Eck, J. (2002). Managing citizen calls to the police: The case of 311. *Criminology and Public Policy, 2,* 97–1245.

McDonald, P. (2002). *Managing police operations.* Belmont, CA: Wadsworth

Meyer, J., & Rowan, C. (1977). Institutionalized organizations. *American Journal of Sociology, 83,* 340–353.

Meyer, J., & Scott, W. R. (1992). Introduction. In J. Meyer & W. R. Scott (Eds.), *Organizational environments.* Newbury Park, CA: Sage.

Morris, N., & Geller, W. (1992). Relations between federal and local police. In M. Tonry & N. Morris (Eds.), *Modern policing* (pp. 231–348). Chicago: University of Chicago Press.

Orlikowski, W. (1992). The duality of technology: Rethinking the concept of technology in organizations. *Organization Science, 3,* 398–427.

Orlikowski, W. (1996). Improvising organizational transformation over time: A situated change perspective. *Information Systems Research, 7*(1), 63–92.

Orlikowski, W. (2000). Using technology and constituting structures: A practice lens for studying technology in organizations. *Organization Science, 11,* 404–428.

Orlikowski, W., & Tyre, M. (1994). Windows of opportunity: Temporal patterns of technological adaptation in organizations. *Organization Science, 5,* 98–118.

Poster, M. (1990). *The mode of information.* Chicago: University of Chicago Press.

Powell, W. W., & DiMaggio, P. (Eds.). (1991). *The new institutionalism in organizational analysis.* Chicago: University of Chicago Press.

Reiss, A. J., Jr. (1992). The police organization in the twentieth century. In M. Tonry & N. Morris (Eds.), *Modern policing.* Chicago: University of Chicago Press.

Reuss-Ianni, E. (1983). *The two cultures of policing.* Rutgers, NJ: Transaction.

Roberts, K., & Grabowski, M. (1996). Organizations, technology, and structuring. In S. Clegg, C. Hardy, & W. Nord (Eds.), *Handbook of organization studies.* London: Sage.

Roy, D. (1952). Quota restriction and goldbricking in a machine shop. *American Journal of Sociology, 57,* 427–442.

Roy, D. (1954). Efficiency and "the fix": Informal intergroup relations in a piecework machine shop. *American Journal of Sociology, 60,* 255–266.

Shearing, C., & Ericson, R. (1991). Culture as figurative action. *British Journal of Sociology, 42,* 481–506.

Silverman, E. (2000). *The NYPD battles crime.* Boston: Northeastern University Press.

Suchman, L. (1991). *Plans and situated actions.* Cambridge, UK: Cambridge University Press.

Thomas, R. (1994). *What machines can't do.* Berkeley: University of California Press.

Thompson, J. D. (1967). *Organizations in action.* New York: McGraw–Hill.

Thompson, V. (1961). *Modern organizations.* New York: Knopf.

Weick, K. (1977). Re-punctuating the problem. In P. Goodman, J. Pennings, & Associates (Eds.), *New perspectives on organizational effectiveness.* San Francisco: Jossey–Bass.

Weick, K. (1995). *Sensemaking in the organization.* Thousand Oaks, CA: Sage.

Weick, K. (2001). *Making sense of the organization.* Malden, MA: Blackwell.

Weisbord, D., Mastrofski, S., McNally, A. M., Greenspan, R., & Willis, J. J. (2003). Reforming to preserve: CompStat and strategic problem-solving in American policing. *Criminology and Public Policy, 2,* 421–456.

Young, M. (1991). *An inside job.* Oxford, UK: Oxford University Press.

Section V

THE FUTURE OF INFORMATION TECHNOLOGY IN THE CRIMINAL JUSTICE SYSTEM

CHAPTER 11

Information, Technology, and Criminal Justice Education

JAMES M. BYRNE AND EVE BUZAWA

One of the axioms of management in both the public and private sectors is that "information is power." In many circles, the management of information is now viewed as a key to effective leadership, particularly in organizations undergoing rapid transformation and change (Gardner, 2004). For managers in the criminal justice sector, the recent advances in information technology (IT) provide opportunities for improvements in operational control, decision making, and strategic planning that are essential to the success of police, court, and correctional agencies. However, changes in IT also create a variety of problems for these same criminal justice managers, particularly regarding the skill development, analytic development, and knowledge development of line staff members, mid-level management, and upper level management. This chapter describes both the opportunities and potential pitfalls (or challenges) of the IT "revolution" in the criminal justice system. It concludes by offering a blueprint for redesigning undergraduate and graduate criminal justice curricula to fully incorporate the knowledge, skills, and analytic tools available in the area of IT. The next generation of criminal justice professionals can and must be both willing and prepared to manage criminal justice agencies using the next generation of criminal justice IT.

INFORMATION, TECHNOLOGY, AND THE CRIMINAL JUSTICE SYSTEM

Advances in IT have already begun to have a profound impact on the administration and management of police, court, and corrections agencies at the federal, state, and local levels in the United States (Boba, 2003; Mamalian and La Vigne, 1999; Meyer, 1998). However, as a recent review by the National Governors Association emphasizes, "Integrating information from 13,000 police departments, 3,100 sheriffs' offices, 2,300 prosecutors, 1,500 corrections agencies, and other justice-related entities poses formidable challenges" (MacLellan, 2004, p. 1).

Perhaps the most direct way in which to evaluate the real and potential impacts of IT on police, court, and corrections agencies is to examine how "information" is used at key decision points throughout the criminal justice (decision-making) process (Gottfredson and Tonry, 1987; Stojkovic, Kalinch, & Klofas, 1998). This section examines the use of IT at key decision points in the criminal justice process. In the process, we discuss both the potential and problems inherent in applying these new technologies in organizations historically resistant to change.

The Police and IT

Police make a number of decisions every day about where to look for crime, who or what to look for, and who to arrest and/or detain. Consider, for a moment, Stojkovic and colleagues' (1998, p. 291) partial listing of police-related decision making:

1. Has a crime occurred in the eyes of a victim or a bystander?

2. Should a crime be reported to the police?

3. Should police be dispatched to the scene?

4. Should police regard the event as a criminal offense?

5. Should investigators be called in?

6. Should an arrest be made?

7. Should search warrants be issued?

8. Should arrest warrants be issued?

9. Should a police officer fire at a suspect?

10. Should an alleged offender be detained in jail?

With the proliferation of community policing programs come an additional set of decisions that can be added to the preceding list:

11. Can "hot spots" for particular types of crime be identified at the neighborhood level?

12. Can and should the concerns of community residents be addressed (and if so, how)?

13. Should the police track the location and movement of known offenders in their community?

Finally, with the advent of global terrorism and the response by federal, state, and local agencies, there is increased recognition that situations and data that may be considered irrelevant (or at least not material) to local law enforcement may have dramatic consequences when reformulated into national or international databases. As a result of the enactment of the Patriot Act of 2001 and similar homeland security-driven measures, the need for enhanced higher level decision-making capabilities is becoming apparent. The tragic events of September 11, 2001, have affected not only the types of information that can be shared across local, state, and federal police agencies but also the (decision-making) policies and practices related to police surveillance and control activities.

Gottfredson (1987) offers an interesting perspective from which to examine police decision making:

> Any decision has three components, namely, a goal, alternative choices, and information. Decisions cannot rationally be made (or studied) if decision-making goals are neither stated nor clear. Unfortunately, goals for criminal justice decisions rarely are stated explicitly, and they often are complex. Rarely is a single goal for a decision given. Without alternatives, there can be no decision problem. Without information on which to base the decision, the "problem" reduces to reliance on chance. (p. 23)

Each of the decisions identified previously requires access to (and analysis of) information before *and* after a decision is made. As Stojkovic and colleagues (1998) observe, "The most important characteristic [of information] is accuracy. The point that improved decisions can be made with accurate information may seem simple, but accuracy of information is a major problem in criminal justice" (p. 301).

Have advancements in IT resulted in more accurate (and timely) information being made available to the police as they consider alternative courses of action and then make decisions? The short answer to this question is *yes*. Meyer (1998), for example, points out that the improvements in security technology have led to the detection of not only more crime (e.g., burglaries) but also different types of crime (e.g., financial crimes). In addition, the recent improvements in the National Crime Information Center (NCIC) have dramatically changed the type of information available to police officers on patrol and on routine traffic stops. Although concerns have been raised about the accuracy (and completeness) of the NCIC database (Barton, 2003; Meyer, 1998), it certainly appears that improvements in this type of IT have "reduced the number of suspects who essentially escaped apprehension by crossing state lines or who were able to surprise officers who were unaware of their violent pasts" (Meyer, 1998, p. 5). In fact, a recent survey of state criminal history information systems revealed that more than 89% of the 64 million criminal history records in state criminal history repositories are automated, and this should improve the country's move toward a comprehensive national criminal history database (Barton, 2003). Nonetheless, there are still a number of problems with existing criminal history databases that must be addressed before data quality is improved to the point where there will be a noticeable and measurable effect on decision making by police. For example, the lag between arrest and data entry is still approximately 12 days on average, and

criminal record updates are often not completed for the disposition of arrests.

IT has also improved the investigative capacity of local, state, and federal policing agencies in a number of important ways. Improved fingerprint technology, DNA testing, the use of the latest photo enhancement technology, and new blood, hair, and fiber technology are just a few examples (Dunworth, 2001; Travis, 1997).

In addition to the detection and investigation of criminal behavior, police departments obviously play an important crime control role in the communities they serve. Strategies such as "profiling" repeat offenders and/or offenders released from prison or jail, identifying and tracking gang members, and identifying, locating, and monitoring known sex offenders (via sex offender registration) are often facilitated by improvements or enhancements in IT (Cadigan, 2001; Gowan, 2001, Mamalian & La Vigne, 1999). As Jeremy Travis, former director of the National Institute of Justice, observes, "These new capabilities pose new challenges to the criminal justice system. Some of those challenges are familiar to us—such as how to balance privacy concerns with the need to conduct criminal investigations—yet these challenges are magnified by the sheer reach of the new information technology" (Travis, 1997, p. 4).

One issue that merits careful consideration is whether police departments have the capacity, not only in terms of technology but also in terms of personnel (e.g., skills, knowledge, training), to use IT to solve problems (e.g., workplace violence, school violence) *proactively* rather than to respond reactively to calls for service and crime. This is the underlying premise of problem-oriented policing, a strategy that has been linked to recent crime drops in major U.S. cities. According to Goldstein (1990), "The problem-oriented approach calls for developing—preferably within the police agency—the skills, procedures, and research techniques to analyze problems and evaluate police effectiveness as an integral continuing part of management" (p. 49, as quoted in Boba, 2003, p. 2).

Recent reviews of the implementation and impact of problem-oriented policing over the past 20 years or so underscore the difficulties inherent in this problem-solving strategy (Boba, 2003; Bynum, 2001; Manning, 2003; Scott, 2000). Stated simply, it appears that police are much better at identifying problems than at solving them (Bynum, 2001). According to Boba (2003), "Analysis and evaluation within police agencies have been the slowest areas to develop, although problem solving and problem-oriented policing have blossomed in both concept and practice" (p. 5).

Another review of problem-oriented policing by Bynum (2001) reaches similar conclusions: "Police often have difficulty clearly defining problems, properly using data sources, conducting comprehensive analysis, and implementing analysis-driven responses" (p. 2, as quoted in Boba, 2003, p. 5). Assuming for the moment that these reviews are accurate, it certainly appears that recent advances in IT must be accompanied by new strategies for educating police personnel on how to use this technology to address the unique crime problems in their communities and broader societal issues of criminal networks crossing municipal or even state jurisdictions. It is our contention that higher education institutions can play an important role in facilitating this process by developing three distinct IT tracks within undergraduate and graduate criminal justice programs: (a) technology-based skill development, (b) technology-based analytic development, and (c) technology-based knowledge development. By integrating these three facets of technology into the undergraduate and graduate criminal justice curricula, we will prepare the next generation of police

management for the challenge of integrating new technology into the workplace. At the same time, we would encourage criminal justice faculty members to design and implement these same technology-based courses for *current* police personnel, perhaps as one component of their departments' ongoing training and development activities.

In terms of technology skills, courses can be offered on crime mapping techniques, database management, and use of the Internet by police. Technology-based courses in analytic development might include courses on the application of a wide range of data analysis techniques and programs for problem solving by police. Finally, technology-based courses in the area of knowledge development would introduce police to the latest developments in IT with current and/or potential applications to current policing problems (Mamalian & La Vigne, 1999) and solutions (National Research Council [NRC], 2004).

The Courts and IT

IT has also had a profound effect on the administration of the federal, state, and local courts in the United States. Because of cutbacks in court budgets, court administrators have been asked to do more (e.g., speedier case processing, creation of specialized courts, backlog reduction, improved collections) with less (e.g., fewer personnel, reduced resources), and this has resulted in an even greater reliance on automated case processing systems along with a wide range of other advances in IT designed to improve the quality, scope, and presentation of information used in court settings (Feinblatt, Berman, & Denckla, 2000; McMillan, 1997). In a white paper on court automation standards, Palmer (2001) observed,

The National Center for State Courts (NCSC) estimates that, collectively, courts spend well in excess of $500 million annually on information technology. These dollars are committed for planning new automated applications, specifying their requirements, purchasing hardware, developing or procuring software, installing new systems, training users how to operate them, and supporting them in operation. (p. 1)

Unfortunately, it appears that in many court systems, court administrators have attempted to change and/or upgrade their existing information systems without a clear understanding of this new technology, its cost (both direct and indirect), and its inherent limitations (McMillan, 1997; Palmer, 2001; Webster, 1997).

To understand the role of IT in a court environment, it makes sense to consider for a moment the basic types of decisions made each day in the nation's courts (as summarized in Stojkovic et al., 1998, p. 291):

1. Should bail be set and at what amount?

2. Should release on recognizance be allowed?

3. Should an alleged offender be prosecuted?

4. Should an alleged offender enter a diversion program?

5. With what priority should prosecution be undertaken?

6. Is an alleged offender competent to stand trial?

7. Should motions be granted?

8. Is an alleged offender guilty?

9. Is an alleged offender not guilty due to insanity?

10. Should an offender be incarcerated or allowed to remain in the community?

11. How long should the sentence be?

12. Should there be special conditions to the sentence?

Of course, the recent development of various "problem-solving" courts in many jurisdictions (e.g., mental health courts, drug courts, family or domestic violence courts, reentry courts) has placed new IT demands on court systems as they monitor (and attempt to change) offenders under their jurisdictions:

13. Have there been measurable changes in the mental health status of targeted offenders?

14. Have there been measurable changes in the substance abuse status of targeted offenders?

15. Have there been measurable changes in the behavior or status of offenders and victims under the jurisdiction of reentry courts?

The challenge for court administrators and judges is to design and implement an IT system that provides answers to these 15 basic questions efficiently and effectively. To make such design choices and implementation decisions, the courts need to know not only about current court IT but also about potential *new* applications of IT to the court decision-making process. According to a review by McMillan (1997),

Courts will have to make some important choices in the next decade. Those choices involve whether to use technology that is available today but is not [yet] being applied by the courts. These choices involve, first, the use of new case management event design as a management tool; second, the use of object technology to extend our information systems into the file room and outside the walls of the courthouse; third, development of shared and communicating systems to both serve and protect information in the justice community; and finally, use of all of the technologies to start to develop automated tools to focus the decision-making process. (p. 1)

We mention the range of choices that will need to be made by court administrators and judges to underscore an important point: The management of IT has become an essential skill for the leaders (e.g., court administrators, judges) of the court system in the United States. Higher education can and should play an important role in preparing the next generation of court leaders to fully use IT by offering courses in the three technology areas identified earlier for police personnel: (a) skill development, (b) analytic development, and (c) knowledge development. At a minimum, courses should be offered on (a) information system design and the courts; (b) strategic planning, IT, and the courts (Webster, 1997); and (c) new (and potential) applications of IT in court settings. In many criminal justice programs at the undergraduate and graduate levels, current faculty members often do not have either the skills or the inclination to teach these types of court-specific courses. This may actually be a good thing because this shortfall may result—by necessity if not by design—in the development of interdisciplinary programs with information science, business, and management faculty members. However, such interdisciplinary efforts will likely fail unless they are preceded by a rigorous cross-training program for interdisciplinary faculty members. Using the skills of this interdisciplinary group, a series of courses on court technology designed for undergraduate and graduate criminal justice majors can be developed.

In addition to such expanded undergraduate and graduate course offerings, it would make sense for universities to offer a series of training programs for current court personnel and management in these same three areas. One strategy that universities might consider is to create an interdisciplinary IT training and education center that could offer courses to the courts in their respective regions. The National Center for State Courts has done a considerable amount of work on the technology issue in general, and on the development of standards for court automation in particular, that could be used

to develop a core curriculum in this area (for an overview, see Palmer, 2001). However, readers are cautioned to keep in mind Webster's (1997) assessment of the IT revolution's impact on the courts:

> We can't substitute technology for training, good management, a decent work environment, adequate compensation, and professional hiring procedures. People make courts work, not computers. Technology can eliminate redundant tasks and speed communication in a court, but it won't solve management problems. It is the combination of intelligent, hardworking, well-trained people and effective tools that produces the best outcomes. Strategic thinkers look first to the people, then to the tools. (p. 6)

It is our view that higher education has an important role to play in the education and training of court personnel and management on the application of IT to problem solving in the court system. But we need to do more than provide an examination of the latest innovations in court technology—from "smart" courtrooms equipped with the latest cameras, DVD players, and audiovisual aids to a review of "best practices" in case flow management (National Center for State Courts, 2004)—by providing courses in the three core areas described earlier: IT skills development, IT analytic development, and IT knowledge development.

Corrections and IT

For a variety of reasons, it appears that the IT revolution has yet to be fully embraced by federal, state, and local corrections systems in the United States (Wright, Brisbee, & Hardyman, 2003). It also appears to lag behind the advances made within law enforcement and even the judicial system, although this may be in part a result of relative funding allocations rather than a philosophical resistance to these types of technological innovations. Nonetheless, both institutional and community corrections administrators have used a variety of IT tools to improve decision making and problem analysis in their agencies (Bogue, 2004; Cadigan, 2001; Hardyman, Austin, & Peyton, 2004; Ogden & Horrocks, 2001; Siegel & Terenzi, 2001). Within the institutional corrections system, there are a number of key decision points where innovations in IT may be helpful (adapted from Stojkovic et al., 1998, p. 291):

At intake:

1. What level of security (and services) does an offender need?

2. To what program (e.g., education, job, counseling) should an offender be assigned?

During incarceration:

3. When and how should the levels of security change?

4. Should an incarcerated offender be transferred?

5. Should disciplinary reports be written?

6. Is an offender guilty of disciplinary infractions?

7. What are the appropriate sanctions for disciplinary violations?

8. Should an offender be transferred (to another facility) or committed to a mental hospital?

On release from prison:

9. Should an incarcerated offender be paroled?

10. How should the offender reentry process be structured?

IT may also improve decision making for offenders supervised in the community (via probation, parole, or some form of intermediate sanction). Similar to institutional corrections, there are intake, case management, and release decisions to be considered:

At intake:

1. What level of community security does an offender need?

2. What (special) conditions of community supervision are needed?

During supervision:

3. Is the offender in compliance with the conditions of his or her release?

4. How will compliance be monitored (e.g., drug/alcohol use, curfews, participation in treatment, registration as sex offender, housing, employment, restitution)?

5. Should disciplinary reports be written?

6. Is the offender guilty of reported infractions?

7. What are the appropriate sanctions for disciplinary violations?

8. Should an offender's probation, parole, or other form of community release be revoked?

On release from community supervision:

9. Should an offender be released or discharged from community supervision?

10. Under various sex offender statutes, most communities receive a record of former inmates residing within their municipal boundaries. If so, whose responsibility is it to keep the database current?

Focusing first on institutional corrections, a number of automated offender classification systems have been developed during recent years, but there are several obstacles that still must be addressed before these are fully operational, including data sharing, data quality, data timeliness, data availability, and (perhaps most important) lack of validation for the risk/need models currently being automated (for a nationwide review of existing classification systems, see Hardyman et al., 2004). Despite these obstacles, the sheer number of new prisoners being classified each month is ample evidence that automation could significantly improve case processing time; the typical male offender spends approximately 40 days in an intake facility, compared with 31 days for the typical female offender. It remains to be seen whether improvements in IT will also improve the quality of these initial intake assessments for the 600,000 admissions each year to the country's state prison system (Hardyman et al., 2004).

Once an offender is classified, he or she leaves the intake facility and is placed in an "appropriate" prison facility based on the offender's security level and programmatic needs. While the offender is in these facilities, a number of decisions are made affecting his or her status (e.g., program placement, categorization of offender behavior, discipline, transfer, release). Unfortunately, it is often quite difficult to get information from prisons on key elements of this decision-making process, and this makes an overall assessment of corrections performance nearly impossible (Wright et al., 2003). A recent survey of the collection and automation of key indicators of the corrections system's performance in four areas (public safety, institutional safety, substance abuse/mental health, and offender profile) is highlighted in the appendix. According to the authors of this review,

> Almost all prison systems across the nation possess the capacity to measure and report about the aggregate prison population under supervision and individual characteristics of that population. Furthermore, most prison agencies collect information about escapes, homicides, and suicides. Beyond these measures, the survey discovered a significant disparity among departments of corrections regarding their capacity to measure and report on all other indicators. (p. 61)

One solution to this information "shortfall" within institutional corrections is the development and implementation of a national performance measurement system. Wright and colleagues (2003) have laid the groundwork for a national data "platform" by defining performance standards, identifying key indicators and data elements, and even providing detailed counting rules. However, they caution that this is a long-term change process (for a summary of key findings from their nationwide review, see the appendix). Indeed, they point out that "as of the summer of 2002, only about 20 to 25 percent of the departments possess integrated information systems that will allow them to participate fully" (p. 63).

In addition to automated prison classification and case management systems and the development and monitoring of performance standards for prisons, other possible applications of IT to the prison setting include the development of sophisticated tracking devices to chart the movement of officers and prisoners within prisons (e.g., through video surveillance, some form of electronic tracking, and/or biometric devices [for a discussion, see Turner & Blackburn, 2002]) along with new methods to detect drug and alcohol use in these settings. Finally, there are a number of ways in which new IT can be applied to the process of offender reentry. For example, even a cursory review of the research on the prevalence of communicable diseases among the U.S. prison population (e.g., nearly half of all offenders released from prison in 2003 had tested positive for either AIDS, hepatitis, or some other serious communicable disease) suggests that *where* an individual offender is released may have an impact on a community that transcends any discussion of individual offender recidivism. Mapping offender reentry patterns is one technique for monitoring the real and potential impacts of concentrations of released offenders on the "health" of neighborhoods. Such a data collection strategy would likely require the sharing of offender-specific release data with police departments and public health departments. Of course, it is one thing to develop interagency agreements to collect these data; it is quite another to develop effective (and ethical) interagency policies and practices to address the serious and significant health problems of offenders released from prison.

Once a decision has been made either to release an offender from prison/jail or to supervise the offender in the community, a number of current and potential IT applications can be identified at each key decision point in the community supervision process. The September 2001 issue of *Federal Probation,* the official journal of the American Probation and Parole Association, was dedicated entirely to this topic. In one article, Siegel and Terenzi (2001) offered a partial listing of possible IT applications:

> The benefits of technology for . . . probation and pretrial services officers include technological tools and capabilities such as mobile computing, immediate access to criminal databases, ankle monitors and remote electronic monitoring, and on-site urinalysis—all to enhance the investigation and supervision of offenders and increase public safety. (p. 31)

There are obviously many other possible applications of IT in community corrections settings. For example, report preparation (e.g., presentence investigations, risk/needs classification) has been automated in several states (Ogden & Horrocks, 2001) using digital dictation and transcription devices and/or computer-based classification devices. In addition, some states (e.g., Utah) are experimenting with the use of kiosks to verify offender location/ identity (via biometric devices that compare an offender's fingerprints on file with those of the "offender" checking in at the kiosk), whereas others are using pagers to facilitate ongoing contact between officers and offenders (Ogden & Horrocks, 2001).

When considering these potential community corrections applications, probation and parole administrators face a number of challenges that can be addressed, at least in part, by working directly with local criminal justice educators. Siegel and Terenzi (2001) describe three basic challenges to the full integration of new advances in IT that bear consideration:

> The first challenge for chiefs . . . is a *mental* one—to believe in technology, not as a panacea for all the challenges in the system, but as a helpful tool to accomplish their daunting responsibilities and to manage their complex operations. . . . The second challenge is a *strategic* one as chiefs consider how to fully exploit the benefits of technology, instead of simply using it to automate high volume bureaucratic routines. . . . [The third challenge] is *implementation*—making things work [through the development of] effective management strategies to manage and develop automation staff. (pp. 31–32)

As the next generation of institutional and community corrections managers is being educated, it certainly makes sense to consider how the three distinct IT tracks discussed earlier—(a) technology-based skill development, (b) technology-based analytic development, and (c) technology-based knowledge development—can be geared to corrections managers and line staff members. In terms of skill development, courses can be offered in database management, information systems design, strategic planning, and management of technical staff members in institutional and community-based corrections agencies. A course focusing on analytic development might examine "how information technology can be used for strategic innovation and not simply for tactical automation" (Siegel and Terenzi, 2001, p. 31), focusing on a wide range of problems currently facing corrections managers in both institutional and community settings (e.g., offender reentry; offender classification for risk, treatment, and/or control; information system integration). Finally, courses emphasizing knowledge development and knowledge use would likely incorporate the most recent "best practices" reviews in the area of IT (e.g., MacLellan, 2004) into the emerging field of evidence-based corrections program development and implementation (Hardyman et al., 2004; McGuire, 2001; Sherman et al., 1998; Taxman, 2002). For example, an examination of electronic monitoring programs would include a critical review not only of the monitoring technology itself but also of the research evaluating the implementation and effectiveness of programs designed to use this technology. A similar approach could also be used to examine a wide range of police–corrections interventions (e.g., reentry), court–corrections interventions (e.g., drug courts), and systemwide interventions (e.g., Break the Cycle).

Information, Technology, and Organizational Change

Currently, many researchers argue that IT has not had a substantial impact on actual organizational practices (Dunworth, 2001; Greene, 2000; Manning, 2003; NRC, 2004). IT is currently regarded as being more likely to merely "supplement" existing sources of knowledge within the organization and facilitate the performance of daily tasks rather than to structurally change organizations and/or become central in decision making. For example, a recent review of "fairness and effectiveness" in policing by the NRC (2004) examined innovations in police IT and found that, despite the claims of dramatic effectiveness (e.g., Bratton & Knobler, 1998; McDonald, 2001), "there is relatively little rigorous study of how, if at all, it is changing police organizations" (p. 167). Based on its comprehensive review, the NRC offers the following recommendations:

> The committee recommends that the National Institute of Justice support a

program of rigorous evaluation of the new crime information technologies in local police agencies. This program should go well beyond describing variation in technologies and whether they "work" in a technical sense; it should track the impact of changes on organizational structures and practices over time in selected departments and compare the impact of these technologies in a variety of departments. (p. 167)

Our own review of the implementation and impact of similar IT innovations in the courts and institutional and community corrections systems suggests that the NRC ultimately would be likely to offer the same recommendation about the need for rigorous evaluations in these systems as well. To some extent, this is the result of a hardly atypical bureaucratized organizational culture present in most criminal justice agencies. To the extent that agency administrators attempt to embrace new technologies, many of their current employees are unfamiliar with the immediate use and full potential of such technologies. Employees often deeply resent the added time and demands that software requires to develop a "data-rich" environment. Efforts to integrate new technologies into an organizational setting often are seen as highly threatening to employees because *they* are not initiating the changes. Many current employees may also be legitimately concerned about "changing the rules" for how accomplishments are measured within the organization, whereas others may be concerned with breaking established organizational routines and practices. In effect, the changes mean that many largely competent employees will feel *less* competent and, at the same time, less likely to know what is expected or the criteria for their own advancement. From these employees' perspectives, such concerns may outweigh benefits that they see as purely theoretical or, at best, only a contingent outcome.

IT and Criminal Justice Education: Issues to Consider

Beyond the inevitable clarion calls for "more research," there are a number of issues that can be raised about the role of higher education in the ongoing efforts to improve criminal justice decision making. Obviously, courses focusing on "knowledge development" in the area of IT applications in criminal justice settings will be designed based on the latest research on the implementation and impact of IT on police, courts, and correctional agencies' performance (e.g., MacLellan, 2004; National Law Enforcement and Corrections Technology Center, 2003; NRC, 2004; Office of Information Technology, 2001; Palmer, 2001).

In the areas of skill development and analytic development, a basic question can be raised: Do we want criminal justice professionals to develop or improve their *own* technology skills and analytic capabilities, or do we want organizations to hire IT "specialists" to perform these functions for their particular needs?

This is a critical issue with obvious implications for curriculum development in criminal justice. Readers who are familiar with the design of research and statistical analysis courses in criminal justice programs are likely to lament that this is "déjà vu all over again." In some programs (e.g., at Rutgers University), separate research methods and data analysis courses were developed for "producers" and "consumers" of research. It appears that the introduction of IT as a core area of a criminal justice curriculum raises the same issue once again. However, it is our view that the next generation of graduates from undergraduate and graduate criminal justice programs should possess skills in the three technology areas identified throughout this chapter: technology skills, technology-based analytic capability, and knowledge of the latest (and most effective) forms of IT used in various criminal justice organizational settings. Although we certainly anticipate debate on the producer versus consumer issue, it is difficult to envision a criminal justice program without a substantial IT component.

A second related issue is the extent to which minimum education standards should be raised for police, court, prison, and community corrections personnel. As the technical skills necessary to function effectively in various criminal justice professions are increased, managers have two basic choices: (a) increase the qualifications (B.A./B.S. degree required) or (b) improve academy and/or in-service training programs in the area of IT. The two venues for education are not, of course, mutually exclusive. Our view is that we need to move decisively in both areas to bridge the gap between the technology available and the capabilities of line staff members and management in police, court, and correction agencies.

A third issue that must be addressed by criminal justice educators is the extent to which the inevitable ethical issues associated with advances in IT are addressed in undergraduate and graduate technology courses. Consider, for example, the use of sex offender registration, the use of DNA collection, the posting of pictures of sex offenders on the Web and in the community, the use of crime mapping techniques to locate sex offenders, and the use of electronic monitoring, pagers, kiosks, and other devices to track the movement of offenders in the community. In each instance, IT is being applied to identify, locate, and monitor a group of offenders who actually pose only a minimal risk to the community, at least in terms of individual offender recidivism. A recent review by Sample and Bray (2003) concludes,

> The overwhelming majority of sex offenders (93%) were *not* rearrested for another sex crime. . . . Based on rates of re-offending, sex offenders do not appear to be more dangerous than other criminal categories

and thereby deserving of the additional institutionalization and surveillance they receive after their judicial punishments have been served. In fact, to the extent that sex offender policies have been enacted based on sex offenders' levels of recidivism, research would indicate that robbers may be better candidates for DNA collection, registration, and community notification than sex offenders. (p. 76)

Whether one agrees or disagrees with Sample and Bray's policy recommendations, the ethical issues associated with these forms of IT cannot be ignored. In many criminal justice programs, criminal justice ethics is now a "core" course that is required for all criminal justice majors.

A strong argument can be made that the next generation of criminal justice professionals needs to be infused not only with technical expertise and skills (particularly in the area of IT), but also with a core set of ethical values and problem-solving strategies. In his recent book, *Changing Minds*, Gardner (2004) coins the term *Good Work* to define this combination of technical skills and morality. He identifies many examples of Good Work, which he describes as follows:

> [It is] work that is at once technically excellent and that seeks outcomes that are ethical, moral, and responsible. . . . Though the ethical quotient for any individual may be contested, there is clearly a difference between individuals who strive to be accountable on the ethical dimension and those for whom only monetary gain or worldly success or power matter. (p. 206)

It is our view that both IT and criminal justice ethics should be required courses in undergraduate criminal justice programs.

CONCLUSIONS: REDESIGNING THE CORE

We believe that criminal justice educators can make a major contribution by preparing students to be familiar with both the current and potential applications of IT in a variety of criminal justice settings. To better accomplish this, it may be helpful for academic professional associations to revisit current recommended educational standards. The general need for educational standards in the discipline were discussed in the 1984 book, *Quest for Quality: A Publication of the Joint Commission of Criminology and Criminal Justice Education and Standards* (Ward & Webb, 1984). In 1994, the Northeast Association of Criminal Justice Sciences first developed criminal justice education standards that were in part a result of its recommendations.

In 1995, the Academy of Criminal Justice Sciences (ACJS) established a committee to examine the possibility of that organization developing minimum standards. After several years of discussion, its recommendations were published in 1998 and titled *Minimum Standards for Criminal Justice Education: Guidelines for College and University-Level Programs* (ACJS, 1998).

These standards were welcomed by the criminal justice academic community as a highly needed guide for both developing and assessing the quality of criminal justice programs and departments. The standards recommended a core focus on the following areas (ACJS, 1998, p. 2):

- Criminal justice and juvenile justice processes (law, crime, and administration of justice)
- Criminology (the causes of crime, typologies, offenders, and victims)
- Law enforcement (police organization, discretion, subculture, and legal constraints)
- Law adjudication (criminal law, prosecution, defense, and court procedures and decision making)
- Corrections (incarceration, community-based corrections, and treatment of offenders)

Although such standards were sound in terms of substantive fields of knowledge within the discipline, it is noteworthy that proficiency in IT (or research methods and data analysis) was not identified as a core component for a criminal justice curriculum. This omission is partially addressed in more recent curricula standards developed at the state level. For example, in July 2002, an amendment to Massachusetts law authorized the Board of Higher Education to establish quality guidelines for police incentive programs (that led to eligibility to receive career incentive pay increases) to be used as a metric to conduct periodic review of criminal justice programs in general. The required areas for course coverage were as follows (Massachusetts Board of Higher Education, 2003, p. 4):

♦ Administration of justice
♦ Corrections
♦ Criminology
♦ Criminal law
♦ Ethics
♦ Policing
♦ Research and analytic methods

We believe that these standards could be further improved through the addition of IT, either as a "core" area in criminal justice curricula or as part of a core course in technology, research, and analytic methods. Such a change would contribute to the development of critical thinking and the ability to apply this knowledge to "related problems and changing fact situations," a stated goal of the ACJS standards (ACJS, 1998, p. 2). If this purpose is interpreted to encompass the ability of students to change organizations as well as situations, it could be argued that providing students with a foundation in IT may be an invaluable additional core area of criminal justice. But providing such a foundation is only a small incremental step toward fully integrating IT into every core course in criminal justice. At a minimum, core subject areas such as police, the courts, and corrections should include separate subject-specific courses in the three areas discussed throughout this chapter: (a) technology skill development, (b) technology-based analytic development, and (c) technology-based knowledge development.

APPENDIX: KEY FINDINGS FROM WRIGHT COLLEAGUES' (2003) NATIONAL SURVEY OF STATE DEPARTMENT OF CORRECTIONS' PERFORMANCE MEASUREMENT SYSTEM

STANDARD I: PUBLIC SAFETY

Key Indicator: Escapes

- Most states keep automated records of escapes.
- Some states have difficulty in distinguishing within their database whether the escape was from within or without.
- Some systems use a legal definition of escape and cannot differentiate between an attempt and a successful escape.
- Nearly all departments could begin to report this information as specified with minor code writing.
- Overall, approximately 21% of the agencies do not have automated information on escapes.

Key Indicator: Escapes from private facilities

- States that place prisoners in private facilities have this information.
- Often the data are not automated (25% of these agencies are not automated).

Key Indicator: Return to prison

- There is considerable variation among responding systems. Some systems already routinely report these data; for other states, it would pose a major undertaking.
- The unified systems would have difficulty in distinguishing among readmission types.
- Overall, approximately 25% of the agencies have no automated information on returns to prison for new convictions.

STANDARD II: INSTITUTIONAL SAFETY

Key Indicator: Prisoner-on-prisoner assaults and victims

- Most departments maintain incident-based records of prisoner assaults. Because the database identifies incidents rather than individuals, some systems would have difficulty in counting the number of assailants. Furthermore, most incident-based systems do not include information on the victim or the extent of injury.
- A few systems could access other records (e.g., medical) to identify the number of victims.
- Information regarding the type of weapon used is frequently not automated but is contained in the written record.
- Few systems link their incident record system with their disciplinary hearing record system, thereby making it impossible to comply with the counting rule that specifies that the assault be substantiated.
- Incident-based records seldom contain follow-up information; rather, they typically record point-in-time information.
- Overall, approximately half of the departments do not have automated data.

Key Indicator: Staff injuries resulting from assaults

- Again, most departments have a critical incident database where incidents in which staff members are attacked by prisoners are tracked.

♦ Because these records tend to be "point-in-time" records, whether injury was sustained and the extent of injury is seldom available.

♦ Many systems would have difficulty in specifying how many staff members were attacked in a single incident.

Key Indicator: Prisoner-on-prisoner sexual assaults

♦ This information is also contained in incident-based data records.

♦ Some states would have difficulty in identifying when there is more than one victim.

♦ Some systems cannot differentiate between types of assaults—sexual or solely physical.

♦ Most data systems lack substantiation.

Key Indicator: Sexual misconduct by staff-on-prisoners

♦ In most departments, staff member misconduct information is not maintained in the primary IT database, which is a prisoner database. Rather, it is contained in records maintained by the internal affairs office, human resources, or the legal department. In nearly all cases, this information is not automated, and if it is, detailed information is lacking.

♦ Identifying the gender of both the staff member and the prisoners, particularly the staff member, would be difficult for most systems.

Key Indicator: Prisoner homicides

♦ Some departments collect information on homicides as part of their information systems.

♦ However, because prisoner-on-prisoner and prisoner-on-staff homicides are such rare occurrences, many states do not have a data field for these events. Most of these states indicated that they could easily produce the information.

Key Indicator: Prisoner suicides

♦ This is the one indicator that all departments can readily produce.

♦ The only caveat is that some departments have difficulty in distinguishing suicides from overdoses because their data lack follow-up information.

Key Indicator: Positive drug tests

♦ Most departments can also produce these data in automated format.

♦ The only difficulty may be whether the department uses the specified threshold level.

Key Indicator: Disturbances

♦ For most departments, reporting major disturbances would be much less difficult than reporting minor disturbances.

♦ Most departments record information regarding disturbances in critical incident reports. Most systems do not automate this information. Of those systems that automate it, most lack the detail required to report this information as specified. Consequently, most states would face a major undertaking to begin to report this information.

STANDARD III: SUBSTANCE ABUSE AND MENTAL HEALTH

Key Indicator: Staff hours of assessment and treatment

♦ Most departments do not collect this information. The only departments that may be able to provide these data are those who have contracts with private providers.
♦ Most respondents indicated that their health departments maintain information regarding assessment and treatment of substance abuse and mental health. These data are seldom automated and are generally contained within traditional hospital jackets. Implementing a data collection system regarding these topics would be a major undertaking.

Key Indicator: Psychiatric beds

♦ Most states can determine how many psychiatric beds are filled on a particular day. However, these data are not always automated.

STANDARD IV: OFFENDER PROFILE

Context Indicator: Commitment type

♦ Most departments can provide information regarding commitment type.
♦ Some departments have difficulty in differentiating between the two categories of offenders returned for violations.
♦ Reporting this information is much more difficult for the unified systems.

Context Indicator: Offense type

♦ Most departments collect offense information, but some would need to recode their data to reflect the categories specified in the counting rules.
♦ Many systems record information according to controlling offenses rather than longest sentences.

Context Indicator: Demographics

♦ Departments can provide information regarding prisoners' age and gender.
♦ Some systems can provide information about whether prisoners are Black or White but cannot separate out Latino/Hispanic prisoners.

Context Indicator: Sentence length

♦ Departments can provide this information with only minor recoding necessary.

Context Indicator: Time served

♦ Most departments can provide this information.
♦ For some departments, separating prisoner groups by admission type will be difficult.

SOURCE: Wright, K., with Brisbee, J., & Hardyman, P. (2003). *Defining and measuring corrections performance; Final report.* Washington, DC: U.S. Department of Justice, pp. 58–60, Table 7.

REFERENCES

Academy of Criminal Justice Sciences. (1998). *Minimum Standards for Criminal Justice Education: Guidelines for college and university-level programs.* Greenbelt, MD: Author.

Barton, S. (2003). *Survey of State Criminal History Information Systems 2001: A criminal justice information policy report.* Washington, DC: U.S. Department of Justice.Boba, R. (2003) *Problem analysis in policing.* Washington, DC: Police Foundation.

Bogue, B. (2004). *Implementing evidence-based practice in community corrections: The principles of effective intervention.* Washington, DC: National Institute of Corrections. Available: www.cjinstitute.org

Bratton, W., with Knobler, P. (1998). *Turnaround.* New York: Random House.

Bynum, T. (2001). *Using analysis for problem-solving: A guidebook for law enforcement.* Washington, DC: Office of Community-Oriented Policing Services.

Cadigan, T. (2001, September). PACTS. *Federal Probation,* pp. 25–30.

Dunworth, T. (2001, September). Criminal justice and the IT revolution. *Federal Probation,* pp. 52–65.

Feinblatt, J., Berman, G., & Denckla, D. (2000). Judicial innovation at the crossroads: The future of problem-solving courts. *The Court Manager, 15*(3), 28–34.

Gardner, H. (2004). *Changing minds: The art and science of changing our own and others' minds.* Boston: Harvard Business School Press.

Goldstein, H. (1990). *Problem-oriented policing.* New York: McGraw–Hill.

Gottfredson, S. (1987). Prediction: An overview of selected methodological issues. In D. Gottfredson & M. Tonry (Eds.), *Prediction and classification: Criminal justice decision making* (pp. 21–51). Chicago: University of Chicago Press.

Gottfredson, D., & Tonry, M. (Eds.). (1987). *Prediction and classification: Criminal justice decision making.* Chicago: University of Chicago Press.

Gowan, D. (2001, September). Remote location monitoring: A supervision strategy to enhance risk control. *Federal Probation,* pp. 38–41.

Greene, J. (2000). *Community policing in America.* In J. Horney (Ed.), *Policies, processes, and decisions of the justice system* (Criminal Justice 2000, Vol. 3). Washington, DC: U.S. Department of Justice.

Hardyman, P., Austin, J., & Peyton, J. (2004). *Prison intake system: Assessing needs and classifying prisoners.* Washington, DC: National Institute of Corrections.

MacLellan, T. (2004). *Improving public safety through justice information sharing.* Washington, DC: National Governors Association.

Mamalian, C., & La Vigne, N. (1999). *The use of computerized crime mapping by law enforcement: Survey results.* Washington, DC: National Institute of Justice.

Manning, P. (2003). *Policing contingences.* Chicago: University of Chicago Press.

Massachusetts Board of Higher Education. (2003, February). *Guidelines for Criminal Justice and Law Enforcement Academic Programs.* Salem: Author.

McDonald, P. (2001). *Managing police operations: Implementing the New York Crime Model–CompStat.* Belmont, CA: Wadsworth.

McGuire, J. (2001). What works in correctional intervention? Evidence and practical implications. In D. Bernfeld & A. Leschied (Eds.), *Offender rehabilitation in practice: Implementing and evaluating effective programs* (pp. 25–43). New York: John Wiley.

McMillan, J. (1997, September). *Court technology in 2007.* Paper presented at the Fifth National Court Technology Conference. Available: www.ncsconline.org/d_ech/ctc/ctc5/supses2.htm

Meyer, J. A. (1998). Tradition and technology: Computers in criminal justice. In L. Moriarty & D. Canter (Eds.), *Criminal justice technology in the 21st century* (pp. 3–46). Springfield, IL: Charles C Thomas.

National Center for State Courts. (2004). *Successful caseflow management techniques.* Washington, DC: Author. Available: www.ncsconline.org

National Law Enforcement and Corrections Technology Center. (2003, Winter). Safe schools: A technology primer. *Tech Beat,* pp. 1–10. Available: www.justnet.org

National Research Council. (2004). *Fairness and effectiveness in policing.* Washington, DC: National Academy Press.

Office of Information Technology. (2001, September). Technology forecast for the federal judiciary. *Federal Probation,* pp. 3–10.

Ogden, T., & Horrocks, C. (2001, September). Pagers, digital audio, and kiosk: Officer assistants. *Federal Probation,* pp. 35–37.

Palmer, K. (2001). *The National Consortium on State Court Automation Standards: A white paper.* Williamsburg, VA: National Center for State Courts. Available: http://ncsconline.org/d_tech/standards/stdwhitepaper.htm

Sample, L., & Bray, T. (2003). *Are sex offenders dangerous? Criminology and Public Policy, 3*(1), 59–82.

Scott, M. (2000). *Problem-oriented policing: Reflections on the first 20 years.* Washington, DC: Office of Community-Oriented Policing Services.

Sherman, L., Gottfredson, D., Mackenzie, D., Eck, J., Rueter, P., & Bushway, S. (1998). *Preventing crime: What works, what doesn't, what's promising.* Washington, DC: U.S. Department of Justice.

Siegel, M., & Terenzi, E. (2001, September). The chief as a technology manager. *Federal Probation,* pp. 31–34.

Stojkovic, S., Kalinch, D., & Klofas, J. (1998). *Criminal justice organizations: Administration and management* (2nd ed.). Belmont, CA: Wadsworth.

Taxman, F. (2002, September). Supervision: Exploring the dimensions of effectiveness. *Federal Probation,* pp. 14–27.

Travis, J. (1997, March). *Technology in criminal justice: Creating the tools for transformation.* Address to the Academy of Criminal Justice Sciences. Available: www.ojp.usdoj.gov/nij/speeches/acjs.htm

Turner, A., & Blackburn, D. (2002, December). Biometrics: Separating myth from reality. *Corrections Today.*

Ward, R. H., & Webb, V. J. (1984). *Quest for quality: A publication of the Joint Commission of Criminology and Criminal Justice Education and Standards.* New York: University Publications.

Webster, L. (1997, September). *Strategic thinking: Essentials for leadership in the next millennium.* Paper presented at the Fifth National Court Technology Conference. Available: www.ncsonline.org/d_tech/ctc/ctc5/supses1.htm

Wright, K., with Bisbee, J., & Hardyman, P. (2003). *Defining and measuring corrections performance: Final report.* Washington, DC: U.S. Department of Justice.

CHAPTER **12**

The Future of Information Technology in Criminal Justice

Prospects and Challenges

APRIL PATTAVINA

The criminal justice system is entering a new era fundamentally transformed by advances in information technology (IT). No longer do most of us in the criminal justice field view technology with a sense of awe and wonder. Through the multitude of technological successes and failures, we are beginning to respect and understand IT for all of its promise, complexity, and challenges. IT will continue to evolve in ways that we have yet to foresee.

Through the articles in this volume, we have come to understand that the development, implementation, and application of IT are influenced by a variety of factors. Some of the factors identified often throughout this book include hardware and software advances; the legal context of information gathering, sharing, and use; the organizational culture in which IT projects are implemented; the quality of information inputs and outputs; the level of involvement in IT projects by agency personnel; and the education and training of line staff members and managers.

Because of this confluence of factors, the computerization of criminal justice has turned out to be more challenging than was anticipated. There are many more challenges that lie ahead as we incorporate the knowledge of past experiences into the future planning of IT projects. Consistent with the issues raised in the other chapters of this book, this chapter identifies the prospects of IT that we can expect in the near future and then discusses some of the significant challenges that lie ahead.

PROSPECTS

What can we say about the future of IT applications to the criminal justice system in general and to criminal justice decision making in particular? It appears that there are five future prospects that can be identified immediately:

1. Advances in computer technology will continue to make information processing easier, faster, and cheaper.

2. Criminal justice agencies will work to facilitate data sharing and continue to integrate systems.

3. New technologies that will change the capacity to commit old crimes (by either supporting or deterring), as well as create opportunites for new crimes, will be developed.

4. New technologies that will support the creation of new methodologies for dealing with criminal activity will be developed.

5. Innovative management strategies to successfully implement technology in police, courts, and corrections agencies will be developed.

When these five prospects are considered together, one thing is certain: What we can expect most for the future of criminal justice IT is change. The pressing question, and one that will continue to challenge us, is how to manage this change in ways that allow us to successfully integrate IT while at the same time balancing the needs, goals, and objectives of the criminal justice system, which can and should change much more slowly.

As computing continues to become easier, cheaper, more powerful, and more convenient, we will continue to increase the amount of information collected and stored pertaining to the lives of individuals, especially those involved in the criminal justice system. Today, many aspects of our lives are documented in various databases. Biologically, there are databases that give information on our physical attributes. These databases include DNA profiles and those that capture biometric measures that can provide information on who we are and what we look like, both inside and out. Economically, there are many databases that track our credit and spending habits. Behaviorally, there are agency databases that contain our criminal histories, driving records, and health records. Intelligence databases created from surveillance technology can even tell where we have been and what we have said.

Given the amount of information that can be collected on persons, there are three important challenges that we should consider as we look to the future of IT: (a) the challenge of technology and research, (b) the challenge of technology and privacy, and (c) the challenge of technology and society. Each of these challenges can be located on a continuum starting with a focused discussion of creating accountability for IT projects and ending with a discussion of some of the larger social and political issues related to advances in technology.

TECHNOLOGY AND RESEARCH: THE FIRST CHALLENGE

Criminal justice goals and objectives are directly related to the development, implementation, and evaluation of IT initiatives in criminal justice agencies. We know, largely from personal experience and anecdotal evidence, that many technology projects have failed to meet initial expectations. Some have suffered from long delays, cost increases, poor performance, and/or even premature obsolescence (Roper & Sullivan, 2003). One of the important lessons we have learned is that it is necessary to develop an assessment system to inform us about successes and failures, particularly during the early stages of IT implementation.

The development of an IT project assessment framework is necessary for several reasons, many of which come from "lessons learned" based on past experiences. Of major importance is the demand for greater accountability. After decades of considerable financial investment in IT by the government and little structured oversight of IT projects, it became apparent that not enough empirical knowledge about failures and successes was being generated to make informed decisions about future investments (Roper & Sullivan, 2003).

The federal government has been a major source of support for state and local criminal justice initiatives. Financial support for many IT projects has come from a variety of U.S. Department of Justice programs, including the Community-Oriented Policing Services (COPS) grant program, the Local Law Enforcement Block Grants program, the Edward Byrne Grant program, and the Juvenile Justice Accountability Incentive Block program. According to a recent overview of past IT projects,

> Traditionally, funding from these programs has been program or purpose specific and has led to the implementation of different computer systems with limited purposes serving the various justice components in state, local, and tribal governments. Many of these "stove-pipe" systems are incapable of sharing information and perpetuate, rather than alleviate, the inefficiency of the justice enterprise. (Bureau of Justice Assistance, 2001, p. 1)

As the integration of justice information and the design of "enterprise-wide" solutions takes priority, it is clear that projects must be initiated with clear, realistic, and measurable goals that participating criminal justice officials can monitor. In a recent report, Roper and Sullivan (2003) make the recommendation that before integration projects are even approved, participants should create performance measures consistent with specific goals. Processes should also be required to collect and analyze data to be used to determine success at various stages in the projects (e.g., design phase, testing phase, implementation phase). This information should be shared on a continual basis with participants, agency officials, and the funding sources. With the establishment of IT performance measures, it will be possible to determine whether or not (a) technology projects are on schedule and within budget, (b) a new system really meets the goals of the initial funding

request, and (c) an integration initiative is a success.

The process of establishing performance measures is informed by stating a business problem, according to Roper and Sullivan (2003). A business problem may be defined as a process or product that appears to be broken. The next issue becomes one of how to relate this business problem to a goal of the criminal justice system. Following are six criminal justice goals and some suggestions to guide the creation of performance measures mentioned in the report (pp. 14–17):

Goal 1: Enhancing public safety

Indicators of goal achievement:
1. Decrease the average response time to establish a positive identification following an arrest.
2. Reduce recidivism.
3. Decrease the amount of time it takes to serve a warrant.

Goal 2: Improving the accountability of the justice system to the general public

Indicators of goal achievement:
1. Increase the number and variety of reports available to the public on the Internet.
2. Increase the number of hours that the public can view the Criminal Justice Information System (CJIS) website.

Goal 3: Improving public trust and confidence in the justice system

Indicators of goal achievement:
1. Reduce the amount of time it takes for a criminal history background check.
2. Increase the percentage of the public that is satisfied that local law enforcement is effectively and efficiently controlling and reducing crime.

Goal 4: Improving caseflow management

Indicators of goal achievement:
1. Reduce the average number of days or hours from arrest to arraignment.
2. Reduce the amount of time it takes for correctional facility intake.

Goal 5: Improving staff efficiencies

Indicators of goal achievement:
1. Reduce the number of hours spent filing documents manually.
2. Increase the number of electronic data transfers between justice agencies.

Goal 6: Enhancing the quality of decision making within the justice system.

Indicators of goal achievement:
1. Reduce the amount of missing information in criminal justice databases.
2. Decrease the number of warrants that never get entered into the state registry.

The establishment of quantifiable performance measures is an important first step to help determine the success of a given criminal justice IT project. However, it is also important that we recognize that IT projects are affected not only by technical issues but also by the political, organizational, and work cultures of any given organization. Although performance indicators may tell us whether a project did or did not meet predetermined goals, we still might not know why a particular project failed in one organization but not in another. This type of information can be gathered only through in-depth studies of how IT is implemented and used in agencies and how it affects the work of individuals within those agencies.

This issue relates to the social aspects of computing. There is a growing body of research that examines the social aspects of computing, although there is a lack of research specifically on IT developments in criminal justice. Some refer to work in this area as social informatics. Kling (1999) defines social informatics as the "interdisciplinary study of the design, uses, and consequences of information technologies that takes into account their interaction with institutional and cultural contexts" (p. 1). Social informatics research is grounded in the notion that the social context of IT influences the way in which people use IT and, therefore, influences their relationship to work, organizations, and other relationships. Unfortunately, to date,

there have been only a handful of studies conducted using this research strategy to study criminal justice.

Peter Manning's work (Chapter 10 in this volume) is an example of this approach. His recent research on crime analysis and crime mapping in police organizations involved in-depth organizational analyses of specific agencies and focused on how technology was actually being used in contrast to how it could be used. Based on observation and interviews, his work in this area is insightful because he found that, in addition to the technical constraints facing crime mapping/analysis technology implementation in organizations, there are cultural issues supported by long-standing work traditions that might not be consistent with the new work processes and objectives imposed by new ITs.

A thorough understanding just how and why IT projects may or may not work will depend on the consideration of interactions among technology (hardware and software), information, people, culture, and organizations. Quantifiable performance measures are certainly one useful means of creating greater accountability. These measures can be used to determine *whether* the technology works. But as Manning's work demonstrates, it is also equally important that we pay attention to the social and organizational cultures in which these projects operate. Without a body of research that sheds needed light on *how* technology works in criminal justice organizations, we will continue to "muddle through" the IT development and implementation process. Manning's work represents one step forward in the process of directly linking research to ongoing IT development and implementation in criminal justice settings.

TECHNOLOGY AND PRIVACY: THE SECOND CHALLENGE

As public awareness of the amount of information being collected by public and private actors that can be used to create personal profiles increases, so does the public's concern about privacy. For example, in a 1999 survey, it was reported that 94% of respondents said that they were concerned about the possible misuse of their personal information. This is a significant increase from 1987, when 66% of respondents were concerned about threats to privacy (Bureau of Justice Statistics, 2001). In the area of privacy, the broad questions of importance are what information to collect, what to do with the information collected, who should be allowed to use the information, and how the information is being used.

Of course, many of the types of data collected by the U.S. government are considered to be matters of public record. Access to this information is crucial to the function of a democratic society for several reasons. According to a 2001 report by SEARCH, the National Consortium for Justice Information and Statistics, public access to criminal justice information promotes government accountability, public safety, First Amendment rights, confidence in the judicial and political systems, private sector accountability, and meritocracy. Of course, there is a potential downside to public access to these data that must also be considered.

Although public access is an important public value, the protection of privacy is also important, and there are laws and policies in place that are intended to protect individual privacy (for a specific discussion of legal issues and privacy, see Kathleen Snavely, Faye Taxman, & Stuart Gordon's chapter in this volume [Chapter 9]). The protection of privacy promotes information practices regarding the use, access, accuracy, right to challenge inaccurate information, and knowledge that the record systems exist (SEARCH, 2001). The challenge is to balance the availability of information made possible by the rapidly changing information environment with the legitimate privacy interests of citizens. As with all balancing

acts, this is an effort that requires constant vigilance.

During the past decade or so, there have been significant changes regarding access to automated information in criminal justice agencies. A report by SEARCH (2001) identified "change drivers" that reflect the technological, cultural, and economic forces that are influencing criminal justice record privacy policies. These change drivers have resulted in a wider circulation of criminal justice information that creates privacy risks for individuals. The following is a summary of the change drivers discussed in the report.

- *Public concern about privacy.* Americans are becoming more concerned about threats to their personal privacy from government and business, while the government is looking to widen the information net significantly in the name of public safety (e.g., the Patriot Act of 2001).

- *Information culture.* Advances in technology, such as powerful personal computers, browsers, search engines, online databases, telecommunications, and the Internet, have led to a demand for, as well as a market in, a wide range of criminal justice case processing information.

- *Systems integration.* The integration of criminal justice information systems across law enforcement, courts, prosecution, and corrections agencies, in conjunction with efforts to merge these systems with other types of personal information (e.g., medical records), has created comprehensive and powerful information sources, but such one-stop shopping for information raises a number of potential privacy concerns.

- *Adoption of a "business model" for the criminal justice system.* Criminal justice agencies are increasingly being required to cooperate with, and be accountable to, the community. The result has been more cooperative community-based relationships between criminal justice agencies and citizens. A significant outcome of this model is that agencies are becoming responsible for providing information to surrounding communities; federal, state, and local agencies; police departments; and other organizations.

- *Commercial compilation and sale.* Private agencies are able to acquire, compile, and market criminal justice information collected from police and courts and are making that information available to those outside the criminal justice system.

- *Government statutes and initiatives.* A number of recent government policies and laws have been established to provide criminal justice information to broader audiences in a more cost-effective and timely manner. An example is "Megan's Law," which facilitated the development of sex offender registries.

- *Intelligence systems.* Criminal justice intelligence systems are being developed and include detailed information for the creation of personal profiles to be used by law enforcement. For example, laws such as the Patriot Act have made it easier for the government to collect and share information on those suspected of supporting terrorism.

The SEARCH (2001) task force report was generated out of concern that changes favoring widespread access to criminal justice information were happening at too fast a pace and before policymakers could respond by developing standards designed to balance privacy with competing demands for criminal justice information. To promote the need to address this issue, the task force made a series of recommendations to guide the development of privacy policy, with a specific emphasis on criminal history information. Some of the major areas identified include the creation of consistent privacy legislation, the use of technology to ensure information accuracy

and security, and communication with those about whom information is collected.

To support legislative initiatives, SEARCH (2001) called for the creation of an advisory board to make recommendations to federal and state legislative, executive, and judicial branches as they proceed to create privacy law and policy that balance the increasing demands for criminal justice information with the privacy risks associated with the collection, management, dissemination, and use of such information. In the interest of information accuracy and security, the recommendation is that legislators and criminal history record information system managers develop, implement, and use the best available technologies to promote data quality and security. Moreover, law and policy should restrict the amalgamation of criminal justice record information with other types of personal information. In the area of communication, the SEARCH report recommends that people who are the subject of criminal history information be told about the practices, procedures, and policies for the collection, maintenance, use, and disclosure of criminal history information. They also should be given the right of access to, as well as procedures to correct, their information. The tasks set forth in the report represent a considerable challenge for the future collection, use, and dissemination of criminal justice information.

Although the establishment of laws and standards regarding the handling of information is important for protecting privacy, bureaucratic issues related to the implementation of IT also warrant consideration. This is especially the case with systems integration initiatives. Systems integration processes will have direct effects on information sharing and privacy issues as they span across the systems. The fact that different agencies and different levels of government may be involved in systems integration complicates the privacy issue considerably.

The National Governors Association (2002) refers to state and local justice systems integration as a process. This process allows the various justice system components, including state and local law enforcement, courts, prosecutors, and corrections agencies, to easily share justice information. Information sharing occurs vertically among different levels of government and horizontally across agencies. Important functions of an integrated system enable agencies to retain control of their information and make it available to authorized users. Protocols and standards are in place to guide the exchange of information. The interagency exchange of information occurs at key decision points in the criminal justice process. It is at these key decision points that privacy guidelines can and will be developed.

The likely problems that may emerge in the creation of integrated systems are less of a technical nature; they are more likely to be directly related to personnel and policy issues. The difficult questions, and ones that relate directly to privacy concerns, are (a) who owns the data, (b) who has access to the data, (c) how the data will be used, (d) where the data will be stored, and (e) who will fund integration projects. These questions are of primary importance and must be addressed. Until answers to these questions are provided, a full discussion of the privacy issues surrounding criminal justice information system integration cannot even begin.

TECHNOLOGY AND SOCIETY: THE THIRD CHALLENGE

What challenges does IT present for the future of our society? From a criminal justice perspective, the question can be framed to focus on the role of IT in crime prevention and control. To that end, the following discussion focuses on the future of policing in the information environment. This is an important issue for contemporary policing, in large part due to the new opportunities for crimes created by technological advances such as the Internet. Moreover, the Internet has added a new challenge to investigative policing because it allows criminals to transcend time, space, and structure—dimensions in which the police have traditionally operated.

In Chapter 3 of this volume, David Wall discusses the Internet as a conduit for criminal activity. He suggests that we carefully consider the law enforcement response to this type of criminal activity. To fashion a reasonable response, he argues, we need to have a thorough understanding of the problem. Our understanding of Internet crime or cybercrime is indeed limited. Much of the research available identifies only businesses as victims. Based on a recent survey of businesses conducted by the Bureau of Justice Statistics, Rantala (2004) reports that close to two thirds of respondents had been the victim of at least one computer virus, one quarter had denial of service attacks, and one fifth reported vandalism or sabotage of their computer systems. Although these numbers provide estimates of cybercrime victimizations, the survey was not a nationally representative survey of all businesses and only 42% of businesses responded. Given that these results may over- or underestimate the cybercrime problem for businesses (and in the absence of other methodologically sound studies), any strategic law enforcement response based on these findings would be premature. But the findings do require law enforcement to look in a new direction (i.e., the Internet) for crime prevention and control.

Newman and Clarke (2003) argue that situational crime prevention may offer a very effective strategy to address Internet crime. With prevention as the major objective, they argue that all we really need to understand are the specific situations that may contribute to crime. Using this model, it is not important to know how much crime there is or even who is committing it to respond effectively.

Newman and Clarke apply the elements of situational crime prevention to e-commerce crime, defined as the conduct of buying and selling in the new environment of IT. Their application of situational crime prevention to e-commerce crime is useful for examining the possibilities for the future of policing in a rapidly changing information environment. In fact, situational crime prevention appears to be one of the few criminological theories that attempt to deal with policing challenges presented by advances in IT.

The application of situational crime prevention to a crime problem involves several steps. The first step is an analysis of the situations in which crime occurs. The second step involves the identification of the opportunities presented in those situations that make the crime possible. The final step involves the development of strategies to alter the criminogenic circumstances of situations in ways that reduce crime opportunities.

The challenge of situational crime prevention is to prevent crime by altering situational circumstances in ways that reduce crime opportunities. Grounded in rational choice and routine activity theories, situational crime prevention assumes that criminals act rationally. Based on this assumption, there are a host of techniques described by Newman and Clarke (2003) that can be used to reduce criminal opportunities. Taken together, these methods seek to "a) increase the effort that the criminal must make in order to commit the crime, b) increase the perceived risk of the crime, c) reduce the anticipated rewards of the crime, and d) remove excuses for the criminal" (p. 19).

By both increasing the effort that criminals must make to complete crimes and increasing the risk for the offenders, situational crime prevention strategies may be effective in reducing this form of criminal behavior. At its core, such a strategy is dependent on the latest innovations in IT as police attempt to (once again) stay one step ahead of cyber criminals.

Situational crime prevention often uses a narrow approach to analyze specific situations and their vulnerability to crime such as the study of transactions that happen in the course of e-commerce activity. However, there is also a broad approach to situational crime prevention that emphasizes the modification of situations and an expanded definition of policing in the information environment.

Policing, according to this expanded definition, involves the mobilization of individuals and organizations that will work together to alter situations in ways that reduce opportunities for crime. Those that might participate include police, merchants, trade associations, consumer groups, corporate security staff members and private policing organizations, human relations and management staff members, Internet service providers, accounting organizations, managers and designers of public spaces, designers of products and services, and collectors and guardians of records.

Situational crime prevention techniques also call for the use of technology and surveillance as means to prevent crime. These techniques, combined with an expanded definition of policing, have caused some concern about the proliferation and ultimate omnipresence of surveillance agents. Such "Big Brother is watching you" concerns focus not only on the influence that these forces may have on public policy but also on the meaning they hold for social control in general and individual behavior in social contexts in particular.

Newman and Clarke (2003) dismiss the Big Brother concern and offer several reasons why they think this critical view is unrealistic. One reason with direct relevance to IT is the claim that it has been impossible to integrate all of the databases that could be used to modify situations. They further suggest that this failure is not the result of technology per se; rather, it is due to the difficulty in getting bureaucracies to work together. A second reason the authors offer is that creating relationships among various stakeholders in efforts to modify situations is very difficult.

This reasoning, along the lines of "It hasn't happened yet, so we should not be concerned," is somewhat surprising, especially given that we know from past experience how difficult it is to predict the future. One of the defining characteristics of technology is that advances sometimes outpace our social preparedness to deal with the consequences. Consider for a moment recent developments in biotechnology that led to cloning, gene mapping, and stem cell research. These developments are hotly debated on legal, social, moral, medical, and economic grounds regarding their impact on the future of humankind. Of course, we cannot create laws and policies before such challenges emerge, but neither should we avoid or reject discussions of the possibilities that technology offers—both good and bad—because they seem outlandish or far-fetched at the moment.

Webster (1997) presented a paper on strategic thinking for the next millennium in which he (borrowing from Joel Barker) highlighted the pitfalls of offering predictions on the subject of IT:

> Thomas J. Watson, chairman of IBM, said in 1943, "I think there is a world market for about five computers." In 1977, Ken Olsen, president of Digital Equipment Corporation, said, "There is no reason for any individual to have a computer in their home." Bill Gates, CEO of Microsoft Corporation, said in 1981, "640K of memory ought to be enough for anybody." (p. 2)

The people who made these comments were leaders in the field of computing, and although each is considered to have contributed significantly to the development of the computer technology industry, each failed to predict how fast and far computing would advance during the decades to come. The point to be made here is not that the future direction of IT is difficult to predict; that is obvious to even the casual observer. Instead, the point is that because it is so difficult to predict the future direction of IT, we must be ready to consider the possible consequences of IT advances—real or imagined—for society because these discussions will help us to identify the ethical and legal issues of IT use.

In the criminal justice field, this issue has been brought to our attention by Marx (2001), who observed a significant increase in the use of science and technology for purposes of social control. As a method of social control, situational crime prevention promotes an engineered society, where the goal is to eliminate or limit crime by design (and control) of the physical and social environments. In situations where that is not possible, deterrence through the threat of detection and apprehension becomes the goal. Some examples of technology that can be used for this purpose include video and audio surveillance, biometrics, DNA analysis, use of computer expert systems, matching and profiling, data mining, mapping, network analysis, and simulation.

Despite the focus on the situations in which crime occurs, situational crime prevention and its reliance on technology cannot be studied in a vacuum. The outcomes of this approach will have implications for other criminal justice system agencies that warrant careful consideration. For example, it may soon become possible for the use of IT to allow for documentation of many infractions, even relatively minor ones. This form of technology would work well in a situational crime prevention context because it would involve increasing the risk of detection for violators. This increase in crimes discovered may overload the police, courts, and corrections systems and may exacerbate the problems of an already overburdened criminal justice system. Consider, for example, the issue of fraudulent identity. This type of offense is likely to increase, according to Marx (1990):

> With the instant availability of computerized information—regardless of whether it is inaccurate or accurate and discrediting—persons may now feel the need to lie about things that in the past were unseen, overlooked, or forgotten. The tightening of the informational net or noose generates structural pressures to fabricate. (p. 153)

How circumstances such as these will be handled in the criminal justice system will force us to confront important questions about what we want as citizens of a democratic society. Some questions raised by Marx in 1990 that are relevant for the current discussion include the following: "How should we view the insatiable demand for more information and documentation and intrusive technologies?" and "What degree of risk and disorder do we want to accept in return for maximizing liberty and privacy?" (p. 164).

CONCLUDING COMMENTS

In this final chapter, a number of predictions have been offered—in the benign form of prospects—about the implementation and impact of the various forms of IT discussed throughout this book. Three potential challenges to the continued application of advances in IT to decision making and problem solving in the criminal justice system were also described (a) research-based challenges, (b) privacy-based challenges, and (c) technological/societal challenges. As we begin to consider the technical, legal, ethical, and practical implications of this new generation of IT, it is critical that we have a firm grasp not only of the potential of the technology itself but also of the inevitable problems associated with any large-scale change in criminal justice.

In essence, the chapters included in this volume share a common theme: Advances in IT provide us with an opportunity to look at old long-standing problems in new ways. However, significant measurable improvements in operational control, decision making, and strategic planning are not likely to occur by improvements in technology alone. For this to occur, we must change the way in which line staff members, managers, and leaders in criminal justice agencies view IT. Byrne and Buzawa (Chapter 11 in this volume) touch on this issue when they argue that higher education can and should play an important role in preparing both the current and next generations of criminal justice professionals to understand and use the latest advances in IT. Ultimately, it comes down to what Gardner (2004) describes as mind change: How do we change our own and other people's minds about a particular problem or issue? If the issue relates directly or indirectly to criminal justice IT, one obvious and self-serving answer to this question is to read this book. However, it is never that simple, and Gardner offers a more likely model of mind change that involves seven layers. Change, he argues, is likely when

> *reason* (often buttressed with *research*), reinforcement through multiple forms of *representation, real world events, resonance,* and *resources* all push in one direction—and resistances can be identified and successfully countered. Conversely, mind changing is unlikely to occur or to consolidate when resistances are strong and most of the other points of leverage are not in place. (p. 211)

The topics discussed in this chapter were intended to raise only some of the important issues that will continue to challenge us in the future. There are many other technology-related issues that are undoubtedly emerging, even as these words are being written.

REFERENCES

Bureau of Justice Assistance. (2001). *Information technology initiatives.* Washington, DC: U.S. Department of Justice.

Bureau of Justice Statistics. (2001). *Public attitudes toward uses of criminal history information: A privacy, technology, and criminal justice information report.* Washington, DC: U.S. Department of Justice.

Gardner, H. (2004). *Changing minds.* Boston: Harvard Business School Press.

Kling, R. (1999, January). What is social informatics and why does it matter? *D-Lib Magazine.* Available: www.dlib.org/dlib/january99/kling/01kling.html

Marx, G. T. (1990). *Fraudulent identity and biography.* In M. J. Lerner (Ed.), *New directions in the study of justice, law, and social control.* New York: Plenum.

Marx, G. T. (2001). *Technology and social control: The search for the illusive silver bullet.* In *International encyclopedia of the social and behavioral sciences.* Oxford, UK: Elsevier.

National Governors Association. (2002). *Issue brief: Improving public safety through justice information sharing.* Washington, DC: Author.

Newman, G. R., & Clarke, R. V. (2003). *Super highway robbery.* Portland, OR: Willan Publishing.

Rantala, R. R. (2004). *Cybercrime against businesses.* Washington, DC: U.S. Department of Justice.

Roper, R., & Sullivan, T. (2003). *Measuring the success of integrated justice: A practical approach* (SEARCH report). Washington, DC: U.S. Department of Justice.

SEARCH. (2001). *Report of the National Task Force on Privacy, Technology, and Criminal Justice Information.* Washington, DC: U.S. Department of Justice.

Webster, L. (1997, September). *Strategic thinking: Essentials for leadership in the next millennium.* Paper presented at the Fifth National Court Technology Conference, Detroit, MI. Available: www.ncsconline.org/d_tech/ctc/ctc5/ supses1.htm

Index

About the Editor

April Pattavina, Ph.D., is Assistant Professor in the Department of Criminal Justice at the University of Massachusetts Lowell. Her interests include the impact of information technology on the criminal justice system and applying spatial analysis techniques to the study of crime. In addition to this book, she has published several journal articles in the area of information technology in general and geographic information systems in particular. One of her most recent articles (with Richard Gore) is "Linking Offender Residence Probability Surfaces to a Specific Incident Location: An Application for Tracking Temporal Shifts in Journey to Crime Relationships and Prioritizing Suspect Lists and Mugshot Order" (*Police Quarterly*). She also works extensively with criminal justice agencies and is currently the principal investigator on a U.S. Department of Justice-funded grant to integrate criminal justice information related to incidents of domestic violence in a local police department.

About the Contributors

Eve Buzawa is Professor and Chairperson of the Department of Criminal Justice at the University of Massachusetts Lowell. She received her B.A. degree from the University of Rochester and her M.A. and Ph.D. degrees from the School of Criminal Justice at Michigan State University. She has been conducting research in the areas of the criminal justice response to family violence and policing for more than 25 years. She is the author and/or coauthor of several books and numerous journal articles. In addition, she has been the recipient of numerous federal, state, and local research grants. She is a past president of the Society of Police and Criminal Psychology, a past president of the Northeast Association of Criminal Justice Sciences, and a former board member of the Academy of Criminal Justice Sciences.

James M. Byrne (M.A., Ph.D., Rutgers University) is a professor in the Department of Criminal Justice at the University of Massachusetts Lowell, where he has taught since 1984. He has written extensively on a wide range of criminal justice topics. Most recently, he served as guest editor for the Fall 2004 special issue of *Federal Probation,* focusing exclusively on the offender reentry problem. His previous publications include *The Social Ecology of Crime* (with Robert Sampson, Springer-Verlag, 1986); *The Effectiveness of the "New" Intensive Supervision Programs* (with Arthur Lurigio and Chris Bond, National Institute of Corrections, 1989); *Smart Sentencing: The Emergence of Intermediate Sanctions* (with Arthur Lurigio and Joan Petersilia, Sage, 1992, 1994); and *Day Reporting Centers* (Vols. 1–2, with Dale Parent et al., National Institute of Justice, 1995). He is currently the Co-principal investigator of an evaluation of the National Institute of Corrections' ongoing Institutional Culture Change Initiative. He is also working on a new text, *Violence in America: Causes, Prevention, and Control* (with Eve Buzawa, Sage).

Lois M. Davis is a Senior Policy Researcher at the RAND Corporation. She has a Ph.D. in public health from the University of California, Los Angeles, and is a former National Institute of Mental Health postdoctoral fellow and a former Pew Health Policy fellow. Her research during the past several years has focused on U.S. emergency preparedness for domestic terrorism. She recently led a nationwide survey of state and local emergency response organizations to evaluate federal weapons of mass destruction preparedness programs in support of a presidential advisory panel. She also conducted a national survey of state and local law enforcement agencies to assess their preparedness for domestic terrorism on behalf of the National Memorial Institute for the Prevention of Terrorism. Currently, she is conducting research on law enforcement intelligence-gathering capabilities. In addition, she participated in a study on citizen preparedness measures for catastrophic terrorism. Her past research has involved assessing the future technology needs of state and local law enforcement agencies. She has served on the U.S. Department of Defense's Military Health tri-service strategic planning committees.

Terence Dunworth is the Director of the Justice Policy Center at the Urban Institute, with responsibility for directing the focus of the center's work, managing its staff members, and overseeing its research projects. He holds a Ph.D. in political science from Michigan State University, an M.A. in political science and international relations from the University of Utah, and a B.A. in politics, economics, and statistics from Durham University in England. Prior to joining the Urban Institute, he was managing vice president of the Law and Public Policy Area of Abt Associates. Before that, he was a senior researcher at the RAND Corporation. His research over the past decade has concentrated on work of a national scope. Under contract with the Administrative Office of the U.S. Courts, he is currently the project executive on a comprehensive study of administrative service delivery in the federal court system. With funding from the National Institute of Justice, he directed the National Evaluation of the Youth Firearms Violence Initiative (1998), the National Impact Assessment of the Federal Weed and Seed Program (1999), and the National Evaluation of the Byrne Formula Grant Program (1997).

Donald Faggiani, Ph.D., is a Senior Research Associate with the Police Executive Research Forum. He is the former executive director of the Wyoming Statistical Analysis Center at the University of Wyoming. He has worked extensively with law enforcement data systems and is recognized as one of the national leaders in research using incident-based police data systems. Several of his most recent publications focus on the practical aspects of the Federal Bureau of Investigation's National Incident-Based Reporting System (NIBRS) for public policy and police use. These publications include "Regional Problem Solving Using the National Incident-Based Reporting System" (in *Solving Crime and Disorder Problems: Current Issues, Police Strategies, and Organizational Tactics*); "Using the National Incident-Based Reporting System for Strategic Crime Analysis" (*Journal of Quantitative Criminology*, July 1999); and "Robbery of Older Adults: A Descriptive Analysis Using the National Incident-Based Reporting System" (*Journal of Research and Policy*, Spring 1999). He has made numerous presentations and conducted several seminars focusing on the use of the NIBRS for policy analysis as well as for tactical and strategic crime analysis. He is one of the few researchers in the country to incorporate the NIBRS with graphical information systems and mapping for research purposes.

Stuart Gordon is a 1972 graduate of the University of Maryland who works as a consultant on editorial and health care policy matters. He holds a J.D. degree and is a member of the Maryland and District of Columbia bars. He was the managing editor of *Under the Dome: A History of the Maryland General Assembly in the 20th Century* (published on Maryland Day 2001 by the Maryland General Assembly).

Roberta E. Griffith works as a research associate to provide data analysis, research, and project management assistance for Project Safe Neighborhoods, a national network committed to reducing gun violence. She received her B.A. in psychology from the University of North Texas, received her M.S. in criminal justice from Northeastern University, and is currently working on her Ph.D. in law, policy, and society at Northeastern University. Her research and interests revolve around dtabase design, analysis, and development as well as privacy legislation and policies. She has published in areas pertaining to the Bureau of Alcohol, Tobacco, Firearms, and Explosives' national firearms tracing system and general information systems as they relate to criminal justice.

David Hirschel is Professor of Criminal Justice at the University of Massachusetts Lowell and Professor Emeritus of Criminal Justice at the University of North Carolina at Charlotte. His primary research and teaching interests are in victims of crime (particularly spouse abuse), international criminal justice, and legal issues in criminal justice. He was principal investigator of the National Institute of Justice (NIJ)-funded Charlotte Spouse Abuse Experiment and is currently principal investigator of another NIJ-funded project titled "Explaining the Prevalence, Context, and Consequences of Dual Arrest in Intimate Partner Cases."

Brian A. Jackson, Ph.D., is a Physical Scientist at the RAND Corporation, where he has been involved in and led studies in the fields of emergency management, homeland security, technology assessment, science policy, and terrorism. His terrorism-related work includes an ongoing study of organizational learning in terrorist groups funded by the National Institute of Justice, participation in a RAND-funded project developing terrorist attack scenarios using hazardous materials, a large-scale study of command and responder protection during responses to major disasters and terrorist attacks, participation in two projects on critical infrastructure protection, and a study of the use of crime-fighting technologies by law enforcement organizations. His key publications in these areas include articles on technology adoption by terrorist organizations and the report, *Protecting Emergency Responders: Lessons Learned From Terrorist Attacks*, examining protection and safety needs of responders to the attacks of September 11, 2001.

Peter K. Manning (Ph.D., Duke University, 1966; M.A., Oxford University, 1982) holds the Elmer V. H. and Eileen M. Brooks Chair in Policing in the College of Criminal Justice at Northeastern University. He has been a fellow of the National Institute of Justice, the Rockefeller Foundation, Balliol and Wolfson Colleges at Oxford, and the Socio-Legal Centre at Oxford. He is listed in *Who's Who in America* and *Who's Who in the World* and has been awarded many contracts and grants. He is the author or editor of 14 books. His research interests include the rationalizing of policing, crime mapping and crime analysis, the uses of information technology, and qualitative methods. The second edition of *Narcs' Game* (Waveland) and his monograph *Policing Contingencies* (University of Chicago Press) both were published in 2003.

Phyllis Parshall McDonald, Ed.D., is Director of Research and Assistant Professor for the Division of Public Safety Leadership at Johns Hopkins University. She is responsible for managing research projects funded by the National Institute of

Justice (school safety), the Federal Transit Administration, the Community-Oriented Policing Services Office (identity theft), and the International Association of Chiefs of Police (post-9/11 policing) as well as for training Baltimore Police Department patrol commanders. She teaches research and evaluation at the undergraduate level, and program evaluation at the graduate level, in the Police Executive Leadership Program. Formerly, she served with the National Institute of Justice and managed research on police operations, police integrity, and measuring police performance. She has nearly 20 years of command experience with local police departments. In the course of her career, she has been responsible for managing three police academies. She has been a consultant to local police agencies and the U.S. Army Military Police in Europe in the areas of police operations, training, and community policing. She has authored several publications, including *Managing Police Operations: Implementing the New York Crime Control Model–CompStat* (Wadsworth, 2001); *Police/Student Relations* (National Education Association), and *Community Policing and Community Prosecution: Differences and Similarities* (National Institute of Justice).

Glenn Pierce, Ph.D., is Interim Director of the Institute for Security and Public Policy and also Principal Research Scientist for the College of Criminal Justice at Northeastern University. At Northeastern University, he has also served as director of strategic planning and research for information services, director of academic computing, and director of the Center of Applied Social Research. He has conducted research on a broad range of social and economic issues and has obtained funding for his research from the National Institute of Mental Health, the National Institute of Justice, the National Science Foundation, the Sage Foundation, the Boston Foundation, and the Bureau of Alcohol, Tobacco, Firearms, and Explosives.

Kathleen R. Snavely (B. A., Ithaca College; M.S., American University) is the Director of Training for the University of Maryland's Bureau of Governmental Research, responsible for development and implementation of training for the HATS Automated Tracking System. Previously, she was the Director of Research for the National Drug Court Institute and served as Managing Editor of NDCI as well. She has also worked as a senior research associate with the District of Columbia Courts and as Project Manager with the Criminal Justice Coordinating Commission in Montgomery County, Maryland. Ms. Snavely has conducted numerous program and criminal justice system evaluations and has worked with juveniles involved with substance abuse.

Faye S. Taxman is Professor at the School of Government and Public Affairs at Virginia Commonwealth University. She is the former Director of the Bureau of Governmental Research (BGR). She has spearheaded a number of initiatives focused on efficacy of interventions and has developed the Recidivism Reduction Laboratory to test ideas and concepts. As BGR director, she was responsible for studies on various aspects of the criminal justice system, including a two-site randomized experiment testing the efficacy of a seamless system of drug treatment services for offenders (National Institute on Drug Abuse) and a four-site study of drug treatment services offered in drug courts (with the University of Southern Maine and funded by the National Institute of Justice). She has published articles in many prominent journals, including the *Journal of Research in Crime and Delinquency* and the *Prison Journal*. In 2002, she received the University of Cincinnati Award from the American Probation and Parole Association for her contributions to the field.

David S. Wall (M.A., M.Phil., York; Ph.D., Leeds) is Professor of Criminal Justice and Director of the Centre for Criminal Justice Studies at the University of Leeds, where he conducts research and teaches in the fields of criminal justice and information technology, policing, and cyberlaw. His specialist area of research is criminal justice and information technology, and he has published a wide range of articles and books on issues related to the field, including *Cybercrimes* (Polity, in press); *Cyberspace Crime* (edited, Ashgate/Dartmouth, 2003); *Crime and the Internet* (edited, Routledge, 2001); and *The Internet, Law, and Society* (coedited with Y. Akdeniz & C. Walker, Longman, 2000). He is currently conducting research on the regulation of deviant behavior on the Internet while he is on an Arts and Humanities Research Board fellowship. He has also published a range of books and articles within the broader field of criminal justice, including *Policy Networks in Criminal Justice* (edited with M. Ryan & S. Savage, Macmillan, 2001); *The British Police: Forces and Chief Officers* (with M. Stallion, Police History Society, 1999); and *The Chief Constables of England and Wales* (Ashgate/ Dartmouth, 1998).